# THE
# ALLYN & BACON
# GUIDE TO WRITING

## Concise Edition

SEVENTH EDITION

**John D. Ramage**
*Arizona State University*

**John C. Bean**
*Seattle University*

**June Johnson**
*Seattle University*

**PEARSON**

Boston   Columbus   Indianapolis   New York   San Francisco   Upper Saddle River
Amsterdam   Cape Town   Dubai   London   Madrid   Milan   Munich   Paris   Montréal   Toronto
Delhi   Mexico City   São Paulo   Sydney   Hong Kong   Seoul   Singapore   Taipei   Tokyo

Senior Acquisitions Editor: Lauren A. Finn
Senior Development Editor: Marion B. Castellucci
Executive Marketing Manager: Roxanne McCarley
Senior Supplements Editor: Donna Campion
Executive Digital Producer: Stefanie A. Snajder
Digital Editor: Sara Gordus
Content Specialist: Erin Jenkins
Project Manager: Savoula Amanatidis
Project Coordination, Text Design, and Electronic Page Makeup: Integra
Cover Designer/Manager: John Callahan
Cover Images: Konstantin Yolshin/Shutterstock
Photo Researcher: Integra
Senior Manufacturing Buyer: Roy L. Pickering, Jr.
Printer and Binder: R. R. Donnelley and Sons Company–Crawfordsville
Cover Printer: Lehigh-Phoenix Color Corporation–Hagerstown

For permission to use copyrighted material, grateful acknowledgment is made to the copyright holders on pp. 372–373, which are hereby made part of this copyright page.

**Library of Congress Cataloging-in-Publication Data**
Ramage, John D., author.
  Allyn & Bacon guide to writing / John D. Ramage, Arizona State University, John C. Bean, Seattle University, June Johnson, Seattle University.—Seventh edition.
     pages cm
  Includes bibliographical references and index.
  ISBN 978-0-321-91422-4
  1. English language—Rhetoric—Handbooks, manuals, etc.   2. English language—Grammar—Handbooks, manuals, etc.   3. Report writing—Handbooks, manuals, etc.   4. College readers. I. Bean, John C., author.   II. Johnson, June, (date) author.   III. Title.   IV. Title: Allyn and Bacon guide to writing.
  PE1408.R18 2015
  808'.042—dc23

                                                                                              2013035650

5    16

www.pearsonhighered.com

**Complete Edition**
ISBN-10: 0-321-91422-8; ISBN-13: 978-0-321-91422-4
**Brief Edition**
ISBN-10: 0-321-91442-2; ISBN-13: 978-0-321-91442-2
**Concise Edition**
ISBN-10: 0-321-91430-9; ISBN-13: 978-0-321-91430-9

# DETAILED CONTENTS

# PART 2   WRITING PROJECTS

# PART 3   A GUIDE TO COMPOSING AND REVISING

# PART 4   A RHETORICAL GUIDE TO RESEARCH

# PREFACE

Through six editions, *The Allyn & Bacon Guide to Writing* has been praised for its groundbreaking integration of composition pedagogy and rhetorical emphasis. In regular, brief, and concise editions, the text has been adopted at a wide range of two- and four-year institutions where instructors admire its appeal to students, its distinctive emphasis on reading and writing as rhetorical acts, its focus on shared problems as the starting point for academic writing, its engaging classroom activities that promote critical thinking, and its effective writing assignments. Reviewers have consistently praised the book's theoretical coherence and explanatory power, which help students produce engaged, idea-rich essays and help composition instructors build pedagogically sound, intellectually stimulating courses shaped by their own strengths, interests, and course goals.

## What's New in the Concise Seventh Edition?

While retaining the signature strengths of earlier editions, the seventh edition features the following key improvements:

- **Expanded coverage of online and multimodal composition** helps students navigate digital environments with rhetorical savvy. Although most of today's students are digital natives, their technological skills often outpace their rhetorical understanding of multimodal communication and their awareness of the legal and ethical dimensions of an interactive online environment.

  - **In Part 1, a new chapter on online and multimodal composition** (Chapter 4) teaches students to analyze the rhetorical use of words, images, and sounds in multimodal texts, to think rhetorically about the interactive Web environment, and to participate responsibly in online discourse.

  - **In Part 3, a new nuts-and-bolts chapter on composing multimodal texts** (Chapter 13) explains the design principles of multimodal composing and guides students to adapt these principles to multimodal genres including posters, speeches with presentation slides, podcasts, and videos.

  - **In each Part 2 chapter, optional Writing Projects for online or multimodal composing** allow instructors to decide the extent to which, if at all, they want to include a multimodal component in their course.

- **A completely revised chapter on analysis and synthesis** (Chapter 8) focuses on the critical thinking and writing moves students need for wrestling with multiple complex texts. This revised chapter streamlines the explanations and uses short professional readings and a new student essay, shown in process, on the timely subject of young adults' search for identity, independence, and security in today's complicated economic and social environment.

- In each assignment chapter, an **"Engaging" activity** provides a classroom exercise that introduces students to the concepts and thinking skills covered in the chapter and awakens students' interest.
- **Many new examples, readings, and student essays** keep the content up-to-date and relevant. New clusters of readings, Web sites, and images focus on the potential risk to children of increasing the role of online education, the controversy over fracking, a proposal for mandatory public service, and the problems of twenty somethings' transitioning into traditional adult roles.

## Distinctive Pedagogical Approach of *The Allyn & Bacon Guide to Writing*

*The Allyn & Bacon Guide to Writing* takes a distinctive pedagogical approach that integrates composition research with rhetorical theory. It treats writing and reading both as rhetorical acts and as processes of problem posing, inquiry, critical thinking, and argument. Its aim is to evoke the kind of deep learning that allows students to transfer compositional and rhetorical skills across disciplines and professional fields. What follows are the distinctive elements of our pedagogical approach to teaching composition:

- **Focus on rhetorical reading.** An often-noted strength of *The Allyn & Bacon Guide to Writing* is its method of teaching rhetorical reading so that students can summarize complex readings and speak back to them through their own analysis and critical thinking. This skill is crucial for writing literature reviews or for doing research in any discipline that uses verbal, visual, or multimodal texts as primary sources. Our instructional approach teaches students to understand the differences between print and cyberspace sources; to analyze the rhetorical occasion, genre, context, intended audience, and angle of vision of sources; to evaluate sources according to appropriate criteria; and to negotiate the World Wide Web with confidence.

- **Focus on transfer of learning into the disciplines.** Recent cognitive research shows that transfer of knowledge and skills from one course to another depends on deep rather than surface learning. *The Allyn & Bacon Guide to Writing* promotes deep learning in a variety of ways. As one example, the text emphasizes four underlying skills that novice academic writers must acquire: (1) how to pose a problem that engages targeted readers; (2) how to summarize the conversation that surrounds the problem; (3) how to produce a thesis that adds something new, challenging, or surprising to the conversation; (4) how to support the thesis with appropriate forms of reasons and evidence. Armed with knowledge of these principles (deep learning), a student entering a new discipline can ask "How does this discipline ask questions? How does it summarize the scholarly conversation surrounding this problem (literature reviews)? What constitutes evidence in this discipline?"

- **Classroom-tested assignments that guide students through all phases of the reading and writing processes and make frequent use of collaboration and peer review.** The Writing Projects promote intellectual growth and stimulate the kind of critical thinking valued in college courses. Numerous "For Writing and Discussion" exercises make it easy to incorporate active learning into a course while deepening students' understanding of concepts. The text's focus on the subject-matter question that precedes the thesis helps students see academic disciplines as fields of inquiry rather than as data banks of right answers.

- **Full coverage of outcome goals for first-year composition from the Council of Writing Program Administrators (WPA).** The correlation of the WPA Outcomes Statement with the Seventh Edition of *The Allyn & Bacon Guide to Writing* appears on the inside back covers of the book and in the *Instructor's Resource Manual*. In addition to helping instructors plan their courses, these correlations help with program-wide internal and external assessments.

## Key Features of *The Allyn & Bacon Guide to Writing*

The modular design of the text is enhanced by regularly recurring pedagogical features that promote easy navigation and consistent reinforcement of key concepts and principles.

- **An organizational structure that offers flexibility to instructors.** The modular organization gives instructors maximum flexibility in designing courses.
  - **Thirteen rhetorical "concepts" in Part 1** provide students with memorable takeaway knowledge about key concepts and principles of rhetoric.
  - **Writing Projects in Part 2,** arranged according to rhetorical aim, teach students the features of a genre while promoting new ways of seeing and thinking.
  - **Modularized lessons in strategies for composing (Part 3)** teach students to develop an effective writing process while gaining expert knowledge for composing closed-form, or multimodal texts.
  - **Modularized lessons for research and writing from sources (Part 4)** teach students expert strategies for conducting academic research in a rhetorical environment.

- **Clearly stated learning outcomes** at the beginning of each chapter preview the chapter's content and motivate learning by nutshelling takeaway concepts.

- **Strategies charts** present suggestions for approaching reading, writing, and research tasks in a handy format for student reference and use.

- **Framework charts showing structural options for writing assignments** help students understand the organizational features of different genres and serve as flowcharts that promote both idea generation and more purposeful ordering of ideas.

## Resources for Instructors and Students

MyWritingLab™ **Now Available for Composition.** *MyWritingLab* is an online homework, tutorial, and assessment program that provides engaging experiences to today's instructors and students. By incorporating rubrics into the writing assignments, faculty can create meaningful assignments, grade them based on their desired criteria, and analyze class performance through advanced reporting. For students who enter the course under-prepared, *MyWritingLab* offers a diagnostic test and personalized remediation so that students see improved results and instructors spend less time in class reviewing the basics. Rich multimedia resources are built in to engage students and support faculty throughout the course. Visit *www.mywritinglab.com* for more information.

**CourseSmart.** Students can subscribe to *The Allyn & Bacon Guide to Writing,* Seventh Edition, as a CourseSmart eText (at CourseSmart.com). The site includes all of the book's content in a format that enables students to search the text, bookmark passages, save their own notes, and print reading assignments that incorporate lecture notes.

*The Instructor's Resource Manual,* **Seventh Edition,** has been revised by Susanmarie Harrington, University of Vermont. The *Instructor's Resource Manual* integrates emphases for meeting the Council of Writing Program Administrators' guidelines for outcome goals in first-year composition courses. It continues to offer detailed teaching suggestions to help both experienced and new instructors; practical teaching strategies for composition instructors in a question-and-answer format; suggested syllabi for courses of various lengths and emphases; chapter-by-chapter teaching suggestions; answers to Handbook exercises; suggestions for using the text with nonnative speakers; suggestions for using the text in an electronic classroom; transparency masters for class use; and annotated bibliographies.

**PowerPoints to Accompany** *The Allyn & Bacon Guide to Writing.* Ideal for hybrid or distance learning courses, the PowerPoint presentation deck offers instructors slides to adapt to their own course needs.

**Accelerated Composition.** Support for acceleration or immersion courses focuses on three fundamental areas: reading, writing, and grammar. Additional questions for professional and student readings help students understand, analyze, and evaluate the strategies writers employ. For each of the text's major Writing Projects, additional activities and prompts encourage students to break down the tasks involved in writing an essay into manageable chunks. Grammar support includes diagnostic, practice, instruction, and mastery assessment. Contact your Pearson representative for access through *MyWritingLab* or for a print workbook.

The reading and writing support for accelerated courses using *The Allyn & Bacon Guide to Writing* is authored by Robert Miller, Associate Professor of English at the Community College of Baltimore County. He has been a member of CCBC's ALP steering committee since its inception and has been teaching the Accelerated Learning Program model for seven years. Professor Miller has presented on Acceleration at numerous conferences including CCCC and the

Conference on Acceleration. He runs www.alp-deved.org, the national ALP Web site and writes the ALP newsletter. He also serves on the national executive board of the Council of Basic Writing.

Contact your Pearson representative for more information on resources for *The Allyn & Bacon Guide to Writing*.

## Acknowledgments

We wish to thank Amy Holly of Front Range Community College for her valuable consulting help as we created the new multimodal material in the seventh edition. Amy's insightful review of the sixth edition inspired us to incorporate more in-depth treatment of multimodal texts into *The Allyn & Bacon Guide to Writing*, and her own innovative use of multimodal assignments in her courses helped stimulate our own thinking. In addition, we would like to thank our former student and current colleague Tiffany Anderson, who in her capacity as Assistant Director of our Writing Center provided research and writing assistance for several of the issues new to this edition.

We give special thanks to the following composition scholars and instructors, who reviewed the sixth-edition text or the manuscript for the seventh edition, helping us understand how they use *The Allyn & Bacon Guide to Writing* in the classroom and offering valuable suggestions for improving the text: Larry Beason, University of South Alabama; Diane Boehm, Saginaw Valley State University; Jenna Caruso, Baker College; Christine Cucciarre, University of Delaware; Heather Salter Dromm, Northwestern State University of Louisiana; Tyler Farrell, Marquette University; Mitch Gathercole, Grand Rapids Community College; Tara Hembrough, Southern Illinois University; Thomas Patrick Henry, Utah Valley University; Guy J. Krueger, University of Mississippi; Lindsay Lewan, Arapahoe Community College; Alison Reynolds, University of Florida; Susan Roach, Purdue University Calumet; Alfred Siha, Harrisburg Area Community College; Ellen Sorg, Owens Community College; Andrea Spofford, University of Southern Mississippi; Richard S. Tomlinson, Richland Community College; and Scott Weeden, Indiana University–Purdue University Indianapolis.

We are particularly grateful to our Pearson team. We especially thank our development editor, Marion Castellucci, who has worked with us through multiple revisions and has become an invaluable part of our team. Her insight, sense of humor, professional experience, and extensive editorial knowledge have once again kept us on track and made the intense work of this revision possible. We thank our production editor, Martha Beyerlein, and have great appreciation for our editor, Lauren Finn, whose comprehensive view of the field, keen insights, and excellent people and communication skills make her a pleasure to work with.

We would also like to thank our Seattle University students who made special contributions to this edition: Michelle Eastman for her short story analysis, Claire Giordano for her classical argument, and Alex Mullen for the story board images and stills from his video production. Most of all, we are indebted to all our students, who have made the teaching of composition such a joy. We thank them for their insights and for their willingness to engage with problems, discuss ideas, and, as they compose and revise, share with us their frustrations and their triumphs. They have sustained our love of teaching and inspired us to write this book.

Finally, John Bean thanks his wife, Kit, also a professional composition teacher, whose dedication to her students as writers and individuals manifests the sustaining values of our unique profession. John also thanks his children, Matthew, Andrew, Stephen, and Sarah, who have grown to adulthood since he began writing textbooks and who continue to give him insights for writing assignments and contemporary issues. June Johnson thanks her husband, Kenneth Bube, a mathematics professor and geophysics consultant, for his insights into the fascinating intersections between learning to think mathematically and the critical thinking and development of writing knowledge and skills in composition. Finally, she thanks her daughter, Jane Ellen, who through her own college coursework in the interdisciplinary field of Environmental Studies has highlighted the importance of academic and civic writing.

JOHN C. BEAN
JUNE JOHNSON

# A RHETORIC FOR WRITERS

This image shows the surrealist painting *Portrait de Famille* (1954) by American painter, artist, and writer Dorothea Tanning (1910–2012). Surrealism was an early twentieth century artistic movement that featured surprise, strange and often disturbing juxtapositions, arresting symbolism, and a blending of reality and the painter's subconscious dreams. These features make interpretation of surrealist art particularly open to speculation. What is surprising, strange, and dreamlike about this painting? What questions does a close look at the figures in this painting inspire you to ask?

# 1 POSING PROBLEMS: THE DEMANDS OF COLLEGE WRITING

## WHAT YOU WILL LEARN

**1.1** To pose subject-matter problems, in which you wrestle with the complexities of your topics.

**1.2** To make decisions about your writing based on purpose, audience, and genre.

**1.3** To use varying rules for "good writing" depending on the rhetorical context.

> It seems to me, then, that the way to help people become better writers is not to tell them that they must first learn the rules of grammar, that they must develop a four-part outline, that they must consult the experts and collect all the useful information. These things may have their place. But none of them is as crucial as having a good, interesting question.
>
> —*Rodney Kilcup, Historian*

Our purpose throughout this textbook is to help you see writers as questioners and problem posers—a view of writing that we believe will lead to your greatest growth as a college-level thinker and writer. In particular, we want you to think of writers as people who pose interesting questions or problems and struggle to work out answers or responses to them. As we show in this chapter, writers pose two sorts of problems: *subject-matter problems* (for example, Should the United States pass stricter gun-control laws?) and *rhetorical problems* (for example, Who are my readers? How much do they already care about gun control? What form and style should I use?).

We don't mean to make this focus on problems sound scary. Indeed, humans pose and solve problems all the time and often take great pleasure in doing so. Psychologists who study critical and creative thinking see problem solving as a productive and positive activity. According to one psychologist, "Critical thinkers are actively engaged with life.... They appreciate creativity, they are innovators, and they exude a sense that life is full of possibilities."* By focusing first on the kinds of problems that writers pose and struggle with, we hope to increase your own engagement and pleasure in becoming a writer.

*Stephen D. Brookfield. *Developing Critical Thinkers: Challenging Adults to Explore Alternative Ways of Thinking and Acting.* (San Francisco: Jossey-Bass, 1987): 5. Academic writers regularly document their quotations and sources. In this text sources are documented either on the page or in the Credits section at the end of the text.

# Why Take a Writing Course?

Before turning directly to the notion of writers as questioners and problem posers, let's ask why a writing course can be valuable for you.

First of all, the skills you learn in this course will be directly transferable to your other college courses. Introductory courses often focus on generalized academic writing, while advanced courses in your major will introduce you to your field's specialized ways of writing and thinking. What college professors value are the kinds of questioning, analyzing, and arguing skills that this course will help you develop. You will emerge from this course as a better reader and thinker and a clearer and more persuasive writer, able to meet the demands of different academic writing situations.

Effective writing skills are also essential for most professional careers. One recent study showed that college graduates in business or professional life spend, on average, 44 percent of their time writing, including (most commonly) letters, memos, short reports, instructional materials, and professional articles and essays.

Besides the pragmatic benefits of college and career success, learning to write well can bring you the personal pleasure of a richer mental life. As we show throughout this text, writing is closely allied to thinking and to the innate satisfaction you take in exercising your curiosity, creativity, and problem-solving ability. Writing connects you to others and helps you discover and express ideas that you would otherwise never think or say. Unlike speaking, writing gives you time to think deep and long about an idea. Because you can revise writing, it lets you pursue a problem in stages, with each new draft reflecting a deeper, clearer, or more complex level of thought. In other words, writing isn't just a way to express thought; it is a way to do the thinking itself. The act of writing stimulates, challenges, and stretches your mental powers and, when you do it well, is profoundly satisfying.

With this background on why a college writing course is important, let's begin with key rhetorical concepts that will serve as the foundation for your study of writing.

# CONCEPT 1.1 **Subject matter problems are the heart of college writing.**

**1.1**
Pose subject-matter problems, in which you wrestle with the complexities of your topics.

From your previous schooling, you are probably familiar with the term **thesis statement**, which is the main point a writer wants to make in an essay. However, you may not have thought much about the question that lies behind the thesis, which is the problem or issue that the writer is wrestling with. An essay's thesis statement is actually the writer's one-sentence summary answer to this question, and it is this question that has motivated the writer's thinking. Experienced writers immerse themselves in subject matter questions in pursuit of answers or solutions. They write to share their proposed solutions with readers who share their interests. Let's look more fully at the kinds of subject matter questions that initiate the writing process.

## Shared Problems Unite Writers and Readers

For college professors, "a good, interesting question" is at the heart of good writing. Professors want students to become gripped by problems because they themselves are gripped by problems. For example, at a workshop for new faculty members, we asked participants to write a brief description of the question or problem that motivated their Ph.D. dissertation or a recent conference paper or article. Here is how a biochemistry professor responded:

> During periods of starvation, the human body makes physiological adaptations to preserve essential protein mass. Unfortunately, these adaptations don't work well during long-term starvation. After the body depletes its carbohydrate storage, it must shift to depleting protein in order to produce glucose. Eventually, this loss of functional protein leads to metabolic dysfunction and death. Interestingly, several animal species are capable of surviving for extensive periods without food and water while conserving protein and maintaining glucose levels. How do the bodies of these animals accomplish this feat? I wanted to investigate the metabolic functioning of these animals, which might lead to insights into the human situation.

As you progress through your college career, you will find yourself increasingly engaged with the kinds of questions that motivate your professors. All around college campuses you'll find clusters of professors and students asking questions about all manner of problems ranging from puzzles in the reproductive cycles of worms and bugs to the changing portrayal of race and gender in American films. At the heart of all these communities of writers and readers is an interest in common questions and the hope for better or different answers. Writers write because they have something new or surprising or challenging to say in response to a question. Readers read because they share the writer's interest in the problem and want to deepen their understanding.

## Where Do Problems Come From?

So where do these problems come from and how can you learn to pose them? The problems that college professors value might be different from what you at first think. Beginning college students typically imagine questions that have right answers. Students ask their professors questions about a subject because they are puzzled by confusing parts of a textbook, a lecture, or an assigned reading. They hope their professors will explain the confusing material clearly. Their purpose in asking these questions is to eliminate misunderstandings, not to open up controversy and debate. Although basic comprehension questions are important, they are not the kinds of inquiry questions that initiate strong college-level writing and thinking.

The kinds of questions that stimulate the writing most valued in college are open-ended questions that focus on unknowns or invite multiple points of view. These are what historian Rodney Kilcup refers to when he says that writers should begin with a "good, interesting question" (see the epigraph to this chapter, p. 2). For Kilcup, a good question sets the writer on the path of inquiry, critical thinking, analysis, and argument.

So how does a writer get hooked on an open-ended problem? Although this "how" question is complex at a philosophical level, we can offer two relatively simple and helpful answers. Sometimes you get caught up in a question that others are already debating—an existing question that is already "out there" in a conversation in the public. Some of these "big questions" have sparked conversations for many hundreds of years: How did the universe get created? Why do good people have to suffer? Do humans have free will? Thousands of narrower subject matter questions are being discussed by communities all the time—in classroom debates, discussion threads on blog sites, or in the pages of scholarly journals or newspapers. When you advance in your major, you'll be drawn into disciplinary problems that may be new to you but not to your professors. In such cases, a problem that is already "out there" initiates your search for a possible answer and invites you to join the conversation.

But sometimes you actually initiate a conversation by posing your own problem fresh from your own brain. For example, you find your own problem whenever you see something puzzling in the natural world, note curious or unexplained features in a cultural phenomenon or artifact, or discover conflicts or contradictions within your own way of looking at the world.

In Table 1.1 we describe some of the ways that writers can become gripped by a problem that may lead to engaged writing.

**TABLE 1.1    How Writers Become Gripped by a Problem**

| Occasion That Leads to Your Posing a Problem | Examples | Your Interior Mental State |
|---|---|---|
| | **The problem is already "out there."** *(You enter a conversation already in progress.)* | |
| You encounter others arguing about a problem, and you don't know where you stand. | Our class discussion has left me uncertain about whether health care should be rationed. In *To Kill a Mockingbird*, I can't decide whether Atticus Finch is a good father. | • You are equally persuaded by different views or dissatisfied with all the views. • Part of you thinks X but another part thinks Y (you feel divided). |
| Your gut instinct tells you that someone else is wrong, but you haven't fully investigated the issue (your instinct may be wrong). | This article's explanation of the causes for anorexia doesn't seem quite right to me. Shanita says that we should build more nuclear power plants to combat global warming, but I say nuclear power is too dangerous. | • Your skepticism or intuition pushes against someone else's view. • Your system of values leads you to views different from some-one else. • *NOTE: You aren't gripped by a problem until you have seen the possible strengths of other views and the possible weaknesses of your own. You must go beyond simply having an opinion.* |
| Someone gives you a question that you can't yet answer. | Your boss asks you whether the company should enact the pro-posed marketing plan. Your history professor asks you, "To what extent does Frederick Jackson Turner's frontier hypothesis reflect a Eurocentric world view?" | • You feel overwhelmed with unknowns. • You feel that you can't begin to answer until you do more exploration and research. • You may be able to propose a few possible answers, but you aren't yet satisfied with them. |

*(continued)*

**TABLE 1.1** *continued*

| Occasion That Leads to Your Posing a Problem | Examples | Your Interior Mental State |
|---|---|---|
| | **You pose the problem yourself.** *(You initiate the conversation.)* | |
| You see something puzzling in a natural or cultural phenomenon. | You note that women's fashion magazines have few ads for computers and begin wondering how you could market computers in these magazines.<br><br>You notice that political activists and protesters are using social media to gain attention and gather adherents. How might social media serve purposes beyond entertainment? | • You begin puzzling about something that other people don't notice.<br>• Your mind plays with possible explanations or new approaches.<br>• You begin testing possible solutions or answers. (Often you want to talk to someone—to start a conversation about the problem). |
| You see something unexpected, puzzling, or unexplained in a poem, painting, or other human artifact. | Why is the person in this advertisement walking two dogs rather than just one?<br><br>My classmates believe that Hamlet really loves Ophelia, but then how do you explain the nunnery scene where he treats her like a whore? | • You can't see why the maker/designer/artist did something in such a way.<br>• You notice that one part of this artifact seems unexpected or incongruous.<br>• You begin trying to explain what is puzzling and playing with possible answers. |
| You identify something inconsistent or contradictory in your own view of the world. | I agree with this writer's argument against consumerism, but I really want a large plasma TV. Is consumerism really bad? Am I a materialist? | • You feel unsettled by your own inconsistent views or values.<br>• You probe more deeply into your own identity and place in the world. |

In each of these cases, the problem starts to spark critical thinking. We'll examine the process of critical thinking in more detail when we discuss "wallowing in complexity" (Chapter 2, Concept 2.1).

**FOR WRITING AND DISCUSSION**

## Finding a Problem

**Background:** Figure 1.1 shows a sculpture by Billie Grace Lynn that was the West Collection 2011 Grand Prize Winner. This electric/hybrid motorcycle made from cow bones, a bicycle frame, and motor is a ridable kinetic sculpture. This activist sculpture is intended to inspire people to think about reducing their consumption of meat. Lynn built a full-sized version of the Mad Cow, which runs on waste vegetable oil, and will be taking the motorcycle on a cross-country tour.

**Task:** Spend several minutes writing down one or more open-ended questions that emerge from looking at the photo of this sculpture. What

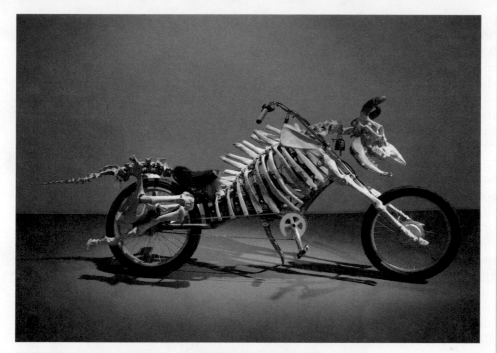

**FIGURE 1.1** *Mad Cow Motorcycle* by Billie Grace Lynn

puzzles you about it? Consider the sculpture's title as well as its appearance and the possible effects the artist hopes to have on viewers. Then share your individual questions with classmates. Speculate about different answers to some of these questions. The best questions will lead to a genuine conversation with different points of view. (If you would like to find out more about Billie Grace Lynn, a quick Web search will yield information about her art training, philosophy of art, and other work.)

In a similar vein, your instructor may ask you to speculate and formulate thought-provoking questions about another puzzling work of art, the surreal painting *Portrait de Famille* (1954) by Dorothea Tanning, which appears on page 1.

## CONCEPT 1.2 **Writers' decisions are shaped by purpose, audience, and genre.**

**1.2**
Make decisions about your writing based on purpose, audience, and genre.

In the introduction to this chapter, we said that writers must address two types of problems: subject matter problems and rhetorical problems. In this section we look at rhetorical problems in more detail. To begin, we'll explain in more detail what we mean by the term *rhetoric*.

### What Is Rhetoric?

At the broadest level, **rhetoric** is the study of how human beings use language and other symbols to influence the attitudes, beliefs, and actions of others. One prominent twentieth-century rhetorician, Kenneth Burke, calls rhetoric "a symbolic means of inducing cooperation in beings that by nature respond to symbols." To understand what Burke means by "symbols," consider the difference in flirting behavior between peacocks and humans. When male peacocks flirt, they spread their fantastic tail feathers, do mating dances, and screech weirdly to attract females, but the whole process is governed by instinct. Peacocks don't have to choose among different symbolic actions such as buying an upscale tail from Neiman Marcus versus a knockoff tail from Walmart. Poor flirting humans, however, must make dozens of symbolic choices, all of which convey meanings to audiences. Consider, for example, the different flirting messages humans send to each other by their choice of clothes, their hairstyles, their accessories, or their song playlists. Even one's word choices (for example, street slang versus intellectual jargon), one's e-mail username (janejones@___.net versus foxychick@___.net) or one's choice of major (chemical engineering versus film studies) gives further hints of a person's identity, values, and social groups. Rhetoricians study, among other things, how these symbols arise within a given culture and how they influence others.

In a narrower sense, rhetoric is the art of making messages persuasive. Perhaps the most famous definition of rhetoric comes from the Greek philosopher Aristotle, who defined rhetoric as "the ability to see, in any particular case, all the available means of persuasion." Effective speakers or writers fruitfully begin by trying to understand their audience's values and beliefs and the kinds of arguments that different audience members might make on a given issue ("all the available means of persuasion"). If we imagine the interaction of several speakers, each proposing different points of view and each analyzing and appreciating others' viewpoints, we can see how mutual understanding might emerge. The study of rhetoric can therefore help humans construct more functional and productive communities.

At an operational level, writers can be said to "think rhetorically" whenever they are consciously aware of writing to an audience for a purpose within a genre. Let's look more closely at each of these in turn.

## How Writers Think about Purpose

In this section, we want to help you think more productively about your purpose for writing. At a specific level, your purpose is to bring something new or contestable to your reader. At a more generalized level, your purpose can be expressed as a rhetorical aim. Let's look at each in turn.

**Purpose as a Desire to Bring Something New or Contestable to Your Reader** One powerful way to think about purpose is to focus on what is new or controversial (contestable—capable of being contested) in your paper. For most essays, you can write a one-sentence, nutshell statement about your purpose.

> My purpose is to give my readers a vivid picture of my difficult struggle with Graves' disease. [What's new: a vivid account of one person's struggle with Graves' disease.]

My purpose is to explain how Thoreau's view of nature differs in important ways from that of contemporary environmentalists. [What's new: a possibly controversial way of thinking about the difference between Thoreau and contemporary environmentalists.]

My purpose is to persuade the general public to ban the sale of assault weapons. [What's new: a contestable argument that some would say narrows the rights conveyed in the Second Amendment.]

This view of purpose will be developed further when we explain how an effective thesis statement tries to bring about some change in the reader's view of the subject (Chapter 2, Concept 2.2). Writers of closed-form prose often place explicit purpose statements in their introductions along with their thesis. In most other forms of writing, the writer uses a behind-the-scenes purpose statement to achieve focus and direction but seldom states the purpose explicitly.

**Purpose as Rhetorical Aim**    It is also possible to think of purpose more broadly by using the concept of **rhetorical aim**. Articulating your rhetorical aim can help you clarify your relationship to your audience and identify typical ways that a piece of writing might be structured and developed. The writing projects in Part 2 of this textbook are based on six different rhetorical aims: to express, to explore, to inform, to analyze/ synthesize, to persuade, and to reflect. Table 1.2 gives you an overview of each of these rhetorical aims and sketches out how different aims typically use different approaches to subject matter, how the writer's task and relationship to readers differ according to aim, and how a chosen aim affects the writing's genre and its position on the spectrum from open to closed forms.

**TABLE 1.2    Purpose as Rhetorical Aim**

| Rhetorical Aim | Focus of Writing | Relationship to Audience | Forms and Genres |
|---|---|---|---|
| **Express or share**<br><br>May also include an artistic aim | Your own life, personal experiences, reflections | You share aspects of your life; you invite readers to walk in your shoes, to experience your insights. | **Form:** Has many open-form features<br>**Sample genres:** journal, blog, personal Web site, or online profile; personal essays or literacy narratives, often with artistic features |
| **Explore or inquire**<br>(Chapter 6) | A significant subject-matter problem that puzzles you | You take readers on your own intellectual journey by showing your inquiry process (raising questions, seeking evidence, considering alternative views). | **Form:** Follows open form in being narrative based; is thesis seeking rather than thesis supporting<br>**Sample genres:** freewriting; research logs; articles and books focused on process of discovery |

*(continued)*

**TABLE 1.2**    *continued*

| Rhetorical Aim | Focus of Writing | Relationship to Audience | Forms and Genres |
|---|---|---|---|
| **Inform or explain** | Factual knowledge addressing a reader's need or curiosity | You provide knowledge that your readers need or want, or you arouse curiosity and provide new, surprising information. You expect readers to trust your authority. | **Form:** Usually has a closed-form structure<br>**Sample genres:** encyclopedia articles; instruction booklets; sales reports; technical reports; informative magazine articles; informative Web sites |
| **Analyze, synthesize, or interpret** (Chapters 7–8) | Complex subject matter that you can break down into parts and put together in new ways for greater understanding | Using critical thinking and possibly research, you challenge readers with a new way of understanding your subject. Skeptical readers expect you to support your thesis with good particulars. | **Form:** Typically has a closed-form structure<br>**Sample genres:** scholarly articles; experimental reports; many kinds of college research papers; public affairs magazine articles; many kinds of blogs |
| **Persuade** (Chapters 9–10) | Subject-matter questions that have multiple controversial answers | You try to convince readers, who may not share your values and beliefs, to accept your stance on an issue by providing good reasons and evidence and attending to alternative views. | **Form:** Usually closed form, but may employ many open-form features for persuasive effect<br>**Sample genres:** letters to the editor; op-ed pieces; advocacy pieces in public affairs magazines; advocacy Web sites; researched academic arguments |
| **Reflect** | Subject matter closely connected to your interests and experience; often involves self-evaluation of an experience | Writing for yourself as well as for a reader, you seek to find personal meaning and value in an experience or course of study. You assume a sympathetic and interested reader. | **Form:** Anywhere on the closed-to-open-form continuum<br>**Sample genres:** memoirs, workplace self-evaluations; introductory letter for a portfolio; personal essays looking back on an experience |

## How Writers Think about Audience

In our discussion of purpose, we have already had a lot to say about audience. What you know about your readers—their familiarity with your subject matter, their level of expertise, their reasons for reading, their values and beliefs—affects most of the choices you make as a writer.

In assessing your audience, you must first determine who that audience is—a single reader (for example, your boss), a select group (a scholarship committee; readers of a particular blog), or a general audience. If you imagine a general audience, you will need to make some initial assumptions about their views and values and about their current attitude toward your subject. Doing so creates an "implied audience," giving you a stable rather than a moving target so that you can make decisions about your own piece of writing. Once you have identified your audience, you can use the following strategies for analysis.

## Strategies for Analyzing Audience

| Questions to Ask about Your Audience | Reasons for Asking the Question |
|---|---|
| How busy are my readers? | • Helps you decide on length, document design, and methods of organization (see Concept 1.3 on open versus closed forms).<br>• In workplace writing, busy readers usually appreciate tightly organized prose with headings that allow for skimming. |
| What are my readers' motives for reading? | • If the reader has requested the document, he or she will probably already be interested in what you say.<br>• In most cases, you need to hook your readers' interest and keep them engaged. |
| What is my relationship with my readers? | • Helps you decide on a formal or informal style<br>• Helps you select tone—polite and serious or loose and slangy |
| What do my readers already know about my topic? Do my readers have more or less expertise than I have, or about the same expertise? | • Helps you determine what will be old/familiar information for your audience versus new/unfamiliar information<br>• Helps you decide how much background and context to include<br>• Helps you decide to use or avoid in-group jargon and specialized knowledge |
| How interested are my readers in my topic? Do my readers already care about it? | • Helps you decide how to write the introduction<br>• Helps you determine how to make the problem you address interesting and significant to your reader |
| What will be my readers' attitudes toward my thesis? Do my readers share my beliefs and values? Will they be skeptical of my argument or even threatened by it? | • Helps you make numerous decisions about tone, structure, reference to alternative views, and use of evidence<br>• Helps you decide on the persona and tone you want to project |

To appreciate the importance of audience, consider how a change in audience can affect the actual content of a piece. Suppose you want voters to approve a bond issue to build a new baseball stadium. For voters who are baseball fans, your argument can appeal to their love of the game and to the improved fan amenities in the new park (more comfortable seats, better sight lines, bigger restrooms, more food options, and so forth). But to reach non-baseball fans, you must take a different tack, appealing to values other than love of baseball. For this new audience, you might argue that the new stadium will bring new tax revenues to the city, clean up a run-down area, revitalize local businesses, or stimulate tourism. Your purpose remains the same—to persuade taxpayers to fund the stadium—but the content of your argument changes if your audience changes.

For college papers, students may think that they are writing to an audience of one—the instructor. But because instructors are captive audiences and because they often know more about the subject matter than the student writer (making it hard for the student writer to bring something "new" to the reader), they often ask students to address real audiences or to role-play addressing hypothetical audiences. They may ask you to blog for a Web audience, publish for classmates on a course Web site, write for community readers in a service learning context, or imagine writing for a particular magazine or journal. As an alternative, they may create case assignments with built-in audiences (for example, "You are an accountant in the firm of Numbers and Fudge; one day you receive a letter from…"). If your instructor does not specify an audience, you can generally assume an audience of student peers who have approximately the same level of knowledge and expertise in the field as you do, who are engaged by the question you address, and who want to read your writing and be surprised in some way.

## How Writers Think about Genre

The term **genre** refers to categories of writing that follow certain conventions of style, structure, approach to subject matter, and document design. Table 1.3 shows different kinds of genres.

The concept of genre creates strong reader expectations, placing specific demands on writers. How you write any given letter, report, or article is influenced by the structure and style of hundreds of previous letters, reports, or articles written

**TABLE 1.3    Examples of Genres**

| Personal Writing | Academic Writing | Popular Culture | Public Affairs, Civic Writing | Professional Writing | Literature |
|---|---|---|---|---|---|
| Letter | Scholarly article | Articles for magazines such as *Seventeen, Ebony,* or *Vibe* | Letter to the editor | Cover letter for a job application | Short story |
| Diary/journal | Research paper | | Newspaper editorial | Résumé | Novel |
| Memoir | Scientific report | Advertisements | Op-ed piece | Business memo | Graphic novel |
| Blog | Abstract or summary | Hip-hop lyrics | Advocacy Web site | Legal brief | Play |
| Text message | Book review | Fan Web sites | Political blog | Brochure | Sonnet |
| E-mail | Essay exam | Bumper stickers | Magazine article on civic issue | Technical manual | Epic poem |
| Facebook profile | Annotated bibliography | Reviews of books, films, plays, music | | Instruction booklet | Literary podcast |
| Personal essay | Textual analysis | | | Proposal | |
| Literacy narrative | | | | Report | |
| Status update | | | | Press release | |
| Tweet | | | | | |

in the same genre. If you wanted to write for *Reader's Digest*, for example, you would have to use the conventions that appeal to its older, conservative readers: simple language, strong reliance on anecdotal evidence in arguments, high level of human interest, and choice of subject matter that reinforces the conservative values of individualism, self-discipline, and family. If you wanted to write for *Seventeen* or *Rolling Stone*, however, you would need to use quite different conventions concerning subject matter, style, and document design. Likewise, the conventions for writing for the Web (blogs, podcasts, Web pages) differ significantly from writing for print.

To illustrate the relationship of a writer to a genre, we sometimes draw an analogy with clothing. Although most people have a variety of clothing in their wardrobes, the genre of activity for which they are dressing (class, concert, party, job interview, wedding) constrains their expression of individuality. A man dressing for a job interview might express his personality through choice of tie or quality and style of business suit; he probably wouldn't express it by wearing a Hawaiian shirt and sandals. Even when people deviate from a convention, they tend to do so in a conventional way. For example, people who do not want to follow typical middle class clothing genres form their own genres of goth, grunge, or hipster. So, by analogy, if you are writing a business memo or an experimental report in APA style, you are constrained by the conventions of the genre. The concept of genre raises intriguing and sometimes unsettling questions about the relationship of the unique self to a social convention or tradition.

In the last ten years, the arrival of Web 2.0 has created a whole range of new genres. Blogs, for example, typically feature links to other Web sites and can include uploaded images, music, or videos. Whereas a print article is stable and fixed, the same article published as a blog can turn rapidly into an on-going conversation as readers post comments first to the original blogger and then to each other. A blog, then, becomes a dynamic conversation site—a genre impossible in print. Note too that if you post a response to someone else's blog, the genre of "blog response" places formidable constraints on outsiders: If you don't reveal the right insider savvy about the conversation, you can be rudely flamed. This dynamic community of readers and writers—along with the hypertext structure— makes Web genres substantially different from print genres.

See Chapter 4 for a fuller discussion of Web genres.

## Thinking about Purpose, Audience, and Genre

**FOR WRITING AND DISCUSSION**

Suppose that you are a political science major researching Second Amendment rights. Suppose further that you generally support the right to own hunting rifles and handguns but that your research has led you to oppose ownership of assault weapons as well as high-capacity ammo clips. Through your research, you have gathered different "means of persuasion" for your position—statistical data, sociological studies of gun violence, political studies of Second Amendment controversies, comparison data with other countries, and anecdotal stories (published in newspapers or on the Web) from witnesses or surviving victims of massacre shootings. You are ready to start writing.

*(continued)*

How would your piece of writing be different under the following conditions related to purpose, audience, and genre?

1. You are an intern for your district's member of the U.S. House of Representatives. She asks you to write a well-documented argument recommending the position she should take on gun control issues.
2. You are an active citizen seriously worried about gun violence. You decide to start a blog devoted to building up public anger against easy access to assault weapons. You now need to write and post your first blog.
3. You are invited by your local newspaper to write an op-ed column on gun control. You have 500 words to make your best case.
4. You've read an argument opposing a ban on assault weapons and high-capacity ammo magazines on a blog site sponsored by the National Rifle Association. You want to post a counter-argument on this blog site—but you want to be taken seriously, not flamed.
5. You seek a broader public for your anti-assault weapon campaign. You decide to send a Twitter tweet as well as create a bumper sticker.

---

**1.3**

Use varying rules for "good writing" depending on the rhetorical context.

## CONCEPT 1.3 The rules for "good writing" vary depending on rhetorical context.

So far we have said that writers must address two types of problems: subject matter problems and rhetorical problems. As we have suggested, rhetorical problems, which influence the writer's decisions about content, organization, and style, often loom as large for writers as do the subject-matter problems that drive their writing in the first place.

In this section, we focus on one important example of a rhetorical problem, an example that will interest all new college writers: Are there "rules" for good college writing? If so, what are they? In our experience, many writers come to college guided by writing rules they learned in high school: "Never use 'I' in a formal paper." "Have a thesis statement." "Use good transitions." "Put a topic sentence in every paragraph." But are these really good rules to follow? Our answer: "Sometimes yes, sometimes no." You'll be able to appreciate this answer for yourself through the following thought exercise.

### A Thought Exercise: Two Pieces of Good Writing That Follow Different "Rules"

Read the following short pieces of nonfiction prose. The first is a letter to the editor written by a professional civil engineer in response to a newspaper editorial arguing for the development of wind-generated electricity. The second short piece is entitled "A Festival of Rain." It was written by the American poet and religious writer Thomas Merton, a Trappist monk. After reading the two samples carefully, proceed to the discussion questions that follow.

## David Rockwood
## A Letter to the Editor

1    Your editorial on November 16, "Get Bullish on Wind Power," is based on fantasy rather than fact. There are several basic reasons why wind-generated power can in no way serve as a reasonable major alternative to other electrical energy supply alternatives for the Pacific Northwest power system.

2    First and foremost, wind power is unreliable. Electric power generation is evaluated not only on the amount of energy provided, but also on its ability to meet system peak load requirements on an hourly, daily, and weekly basis. In other words, an effective power system would have to provide enough electricity to meet peak demands in a situation when the wind energy would be unavailable—either in no wind situations or in severe blizzard conditions, which would shut down the wind generators. Because wind power cannot be relied on at times of peak needs, it would have to be backed up by other power generation resources at great expense and duplication of facilities.

3    Secondly, there are major unsolved problems involved in the design of wind generation facilities, particularly for those located in rugged mountain areas. Ice storms, in particular, can cause sudden dynamic problems for the rotating blades and mechanisms which could well result in breakdown or failure of the generators. Furthermore, the design of the facilities to meet the stresses imposed by high winds in these remote mountain regions, in the order of 125 miles per hour, would indeed escalate the costs.

4    Thirdly, the environmental impact of constructing wind generation facilities amounting to 28 percent of the region's electrical supply system (as proposed in your editorial) would be tremendous. The Northwest Electrical Power system presently has a capacity of about 37,000 megawatts of hydro power and 10,300 megawatts of thermal, for a total of about 48,000 megawatts. Meeting 28 percent of this capacity by wind power generators would, most optimistically, require about 13,400 wind towers, each with about 1,000 kilowatt (one megawatt) generating capacity. These towers, some 100 to 200 feet high, would have to be located in the mountains of Oregon and Washington. These would encompass hundreds of square miles of pristine mountain area, which, together with interconnecting transmission facilities, control works, and roads, would indeed have major adverse environmental impacts on the region.

5    There are many other lesser problems of control and maintenance of such a system. Let it be said that, from my experience and knowledge as a professional engineer, the use of wind power as a major resource in the Pacific Northwest power system is strictly a pipe dream.

## Thomas Merton
## A Festival of Rain

1    Let me say this before rain becomes a utility that they can plan and distribute for money. By "they" I mean the people who cannot understand that rain is a festival, who do not appreciate its gratuity, who think that what has no price has no

(continued)

value, that what cannot be sold is not real, so that the only way to make something *actual* is to place it on the market. The time will come when they will sell you even your rain. At the moment it is still free, and I am in it. I celebrate its gratuity and its meaninglessness.

2    The rain I am in is not like the rain of cities. It fills the woods with an immense and confused sound. It covers the flat roof of the cabin and its porch with insistent and controlled rhythms. And I listen, because it reminds me again and again that the whole world runs by rhythms I have not yet learned to recognize, rhythms that are not those of the engineer.

3    I came up here from the monastery last night, sloshing through the corn fields, said Vespers, and put some oatmeal on the Coleman stove for supper.... The night became very dark. The rain surrounded the whole cabin with its enormous virginal myth, a whole world of meaning, of secrecy, of silence, of rumor. Think of it: all that speech pouring down, selling nothing, judging nobody, drenching the thick mulch of dead leaves, soaking the trees, filling the gullies and crannies of the wood with water, washing out the places where men have stripped the hillside! What a thing it is to sit absolutely alone, in a forest, at night, cherished by this wonderful, unintelligible, perfectly innocent speech, the most comforting speech in the world, the talk that rain makes by itself all over the ridges, and the talk of the watercourses everywhere in the hollows!

4    Nobody started it, nobody is going to stop it. It will talk as long as it wants, this rain. As long as it talks I am going to listen.

5    But I am also going to sleep, because here in this wilderness I have learned how to sleep again. Here I am not alien. The trees I know, the night I know, the rain I know. I close my eyes and instantly sink into the whole rainy world of which I am a part, and the world goes on with me in it, for I am not alien to it.

---

**FOR WRITING AND DISCUSSION**

## Comparing Rockwood's and Merton's Writing

Working as a whole class or in small groups, share your answers to the following questions:

1. What are the main differences between the two types of writing?
2. Create a metaphor, simile, or analogy that best sums up your feelings about the most important differences between Rockwood's and Merton's writing: "Rockwood's writing is like..., but Merton's writing is like...."
3. Explain why your metaphors are apt. How do your metaphors help clarify or illuminate the differences between the two pieces of writing?

Working as a whole class or in small groups, share your answers to the above questions.

## Distinctions between Closed and Open Forms of Writing

Here now is our own brief analysis of the differences between these two pieces. David Rockwood's letter and Thomas Merton's mini-essay are both examples of nonfiction prose. But as these examples illustrate, nonfiction prose can vary enormously in form and style. When we give this exercise to our students, they have no trouble articulating the differences between the two pieces of writing. Rockwood's piece has an explicit thesis statement, unified and coherent paragraphs with topic sentences, evidence to support each topic sentence, and strong transitions between each paragraph. Merton's piece, in contrast, seems to ignore these rules; it is more artistic, more creative, more like a story. (Among our students, one group said that Rockwood's piece is like riding a train on a track while Merton's piece is like floating down a river on an inner tube.) One way to label these differences is to say that Rockwood's piece is thesis-based while Merton's piece is narrative-based. But another way to distinguish between them is to place them on a continuum from closed-form prose to open-form prose (see Figure 1.2).

**Closed-Form Prose**    Rockwood's letter illustrates tightly **closed-form prose** (far left on the continuum), which we can define as writing with a hierarchical structure of points and details in support of an explicit thesis. It is characterized by unified and coherent paragraphs, topic sentences, transitions between sentences and paragraphs, and forecasting of the whole before presentation of the parts. Once Rockwood states his thesis ("Wind-generated power isn't a reasonable alternative energy source in the Pacific Northwest"), readers know the point of the essay and can predict its structure: a series of paragraphs giving reasons and evidence in support of the thesis. We say that this form is "closed" because it doesn't allow any digressions or structural surprises. Because its structure is predictable, its success depends entirely on the quality of its ideas, which must bring something new to readers or challenge them with something contestable. Closed-form prose is what most college professors expect from their students on most occasions; likewise it is often the most effective form of writing in professional and business settings. (Note that the five-paragraph essay, common in many high schools, is a by-the-numbers approach for teaching closed-form prose.)

**Open-Form Prose**    In contrast, Merton's "A Festival of Rain" falls toward the right end of the closed-to-open continuum. **Open-form prose** resists reduction to a single, summarizable thesis. It is characterized by narrative or story-like structure, sometimes with abrupt transitions, and uses various literary techniques to make the prose memorable and powerful. Although Merton is gladdened by rain, and clearly opposes the consumer culture that will try to "sell" you the rain, it is hard to pin down exactly what he means by "festival of rain" or by rain's "gratuity and its meaninglessness." The main organizing principle of Merton's piece, like that of most open-form prose, is a story or narrative—in this case the story

**FIGURE 1.2**
A Continuum
of Essay Types:
Closed to Open
Forms

**Closed Forms**

**Top-down thesis-based prose**
- thesis explicitly stated in introduction
- all parts of essay linked clearly to thesis
- body paragraphs develop thesis
- body paragraphs have topic sentences
- structure forecasted

**Delayed-thesis prose**
- thesis appears near end
- text reads as a mystery
- reader held in suspense

of Merton's leaving the monastery to sleep in the rain-drenched cabin. Rather than announce a thesis and support it with reasons and evidence, Merton lets his point emerge suggestively from his story and his language. Open-form essays still have a focus, but the focus is more like a theme in fiction than like a thesis in argument. Readers may argue over its meaning in the same way that they argue over the meaning of a film or poem or novel. Consider also the extent to which Merton violates the rules for closed-form prose. Instead of using transitions between paragraphs, Merton juxtaposes narrative passages about his camping trip ("I came up here from the monastery last night...") with passages that make cryptic, interpretive comments about his experience ("The rain I am in is not like the rain of cities"). Unlike paragraphs in closed-form prose, which typically begin with topic sentences and are developed with supporting details, the paragraphs in Merton's piece have no clear hierarchical structure; paragraph four, in fact, has only twenty-nine words. Features of open-form prose often appear in personal essays, in popular magazine articles, in exploratory or reflective writing, or in character profiles that tell stories of a person's life. Open-form prose usually has an artistic or aesthetic appeal, and many examples are classified as literary nonfiction or creative nonfiction.

## Flexibility of "Rules" along the Continuum

As you can see from the continuum in Figure 1.2, essays can fall anywhere along the scale. Not all thesis-with-support writing has to be top down, stating its thesis explicitly in the introduction. In some cases writers choose to delay the thesis, creating a more exploratory, open-ended, "let's think through this together" feeling before finally stating the main point late in the essay. In some cases writers explore a problem without *ever* finding a satisfactory thesis, creating an essay that seeks a thesis rather than supporting one. Because exploratory essays are aimed at deepening the reader's engagement with a question and resisting easy answers, they often include digressions, speculations, conjectures, multiple perspectives, and occasional invitations to the reader to help solve the problem. When writers reach the far right-hand position on the continuum, they no longer state an

Open Forms

**Thesis-seeking prose**
- essay organized around a question rather than a thesis
- essay explores the problem or question, looking at it in many ways
- writer may or may not arrive at thesis

**Theme-based narrative**
- often organized chronologically or has storylike elements
- often used to heighten or deepen a problem, or show its human significance
- often has an implicit theme rather than a thesis
- often violates rules of closed-form prose by using literary techniques

explicit thesis. Instead, like fiction writers, they embed their points in plot, character, imagery, and dialogue, leaving their readers to *infer* a theme from the text.

## Where to Place Your Writing along the Continuum

Clearly, essays at opposite ends of this continuum operate in different ways and obey different rules. Because each position on the continuum has its appropriate uses, the writer's challenge is to determine which sort of writing is most appropriate in a given situation. Most college papers (but not all) and much professional writing are written in closed form. Thus if you were writing a business proposal, a legal brief, or an academic paper for a scholarly audience, you would typically choose a closed-form structure, and your finished product would include elements such as the following:

- An explicit thesis in the introduction
- Forecasting of structure
- Cohesive and unified paragraphs with topic sentences
- Clear transitions between sentences and between parts
- No digressions

But if you were writing, say, to express your conflicted relationship with a parent, your first discovery of evil, or your life-changing encounter with a stranger, you would probably rely on juxtaposed narratives and stories, moving toward the open end of the continuum and violating one or more of these closed-form conventions.

What is important to see is that having a thesis statement, topic sentences, good transitions, and unified and coherent paragraphs is not a mark of "good prose" but simply of "closed-form" prose. What makes closed-form prose good is the quality of its ideas. In contrast, powerful open-form prose often ignores closed-form rules. It's not that open-form prose doesn't have rules; it's that the rules are different, just as the rules for jazz are different from the rules for a classical sonata. Whether the writer chooses a closed-form or an open-form approach depends on the intended audience of the piece and the writer's purpose.

> ### Thinking Personally about Closed and Open Forms
>
> Do you and your classmates most enjoy writing prose at the closed or at the more open end of the continuum? Recall a favorite piece of writing that you have done in the past. Jot down a brief description of the kind of writing this was (a personal-experience essay, a piece of workplace writing, a research paper, a blog post, a persuasive argument) and explain why you liked it. Where would you place this piece of writing on the closed-to-open continuum? Are you at your best in closed-form writing that calls for an explicit thesis statement and logical support? Or are you at your best in more open, creative, and personal forms? Share your preferences with those of classmates.

## Chapter Summary

This chapter has introduced you to three useful rhetorical concepts connected to the demands of college writing.

- *Concept 1.1 Subject matter problems are the heart of college writing.* The starting place of college writing is a subject matter problem that interests both the writer and the reader. Writers write because they have something new, surprising, or challenging to say in response to that problem. Writers can pose their own problematic questions about a subject or become engaged in controversies or issues that are already "out there."
- *Concept 1.2 Writers' decisions are shaped by purpose, audience, and genre.* To articulate purpose, writers focus on what is new or contestable in their intended work or, at a more general level, consider their rhetorical aim. To think about audience, they analyze how much their readers already know about (and care about) their subject and assess their readers' values, beliefs, and assumptions. Writers attend to genre by thinking about the conventions of content, structure, and style associated with the kind of document they are writing.
- *Concept 1.3 The rules for good writing vary according to rhetorical context.* Good writing can vary along a continuum from closed to open forms. Closed-form prose has an explicit thesis statement, unified and coherent paragraphs with topic sentences, and good transitions. Closed-form prose is "good" only if its ideas bring something new or challenging to the reader. At the other end of the continuum, open-form prose often uses narrative techniques such as storytelling, evocative language, surprising juxtapositions, and other features that violate the conventions of closed-form prose.

## Two Messages for Different Purposes, Audiences, and Genres

The purpose of this brief write-to-learn assignment is to let you experience first-hand how rhetorical context influences a writer's choices. The whole assignment, which has three parts, should not be more than two double-spaced pages long.

1. *A Text Message to a Friend.* Write a cell phone text message to a friend using the abbreviations, capitalization, and punctuation style typically used for text messages. Explain that you are going to miss Friday's social event (movie, pizza night, dance, party) because you have to fly home to attend a funeral. Ask your friend about another time for a get-together. (Make up details as you need them.)

2. *An E-Mail Message to a Professor.* Compose an e-mail message to your professor explaining that you are going to miss Friday's field trip because you have to fly home to attend a funeral. You are asking how you can make up for this missed field trip. (Use the same details as in item 1.) Create a subject line appropriate for this new context.

3. *Reflection on the Two Messages.* Using Items 1 and 2 as illustrative examples, explain to someone who has not read Chapter 1 of this text why a difference in your rhetorical context caused you to make different choices in these two messages. In your explanation, use the terms "purpose," "audience," and "genre." Your goal is to teach your audience the meanings of these terms.

# 2

# EXPLORING PROBLEMS, MAKING CLAIMS

## WHAT YOU WILL LEARN

**2.1** To "wallow in complexity" in order to determine your thesis.

**2.2** To write a strong thesis that surprises readers with something new or challenging.

**2.3** To begin a typical closed-form introduction with the problem, not the thesis.

> **"In management, people don't merely 'write papers,' they solve problems," said [business professor A. Kimbrough Sherman]. . . . He explained that he wanted to construct situations where students would have to "wallow in complexity" and work their way out, as managers must.**
>
> —A. Kimbrough Sherman, Management Professor, Quoted by
> Barbara E. Walvoord and Lucille P. McCarthy

n the previous chapter we explained how writers become engaged with subject matter problems, how writers think rhetorically about their purpose, audience, and genre, and how the rules for good writing vary along a continuum from closed to open forms. In this chapter we show how writers think rhetorically about their subject matter during the process of exploring a problem and determining a possible claim.* Because this chapter concerns academic writing, we focus on closed-form prose—the kind of thesis-governed writing most often required in college courses and in civic and professional life.

## CONCEPT 2.1  **To determine their thesis, writers must often "wallow in complexity."**

As we explained in the previous chapter, the starting point of academic writing is a "good, interesting question." At the outset, we should say that these questions may lead you toward new and unfamiliar ways of thinking. Beginning college

*In this text we use the words *claim* and *thesis statement* interchangeably. In courses across the curriculum, instructors typically use one or the other of these terms. Other synonyms for *thesis statement* include *proposition, main point,* or *thesis sentence.*

students typically value questions that have right answers. Students ask their professors questions because they are puzzled by confusing parts of a textbook, a lecture, or an assigned reading. They hope their professors will explain the confusing material clearly. Their purpose in asking these questions is to eliminate misunderstandings, not to open up controversy and debate. Although basic comprehension questions are important, they are not the kinds of inquiry questions that lead to strong college-level writing and thinking.

Instead, the kinds of questions that stimulate the writing most valued in college are open-ended questions that focus on unknowns or uncertainties (what educational researcher Ken Bain calls "beautiful problems") rather than factual questions that have single, correct answers.* Good open-ended questions invite multiple points of view or alternative hypotheses; they stimulate critical thinking and research. Our way of thinking about problems has been motivated by the South American educator Paulo Freire, who wanted his students (often poor, illiterate villagers) to become *problematizers* instead of memorizers. Freire opposed what he called "the banking method" of education, in which students deposit knowledge in their memory banks and then make withdrawals during exams. The banking method, Freire believed, left third world villagers passive and helpless to improve their situations in life. Using the banking method, students being taught to read and write might learn the word *water* through drill-and-skill workbook sentences such as, "The water is in the well." With Freire's problematizing method, students might learn the word *water* by asking, "Why is the water dirty and who is responsible?" Freire believed that good questions have stakes and that answering them can make a difference in the world.

## Learning to Wallow in Complexity

This focus on important problems explains why college professors want students to go beyond simply understanding course concepts as taught in textbooks and lectures. Such comprehension is important, but it is only a starting point. As management professor A. Kimbrough Sherman explains in the epigraph to this chapter, college instructors expect students to wrestle with problems by applying the concepts, data, and thought processes they learn in a course to new situations. As Sherman puts it, students must learn to "wallow in complexity" and work their way out. To put it another way, college professors want students to "earn" their thesis. (Earning a thesis is very different from simply stating your opinion, which might not be deeply examined at all.) Because college professors value this kind of complex thinking, they often phrase essay exam questions or writing assignments as open-ended problems that can be answered in more than one way. They are looking not for the right answer, but for well-supported arguments that acknowledge alternative views. A C paper and an A paper may have

---

*Cognitive psychologists call these beautiful problems "ill-structured." An ill-structured problem has competing solutions, requiring the thinker to argue for the best solution in the absence of full and complete data or in the presence of stakeholders with different backgrounds, assumptions, beliefs, and values. In contrast, a "well-structured" problem eventually yields a correct answer. Math problems that can be solved by applying the right formulae and processes are well structured; they yield single, agreed upon "right answers."

the same "answer" (identical thesis statements), but the C writer may have waded only ankle deep into the mud of complexity, whereas the A writer wallowed in it and worked a way out.

What skills are required for successful wallowing? Specialists in critical thinking have identified the following:

### CRITICAL THINKING SKILLS NEEDED FOR "WALLOWING IN COMPLEXITY"

- The ability to pose problematic questions
- The ability to analyze a problem in all its dimensions—to define its key terms, determine its causes, understand its history, appreciate its human dimension and its connection to one's own personal experience, and appreciate what makes it problematic or complex
- The ability (and determination) to find, gather, and interpret facts, data, and other information relevant to the problem (often involving library, Internet, or field research)
- The ability to imagine alternative solutions to the problem, to see different ways in which the question might be answered and different perspectives for viewing it
- The ability to analyze competing approaches and answers, to construct arguments for and against alternatives, and to choose the best solution in light of values, objectives, and other criteria that you determine and articulate
- The ability to write an effective argument justifying your choice while acknowledging counterarguments

We discuss and develop these skills throughout this text.

## Seeing Each Academic Discipline as a Field of Inquiry and Argument

In addition to these general thinking abilities, critical thinking requires what psychologists call "domain-specific" skills. Each academic discipline has its own characteristic ways of approaching knowledge and its own specialized habits of mind. The questions asked by psychologists differ from those asked by historians or anthropologists; the evidence and assumptions used to support arguments in literary analysis differ from those in philosophy or sociology. As illustrations, here are some examples of how different disciplines might pose different questions about hip-hop:

- *Psychology:* To what extent do hip-hop lyrics increase misogynistic or homophobic attitudes in male listeners?
- *History:* What was the role of urban housing projects in the early development of hip-hop?
- *Sociology:* How does the level of an individual's appreciation for rap music vary by ethnicity, class, age, geographic region, and gender?
- *Rhetoric/Composition:* What images of urban life do the lyrics of rap songs portray?
- *Marketing and Management:* How did the white media turn a black, urban phenomenon into corporate profits?

- *Women's Studies:* What influence does hip-hop music have on the self-image of African-American women?
- *Global Studies:* How are other countries adapting hip-hop to their cultures?

As these questions suggest, when you study a new discipline, you must learn not only the knowledge that scholars in that discipline have acquired over the years, but also the processes they used to discover that knowledge. It is useful to think of each academic discipline as a network of conversations in which participants exchange information, respond to each other's questions, and express agreement and disagreement. As each discipline evolves and changes, its central questions evolve also, creating a fascinating, dynamic conversation that defines the discipline. Table 2.1 provides examples of questions that scholars have debated over the years as well as questions they are addressing today.

**TABLE 2.1    Scholarly Questions in Different Disciplines**

| Field | Examples of Current Cutting-Edge Questions | Examples of Historical Controversies |
|---|---|---|
| Anatomy | What is the effect of a pregnant rat's alcohol ingestion on the development of fetal eye tissue? | In 1628, William Harvey produced a treatise arguing that the heart, through repeated contractions, causes blood to circulate through the body. His views were attacked by followers of the Greek physician Galen. |
| Literature | To what extent does the structure of a work of literature, for example, Conrad's *Heart of Darkness*, reflect the class and gender bias of the author? | In the 1920s, a group of New Critics argued that the interpretation of a work of literature should be based on close examination of the work's imagery and form and that the intentions of the writer and the biases of the reader were not important. These views held sway in U.S. universities until the late 1960s, when they came increasingly under attack by deconstructionists and other postmoderns, who claimed that author intentions and reader's bias were important parts of the work's meaning. |
| Rhetoric/ Composition | How does hypertext structure and increased attention to visual images in Web-based writing affect the composing processes of writers? | Prior to the 1970s, college writing courses in the United States were typically organized around the rhetorical modes (description, narration, exemplification, comparison and contrast, and so forth). This approach was criticized by the expressivist school associated with the British composition researcher James Britton. Since the 1980s, composition scholars have proposed various alternative strategies for designing and sequencing assignments. |
| Psychology | What are the underlying causes of gender identification? To what extent are differences between male and female behavior explainable by nature (genetics, body chemistry) versus nurture (social learning)? | In the early 1900s under the influence of Sigmund Freud, psychoanalytic psychologists began explaining human behavior in terms of unconscious drives and mental processes that stemmed from repressed childhood experiences. Later, psychoanalysts were opposed by behaviorists, who rejected the notion of the unconscious and explained behavior as responses to environmental stimuli. |

## Using Exploratory Writing to Help You Wallow in Complexity

One of the important discoveries of research in rhetoric and composition is the extent to which experienced writers use writing to generate and discover ideas. Not all writing, in other words, is initially intended as a final product for readers. The very act of writing—often without concern for audience, structure, or correctness—can stimulate the mind to produce ideas. Moreover, when you write down your thoughts, you'll have a record of your thinking that you can draw on later. In Chapter 11 we explain this phenomenon more fully, showing you how to take full advantage of the writing process for invention of ideas and revision for readers. In this section we describe five strategies of exploratory writing and talking: freewriting; focused freewriting; idea mapping; dialectic talk in person, in class discussions, or in electronic discussion boards; and playing the believing and doubting game.

**Freewriting**  *Freewriting*, also sometimes called *nonstop writing* or *silent, sustained writing*, asks you to record your thinking directly. To freewrite, put pen to paper (or sit at your computer screen, perhaps turning *off* the monitor so that you can't see what you are writing) and write rapidly, *nonstop*, for ten to fifteen minutes at a stretch. Don't worry about grammar, spelling, organization, transitions, or other features of edited writing. The object is to think of as many ideas as possible. Some freewriting looks like stream of consciousness. Some is more organized and focused, although it lacks the logical connections and development that would make it suitable for an audience of strangers.

Many freewriters find that their initial reservoir of ideas runs out in three to five minutes. If this happens, force yourself to keep your fingers moving. If you can't think of anything to say, write, "Relax" over and over (or "This is stupid" or "I'm stuck") until new ideas emerge.

What do you write about? The answer varies according to your situation. Often you will freewrite in response to a question or problem posed by your instructor. Sometimes you will pose your own questions and use freewriting to explore possible answers or simply generate ideas.

The following freewrite, by student writer Kent Ansen, formed the starting point for his later exploration of mandatory public service. It was written in response to a class discussion of service learning. We will return to Kent's story occasionally throughout this text. You can read his final paper in Chapter 10, pages 259–268, where he proposes that the United States should require public service for all young adults. You can also read his exploratory paper (Chapter 6, pp. 136–140), which narrates the evolution of his thinking as he researched issues connected to public service programs.

### KENT ANSEN'S INITIAL FREEWRITE

The class discussion of service learning was interesting. Hmmm. What do young people gain from community service? I gained a lot from my own volunteer activities in high school. They taught me about my neighbors and myself. Would it be a good idea for every American citizen to have some kind of public service experience? But that would make it mandatory. Interesting idea—mandatory community service program, sort of like the draft. Hmmm. What could it offer the country and young adults? The word that keeps catching my attention is "mandatory." The immediate connection that comes to mind is the military draft during the Vietnam War and all of the protests that went along with it. I think what really bothered people was that they didn't want to be forced to risk their lives for what they considered to be an unjust war. As a contemporary example, Israel requires a term of military service from its young citizens, although I am not sure of the particulars or of its level of support among young people and society at large. Mandatory *civil* service, on the other hand, would be controversial for different reasons. While the program would not ask people to risk their lives, it would still impose a requirement that significantly affects a person's life. I can hear the outcry already from those who oppose government involvement in citizens' choices and lives. I am not sure I disagree with them on this issue, particularly as I consider what I assume would be the high cost of a mandatory national service program and the major federal budget cuts that recently went into effect. On the other hand, when I think of how much money went into the Iraq War, I wonder why it at times seems less controversial to fund activities that tear communities apart rather than something like national service, which would probably make our communities a better place. I wonder [out of time]

Note how this freewrite rambles, moving associatively from one topic or question to the next. Freewrites often have this kind of loose, associative structure. The value of such freewrites is that they help writers discover areas of interest or rudimentary beginnings of ideas. When you read back over one of your freewrites, try to find places that seem worth pursuing. Freewriters call these places "hot spots," "centers of interest," "centers of gravity," or simply "nuggets" or "seeds." Because we believe this technique is of great value to writers, we suggest that you use it to generate ideas for class discussions and essays.

**Focused Freewriting** Freewriting, as we have just described it, can be quick and associational, like brainstorming aloud on paper. Focused freewriting, in contrast, is less associational and aimed more at developing a line of thought. You wrestle with a specific problem or question, trying to think and write your way into its complexity and multiple points of view. Because the writing is still informal, with the emphasis on your ideas and not on making your writing grammatically or stylistically polished, you don't have to worry about spelling, punctuation, grammar, or organizational structure. Your purpose is to deepen and extend your thinking on the problem. Some instructors will create prompts or give you specific questions to ponder, and they may call this kind of exploratory writing "focused freewriting," "learning log responses," "writer's notebook entries," or "thinking pieces."

**Idea Mapping** Another good technique for exploring ideas is *idea mapping*, a more visual method than freewriting. To make an idea map, draw a circle in the center of a page and write down your broad topic area (or a triggering question or your thesis) inside the circle. Then record your ideas on branches and subbranches that extend out from the center circle. As long as you pursue one train of thought, keep recording your ideas on subbranches off the main branch. But as soon as that chain of ideas runs dry, go back and start a new branch.

Often your thoughts will jump back and forth between one branch and another. This technique will help you see them as part of an emerging design rather than as strings of unrelated ideas. Additionally, idea mapping establishes at an early stage a sense of hierarchy in your ideas. If you enter an idea on a sub-branch, you can see that you are more fully developing a previous idea. If you return to the hub and start a new branch, you can see that you are beginning a new train of thought.

An idea map usually records more ideas than a freewrite, but the ideas are not as fully developed. Writers who practice both techniques report that they can vary the kinds of ideas they generate depending on which technique they choose. Figure 2.1 shows a student's idea map made while he was exploring issues related to the grading system.

**Dialectic Conversation**  Another effective way to explore the complexity of a topic is through dialectic discussions with others, whether in class, over coffee in the student union, late at night in bull sessions, or online in blogs or discussion boards.

**FIGURE 2.1**  Idea Map on Problems with the Grading System

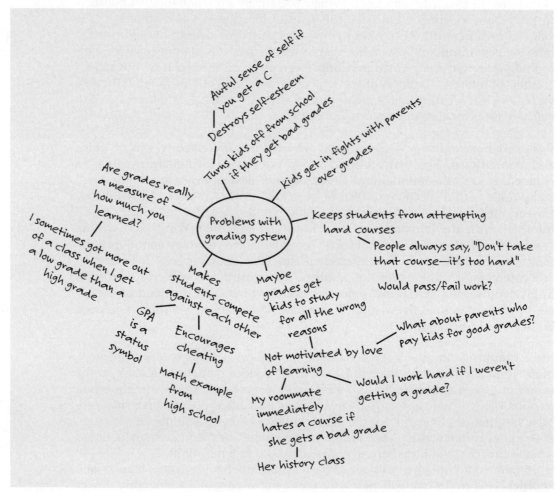

Not all discussions are productive; some are too superficial and scattered, others too heated. Good ones are *dialectic*—participants with differing views on a topic try to understand each other and resolve their differences by examining contradictions in each person's position. The key to dialectic conversation is careful listening, which is made possible by an openness to each other's views. A dialectic discussion differs from a talk show shouting match or a pro/con debate in which proponents of opposing positions, their views set in stone, attempt to win the argument. In a dialectic discussion, participants assume that each position has strengths and weaknesses and that even the strongest position contains inconsistencies, which should be exposed and examined. When dialectic conversation works well, participants scrutinize their own positions more critically and deeply, and often alter their views. True dialectic conversation implies growth and change, not a hardening of positions.

Dialectic discussion can be particularly effective online through electronic discussion boards, chat rooms, blogs, or other digital sites for informal exchange of ideas. If your goal is to generate ideas, your stance should be the exact opposite of the flamer's stance. A flamer's intention is to use brute rhetorical power (sometimes mindlessly obscene or mean, sometimes clever and humorous) to humiliate another writer and shut off further discussion. In contrast, the dialectician's goal is to listen respectfully to other ideas, to test new ways of thinking, to modify ideas in the face of other views, and to see an issue as fully and complexly as possible. If you go on to a discussion board to learn and change, rather than to defend your own position and shut off other views, you will be surprised at how powerful this medium can be.

**Playing the Believing and Doubting Game** One of the best ways to explore a question is to play what writing theorist Peter Elbow calls the "believing and doubting game." This game helps you appreciate the power of alternative arguments and points of view by urging you to formulate and explore alternative positions. To play the game, you imagine a possible answer to a problematic question and then systematically try first to believe that answer and then to doubt it. The game stimulates your critical thinking, helping you wallow in complexity and resist early closure.

When you play the believing side of this game, you try to become sympathetic to an idea or point of view. You listen carefully to it, opening yourself to the possibility that it is true. You try to appreciate why the idea has force for so many people; you try to accept it by discovering as many reasons as you can for believing it. It is easy to play the believing game with ideas you already believe in, but the game becomes more difficult, sometimes even frightening and dangerous, when you try believing ideas that seem untrue or disturbing.

The doubting game is the opposite of the believing game. It calls for you to be judgmental and critical, to find fault with an idea rather than to accept it. When you doubt a new idea, you try your best to falsify it, to find counterexamples that disprove it, to find flaws in its logic. Again, it is easy to play the doubting game with ideas you don't like, but it, too, can be threatening when you try to doubt ideas that are dear to your heart or central to your own worldview.

Here is how one student played the believing and doubting game with the following assertion from professional writer Paul Theroux that emphasizing sports is harmful to boys.

Just as high school basketball teaches you how to be a poor loser, the manly attitude towards sports seems to be little more than a recipe for creating bad marriages, social misfits, moral degenerates, sadists, latent rapists and just plain louts. I regard high school sports as a drug far worse than marijuana.

## Believing and Doubting Paul Theroux's Negative View of Sports

### Believe

1    Although I am a woman I have a hard time believing this because I was a high school basketball player and believe high school sports are *very* important. But here goes. I will try to believe this statement even though I hate it. Let's see. It would seem that I wouldn't have much first-hand experience with how society turns boys into men. I do see though that Theroux is right about some major problems. Through my observations, I've seen many young boys go through humiliating experiences with sports that have left them scarred. For example, a 7-year-old boy, Matt, isn't very athletic and when kids in our neighborhood choose teams, they usually choose girls before they choose Matt. I wonder if he sees himself as a sissy and what this does to him? I have also experienced some first-hand adverse effects of society's methods of turning boys into men. In our family, my dad spent much of his time playing football, basketball, and baseball with my brother. I've loved sports since I was very young so I was eager to play. In order to play with them, I had to play like a boy. Being told you threw or played like a girl was the worst possible insult you could receive. The phrase, "be tough" was something I heard repeatedly while I was growing up. Whenever I got hurt, my dad would say, "Be tough." It didn't matter how badly I was hurt, I always heard the same message. Today, I think, I have a very, very difficult time opening up and letting people get to know me, because for so long I was taught to keep everything inside. Maybe sports does have some bad effects.

### Doubt

2    I am glad I get to doubt this too because I have been really mad at all the sports bashing that has been going on in class. I think much of what Theroux says is just a crock. I know that the statement "sports builds character" is a cliché, but I really believe it. It seems to me that the people who lash out at sports clichés are those who never experienced these aspects of athletics and therefore don't understand them. No one can tell me that sports didn't contribute to some of my best and most meaningful friendships and growing experiences. I am convinced that I am a better person because through sports I have had to deal with failure, defeat, frustration, sacrificing individual desires for the benefit of the team, and so on. After my last high school basketball game when after many years of mind games, of hating my coach one minute and the next having deep respect for him, of big games lost on my mistakes, of hours spent alone in the gym, of wondering if the end justifies the means, my coach put his arm around me and told me he was proud. Everything, all the pain, frustration, anxiety, fear, and sacrifice of the past years seemed so worthwhile. You might try to tell

> me that this story is hackneyed and trite, but I won't listen because it is a part of me, and some thing you will never be able to damage or take away. I think athletes share a special bond. They know what it is like to go through the physical pain of practice time and again. They understand the wide variety of emotions felt (but rarely expressed). They also know what a big role the friendships of teammates and coaches play in an athlete's life.

We admire this writer a great deal—both for the passion with which she defends sports in her doubting section and for the courage of walking in a sports basher's shoes in the believing section. This exercise clearly engaged and stretched her thinking.

## Using Exploratory Writing and Talking to Generate Ideas

**FOR WRITING AND DISCUSSION**

The following task is based on e. e. cummings' poem "next to of course god america I." You could do the same exercise focused on Billie Grace Lynn's sculpture (page 7) or on a puzzling phenomenon, artifact, or question supplied by your instructor.

### next to of course god america i

"next to of course god america i
love you land of the pilgrims' and so forth oh
say can you see by the dawn's early my
country 'tis of centuries come and go

and are no more what of it we should worry
in every language even deafanddumb
thy sons acclaim your glorious name by gorry
by jingo by gee by gosh by gum
why talk of beauty what could be more beautiful than these heroic happy dead
who rushed like lions to the roaring slaughter
they did not stop to think they died instead
then shall the voice of liberty be mute?"

He spoke. And drank rapidly a glass of water

—*e. e. cummings*

1. ***Using freewriting, idea mapping, and dialectic discussion to stimulate thinking.*** On your own, read e. e. cummings' poem three or four times, trying to make as much sense of it as you can. Then using freewriting or idea-mapping, spend five minutes in response to this prompt: *What do you find puzzling, thought-provoking, meaningful, or disturbing about e. e. cummings' poem?* Let the ideas flow through your fingers. You are trying to

*(continued)*

identify aspects of the poem that you personally find puzzling or thought-provoking or that speak meaningfully to you (or against you). What is e. e. cummings trying to say or do in this poem? How does the poem affect you? As you pose questions, also explore possible ways that you might try to "answer" some of them.

***Dialectic conversation:*** Share some of the questions or ideas raised in your freewrites or idea maps and see how the exchange with classmates inspires more ideas.

2. ***Playing "the believing and doubting game."*** On your own, play the believing/doubting game with one of the following controversial assertions or another assertion provided by your instructor. First spend at least five minutes "believing" the assertion. Then reverse directions and spend the same amount of time "doubting" the assertion.

- My choice of clothing on any given day is an expression of my free will.
- It is always wrong to tell a lie.
- Athletes should be allowed to use steroids and other performance-enhancing drugs.
- In his poem ""next to of course god america I" e. e. cummings shows that he hates America.

***Dialectic conversation.*** Share ideas you discovered during this process with your classmates. Also share reflections on whether (for you) playing the "believing" or the "doubting" side was more difficult and why. Which side was most helpful for extending your thinking?

## 2.2
Write a strong thesis that surprises readers with something new or challenging.

# CONCEPT 2.2  A strong thesis statement surprises readers with something new or challenging.

The strategies for exploring ideas that we offered in the previous section can prepare you to move from posing problems to proposing your own solutions. Your answer to your subject-matter question becomes your **thesis statement**. In this section we show that a good thesis surprises its readers either by bringing something new to the reader or by pushing against other possible ways to answer the writer's question.

Thus a strong thesis usually contains an element of uncertainty, risk, or challenge. A strong thesis implies a naysayer who could disagree with you. According to composition theorist Peter Elbow, a thesis has "got to stick its neck out, not just hedge or wander. [It is] something that can be quarreled with." Elbow's sticking-its-neck-out metaphor is a good one, but we prefer to say that a strong thesis *surprises* the reader with a new, unexpected, different, or challenging view of the writer's topic. By surprise, we intend to connote, first of all, freshness or newness for the reader. Many kinds of closed-form prose don't have a sharply contestable thesis of the sticking-its-neck-out kind highlighted by Elbow. A geology report, for example, may provide readers with desired information about rock strata in an exposed cliff, or a Web page for diabetics may explain how to coordinate meals and insulin injections during a plane trip across time zones. In these cases, the information is surprising because it brings something new and significant to intended readers.

In other kinds of closed-form prose, especially academic or civic prose address-ing a problematic question or a disputed issue, surprise requires an argumentative, risky, or contestable thesis. In these cases also, surprise is not inherent in the mate-rial but in the intended readers' reception; it comes from the writer's providing an adequate or appropriate response to the readers' presumed question or problem.

In this section, we present two ways of creating a surprising thesis: (1) trying to change your reader's view of your subject; and (2) giving your thesis tension.

## Trying to Change Your Reader's View of Your Subject

To change your reader's view of your subject, you must first imagine how the reader would view the subject *before* reading your essay. Then you can articulate how you aim to change that view. A useful exercise is to write out the "before" and "after" views of your imagined readers:

Before reading my essay, my readers think this way about my topic: _____
_____

After reading my essay, my readers will think this different way about my topic:
_____

You can change your reader's view of a subject in several ways.*

1. ***You can enlarge your reader's view.*** Writing that enlarges a view is primar-ily informational. It provides new ideas and data to a reader's store of knowl-edge about the subject. For example, suppose you are interested in the prob-lem of storing nuclear waste (a highly controversial issue in the United States) and decide to investigate how France stores radioactive waste from its nuclear power plants. You could report your researched findings on this problem in an informative paper. (Before reading my paper, readers would be uncertain how France stores nuclear waste. After reading my paper, my readers would under-stand the French methods, possibly helping us better understand our options in the United States.)

2. ***You can clarify your reader's view of something that was previously fuzzy, tentative, or uncertain.*** Writing of this kind often explains, ana-lyzes, or interprets. This is the kind of writing you do when you analyze a short story, a painting, an historical document, a set of economic data, or other puz-zling phenomena or when you speculate on the cause, consequence, purpose, or function of something. Suppose you are analyzing the persuasive strategies used by various clothing ads. You are intrigued by a jeans ad that you "read" differently from your classmates. (Before reading my paper, my readers will think that this jeans ad reveals a liberated woman, but after reading my paper they will see that the ad reinforces traditional gender stereotypes.)

*Our discussion of how writing changes a reader's view of the world is indebted to Richard Young, Alton Becker, and Kenneth Pike, *Rhetoric: Discovery and Change* (New York: Harcourt Brace & Company, 1971).

3. ***You can restructure readers' whole view of a subject.*** Such essays persuade readers to change their minds or urge them to action. For example, engineer David Rockwood, in his letter to the editor, wants to change readers' views about wind power (see Chapter 1, p. 15). (Before reading my letter, readers will believe that wind-generated electricity can solve our energy crisis, but after reading my letter, they will see that the hope of wind power is a pipe dream.)

Surprise, then, is the measure of change an essay brings about in a reader. Of course, to bring about such change requires more than just a surprising thesis; the essay itself must persuade the reader that the thesis is sound as well as novel.

## Giving Your Thesis Tension through "Surprising Reversal"

Another element of a surprising thesis is tension. By *tension* we mean the reader's sensation of being pulled away from familiar ideas toward new, unfamiliar ones. A strategy for creating this tension—a strategy we call "surprising reversal"—is to contrast your surprising answer to a question with your targeted audience's common answer, creating tension between your own thesis and one or more alternative views. Its basic template is as follows:

> *"Many people believe X (common view), but I am going to show Y (new, surprising view)."*

The concept of surprising reversal spurs the writer to go beyond the commonplace to change the reader's view of a topic.

One of the best ways to employ this strategy is to begin your thesis statement with an "although" clause that summarizes the reader's "before" view or the counterclaim that your essay opposes; the main clause states the surprising view or position that your essay will support. You may choose to omit the *although* clause from your actual essay, but formulating it first will help you achieve focus and surprise in your thesis. The examples that follow illustrate the kinds of tension we have been discussing and show why tension is a key requirement for a good thesis.

| | |
|---|---|
| **Question** | What effect has the cell phone had on our culture? |
| **Thesis without Tension** | The invention of the cell phone has brought many advantages to our culture. |
| **Thesis with Tension** | Although the cell phone has brought many advantages to our culture, it may also have contributed to an increase in risky behavior among boaters and hikers. |
| **Question** | Do reservations serve a useful role in contemporary Native American culture? |
| **Thesis without Tension** | Reservations have good points and bad points. |
| **Thesis with Tension** | Although my friend Wilson Real Bird believes that reservations are necessary for Native Americans to preserve their heritage, the continuation of reservations actually degrades Native American culture. |

In the first example, the thesis without tension (cell phones have brought advantages to our culture) is a truism with which everyone would agree and hence lacks surprise. The thesis with tension places this truism (the reader's "before" view) in an *although* clause and goes on to make a surprising or contestable assertion. The idea that the cell phone contributes to risky behavior among outdoor enthusiasts alters our initial, complacent view of the cell phone and gives us new ideas to think about.

In the second example, the thesis without tension may not at first seem tensionless because the writer sets up an opposition between good and bad points. But *almost anything* has good and bad points, so the opposition is not meaningful, and the thesis offers no element of surprise. Substitute virtually any other social institution (marriage, the postal service, the military, prisons), and the statement that it has good and bad points would be equally true. The thesis with tension, in contrast, is risky. It commits the writer to argue that reservations have degraded Native American culture and to oppose the counterthesis that reservations are needed to *preserve* Native American culture. The reader now feels genuine tension between two opposing views.

Tension, then, is a component of surprise. The writer's goal is to surprise the reader in some way, thereby bringing about some kind of change in the reader's view. As you are wallowing in complexity about your subject-matter problem, try the following strategies for bringing something new, surprising, or challenging to your targeted readers:

## Strategies for Creating a Thesis with Tension or Surprise

| How You Became Gripped with a Problem | Example of a Problem | Your Strategy While You "Wallow in Complexity" | Possible Thesis with Tension or Surprise |
|---|---|---|---|
| **The problem is already "out there."** *(You enter a conversation already in progress.)* | | | |
| You don't know where you stand on an issue. | Should health care be rationed? | Look at all sides of the issue, including all the available data, to determine where you stand based on your own examined values. | Although rationing health care at first seems inhumane, it may be the only ethical way to provide affordable health care to all citizens. |
| You do know where you stand on an issue but your position hasn't yet been "earned." *[You need to move from an opinion to an earned thesis.]* | Shanita says that we should build more nuclear power plants to combat global warming, but I say nuclear power is too dangerous. | Research the strengths of the opposing views and the weaknesses of your own view. (*Note: You may change your mind.*) | Although nuclear power poses danger from storage of waste or possible meltdown, the benefits of reducing greenhouse gases and cutting coal pollution outweigh the dangers. |

*(continued)*

| How You Became Gripped with a Problem | Example of a Problem | Your Strategy While You "Wallow in Complexity" | Possible Thesis with Tension or Surprise |
|---|---|---|---|
| Someone gives you a question that you can't yet answer. | Your boss asks you whether the company should enact the proposed marketing plan. | Do the research, critical thinking, and analysis needed to propose the "best solution" to the boss's question. | The marketing team's proposal, despite its creative use of advertising, is too risky to undertake at this time. |
| **You pose the problem yourself.** *(You initiate the conversation.)* | | | |
| You see something puzzling in a natural phenomenon or a cultural activity or artifact. | Why does Merton call rain "meaningless"? | Through critical thinking and research, try to figure out a plausible "best solution" to your question. | Merton's puzzling use of "meaningless" in reference to the rain can perhaps be explained by his admiration for Buddhism. |
| You discover something inconsistent or contradictory in your own view of the world. | I agree with Merton's argument against consumerism, but I really want a large plasma TV. Is consumerism really bad? Am I a materialist? | Reflect on your own values and beliefs; try to achieve a consistent stand with regard to enduring social or ethical issues. | Although Merton makes me consider the potential shallowness of my desire for a huge plasma TV, I don't think I'm necessarily a materialist. |

**FOR WRITING AND DISCUSSION**

## Developing Thesis Statements Out of Questions

Writers can't be asked to create thesis statements on the spot because a writer's thesis grows out of extended intellectual struggle with a problem. However, in response to a question one can often propose a hypothetical claim and treat it as a tentative thesis statement for testing. This exercise asks you to try this approach—formulate a surprising thesis statement that you could then test further through more exploration. We provide three possible questions for exploration. Your instructor might give you a different question. In formulating your claim, also imagine a targeted audience that would find your claim new, challenging, or otherwise surprising. Finally, speculate on the kinds of evidence you would need to support your thesis.

1. What can an individual do, if anything, to combat climate change? (Note: Your thesis will have no tension or surprise if you say just the obvious—take the bus or change light bulbs.)

2. What should the federal government do, if anything, to help prevent mass killings enacted with rapid-fire semi-automatic weapons?
3. What is e. e. cummings' attitude toward America in "next to of course god america i" (p. 31)?

Here is an example:

*Problematic question:* What can cities do to prevent traffic congestion?

*One possible thesis:* Although many people think that little can be done to get people out of their beloved cars, new light-rail systems in many cities have attracted former car commuters and alleviated traffic problems.

*Intended audience:* Residents of cities concerned about traffic congestion but skeptical about light-rail

*Kinds of evidence needed to support thesis:* Examples of cities with successful light-rail systems; evidence that many riders switched from driving cars; evidence that light-rail alleviated traffic problems

## CONCEPT 2.3  In closed-form prose, a typical introduction starts with the problem, not the thesis.

2.3
Begin a typical closed-form introduction with the problem, not the thesis.

In Concept 2.2 we explained that in closed-form prose a writer's thesis statement is a tentative, contestable, and surprising answer to a question or problem that the writer shares with the reader. Before readers can understand or appreciate a writer's thesis, they must first know the problem or question that the thesis addresses. Typically a writer's thesis statement comes at the *end* of the introduction. What precedes the thesis is the writer's explanation of the problem that she is addressing or the conversation that she is joining. This problem-before-thesis-structure follows a principle of closed-form prose called "the old/new contract," which helps readers connect new information to previously stated old information. In closed-form prose, your thesis statement summarizes the "new information" that makes your argument surprising, new, or challenging. The "old information" that must precede the thesis is the question or problem that your thesis addresses.

See Chapter 12, pp. 291–293, where the old/ new contract is explained in detail.

It follows then that a primary function of most closed-form introductions is to present the problem that you are addressing and to motivate your readers' interest in it. (If they aren't interested, they'll quit reading.) The length of the introduction is a function of how much your reader already knows and cares about your problem. The less they know or care, the more your introduction needs to provide background and answer the "so what?" question that motivates caring. Once readers are on board with you about the problem being addressed and about why the problem matters, they are prepared for your thesis statement.

### A Typical Introduction

In the following example of a typical closed-form introduction, note how student writer Jackie Wyngaard first presents a question and then moves, at the end of the introduction, to her thesis statement.

### EMP: MUSIC HISTORY OR MUSIC TRIVIA?

Along with other college students new to Seattle, I wanted to see what cultural opportunities the area offers. I especially wanted to see billionaire Paul Allen's controversial Experience Music Project (known as EMP), a huge, bizarre, shiny, multicolored structure that is supposed to resemble a smashed guitar. Brochures say that EMP celebrates the creativity of American popular music, but it has prompted heated discussions among architects, Seattle residents, museum goers, and music lovers, who have questioned its commercialism and the real value of its exhibits. My sister recommended this museum to me because she knows I am a big music lover and a rock and roll fan. Also, as an active choir member since the sixth grade, I have always been intrigued by the history of music. I went to EMP expecting to learn more about music history from exhibits that showed a range of popular musical styles, that traced historical connections and influences, and that enjoyably conveyed useful information. However, as a museum of rock history, EMP is a disappointing failure.

## Features of an Effective Introduction

Wyngaard's introduction, which shares the structure of many professionally written closed-form introductions, includes the following typical features:

- ***Topic area and context.*** Readers need early on to know the specific topic area of the paper they are about to read—in this case a paper about the Experience Music Project in Seattle rather than, say, shower mold or medieval queenship. Sometimes writers also use a startling scene or statistic as an "attention grabber" as part of the opening context.
- ***A direct or implied question.*** As soon as possible, readers need to know how the topic area gives rise to a problem, question, or issue that the writer will examine. In this case, Jackie Wyngaard implies her question: Will EMP live up to my expectations as a museum of rock history? Note that her question appears directly in her title: "EMP: Music History or Music Trivia?"
- ***An indication of how the question invites tension, has evoked controversy, or is otherwise problematic.*** Jackie indicates that the EMP has generated "heated discussions" among a range of audiences about its commercialism and the value of its exhibits. She gives the question further tension by contrasting her initial expectations with her later disappointment.
- ***An indication of how the question is significant or worth examining.*** In order to avoid a "so what?" response, writers must motivate readers' interest in the question. Somebody might say, "Who cares about EMP anyway?" Jackie's strategy is to imagine an audience who shares her interest in rock and roll music and her love of music history. These are the readers who will care whether it is worth big bucks to spend an afternoon in EMP. Readers who identify with Jackie's enthusiasm for rock history will share her engagement with the question.
- ***The writer's thesis, which brings something new to the audience.*** Once readers are hooked on the writer's question, they are ready for the writer's answer. In this case, Jackie makes the claim that EMP fails as a rock history museum.

Additional nuts-and-bolts advice for composing an effective closed-form introduction is found in Chapter 12, pp. 300–303.

For a fuller overview of how to think about introductions from a rhetorical perspective (hooking up with your reader, motivating your reader to continue reading), consider the following strategies chart:

| Strategies for Introducing Your Problem to Targeted Readers | |
| --- | --- |
| **Situation** | **Strategies** |
| **The problem is already "out there."** *(You enter a conversation already in progress.)* | *If readers are already familiar with the problem and care about it, use a mix of the following strategies:*<br>• Provide background where needed<br>• State the problem directly (often as a grammatical question ending with a question mark) or imply the question through context<br>• Summarize the different points of view on the problem (or)<br>• Summarize the particular point of view you intend to "push against"<br><br>*If readers are less familiar with the problem:*<br>• Summarize controversy in more depth<br>• Explain why the problem is problematic (show why there are no easy answers to the problem; point out weaknesses in proposed answers; show the history of attempts to solve the problem)<br><br>*If readers don't already care about the problem:*<br>• Show why the problem is important (answer the "so what?" question)<br>• Show how solving the problem will bring good consequences (or)<br>• Show how answering the question will help us begin to answer a larger question |
| **You pose the problem yourself.** *(You initiate the conversation.)* | • Describe the artifact or phenomenon you are writing about and point to the specific features where you see an inconsistency, gap, or puzzle<br>• State the problem directly (often as a grammatical question ending with a question mark)<br>• Show how there isn't any immediate, easy answer to the question or problem or how the question can invite controversy/discussion; you can often employ a template such as the following:<br>  • Some people might think..., but closer observation shows that....<br>  • At first I thought..., but later I saw that....<br>  • Part of me thinks..., but another part of me thinks that....<br>  • I expected...; but what I actually found was....<br>• Show why the problem is important (answer the "so what?" question)<br>• Show how solving the problem will bring good consequences (or)<br>• Show how answering this question will help us begin to answer a larger question |

## Examining the Problem–Thesis Structure of Introductions

**Background:** Although introductions to closed-form essays don't always follow the typical structure we just described, many do. In this exercise, we invite you to analyze additional introductions.

**Task:** Look at the following introductions. In each case, analyze the extent to which the introduction follows or varies from the typical introductions we have described in Concept 2.3.

1. Paragraphs 1–2 of Ross Taylor's "Paintball: Promoter of Violence or Healthy Fun?" (pp. 230–233)
2. Paragraph 1 of Claire Giordano's "Virtual Promise: Why Online Courses Will Not Adequately Prepare Us for the Future" (pp. 234–243)
3. Paragraphs 1–3 of Kent Ansen's "Engaging Young Adults to Meet America's Challenges: A Proposal for Mandatory National Service" (pp. 263–272)

## Chapter Summary

This chapter has introduced you to three concepts that will enable you to think about your subject matter from a rhetorical perspective.

- *Concept 2.1 To determine their thesis, writers must often "wallow in complexity."* What typically initiates the writing process is a problematic question that invites the writer to explore the problem's complexity. To do so, experienced writers often use exploratory techniques such as freewriting, idea mapping, dialectic talk, and the believing and doubting game to generate ideas.
- *Concept 2.2 A strong thesis surprises readers with something new or challenging.* A good thesis tries to change the reader's view of the subject and often creates tension by pushing against alternative views.
- *Concept 2.3 In closed-form prose, a typical introduction starts with the problem, not the thesis.* Readers need to be engaged with the writer's question before they can understand the thesis.

## Playing the Believing and Doubting Game

The For Writing and Discussion exercise in Concept 2.2 (p. 32) asks you to play the believing and doubting game as a freewriting exercise. Because this game is so helpful for developing critical thinking skills and learning to wallow in complexity, we repeat it here as a brief writing assignment. Your instructor will explain whether this assignment will be graded formally (in which case grammar and organization matter) or informally (in which case you will just freewrite to explore ideas.)

***Part 1. The Game.*** Play the believing and doubting game with one of the assertions listed here (or with another assertion provided by your instructor). Include at least one full paragraph or page (ask your instructor about length) believing the assertion and then an equivalent stretch of prose doubting the assertion. When you believe an assertion, you agree, support, illustrate, extend, and apply the idea. When you doubt an assertion, you question, challenge, rebut, and offer counterreasons and counterexamples to the assertion.

1. Grades are an effective means of motivating students to do their best work.
2. Facebook or other social media provide a good way to make new friends.
3. In recent years, advertising has made enormous gains in portraying women as strong, independent, and intelligent.
4. If there is only one kidney available for transplant and two sick persons need it, one in her thirties and one in her sixties, the kidney should go to the younger person.
5. The United States should reinstate the draft.

***Part 2. Reflection.*** Write a reflective paragraph in which you assess the extent to which the believing and doubting game extended or stretched your thinking. Particularly, answer these questions:

1. What was difficult about this writing activity?
2. To what extent did it make you take an unfamiliar or uncomfortable stance?
3. How can believing and doubting help you wallow in complexity?

# 3 HOW MESSAGES PERSUADE

**WHAT YOU WILL LEARN**

**3.1** To analyze how messages persuade through their angle of vision.

**3.2** To analyze how messages persuade through appeals to *logos, ethos*, and *pathos*.

**3.3** To analyze how messages persuade through style and document design.

**3.4** To analyze how nonverbal texts persuade through visual rhetorical strategies.

**A way of seeing is also a way of not seeing.**

—*Kenneth Burke, Rhetorician*

The goal of this chapter is to help you analyze the rhetorical strategies that make messages persuasive. When you understand how messages achieve their effects, you will be better prepared to analyze and evaluate them and to decide whether to resist their arguments or accede to them. You'll also be better prepared to use these rhetorical strategies effectively and ethically in your own writing.

**3.1**
Analyze how messages persuade through their angle of vision.

## CONCEPT 3.1 Messages persuade through their angle of vision.

One way that messages persuade is through their **angle of vision**, which causes a reader to see a subject from one perspective only—the writer's. Writers create an angle of vision through strategies such as the following:

- Stating point of view directly
- Selecting some details while omitting others
- Choosing words or figures of speech with intended connotations
- Creating emphasis or de-emphasis through sentence structure and organization

The writer's angle of vision—which might also be called a lens, a filter, a perspective, or a point of view—is persuasive because it controls what the reader "sees." Unless readers are rhetorically savvy, they can lose awareness that they are seeing the writer's subject matter through a lens that both reveals and conceals.

A classic illustration of angle of vision is the following thought exercise:

**THOUGHT EXERCISE ON ANGLE OF VISION**

Suppose you attended a fun party on Saturday night. (You get to choose what constitutes "fun" for you.) Now imagine that two people ask what you did on Saturday night. Person A is a close friend who missed the party. Person B is your parent. How would your descriptions of Saturday night differ?

Clearly there isn't just one way to describe this party. Your description will be influenced by your purpose and audience. You will have to decide:

- What image of myself should I project? (For your friend you might construct yourself as a party animal; for your parent, as a more detached observer.)
- How much emphasis do I give the party? (You might describe the party in detail for your friend while mentioning it only in passing to your parent, emphasizing instead all the homework you did over the weekend.)
- What details should I include or leave out? (Does my parent really need to know that the neighbors called the police?)
- What words should I choose? (The slang you use with your friend might not be appropriate for your parent.)

You'll note that our comments about your rhetorical choices reflect common assumptions about friends and parents. You might actually have a party-loving parent and a geeky friend, in which case your party descriptions would be altered accordingly. In any case, you are in rhetorical control; you choose what your audience "sees" and how they see it.

## Recognizing the Angle of Vision in a Text

This thought exercise illustrates a key insight of rhetoric: There is always more than one way to tell a story, and no single way of telling it constitutes the whole truth. By saying that a writer writes from an "angle of vision," we mean that the writer cannot take a godlike stance that allows a universal, unfiltered, totally unbiased or objective way of knowing. Rather, the writer looks at the subject from a certain location, or, to use another metaphor, the writer wears a lens that colors or filters the topic in a certain way. The angle of vision, lens, or filter determines what part of a topic gets "seen" and what remains "unseen," what gets included or excluded, what gets emphasized or de-emphasized, and so forth. It even determines what words get chosen out of an array of options—for example, whether the writer says "panhandler" or "homeless person," "torture" or "enhanced interrogation," "universal health care" or "socialized medicine."

As an illustration of angle of vision, consider the cartoon in Figure 3.1, which shows different ways that stakeholders "see" sweatshops. For each stakeholder, some aspects of sweatshops surge into view, while other aspects remain unseen or invisible. An alert reader needs to be aware that none of these stakeholders can portray sweatshops in a completely "true" way. Stockholders and corporate leaders emphasize reduced labor costs and enhanced corporate profits and retirement portfolios while de-emphasizing (or omitting entirely) the working conditions in

**FIGURE 3.1** Different Angles of Vision on "Sweatshops"

sweatshops or the plight of American workers whose jobs have been outsourced to developing countries. Consumers enjoy abundant low-cost goods made possible by sweatshops and may not even think about where or how the products are made. Opponents of sweatshops focus on the miserable conditions of sweatshop workers, their low wages, the use of child labor, and the "obscene" profits of corporations. Meanwhile, as the American union worker laments the loss of jobs in the United States, third world workers and their children may welcome sweatshops as a source of income superior to the other harsh alternatives such as scavenging in dumps or prostitution. The multiple angles of vision show how complex the issue of sweatshops is. In fact, most issues are equally complex, and any one view of the issue is controlled by the writer's angle of vision.

To get a hands-on feel for how a writer creates an angle of vision, try doing the following U. R. Riddle activity, which invites you to write a letter of recommendation for a student.

## U. R. Riddle Letter

**Background:** Suppose that you are a management professor who regularly writes letters of recommendation for former students. One day you receive a letter from a local bank requesting a confidential evaluation of a former student, Uriah Rudy Riddle (U. R. Riddle), who has applied for a job as a management trainee. The bank wants your assessment of Riddle's intelligence, aptitude, dependability, and ability to work with people. You haven't seen U. R. for several years, but you remember him well. Here are the facts and impressions you recall about Riddle:

- Very temperamental student, seemed moody, something of a loner
- Long hair and very sloppy dress—seemed like a misplaced street person; often twitchy and hyperactive
- Absolutely brilliant mind; took lots of liberal arts courses and applied them to business
- Wrote a term paper relating different management styles to modern theories of psychology—the best undergraduate paper you ever received. You gave it an A+ and remember learning a lot from it yourself.
- Had a strong command of language—the paper was very well written
- Good at mathematics; could easily handle all the statistical aspects of the course
- Frequently missed class and once told you that your class was boring
- Didn't show up for the midterm. When he returned to class later, he said only that he had been out of town. You let him make up the midterm, and he got an A.
- Didn't participate in a group project required for your course. He said the other students in his group were idiots.
- You thought at the time that Riddle didn't have a chance of making it in the business world because he had no talent for getting along with people.
- Other professors held similar views of Riddle—brilliant, but rather strange and hard to like; an odd duck.

You are in a dilemma because you want to give Riddle a chance (he's still young and may have had a personality transformation of some sort), but you also don't want to damage your own professional reputation by falsifying your true impressions.

**Individual task:** Working individually for ten minutes or so, compose a brief letter of recommendation assessing Riddle; use details from the list to support your assessment. Role-play that you have decided to take a gamble with Riddle and give him a chance at this career. Write as strong a recommendation as possible while remaining honest. (To make this exercise more complex, your instructor might ask half the class to role-play a negative angle of vision in which you want to warn the bank against hiring Riddle without hiding his strengths or good points.)

(continued)

> **Task for group or whole-class discussion:** Working in small groups or as a whole class, share your letters. Then pick representative examples ranging from the most positive to the least positive and discuss how the letters achieve their different rhetorical effects. If your intent is to support Riddle, to what extent does honesty compel you to mention some or all of your negative memories? Is it possible to mention negative items without emphasizing them? How?

## Analyzing Angle of Vision

Just as there is more than one way to describe the party you went to on Saturday night or to write about sweatshops, there is more than one way to write a letter of recommendation for U. R. Riddle. The writer's angle of vision determines what is "seen" or "not seen" in a given piece of writing—what gets slanted in a positive or negative direction, what gets highlighted, what gets thrown into the shadows. As rhetorician Kenneth Burke claims in the epigraph for the chapter, "A way of seeing is also a way of not seeing." Note how the writer controls what the reader "sees." As Riddle's former professor, you might in your mind's eye see Riddle as long-haired and sloppy, but if you don't mention these details in your letter, they remain unseen to the reader. Note too that your own terms "long-haired and sloppy" interpret Riddle's appearance through the lens of your own characteristic way of seeing—a way that perhaps values business attire and clean-cut tidiness. Another observer might describe Riddle's appearance quite differently, thus seeing what you don't see.

In an effective piece of writing, the author's angle of vision often works so subtly that unsuspecting readers—unless they learn to think rhetorically—will be drawn into the writer's spell and believe that the writer's prose conveys the "whole picture" of its subject rather than a limited picture filtered through the screen of the writer's perspective.

**Contrasting Angles of Vision in Two Texts**  Consider the differences in what gets seen in the following two descriptions of the Arctic National Wildlife Refuge in Alaska (the ANWR), where proponents of oil exploration are locked in a fierce battle with anti-exploration conservationists. The first passage is from a pro-exploration advocacy group called Arctic Power; the second is from former President Jimmy Carter.

### ARCTIC POWER'S DESCRIPTION OF THE ANWR

On the coastal plain [of the ANWR], the Arctic winter lasts for 9 months. It is dark continuously for 56 days in midwinter. Temperatures with the wind chill can reach –110 degrees F. It's not pristine. There are villages, roads, houses, schools, and military installations. It's not a unique Arctic ecosystem. The coastal plain is only a small fraction of the 88,000 square miles that make up the North Slope. The same tundra environment and wildlife can be found throughout the circumpolar Arctic regions. The 1002 Area [the legal term for the plot of coastal plain being contested] is flat. That's why they call it a plain. [...]

Some groups want to make the 1002 Area a wilderness. But a vote for wilderness is a vote against American jobs.

**JIMMY CARTER'S DESCRIPTION OF THE ANWR**

Rosalynn [Carter's wife] and I always look for opportunities to visit parks and wildlife areas in our travels. But nothing matches the spectacle of wildlife we found on the coastal plain of America's Arctic National Wildlife Refuge in Alaska. To the north lay the Arctic Ocean; to the south rolling foothills rose toward the glaciated peaks of the Brooks Range. At our feet was a mat of low tundra plant life, bursting with new growth, perched atop the permafrost.

As we watched, 80,000 caribou surged across the vast expanse around us. Called by instinct older than history, this Porcupine (River) caribou herd was in the midst of its annual migration. To witness this vast sea of caribou in an uncorrupted wilderness home, and the wolves, ptarmigan, grizzlies, polar bears, musk oxen and millions of migratory birds, was a profoundly humbling experience. We were reminded of our human dependence on the natural world.

Sadly, we were also forced to imagine what we might see if the caribou were replaced by smoke-belching oil rigs, highways and a pipeline that would destroy forever the plain's delicate and precious ecosystem.

—Jimmy Carter. From "Make This Natural Treasure a National Monument" from The New York Times, December 29, 2000. © 2000 The New York Times. All rights reserved. Used by permission and protected by the Copyright Laws of the United States. The printing, copying, retransmission of this Content without express written permission is prohibited.

**How Angle of Vision Persuades** To understand more clearly how angle of vision persuades, you can analyze the language strategies at work. Some strategies that writers employ consciously or unconsciously are described below.

## Strategies for Constructing an Angle of Vision

| Strategy | ANWR Example | U. R. Riddle Example |
|---|---|---|
| State your intention directly. | • Earlier passages in the preceding excerpts directly state Arctic Powers' pro-drilling and Carter's anti-drilling stances. | • You might say "Riddle would make an excellent manager" or "Riddle doesn't have the personality to be a bank manager." |
| Select details that support your intentions; omit or de-emphasize others. | • Arctic Power writer (AP)"sees" the cold, barren darkness of the ANWR; Carter sees the beauty.<br>• AP spotlights the people who live on the coastal plain while making the animals invisible; Carter spotlights the caribou while omitting the people.<br>• To AP, drilling means jobs; to Carter it means destructive oil rigs. | • A positive view of Riddle would select and emphasize Riddle's good traits and de-emphasize or omit his bad ones.<br>• A negative view would take the opposite tack. |

(continued)

| Strategy | ANWR Example | U. R. Riddle Example |
|---|---|---|
| Choose words that frame your subject in the desired way or have desired connotations. | • AP frames the ANWR as the dreary "1002 Area"; Carter frames it as a "spectacle of wildlife," a unique "delicate and precious ecosystem."<br><br>• Arctic Power uses words with negative connotations ("wind chill"); Carter uses words connoting life and growth ("a mat of low tundra plant life"). | • "Riddle is an independent thinker who doesn't follow the crowd" (frames him positively in value system that favors individualism).<br><br>• "Riddle is a loner who thinks egocentrically" (frames him negatively in value system favoring consensus and social skills).<br><br>• You could say, "Riddle is forthright" or "Riddle is rude"—positive versus negative connotations. |
| Use figurative language (metaphors, similes, and analogies) that conveys your intended effect. | • AP avoids figurative language, claiming objective presentation of facts.<br><br>• Carter uses positive metaphors to convey ANWR's vitality (tundra "bursting with new growth") and negative metaphors for drilling ("smoke-belching oil rigs"). | • To suggest that Riddle has outgrown his alienating behavior, you could say, "Riddle is a social late bloomer."<br><br>• To recommend against hiring Riddle while still being positive, you could say, "Riddle's independent spirit would feel caged in by the routine of a bank." |
| Use sentence structure to emphasize and de-emphasize your ideas. *(Emphasize an idea by placing it at the end of a long sentence, in a short sentence, or in a main clause.)* | • AP uses short sentences to emphasize main points: "It's not pristine." "It's not a unique ecosystem." "That's why they call it a plain."<br><br>• Carter uses longer sentences for description, with an occasional short sentence to make a point: "We were reminded of our human dependence on the natural world." | Consider the difference between the following:<br>• "Although Riddle had problems relating to other students, he is a brilliant thinker."<br><br>• "Although Riddle is a brilliant thinker, he had problems relating to other students in the class." |

## 3.2
Analyze how messages persuade through appeals to *logos, ethos,* and *pathos.*

# CONCEPT 3.2  **Messages persuade through appeals to *logos, ethos,* and *pathos.***

Another way to think about the persuasive power of texts is to examine the strategies writers or speakers use to sway their audiences toward a certain position on an issue. To win people's consideration of their ideas, writers or speakers can appeal to what the classical philosopher Aristotle called *logos, ethos,* and *pathos.*

Developing the habit of examining how these appeals are functioning in texts and being able to employ these appeals in your own writing will enhance your ability to read and write rhetorically. Let's look briefly at each:

A fuller discussion of these classical appeals appears in Chapter 9, "Writing a Classical Argument."

- **Logos *is the appeal to reason.*** It refers to the quality of the message itself—to its internal consistency, to its clarity in asserting a thesis or point, and to the quality of reasons and evidence used to support the point.
- **Ethos *is the appeal to the character of the speaker/writer.*** It refers to the speaker/writer's trustworthiness and credibility. One can often increase one's *ethos* in a message by being knowledgeable about the issue, by appearing thoughtful and fair, by listening well, and by being respectful of alternative points of view. A writer's accuracy and thoroughness in crediting sources and professionalism in caring about the format, grammar, and neat appearance of a document are part of the appeal to *ethos.*
- **Pathos *is the appeal to the sympathies, values, beliefs, and emotions of the audience.*** Appeals to *pathos* can be made in many ways. *Pathos* can often be enhanced through evocative visual images, frequently used in Web sites, posters, and magazine or newspaper articles. In written texts, the same effects can be created through vivid examples and details, through connotative language, and through empathy with the audience's beliefs and values.

To see how these three appeals are interrelated, you can visualize a triangle with points labeled *Message, Audience,* and *Writer* or *Speaker.* Rhetoricians study how effective communicators consider all three points of this *rhetorical triangle.* (See Figure 3.2.)

**FIGURE 3.2** Rhetorical Triangle

Message
***Logos:*** *How can I make my ideas internally consistent and logical? How can I find the best reasons and support them with the best evidence?*

Audience
***Pathos:*** *How can I make the readers open to my message? How can I best engage my readers' emotions and imaginations? How can I appeal to my readers' values and interests?*

Writer or Speaker
***Ethos:*** *How can I present myself effectively? How can I enhance my credibility and trustworthiness?*

We encourage you to ask questions about the appeals to *logos, ethos,* and *pathos* every time you examine a text. For example, is the appeal to *logos* weakened by the writer's use of scanty and questionable evidence? Has the writer made a powerful appeal to *ethos* by documenting her sources and showing that she is an authority on the issue? Has the writer relied too heavily on appeals to *pathos* by using numerous heart-wringing examples? Later chapters in this textbook will help you use these appeals competently in your own writing as well as analyze these appeals in others' messages.

**3.3**
Analyze how messages persuade through style and document design.

## CONCEPT 3.3  Messages persuade through writers' choices about style and document design.

So far we have shown how messages persuade through angle of vision and appeals to *logos, ethos,* and *pathos.* In this section we explain the persuasive power of style and document design, which are themselves factors in the creation of a message's angle of vision and contribute to its logical, ethical, or emotional appeals.

### Understanding Factors That Affect Style

**Style** refers to analyzable features of language that work together to create different effects. As shown in Figure 3.3, style can be thought of as a mixture of four factors:

- *Ways of shaping sentences,* such as length or complexity of sentence structure
- *Word choice,* such as abstract versus concrete or formal versus colloquial
- *Voice, or persona,* which refers to the reader's impression of the writer as projected from the page: expert versus layperson or scholarly voice versus popular voice
- *Tone,* which refers to the writer's attitude toward the subject matter or toward the reader, such as cold or warm, humorous or serious, detached or passionate

**FIGURE 3.3**  Ingredients of Style

| Ways of shaping sentences | Types of words | Voice or persona | Tone |
|---|---|---|---|
| Long/short<br>Simple/complex<br>Many modifiers/few modifiers<br>Normal word order/frequent inversions or interruptions<br>Mostly main clauses/many embedded phrases and subordinate clauses | Abstract/concrete<br>Formal/colloquial<br>Unusual/ordinary<br>Specialized/general<br>Metaphorical/literal<br>Scientific/literary | Expert/layperson<br>Scholar/student<br>Outsider/insider<br>Political liberal/ conservative<br>Neutral observer/ active participant | Intimate/distant<br>Personal/impersonal<br>Angry/calm<br>Browbeating/sharing<br>Informative/ entertaining<br>Humorous/serious<br>Ironic/literal<br>Passionately involved/aloof |

What style you adopt depends on your purpose, audience, and genre. Consider, for example, the differences in style in two articles about the animated sitcom *South Park*. The first passage comes from an academic journal in which the author analyzes how race is portrayed in *South Park*. The second passage is from a popular magazine, where the author argues that despite *South Park*'s vulgarity, the sitcom has a redeeming social value.

### PASSAGE FROM SCHOLARLY JOURNAL

In these cartoons, multiplicity encodes a set of nonwhite identities to be appropriated and commodified by whiteness. In the cartoon world, obscene humor and satire mediate this commodification. The whiteness that appropriates typically does so by virtue of its mobile positioning between and through imagined boundaries contrarily shown as impassible to black characters or agents marked as black. Let me briefly turn to an appropriately confusing example of such a character in *South Park*'s scatological hero extraordinaire, Eric Cartman....Eric Cartman's yen for breaking into Black English and interactions with black identities also fashion him an appropriator. However, Cartman's voice and persona may be seen as only an avatar, one layer of textual identity for creator Trey Parker, who may be regarded in one sense as a "black-voice" performer.

—Michael A. Chaney, "Representations of Race and Place in *Static Shock, King of the Hill,* and *South Park*"

### PASSAGE FROM POPULAR MAGAZINE

Despite the theme song's chamber of commerce puffery, *South Park* is the closest television has ever come to depicting hell on earth. Its inhabitants are, almost without exception, stupid, ignorant or venal—usually all three. Its central characters are four eight-year-olds: Stan, the high-achiever, Kyle, the sensitive Jew, Kenny, whose grisly death each week prompts the tortured cry, "Oh my God! They've killed Kenny! Those bastards!" and Eric Cartman, who has become the Archie Bunker of the '90s, beloved by millions. My 12-year-old son informs me that many of his schoolmates have taken to speaking permanently in Cartman's bigoted and usually furiously inarticulate manner. A (mild) sample: any display of human sensitivity is usually met by him with the rejoinder: "Tree-hugging hippie crap!" This has led to predictable calls for *South Park*, which is usually programmed late in the evening, to be banned altogether.

—Kevin Michael Grace, "*South Park* Is a Snort of Defiance Against a World Gone to Hell"

## Analyzing Differences in Style

**FOR WRITING AND DISCUSSION**

Working in small groups or as a whole class, analyze the differences in the styles of these two samples.

1. How would you describe differences in the length and complexity of sentences, in the level of vocabulary, and in the degree of formality?
2. How do the differences in styles create different voices, personas, and tones?

*(continued)*

3. Based on clues from style and genre, who is the intended audience of each piece? What is the writer's purpose? How does each writer hope to surprise the intended audience with something new, challenging, or valuable?
4. How are the differences in content and style influenced by differences in purpose, audience, and genre?

Your stylistic choices can enhance your appeals to *logos* (for example, by emphasizing main ideas), to *pathos* (by using words that evoke emotional responses and trigger networks of associations), and to *ethos* (by creating an appropriate and effective voice). In the rest of this section we'll show how these strategies can make your own style more effective.

### Using Sentence Structure to Emphasize Main Ideas

Experienced writers make stylistic choices that emphasize main ideas. For example, you can highlight an idea by placing it in a main clause rather than a subordinate clause or by placing it in a short sentence surrounded by longer sentences. We illustrated this phenomenon in our discussion of the U. R. Riddle exercise on angle of vision (pp. 45–46), where variations in sentence structure created different emphases on Riddle's good or bad points:

> Although Riddle is a brilliant thinker, he had problems relating to other students in my class. (Emphasizes Riddle's personal shortcomings.)
> Although Riddle had problems relating to other students in my class, he is a brilliant thinker. (Emphasizes Riddle's intelligence.)

Neither of these effects would have been possible had the writer simply strung together two simple sentences:

> Riddle had problems relating to other students in my class. He is also a brilliant thinker.

In this version, both points about Riddle are equally emphasized, leaving the reader uncertain about the writer's intended meaning (a problem of *logos*). If you string together a long sequence of short sentences—or simply join them with words like *and, or, so,* or *but*—you create a choppy effect that fails to distinguish between more important and less important material. Consider the following example:

| Every Idea Equally Emphasized | Main Ideas Emphasized | Comment |
|---|---|---|
| I am a student at Sycamore College, and I live in Watkins Hall, and I am enclosing a proposal that concerns a problem with dorm life. There is too much drinking, so nondrinking students don't have an alcohol-free place to go, and so the university should create an alcohol-free dorm, and they should strictly enforce this no-alcohol policy. | As a Sycamore College student living in Watkins Hall, I am enclosing a proposal to improve dorm life. Because there is too much drinking on campus, there is no place for nondrinking students to go. I propose that the university create an alcohol-free dorm and strictly enforce the no-alcohol policy. | In the left-column version, every idea gets equal weight because every idea is in a main clause. In the middle-column version, subordinate ideas are tucked into phrases or subordinate clauses and the main ideas (the problem and the proposed solution) are placed in main clauses for emphasis. |

**Where Appropriate, Including Details Low on the Ladder of Abstraction** In previous writing courses, you might have been told to use concrete, specific language or to "show, not tell." Our advice in this section follows the same spirit: to write as low on the ladder of abstraction as your context allows.

We use the metaphor of a ladder to show how words can vary along a continuum from the abstract ("harm the environment") to the more specific and concrete ("poisoning thousands of freshwater trout with toxic sludge"). As a general rule, details that are low on the ladder of abstraction provide specific factual data as evidence (appeals to *logos*) or trigger vivid images with emotional associations (appeals to *pathos*). As an illustration, consider Figure 3.4, which depicts a "ladder of abstraction" descending from abstract terms at the top toward more specific ones at the bottom.

Choosing words low on the ladder of abstraction is particularly effective for descriptive writing, where your goal is to create a vivid mental image for readers—hence the maxim "Show, don't tell." *Tell* words interpret a scene or tell readers what to feel about a scene without describing it. ("The food for the tailgate party smells wonderful.") In contrast, *show* words describe a scene through sensory details. ("The tantalizing smell of grilled hamburgers and buttered corn on the cob wafts from tailgate party barbecues, where men in their cookout aprons wield forks and spatulas and drink Budweisers.") The description itself evokes the desired effect without requiring the writer to interpret it overtly.

Of course, not all writing needs to be this low on the ladder of abstraction. Our advice, rather, is that the supporting details for a paper should come from as low on the ladder as your context allows. Even the most abstract kind of prose will move up and down between several rungs on the ladder. In closed-form prose, writers need to make choices about the level of specificity that will be most

**FIGURE 3.4** Ladder of Abstraction

| Level on Ladder | Clothing Example | Charity Example | Global Agriculture Example | Gendered Play Examples |
|---|---|---|---|---|
| **High level:** abstract or general | Footwear | Love your neighbor | Traditional crops versus commercial crops | Sam exhibited gendered play behavior. |
| **Middle level** | Flip flops | Help/feed the poor | Crops grown by traditional Indian farmers versus genetically engineered crops | Sam played with trucks and fire engines. |
| **Low level:** specific or concrete | Purple platform flip-flops with rhinestones | Chop vegetables for the Friday night soup kitchen dinner on 3rd Avenue | In Northern India, traditional mandua and jhangora versus genetically modified soy beans | Sam gleefully smashed his toy Tonka fire engine into the coffee table. |

effective based on their purpose, audience, and genre. Note the differences in the levels of abstraction in the following passages:

**PASSAGE 1: FAIRLY HIGH ON LADDER OF ABSTRACTION**

*Point sentence*

*Details relatively high on ladder of abstraction*

Although lightning produces the most deaths and injuries of all weather-related accidents, the rate of danger varies considerably from state to state. Florida has twice as many deaths and injuries from lightning strikes as any other state. Hawaii and Alaska have the fewest.

—*Passage from a general interest informative article on weather-related accidents*

**PASSAGE 2: LOWER ON LADDER OF ABSTRACTION**

*Point sentence*

*Details at middle level on ladder*

*Details at lower level on ladder*

Florida has twice as many deaths and injuries from lightning strikes as any other state, with many of these casualties occurring on the open spaces of golf courses. Florida golfers should carefully note the signals of dangerous weather conditions such as darkening skies, a sudden drop in temperature, an increase in wind, flashes of light and claps of thunder, and the sensation of an electric charge on one's hair or body. In the event of an electric storm, golfers should run into a forest, get under a shelter, get into a car, or assume the safest body position. To avoid being the tallest object in an area, if caught in open areas, golfers should find a low spot, spread out, and crouch into a curled position with feet together to create minimal body contact with the ground.

—*Passage from a safety article aimed at Florida golfers*

Both of these passages are effective for their audience and purpose. The first passage might be compared to a distant shot with a camera, giving an overview of lightning deaths in the United States, while the second zooms in for a more detailed look at a specific case, Florida golf courses. Sometimes, low-on-the-ladder particulars consist of statistics or quotations rather than sensory details. For example, civil engineer David Rockwood uses low-on-the-ladder numerical data about the size and number of wind towers to convince readers that wind genera- tion of electricity entails environmental damage. Your rhetorical decisions about level of abstraction are important because too much high-on-the-scale writing can become dull for readers, while too much low-on-the-scale writing can seem overwhelming or pointless.

See Rockwood's letter to the editor on p. 15.

---

**FOR WRITING AND DISCUSSION**

### Choosing Details for Different Levels on the Ladder of Abstraction

The following exercise will help you appreciate how details can be chosen at different levels of abstraction to serve different purposes and audiences. Working in small groups or as a whole class, invent details at appropriate posi- tions on the ladder of abstraction for each of the following point sentences.

1. *Yesterday's game was a major disappointment.* You are writing an e-mail message to a friend who is a fan (of baseball, football, basketball, another sport) and missed the game; use midlevel details to explain what was disappointing.

2. *Although the game stank, there were some great moments.* Switch to low-on-the-ladder specific details to describe one of these "great moments."

3. *Advertising in women's fashion magazines creates a distorted and unhealthy view of beauty.* You are writing an analysis for a college course on popular culture; use high-to-midlevel details to give a one-paragraph overview of several ways these ads create an unhealthy view of beauty.

4. *One recent ad, in particular, conveys an especially destructive message about beauty.* Choose a particular ad and describe it with low-on-the-ladder, very specific details.

## Creating a Voice Matched to Your Purpose, Audience, and Genre

College students often wonder what style—and particularly, what voice—is appropriate for college papers. For most college assignments, we recommend that you approximate your natural speaking voice to give your writing a conversational academic style. By "conversational," we mean a voice that strives to be plain and clear while retaining the engaging quality of a person who is enthusiastic about the subject. Of course, as you become an expert in a discipline, you may need to move toward a more scholarly voice. For example, the prose in an academic journal article can be extremely dense with technical terms and complex sentence structure, but expert readers in that field understand and expect this voice.

Students sometimes try to imitate a dense academic style before they have achieved the disciplinary expertise to make the style sound natural. The result can seem pretentious or phony. At the other extreme, students sometimes adopt an overly informal or street slang voice that doesn't fit an academic context. Writing with clarity and directness within your natural range will usually create the most effective and powerful voice. Consider the difference in the following examples:

| Overly Academic Voice | Conversational Academic Voice | Overly Informal Voice |
|---|---|---|
| As people advance in age, they experience time-dependent alterations in their ability to adapt to environmental change. However, much prior research on the aging process has failed to differentiate between detrimental changes caused by an organism's aging process itself and detrimental changes caused by a disease process that is often associated with aging. | As people get older, they are less able to adapt to changes in their environment. Research on aging, however, hasn't always distinguished between loss of function caused by aging itself and loss caused by diseases common among older people. | Old folks don't adapt well to changes in their environments. Some scientists who studied the cane and walker crowd found out that it was hard to tell the difference between bad stuff caused by age versus bad stuff caused by disease. |

Although the "conversational academic voice" style is appropriate for most college papers, especially those written for lower-division courses, many professors construct assignments asking you to adopt different voices and different styles. It is thus important to understand the professor's assignment and to adopt the style and voice appropriate for the assigned rhetorical situation.

## Making Purposeful Choices about Document Design

Document design, which refers to the format of a text on the page including use of graphics or visual images, can have a surprising impact on the effectiveness of a message. In an academic context, writers usually produce manuscript (keyboarded pages of typed text presented electronically or in hard copy held together with a staple or folder) rather than a "camera ready" document created through desktop-publishing software. With manuscripts, your document design choices mainly concern margins, font style and size, line spacing, and headers or footers (page number, document identification, date). Generally these choices are dictated by the style guidelines of an academic discipline such as American Psychological Association (APA). If you deviate from the expected document design (for example, by using a specialty font or by designing a decorative cover page for an academic paper) you undergo the risk either of appearing unaware of academic conventions or of flaunting them to get noticed—like wearing a jump-suit to a job interview. Attention to document design and the appearance of your manuscripts thus signals your membership in an academic or professional community. An inappropriately formatted or sloppy paper can hurt your *ethos* and may send a message that you are unprofessional.

For more on these issues, see Chapter 4 on composing in a digital environment and Chapter 7 on analyzing visual images.

In contrast, desktop-published, "camera ready" works require elaborate decisions about document design to give them a professional visual appeal ready for print or the Web. For desktop-published documents, design is closely related to genre and involves rhetorical decisions about font styles, use of space and layout, color, and graphics or images. Table 3.1 lists some of the variables associated with document design when writers move from a "manuscript" environment to a "desktop-published" or multimedia environment.

**TABLE 3.1    Features of Document Design in Scholarly versus Popular Genres**

| Design Feature | Typical Use in Scholarly Journal | Variations in Popular Genres |
|---|---|---|
| Fonts | • Conservative, highly readable (Times New Roman)<br>• Boldface for headings or occasional emphasis<br>• Italics or underlining governed by disciplinary conventions | • Playful use of fonts in titles and introductions<br>• Different font styles in sidebars or boxes<br>• Larger font sizes at start of articles |
| Use of white space (margins, spacing, placement of titles and visuals, single versus double columns) | • Consistent use of white space in each journal article to achieve orderly effect<br>• Table of contents often on cover<br>• Double columns often used to maximize amount of readable prose per page | • Wide variations in use of white space<br>• Text may be wrapped around visuals<br>• Distinction between articles and advertisements sometimes blurred<br>• Table of contents often buried among advertisements |

| **TABLE 3.1**   *continued* | | |
|---|---|---|
| **Design Feature** | **Typical Use in Scholarly Journal** | **Variations in Popular Genres** |
| Color | • Minimal use of color<br>• Some color in graphics and charts to set off main ideas or highlight categories | • Playful and artistic use of color to create mood, draw eye to certain locations, create variety, or achieve desired emphasis |
| Visuals | • Primarily graphics or illustrations with focus on clarity and logic<br>• Visuals are called "Tables" or "Figures"; all axes and variables are clearly labeled | • Often playful use of visuals to illustrate content or theme<br>• Often uses drawings or photoshopped images to illustrate themes |

**FOR WRITING AND DISCUSSION**

### Analyzing Rhetorical Effect

Using examples of different kinds of published documents—scholarly articles, popular magazine articles, newspapers, pamphlets, and so forth—and images of various Web documents or multimedia products, analyze differences in document design. In each case, how is document design related to genre? How does it contribute to the document's effectiveness?

## CONCEPT 3.4  Nonverbal messages persuade through visual strategies that can be analyzed rhetorically.

**3.4**
Analyze how nonverbal texts persuade through visual rhetorical strategies.

Just as you can think rhetorically about texts, you can think rhetorically about photographs, drawings, and other images as well as artifacts such as clothing.

### Visual Rhetoric

The persuasive power of images shapes our impressions and understanding of events. Take, for instance, the 2010 BP oil spill in the Gulf of Mexico that pumped millions of barrels of crude oil into the Gulf for three months. Aerial photos of the spreading brown oil plumes in the water conveyed the seriousness and magnitude of the problem, which was further driven home by photos of animals coated in sticky brown oil—sea turtles, crabs, pelicans, other birds, and fish—almost unrecognizable as animals. These photos made the logical argument (*logos*) that underwater oil extraction needs more stringent regulation. They also appealed powerfully to viewers' emotions (*pathos*) in their vivid and immediate depiction of suffering and dying animals and of damage to the environment. These photos helped galvanize public opposition to expanded offshore drilling. Think also of how the images of the destruction of superstorm Sandy drove home to Americans the need to prepare for extreme weather and raised awareness of the effects of climate change. Or think of the way frequent news photos of hundreds

Chapter 7 deals extensively with visual rhetoric, explaining how visual elements work together to create a persuasive effect.

of thousands of angry protestors in Egypt have continued to arouse American anxiety about political instability in the Middle East and Northern Africa.

What gives these images this persuasive power? For one thing, they can be apprehended at a glance, condensing an argument into a memorable scene or symbol that taps deeply into our emotions and values. Images also persuade by appealing to *logos*, *ethos*, and *pathos*. They make implicit arguments (*logos*) while also appealing to our values and emotions (*pathos*) and causing us to respond favorably or unfavorably to the artist or photographer (*ethos*). Like verbal texts, images have an angle of vision, which can be crafted by selecting, manipulating, and often photoshopping images to control what viewers see and thus influence what they think. (Note that "angle of vision" is itself a visual metaphor.) Through the location and angle of the camera, the distance from the subject, and the framing, cropping, and filtering/lighting of the image, the photographer steers us toward a particular view of the subject, influencing us to forget, at least momentarily, that there are other ways of seeing the same subject. For example, opponents of building the Keystone Pipeline linking Canada's Alberta tar sands oil with refineries in Texas used photos of contaminated sludge ponds and damaged boreal forests while supporters used up-close photos of workers benefiting from high-paying jobs.

Although images can have powerful rhetorical effects, these effects may be less controllable and more audience-dependent than those of verbal texts. Consider, for example, the photo in Figure 3.5 of a vast iceberg, a common image

**FIGURE 3.5** Floating Iceberg

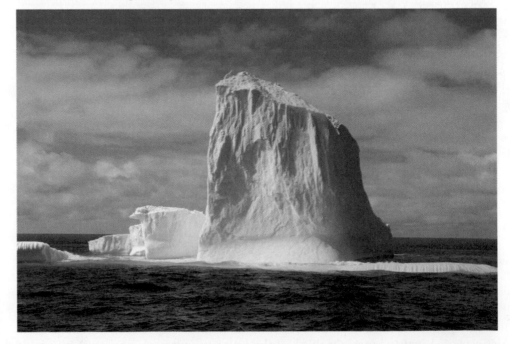

recently in newspapers and magazines. This photo resembles those taken by environmental photographer James Balog for his Extreme Ice Survey, documenting the recent rapid melting of glaciers around the world. (Balog's work is featured in the award-winning documentary *Chasing Ice*.) In this photo, the iceberg towers above the water and glistens in the sun. When these photographs are used in the climate change debate, the intention is to document the rapid melting of Arctic and Antarctic ice—as shown by the size of the iceberg and the vast expanse of water in which it is floating. Viewers familiar with the context of shrinking glaciers and spectacular icebergs breaking off the glaciers will interpret the *logos* of this photo as evidence for global warming, which in a matter of years is shrinking glaciers that took tens of thousands of years to form. In contrast, other viewers might find that the striking aesthetic beauty of this image distracts them from the global warming message. For them, the photographer's angle of vision and use of visual techniques have created a work of art that undermines its ability to convey scientific information in support of the global climate change crisis. Interpreted in this way, the photo could be seen to use *pathos* to attract viewers to the magnificent, strange beauty of this part of the world, perhaps as a potential part of a travel brochure. Because images are somewhat open in the way they create arguments, writers of texts that include images should anticipate viewers' possible alternative interpretations and consider the importance in many cases of contextualizing images.

For a photo of melting glaciers that participates in the climate change debate, see the image on p. 275. That photo makes different appeals to *logos*, *ethos*, and *pathos*.

For further discussion of how to use words to guide viewers' interpretation of images, see Chapter 13, Skill 13.2.

## Analyzing Images

**FOR WRITING AND DISCUSSION**

The following exercise asks you to think about the rhetorical effects of different images of wolves and particularly about how they can create implicit arguments in the public controversy about hunting wolves in western states. The gray wolf had been on the federal Endangered Species list but was removed in 2012 when the wolf population had grown. However, "wolf wars" have flared in Montana, Wyoming, and especially Minnesota since then. Ranchers and hunters argue that wolves are too numerous and aggressive in hunting livestock and game and have lobbied for hunting permits from state governments to kill hundreds of wolves. In contrast, animal rights groups, environmental organizations, and the Ojibwe/Anishinaabe and Sioux have lobbied against these hunting permits, arguing that wolf populations should be allowed to grow in order to sustain a natural ecological system in which wolves help keep deer and other wild animal populations in balance.

**Analyzing the Photos.** As you imagine the use of images in Figures 3.6–3.9, explore the rhetorical effects of these images, noting how the effect may differ from person to person. In each photograph, on what details has the photographer chosen to focus? How do the details and angle of vision contribute to the dominant impression of wolves conveyed by the whole photograph? How

*(continued)*

**FIGURE 3.6** Wolf in a Field of Grass

**FIGURE 3.7** Four Wolves in Winter

**FIGURE 3.8** Wolves with Deer Carcass

**FIGURE 3.9** Wolf with Rabbit

does the photograph affect you emotionally? How does it shape your attitude toward wolves? How would you rank these images in terms of their favorable or unfavorable impression of wolves and their emotional appeal?

**Using the Photos.** Now imagine that you are creating a flyer for each of the following audiences and purposes. Which photo or photos would help you make the most compelling argument (consider *logos*, *ethos*, and *pathos*) for each group and purpose? Explain your rationale.

A. An organization consisting of hunters and ranchers has commissioned you to create a flyer that seeks to make the public more tolerant of hunting wolves now that the gray wolf has been taken off the Endangered Species list.

B. An environmental organization has asked you to create a flyer for the general public that seeks to generate appreciation for gray wolves' role in western ecosystems and to spark sympathy for them in protest against the reinstated wolf hunting permits.

## The Rhetoric of Clothing and Other Consumer Items

Not only do photographs, paintings, and drawings have rhetorical power, but so do the images projected by many of our consumer choices. Consider, for example, the rhetorical thinking that goes into our choice of clothes. We choose our clothes not only to keep ourselves covered and warm but also to project visually our identification with certain social groups and subcultures. For example, if you want to be identified as a skateboarder, a preppy, a geek, a NASCAR fan, or a junior partner in a corporate law firm, you know how to select clothes and accessories that convey that identification. The way you dress is a code that communicates where you fit (or how you want to be perceived as fitting) within a class and social structure. For the most part, clothing codes are arbitrary, based on a system of differences. For example, there is no universal "truth" saying that long, baggy basketball shorts are more attractive than short basketball shorts, even though one style may feel current and the other out-of-date.

How do these symbolic codes get established? They can be set by fashion designers, by advertisers, or by trendy groups or individuals. The key to any new clothing code is to make it look different in some distinctive way from an earlier code or from a code of another group. Sometimes clothing codes develop to show rebellion against the values of parents or authority figures. At other times they develop to show new kinds of group identities.

Clothing codes are played on in conscious ways in fashion advertisements so that consumers become very aware of what identifications are signaled by different styles and brands. This aspect of consumer society is so ubiquitous that one of the marks of growing affluence in third world countries is people's attention to the rhetoric of consumer goods. Buying a certain kind of consumer good projects a certain kind of status or group or class identity. Our point, from a rhetorical perspective, is that in making a consumer choice, many people are concerned not only with the quality of the item itself but also with its rhetorical symbolism. Note that the same item can send quite different messages to different groups: A Rolex watch might enhance one's credibility at a corporate board meeting while undercutting it at a company picnic for workers.

---

### Clothing as Visual Arguments

FOR WRITING AND DISCUSSION

Working in small groups or as a whole class, do a rhetorical analysis of the consumer items shown in Figures 3.10 through 3.13.

1. In each case, see if you can reach consensus on why these people might have chosen a particular way of dressing. How does the clothing style project a desire to identify with certain groups or to shock or reject certain groups? How do the clothing choices help establish and enhance the wearer's sense of identity?

*(continued)*

**FIGURE 3.10**

**FIGURE 3.11**

**FIGURE 3.12**

**FIGURE 3.13**

2. When you and your friends make consumer purchases, to what extent are you swayed by the quality of the item (its materials and workmanship) versus the rhetorical messages it sends to an audience (its signals about social identity and standing)?

3. How does the rhetoric of clothing extend to other consumer items such as cell phones, cars, vacations, recreational activities, home furnishings, music, and so forth?

4. Suppose that you are interviewing for a job in one or more of these job settings: barista in a coffee shop, retail sales clerk, intern at a corporate law office, or some other workplace setting of your choice. What clothing would be appropriate for your interview and why? Be as specific as possible for all items of clothing including shoes and accessories.
5. To what extent are dress codes for women more complex than those for men?

## Chapter Summary

In this chapter we have looked briefly at rhetorical theory in order to explain the persuasive power of both verbal and visual texts.

- *Concept 3.1 Messages persuade through their angle of vision.* Any text necessarily looks at its subject from a perspective—an angle of vision—that selects and emphasizes some details while omitting or minimizing others. You can analyze writers' angle of vision by considering their direct statements of intention, their selection of details, their word choice, their figures of speech, and their manipulation of sentence structure to control emphasis.
- *Concept 3.2 Messages persuade through appeals to* **logos, ethos,** *and* **pathos.** *Logos* refers to the power of the writer's reasons and evidence; *pathos* to the way the writer connects to the reader's sympathies, emotions, values, and beliefs; and *ethos* to the way the writer portrays himself or herself as trustworthy and credible.
- *Concept 3.3 Messages persuade through writers' choices about style and document design.* Stylistic features such as sentence structure, word choice, voice, and tone work together to create different rhetorical effects. An effective style highlights key ideas, moves down the ladder of abstraction for details, and establishes an appropriate voice. Document design also contributes to a message's effect. Academic articles generally adopt a conservative design while more popular genres approach design playfully and artistically.
- *Concept 3.4 Nonverbal messages persuade through visual strategies that can be analyzed rhetorically.* Like verbal texts, visual texts have an angle of vision created by the way the image is framed and by the perspective from which it is viewed. Images also make implicit arguments (*logos*), appeal to the viewer's emotions and values (*pathos*), and suggest the creator's character and trustworthiness (*ethos*). One can also analyze consumer choices (clothing, jewelry, cars) rhetorically because such choices make implicit arguments about the consumer's desired identity.

## Two Contrasting Descriptions of the Same Scene

**BRIEF**

**WRITING PROJECT**

This brief writing project is a write-to-learn task that will help you appreciate how writers construct an "angle of vision" (see Concept 3.1) through selection of low-on-the-ladder details, word choice, and other means.

Write two descriptions of the same scene. Here is the catch. Your two descriptions must illustrate contrasting angles of vision. Your first description must convey a favorable impression of the scene, making it appear pleasing or attractive. The second description must convey a negative or unfavorable impression, making the scene appear unpleasant or unattractive. Both descriptions must contain only factual details and must describe exactly the same scene from the same location at the same time. It's not fair, in other words, to describe the scene in sunny weather and then in the rain or otherwise to alter factual details. Each description should be one paragraph long (approximately 125–175 words).

To get into the spirit of this unusual assignment, you need to create a personal rationale for why you are writing two opposing descriptions. You might think of yourself being in two different moods so that you look at the scene first through your "happy glasses" and then through your "sad glasses." Or you could simply think of yourself as a word wizard consciously trying to create, in the spirit of a game, two different effects on readers for two different rhetorical purposes.

Once you have chosen your scene, you'll need to observe and take notes in preparation for writing the focused descriptions of the scene. You need to compose descriptions that are rich in sensory detail (low on the ladder of abstraction)—sights, sounds, smells, textures, even on occasion tastes—all contributing to a dominant impression that gives the description focus.

You can train yourself to notice sensory details by creating a two-column sensory chart and noting details that appeal to each of the senses. Then try describing them, first positively (left column) and then negatively (right column). One student, observing a scene in a local tavern, made these notes in her sensory chart:

| Positive Description | Negative Description |
| --- | --- |
| **Taste** | |
| salted and buttered popcorn | salty, greasy popcorn |
| frosty pitchers of beer | half-drunk pitchers of stale, warm beer |
| big bowls of salted-in-the-shell peanuts on the tables | mess of peanut shells and discarded pretzel wrappers on tables and floor |
| **Sound** | |
| hum of students laughing and chatting | din of high-pitched giggles and various obnoxious frat guys shouting at each other |
| the jukebox playing oldies but goodies from the early Beatles | jukebox blaring out-of-date music |

## Student Example

We conclude with a student example of this assignment.

### DESCRIPTION 1—POSITIVE EFFECT

Light rain gently drops into the puddles that have formed along the curb as I look out my apartment window at the corner of 14th and East John. Pedestrians layered in sweaters, raincoats, and scarves and guarded with shiny rubber boots and colorful umbrellas sip their steaming hot triple-tall lattes. Some share smiles and pleasant exchanges as they hurry down the street, hastening to work where it is warm and dry. Others, smelling the aroma of French roast espresso coming from the coffee bar next to the bus stop, listen for the familiar rumbling sound that will mean the 56 bus has arrived. Radiant orange, yellow, and red leaves blanket the sidewalk in the areas next to the maple trees that line the road. Along the curb a mother holds the hand of her toddler, dressed like a miniature tugboat captain in yellow raincoat and pants, who splashes happily in a puddle.

### DESCRIPTION 2—NEGATIVE EFFECT

A solemn grayness hangs in the air, as I peer out the window of my apartment at the corner of 14th and East John. A steady drizzle of rain leaves boot-drenching puddles for pedestrians to avoid. Bundled in rubber boots, sweaters, coats, and rain-soaked scarves, commuters clutch Styrofoam cups of coffee as a defense against the biting cold. They lift their heads every so often to take a small sip of caffeine, but look sleep-swollen nevertheless. Pedestrians hurry past each other, moving quickly to get away from the dismal weather, the dull grayness. Some nod a brief hello to a familiar face, but most clutch their overcoats and tread grimly on, looking to avoid puddles or spray from passing cars. Others stand at the bus stop, hunched over, waiting in the drab early morning for the smell of diesel that means the 56 bus has arrived. Along the curb an impatient mother jerks the hand of a toddler to keep him from stomping in an oil-streaked puddle.

# 4 MULTIMODAL AND ONLINE COMMUNICATION

**WHAT YOU WILL LEARN**

**4.1** To analyze the rhetorical use of words, images, and sounds in multimodal texts.

**4.2** To think rhetorically about the interactive Web environment with shifting audiences, purposes, genres, and authorial roles.

**4.3** To participate responsibly in online discourse by understanding intellectual property rights and by constructing an ethical persona.

**Everything is a remix.**

—*Kirby Ferguson, filmmaker*

We examined the rhetorical power of images in Chapter 3 (Concept 3.4). In this chapter we expand our discussion of visual rhetoric to include a range of **multimodal texts**, by which we mean any text that supplements words with another mode of communication such as images, sounds, or even the rhetorical use of page design. The word *multimodal* combines the concepts of "multi" (more than one) and "modality" (a channel, medium, or mode of communication). The use of multimodal texts has increased dramatically in the digital age, but multimodal texts that combine words and images have a long history. Medieval scriptures often had vivid religious scenes painted in the margins (called "illuminations"), and Charles Darwin's field notes combine words with carefully drawn images of flora and fauna. Many of the multimodal compositions in this text combine words and images in ways that require no digital technology—see the poster arguing that high heel shoes are harmful to feet (p. 328) or the advocacy ad arguing that black kids are more likely than white kids to go to prison (p. 246).

What is new in the digital age is the predominance of online multimodal texts with full-color images, videos, animations, and sounds as well as embedded hyperlinks that allow readers to jump from one location to another. The resulting interactive Web environment differs substantially from print text—usually black letters on white paper—that you read linearly from left to right, top to bottom. How to think rhetorically about this interactive multimodal environment is the subject of this chapter. It is one thing to post a video of cute kittens or funny golf swings on YouTube; it is quite another thing to compose a purposeful multimodal text that effectively uses rhetorical principles to move an audience. Moreover, Web environments complicate our understanding of audiences, purposes, genres, and authors while also raising legal issues about intellectual property and ethical issues about online etiquette and personas.

## CONCEPT 4.1  **Composers of multimodal texts use words, images, and sounds rhetorically to move an audience.**

**4.1**
Analyze the rhetorical use of words, images, and sounds in multimodal texts.

Research suggests that Internet surfers view a Web page for only a second or two before they move on to something else. Effective Web communicators have to negotiate this competitive, short-attention-span environment by hooking audiences quickly and then keeping them engaged with high-level content.

### Hooking Audiences with Images and "Nutshell" Text

Readers on the Web typically don't read from beginning to end as they might in a print text. They jump from page to page, influenced by multisensory stimuli urging them to pause on an image, scan a verbal text, or click on a link. Texts in multimodal forms are layered, shuffled, combined, and recombined in ways that make it difficult for authors to predict how readers will navigate a Web site or what they will choose to read or view.

In such a busy environment, composers often use images for immediate appeals to *pathos*. Because Web composers have but a split second to hook the reader's interest, they often use emotion-evoking or interest-arousing images, which have an immediacy that verbal texts can't match, as we explained in Concept 3.4. Such images invoke in audiences a kind of non-rational investment in a subject, an investment that precedes attention to a page's more logical appeals often conveyed by words. For an illustration of how Web composers use images to hook readers, see the competing Web sites about fracking in Chapter 14 (p. 347).

Another way to attract a reader's attention is through pithy "nutshell" sentences that convey the "take away" point of a page. These nutshell sentences, often highlighted by a different color, enlarged font, or placement in a call-out box, are the multimodal equivalent of a thesis statement or paragraph topic sentence in purely verbal text. Because long chunks of text look deadly dull on a screen, skilled Web composers produce easily readable, concise texts that are often broken up by spacing, text boxes, or bullets. Often, too, Web composers use the journalistic inverted pyramid, so that the opening paragraph of a story summarizes the whole story. The goal of nutshell sentences and inverted pyramids is to send readers the complete take-away message of a text quickly in case the reader jumps to something else. In the fracking Web sites shown in Chapter 14, page 347, note nutshell phrases and sentences such as the following: "Shale: The energy to do it right" and "Keep North Carolina frack-free."

## Holding Readers through Strong Content

Once readers are hooked by a site, they will continue only if the site delivers good content—that is, only if it gives them something new, challenging, surprising, or otherwise interesting or entertaining. Sometimes this content is conveyed entirely through verbal text to be read on the screen. But often the content is presented in multimodal texts such as audio podcasts, slide shows set to music, videos of lectures containing PowerPoint or Prezi slides, animations, or videos produced with rhetorical sophistication to make a point. Because simple videos can be made with smartphone and digital cameras and relatively easy-to-learn editing programs, many students are trying their hand at this powerful new genre. Although it is beyond the scope of this text to discuss the technology of video-making, we can introduce you to the rhetorical thinking that underlies an effective video.

## Designing Video Narratives that Move Viewers

An effective video calls for a full range of visual analysis. A video can be paused at any moment to freeze single frames, each of which can be analyzed rhetorically as a still image using the strategies introduced in Concept 3.4 and developed more fully in Chapter 7, "Analyzing Images." In the "play" mode, however, videos add the dimension of motion (narration, movement through time) as well as the power of sound (dialogue, background sounds, music, voice-over) to achieve desired effects.

Visually, a video makes its narrative impact along two channels. First, a video's "story" is told through the narrative action and dialogue—the content of the video. But the story is also told through the visual grammar deployed through camera placement and technique. Teachers of video production say that beginning camera users tend to photograph the action from one camera position only— usually a distance or mid-distance shot—that requires minimal editing. In contrast, experienced videographers shoot from several positions and purposely use cutting and splicing techniques to narrate the action through the perspective of different camera positions. They choose each position for a rhetorical purpose in order to emphasize some parts of the action and deemphasize others. Their goal is to *design* or *compose* a video sequence that has a narrative arc and shape. Film scholars have shown that camera positions can generally be classified into three types:

- *Establishing shots,* which set the narrative in a context showing location and setting.
- *Reaction shots,* which show a close-up, often of a face, to register a character's emotional reaction.
- *Point of view shots,* which look at a scene through the eyes of one of the characters.

These three kinds of shots are illustrated in Figure 4.1, which shows still frames from a student video of an urban gardener gathering eggs from her backyard chicken coop. The first image is an establishing shot showing the chicken coop, some chickens, and the woman lifting the coop door to retrieve the day's eggs.

Establishing shot

Point of view shot

Reaction shot

**FIGURE 4.1** Urban Gardener Video

Next we see a point of view shot (looking through the woman's eyes) of the eggs up close including the woman's hand grasping one of the eggs. Finally, we see a reaction shot showing the woman's smiling face expressing happiness for the eggs and gratitude toward her hens. These different camera positions create a brief narrative arc of the urban gardener's anticipation and satisfaction at getting eggs from her free range backyard chickens.

## Analyzing a Video Sequence

FOR WRITING AND DISCUSSION

Watch and then analyze a short video assigned by your instructor or chosen by yourself. The video should use different camera positions as well as sounds for rhetorical effect.

1. ***Analyzing editing choices:*** After playing the whole clip several times, pause the video at each of the edits where the camera position shifts.

*(continued)*

Consider the following questions: How does the videographer use establishing, point of view, and reaction shots to achieve a desired effect on viewers? What is the rhetorical purpose of each camera position? What is emphasized in each camera position? How does the sequence create a thematic point or meaning?

2. ***Analyzing still frames:*** Pause the video on several frames that can be analyzed rhetorically like a photograph. How is the scene framed? How is it lighted or filtered? What is the camera angle and distance? What is the subject matter of the scene? If the scene contains people, what is the rhetorical effect of the characters' clothing and accessories, hairstyle, gestures, poses, and positioning? How would you analyze the scene in terms of gender, social class, or implied values?

3. ***Analyzing sound:*** Finally, play the clip again, this time paying attention to sounds. If the video includes music, what is the effect of the musical choices? If the clip has a voice-over, what is the effect of the choices about gender, vocal register, accent, pacing, and so forth? What sounds are emphasized in the video? What sounds might have been filtered out?

See Chapter 7, pp. 146–152, for advice on how to analyze a still image.

---

**4.2**
Think rhetorically about the interactive Web environment with shifting audiences, purposes, genres, and authorial roles.

## CONCEPT 4.2  Online environments are rhetorically interactive with shifting audiences, purposes, genres, and authorial roles.

Consider the difference between reading a print version of a news story and the same newspaper's online version. Here is the headline from a recent front page print story in a city newspaper: "**INTRUDER TERRIFIES STUDENTS.**" According to the print story, a man wearing a trench coat and eating an ice cream cone entered a classroom at a local university and "frightened students with his bizarre behavior." When the intruder refused to leave the classroom, the professor called campus security and dismissed the class. According to the newspaper, campus security was slow to respond; meanwhile, students were terrified as they watched the man "talking incoherently and turn[ing] over tables and other classroom furniture." Once campus security arrived, the man was arrested and booked into the county jail. (He was unarmed.)

If you read the story only in the print version, you would think the campus barely escaped a disaster. But how accurate was the story? In the newspaper's online version, the same story was accompanied by comment posts from students who were in the classroom at the time. Many of these posts contradicted the newspaper's story, saying that the intruder was odd, but not threatening, that campus security arrived within one minute of being called, and that students, rather than fleeing the classroom in terror, lingered out of curiosity. One commenter said that the intruder seemed to be enjoying his ice cream cone. Another said that he couldn't have possibly tipped over tables because the classroom furniture was fixed to the floor. Whereas the newspaper's "angle of vision" portrayed the incident as frightening and dangerous, the posts portrayed it collectively as a bizarre but harmless encounter with a possibly mentally ill street person. Within a day, more than a hundred posts contributed to the story. The ensuing discussion thread evolved from concerns about what happened in the classroom to a larger conversation about the best way to respond to threats. One respondent said it was lucky that no one in the class carried a concealed weapon because an armed student might have killed the intruder (or accidentally shot a classmate), turning a harmless incident into a tragedy. The discussion thread was then dominated by heated exchanges over the advisability of armed citizens.

Our point in recounting this episode is that the Web creates an interactive participatory news environment very unlike that of traditional print newspapers and news magazines. Because Web readers are often Web writers, content published online can receive reader responses within minutes. These responses in turn can alter the way readers read the original content so that the "message" itself begins to evolve. This participatory environment has many implications for reading online communication rhetorically.

## Shifting and Evolving Rhetorical Contexts Online

We can see the rhetorical implications of an online environment if we return for a moment to the rhetorical triangle (audience, writer, message) that we introduced in Concept 3.2 , page 48. Consider how an online environment destabilizes each point of the triangle.

**Shifting Audiences** When you publish something online (say an e-mail or a Yelp! restaurant review), who are your readers? In some cases, you might think you can identify your audience precisely. If you send an e-mail, for example, you assume that your audience is the person addressed. But sometimes recipients forward e-mails without your knowledge or consent, or sometimes, to your great embarrassment, you might hit "reply all" when you intended to hit "reply." Moreover, e-mails are always stored somewhere on servers and may be leaked by a whistleblower or read by attorneys who subpoena them in legal proceedings. (Almost every week produces news stories of scandals or lawsuits initiated by leaked e-mails.) Likewise you might believe your Facebook audience is limited to "friends" only. However, unless you set your privacy codes very narrowly, one of your friends can "like" or "share" one of your posts, sending it to a whole new network of that person's friends. One of your posts or pictures may well be viewed by hundreds of strangers including your boss or your teacher. (And we know, of course, that "friends" on a Facebook site are often not really friends at all, and sometimes not even acquaintances.)

Variability of audiences occurs in different ways if you write a blog, upload a video to YouTube, or create your own Web site. In such cases, you cast your net for readers or viewers, probably hoping for a large audience. Although a given post can sometimes go viral by spreading exponentially through social media, often you are thankful for a small readership that you hope will grow. Sometimes your post may be read by audiences that you didn't intend to target—people who disagree with you, for example—and these people may forward your work to a largely hostile audience. At other times, however, online communities often work paradoxically to shut off outside readers by creating "insider" discussion threads that reinforce insider views and make outsiders feel unwelcome. Sometimes, in fact, members of these communities will flame an outsider who posts unwittingly on a thread. The community thus tries to stabilize its audience through self-policing, but in the process often limits a real exchange of communication across differences. Wise online writers, we believe, will in most cases try to enlarge their audiences rather than limit them. This desire to reach more readers puts the burden on the writer to use the appeals of *logos*, *pathos*, and *ethos* to draw in readers rather than shut them out.

**Shifting Writers** Just as the Web environment destabilizes our conception of "audience," so can it destabilize the concept of "writer." Online environments often blur the concept of the single, authoritative writer by creating texts written by communities. Through wikis, for example, writers who may not even know each other can build collaborative texts that cannot be identified with any individual writer. Although wiki writers don't produce texts in quite the way that bees build a hive—as if some group mind generates the words and makes the rhetorical decisions rather than an individual—the text seems to emerge collaboratively without a controlling lead author. In an analogous way, discussion threads on blog sites can be said to blur the individual writer. Although an originating blogger may have a strong individual identity, the responses posted by readers bring other voices to the original blogger's message, creating a kind of larger and more complex "co-created" message. We saw this phenomenon in our example of the news story about the ice-cream cone eating classroom intruder: That story's "truth content" was not controlled by the original author (the news reporter) but by the collective weight of all readers who posted responses to the story. Finally, the concept of the writer is blurred by the anonymity created by the use of pseudonyms or avatars, which often make it difficult to identify texts with the actual human author.

**Evolving Messages** Very few pieces of content published on the Web are stable or permanent. Items appear and quickly disappear. An author can post a story or article on a Web site, make corrections or revisions, and then quickly repost the altered version. (This impermanence explains why academic conventions for citing and documenting sources sometimes require you to indicate the date on which you viewed the site.) Also readers often don't read Web texts linearly from beginning to end in the stabilizing way they read print-based text. Rather they are apt to click on embedded hyperlinks, jumping from text to text. Thus a message will be perceived differently by different readers according to their pathway through it. Messages evolve in still another way within threaded discussion sites where the reader's view of the subject is gradually modified by the cumulative impact of all the posts. Moreover, even an individual writer's view might evolve as the discussion continues. A given writer who expresses one view early on in a thread may express a quite different view later.

## Online Variations in Purposes, Genres, and Authorial Roles

Another way to think rhetorically about online communication is to consider how a writer's choice of genre or medium affects the writer's purpose and authorial role. To see what we are talking about, consider the following thought experiment:

**THOUGHT EXPERIMENT**

Suppose that next year you plan to do something unusual (take a road trip, do a service project in an impoverished area, live in a foreign country) and want to keep your friends posted about your activities. How could you best do so? An old technology approach would be to send them postcards once a week. New technology approaches include e-mail (you could set up an address list), Facebook (you already have "friends" established), tweets, or a personal blog. How would each choice influence your role and purpose in constructing a message? How would each choice affect the size and composition of your audience? Which would you choose and why?

When we discuss this thought experiment with our own students, they reveal many variables among these choices. They surmise that the blog invites the most serious, reflective, and in-depth writing. Writers would be apt to compose a blog in a word-processing program, revise and proof it, and then post it to the blog site. Their purpose would be to bring interesting insights and points of view to willing readers. In contrast, the least reflective genres or media would be tweets (requiring "sound bites" with 140 or fewer characters) or old-technology postcards, which have limited space and have traditionally invited clichés such as "wish you were here" or "check out the pic on the back—we were there yesterday." In between is e-mail, which hypothetically could be as reflective as a blog, but is more likely to be breezier and less formal—probably composed in the e-mail program itself and limited in length.

Another important variable concerns audience. Our students surmise that the blog is apt to have the fewest readers among your friends. Your friends would have to know about it and be motivated to find and read it. However, the blog is the most apt to attract outside readers if your subject matter and style were interesting and if enough initial readers "liked" you and began spreading the word. In contrast, e-mail has a captive audience, but raises awkward decisions about whom to include in your mailing list. Sending an e-mail seems to tell recipients that your message is worth their time. Some might resent having an e-mail from you every day, yet feel obligated at least to skim it. Others might be excited to follow your every word. Tweets have different audiences still. If your friends just want quick updates on your travels, then tweets serve that purpose well. Friends can follow you on Twitter as they like without having to log into a blog or get annoyed with your clogging their e-mail inbox. The worst option for reaching a wide audience, everyone agrees, is the old technology postcard, which requires you to write to each recipient separately in long hand, address the postcard, add a stamp, and mail it.

Of special consideration is Facebook. Our students think most people would use Facebook to post photographs of a trip and to send brief sound bite messages, but they would not use Facebook as a way to share the reflections that would be put into a blog. Facebook seems to invite triviality more than depth.

## How Do You Read and Write the Web?

In small groups or as a whole class, share how you currently use the Web for reading and writing. When you are online, what do you typically view or read? Do you use social media? How? Do you post photos on Flickr? Have you ever uploaded a video on YouTube? Have you ever tweeted? Do you use e-mail? (If so, how do you use it differently from text messaging on a phone?) Have you ever blogged? Created a Web site? Created a multimodal text? Have you ever responded to a blog or otherwise posted on a discussion thread? Have you ever written an online review? Have you ever contributed to a wiki? Your goal here is to share the various ways that you and members of your class read and write on the Web.

## Maintaining Appropriate Online Privacy

As we have suggested, the Internet goes on forever. Therefore, it is important that writers are careful about what personal information they bring into the cyber universe. What writers publish in their early teens may come back to haunt them as they pursue careers later in life. Even the youngest writers must remember that the persona they cultivate in their earliest online publications will continue to exist online for decades to come. One good strategy is to follow the Parent/Boss/Teacher Rule. Before posting something online, ask yourself, is this something I would want my parent/boss/teacher to see? If the answer is no, there's a good chance it might pose problems for you later.

That said, we also want to emphasize that sharing online is not a bad thing. Quite the contrary, the willingness of ordinary people to share information and perspectives online has made the Internet a powerful tool for democracy. Individuals feel less isolated when they can interact with interested readers. When you are willing to share your views and knowledge online—honestly, albeit carefully—you contribute to increased democratic interaction around the globe. This kind of sharing ranges from the most mundane Facebook posts to more sophisticated participation in blog sites devoted to political or social issues. Online chat rooms can blossom into fully-formed support groups that help people overcome adversities and promote justice.

**4.3**
Participate
responsibly in
online discourse
by understanding
intellectual
property
rights and by
constructing an
ethical persona.

## CONCEPT 4.3  Responsible participation in online discourse requires understanding intellectual property rights and constructing an ethical persona.

To understand concerns about "intellectual property," consider the case of a student-produced scientific poster that reports a student team's findings about gender stereotypes in Mickey Mouse versus SpongeBob Squarepants cartoons. In the upper corners of their original poster, the students included a downloaded image of a smiling SpongeBob Squarepants as well as an iconic image of Mickey Mouse.

Our reproduction of the poster in one of our textbooks omits these images because the copyright owners refused to grant us permission to use them. Probably these corporate copyright owners would grant a "fair use" exception to students who download the images for a one-time class project that wasn't later posted to the Web, but they would certainly not grant this exception to a textbook company.

We say "probably" in the preceding sentence about student use of copyrighted images because "fair use" exceptions to copyright laws are continually being tested in court and often remain uncertain and evolving. Intellectual property laws often seem undemocratic to digital natives who consider downloading and remixing of Web materials as artistic "sharing." Many Web authors in fact seem uninterested in intellectual property rights. They may not even take credit for their work, choosing to publish under a pseudonym or by first name only. A growing community of Web authors, committed to what has come to be called the "creative commons," embrace a view of originality as **remixing**—combining or editing existing materials to produce something new. According to filmmaker Kirby Ferguson, who advocates for the creative commons, "Everything is a remix" (see the epigraph to this chapter).

It's no wonder that for many students traditional rules about intellectual property or plagiarism seem opposed to their own personal experience in reading and writing online. They've grown up in a digital culture marked by video sharing sites such as Flickr and YouTube and by "blurred authorship" media that includes CNN iReports (where every citizen is a news reporter with a camera) and shows like *Ridiculousness* or *Tosh.O*, which cite their video sources by first name only if at all. This is a culture of sampling, remixing, and mashups, where it seems impossible to mark off someone's "intellectual property." Nevertheless, the issue of intellectual property and plagiarism is real as evidenced by disputes about plagiarism in print texts or disputes in the music industry, where the desire of individuals to download songs for free on the Web conflicts with the rights of artists to profit financially from their intellectual work.

## Understanding Issues of Copyright, Fair Use, and Creative Commons Licenses

Although it takes a lawyer to understand the intricacies of copyright law, ethical students need to be familiar with the issues surrounding intellectual property:

- *Copyright laws* The right to protection of one's intellectual property is guaranteed in the U.S. Constitution and, like patent law that protects inventions, is essential for providing financial reward to creative people for their work. Copyright laws cover nonfiction articles and books, fictional works including plays and poems, film scripts, paintings, drawings, photographs, videos, music, dance, sculpture, print or digital designs, computer programs, and any other kind of intellectual or creative work. Copyright laws are particularly enforced in commercial situations to prevent one person from using a second person's work for financial gain without the second person's knowledge and permission. Copyright laws tend to see "borrowing" as "stealing."

See also the discussion of plagiarism in Chapter 14, pp. 355–358.

- *Fair use* Fair use doctrine specifies occasions where someone can use another person's work without permission. Fair use, however, always requires citation and attribution—that is, the person must identify work done by others, credit that work, and cite the source from which the borrowed material was obtained. For multimodal projects produced for a class assignment, fair use doctrine usually allows students one-time use of copyrighted material, but it does not allow the student to "publish" the project on the Web.

- ***Creative commons*** The digital age has given rise to a highly democratic community of writers and artists who have formed what is called a "creative commons." (To learn more, type "creative commons" into your Web search engine.) These writers and artists wish to make their works freely available for downloading and remixing so long as the purposes are non-commercial and the borrowers properly acknowledge and cite their sources. A well known creative common site for images is Flickr, which allows you to use images for free without having to obtain written permission from the copyright holder. You must, however, cite the source according to the level of restrictions specified for each image on the Flickr site.

## Using Images and Sound Ethically in Your Multimodal Projects

The ethics of multimodal production involves three principles: Get permission from any persons whom you photograph or audio-record; compile a complete bibliography of all borrowed texts, images, and sounds that you use in your work; and follow all intellectual property laws as they apply to your particular situation, rhetorical context, and source.

**Obtaining Permission** The first two of these principles apply in all situations. Anytime you take your own photographs, shoot your own videos, or audio-record sounds or voices, you need permission from the people being photographed or audio-recorded. (If they are under 18 years of age, you must get a parent's permission.)

Bibliographic instructions for documenting sources are shown on pp. 359–366 (MLA) and 367–371 (APA).

**Compiling a Complete Bibliography** You must also be meticulous in citing the source of all material that you borrow from others—verbal text from other people's work (see discussion of plagiarism, pp. 355–358); images, videos, or music downloaded from the Web; photographs scanned into your own files; your own CD or vinyl music collections; and so forth.

When you submit a multimodal project, include a complete bibliography of all sources. In videos or photo galleries, you can include the bibliography in final credits or as a final slide.

**Following Intellectual Property Law** The third of these principles requires you to negotiate the distinction between copyright law, which requires permission from the copyright holder, and possible exceptions to copyright law allowed by "fair use" or the creative commons. If you produce a multimodal project for a course assignment and submit it as a one-time class project in print form (a brochure, a poster), on a jump drive or CD, or on a password protected course Web site, then your project may meet the criteria for fair use. If you publish your project on the Web, however, full national and international copyright law is apt to apply. You will need to consult your instructor for guidance.

## Creating an Ethical Online Persona

In addition to ethical use of sources, online ethics includes other considerations. As we all know, sometimes people say—or write—things they don't really mean. And sometimes the anonymity of the Web (if we compose under a pseudonym or an avatar) can bring out our dark sides, leading to mean-spirited flaming, to name-calling, or even to cyber-bullying. In many cases, it is not our dark sides that we later regret expressing, but simply our impolite or non-respectful selves. For example, we may create offensive stereotypes of political opponents—stereotypes that may play well on a Web site that attracts mostly like-minded people, but that may be deeply offensive to readers you weren't anticipating. Thus, given the instantaneous and global nature of the Web, writers can easily publish something online they might later regret. Because writing online is not usually restrained by editorial oversight, authors must become their own editors—not only for thought-intensive blog posts but for the most hastily composed tweet, status update, or e-mail.

In our view, it is not okay to write something offensive online and imagine that no one on the other side is affected by what you say. The democratic potential of the Web depends on promoting communication across differences rather than shutting people off into their own self-selected portion of the Web. You can be an agent for change simply by creating an online persona who listens to others respectfully and advances conversations with politeness and integrity. (For what we might call "problematic personae," see the cartoon in Figure 4.2.)

**FIGURE 4.2** Problematic Online Personae

We end this chapter by inviting you to think more fully about your own online persona. If you compose regularly on the Web, you will find it all too easy to move in and out of "multiple personalities." Writers may take on a different persona for each different writing situation—a persona for their Facebook presence, a different persona for writing product reviews, a still different persona for blogging or for posting comments on someone else's blog. However, we suggest that it is good for new Web writers to avoid "multiple personality disorder." Writers will be taken more seriously in the long run if they build toward an overall body of work characterized by a consistent, respectful, and sustainable persona.

## Chapter Summary

This chapter has introduced you to three rhetorical concepts useful for analyzing and producing multimodal and other online texts.

- *Concept 4.1 Composers of multimodal texts use words, images, and sounds rhetorically to move an audience.* Online communication is typically hyperlinked and multimodal so that it is difficult for authors to predict how viewers will navigate their work. Web communicators have to hook audiences quickly and then keep them engaged with high level content. Effective messages often combine verbal text with rhetorically effective images and sounds that make immediate appeals to *pathos, logos*, and *ethos*. Effective videos combine the rhetorical power of still images with the storytelling effect of moving images and sound.
- *Concept 4.2 Online environments are rhetorically interactive with shifting audiences, purposes, genres, and authorial roles.* Online communication frequently destabilizes all three points of the rhetorical triangle—audience, writer, and message. Audiences for online texts can shift rapidly because a reader can forward messages to new readers or post a message to a new site. The "writer" of on online text can be blurred through communally produced wiki texts or through the anonymity of pseudonyms and avatars. Online messages are ephemeral, frequently revised, and nuanced through the cumulative effect of posted reader responses. Also different genres and media (such as e-mail, blogs, Facebook, or Twitter) invite different purposes and authorial roles.
- *Concept 4.3 Responsible participation in online discourse requires understanding of intellectual property rights and the construction of an ethical online persona.* Because online environments celebrate sampling and remixing while blurring boundaries of intellectual property, responsible Web communicators must respect copyright laws, understand when fair use exceptions may be permissible, and appreciate the democratic value of creative commons sites. Additionally, multimodal texts must be accompanied by a complete bibliography of all borrowed texts, images, and sounds. Finally, responsible Web communicators should try to create a respectful, consistent online persona that promotes dialog across differences.

## Option 1: Description and Reflection on Your Online Communications

Consider recent examples of your own online communications (writing a blog, post-ing comments on a blog or news site, posting a product or book review, maintaining a Facebook page, collaborating on a Wiki, sending a tweet, or even sending e-mails). Consider also any responses you may have received from these communications.

- Part 1. Describe one or more of these communications. What was the occasion? What was your purpose or motivation? Who was your targeted audience? What was the content of the message (in summary form)? What effort went into the communication in terms of planning or drafting? What responses did you receive, if any?
- Part 2. Reflect on these online experiences based on the ideas and concepts in this chapter. How much did you think about audience and purpose as you composed your communication? What persona were you conscious of try-ing to convey? What kind of audience response did you anticipate or hope for? What kinds of insights into your experience have you gotten from this chapter? How might the concepts in this chapter influence your online com-munications from here on?

## Option 2: Description and Reflection on Your Creation of a Multimodal Composition

If you have ever created a multimodal text (involving any combination of verbal text, images, video, or sound), either for a class or for personal reasons, this brief assignment asks you to describe your creation and reflect on it.

- Part 1. Describe the multimodal text that you created—for example, a poster or brochure, a research report that incorporated graphs and images, a podcast, a video, a slideshow set to music, and so forth). Describe your multimodal creation. What was its core message? What was its rhetorical context—your purpose, and audience? What were you trying to accomplish with this multi-modal text?
- Part 2. Reflect on why you designed it the way you did and on the responses that you received. Particularly explain the challenges of creating this text and the effect you wanted this text to have on your audience. Think about the concepts in this chapter and explain which ones particularly relate to the challenges you faced and the degree of success you had with this text.

# WRITING PROJECTS

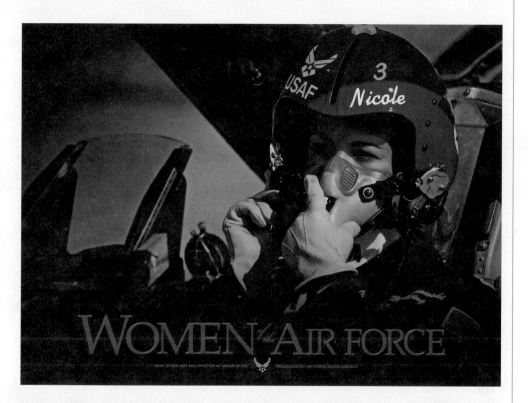

This U.S. Air Force poster represents a strong voice in the ongoing national discussion of women's role in the military. In 2013, the Pentagon lifted the ban on women in combat, recognizing their active role and high performance in modern irregular warfare. However, opponents continue to argue that women lack the fitness and stamina to keep up with men and that they compromise the standards and morale of fighting units. Examine the image of this woman carefully—how she looks and what she is doing. To what extent does this poster support gender equality, the argument that women can play key roles in combat operations? To what extent does it complicate our response to the issue of women's leadership roles in modern warfare?

# 5 | READING RHETORICALLY
## The Writer as Strong Reader

**WHAT YOU WILL LEARN**

**5.1** To carefully read a text, analyze its parts and their functions, and summarize its ideas.

**5.2** To write strong responses to texts by interacting with them, either by agreeing with, questioning, or actively challenging them.

Many new college students are surprised by the amount, range, and difficulty of reading they have to do in college. Every day they are challenged by reading assignments ranging from scholarly articles and textbooks on complex subject matter to primary sources such as Plato's dialogues or Darwin's *Voyage of the Beagle*.

To interact strongly with challenging texts, you must learn how to read them both with and against the grain. When you read *with the grain* of a text, you see the world through its author's perspective, open yourself to the author's argument, apply the text's insights to new contexts, and connect its ideas to your own experiences and personal knowledge. When you read *against the grain* of a text, you resist it by questioning its points, raising doubts, analyzing the limits of its perspective, or even refuting its argument.

We say that readers read *rhetorically* when they are aware of the effect a text is intended to have on them. Strong rhetorical readers analyze how a text works persuasively, and they think critically about whether to accede to or challenge the text's intentions. The two writing projects in this chapter, both of which demand rhetorical reading, introduce you to several of the most common genres of academic writing: the **summary**, and various kinds of **strong response essays**, which usually incorporate a summary of the text to which the writer is responding. This chapter will help you become a more powerful reader of academic texts, prepared to take part in the conversations of the disciplines you study.

## Engaging Rhetorical Reading

Imagine that you are investigating different strategies that individual Americans might take to protect the environment. In doing your research, you have encountered Michael Pollan's 2008 article, "Why Bother?" from the *New York Times Magazine*.

Pollan, a professor of journalism at the University of California Berkeley Graduate School of Journalism, is known for his popular books on reforming our food production system for the benefit of humans, animals, and the environment: *The Omnivore's Dilemma: A Natural History of Four Meals* (2007), *In Defense of Food: An Eater's Manifesto* (2009), and *Food Rules* (2010). Shortly we'll ask you to read Pollan's article, but before you do so, respond to the following opinion survey, using a 1 to 5 scale, with 1 meaning "strongly agree" and 5 meaning "strongly disagree."

| Item | Strongly agree | Agree | Neutral | Disagree | Strongly disagree |
|---|---|---|---|---|---|
| 1. Global warming is a very serious problem. | 1 | 2 | 3 | 4 | 5 |
| 2. Going green in my own lifestyle will have no effect on climate change—the magnitude of the problem is too great. | 1 | 2 | 3 | 4 | 5 |
| 3. The only way to make a real difference in climate change is through hugely expensive actions taken by governments and businesses. | 1 | 2 | 3 | 4 | 5 |
| 4. The best way to combat global warming is for individual Americans to go green in their own consumer choices. | 1 | 2 | 3 | 4 | 5 |
| 5. Environmentally conscious people should change the way they eat. | 1 | 2 | 3 | 4 | 5 |

Once you have finished rating your degree of agreement with these statements, please read Pollan's article on pages 114–119. (We'll refer to Pollan's article regularly throughout this chapter.) As you read, use whatever note-taking, underlining, or highlighting strategies you normally use when reading for a class. When you have finished reading, please explore how this article may have influenced your ideas about what we might do to combat global warming.

## ON YOUR OWN

1. In three or four sentences, summarize Michael Pollan's main points.
2. Freewrite a response to these questions: In what way has Pollan's article caused me to reconsider one or more of my answers to the survey above? From my perspective, what are the most insightful or provocative points in the article? If I were engaging Pollan in conversation, which of his views would I agree with? Where would I raise questions, doubts, or counterarguments?

## IN CONVERSATION

1. To help you become more aware of your thinking processes as you read, compare your note-taking strategies with those of your classmates. How many people wrote marginal notes, underlined, or highlighted passages? Did people highlight the same passages or different ones? Why did you write or mark what you did?

**2.** What passages did you and your classmates choose as important? How did this article influence people's thinking about the impact of individual actions and lifestyles on climate change? As a result of reading Pollan's article, are you more apt to try growing some of your own vegetables either now or in the future?

**5.1**

Carefully read a text, analyze its parts and their functions, and summarize its ideas.

# Understanding Rhetorical Reading

In this section, we explain why college-level reading is often difficult for new students and offer suggestions for improving your reading process based on the reading strategies of experts.

## What Makes College-Level Reading Difficult?

The difficulty of college-level reading stems in part from the complexity of new subject matter. Whatever the subject—from international monetary policies to the intricacies of photosynthesis—you have to wrestle with new and complex materials that might perplex anyone. But in addition to the daunting subject matter, several other factors contribute to the difficulty of college-level reading:

- **Vocabulary.** Many college-level readings contain unfamiliar technical language such as the economic terms *assets*, or *export subsidy* or the philosophic terms *hermeneutics* or *Neo-Platonism*. Even nontechnical readings and civic writing for the general public can contain unfamiliar terms. For example, in the Pollan article, the literary term *doppelgänger* or the ecological terms *feedback loops* or *pollution-trading systems* may have given you pause. In academia, words often carry specialized meanings that evoke a whole history of conversation and debate that may be inaccessible, even through a specialized dictionary. Good examples might be *postmodernism, string theory,* or *cultural materialism.* You will not fully understand these terms until you are initiated into the disciplinary conversations that gave rise to them.
- **Unfamiliar rhetorical context.** As we explained in Part 1, writers write to an audience for a purpose arising from some motivating occasion. Knowing an author's purpose, occasion, and audience may clarify confusing parts of a text. For example, Pollan's article was published in the *New York Times Magazine*, which attracts a liberal, well-educated audience. Pollan assumes that his audience already takes climate change seriously. In fact, they may be so overwhelmed with the problem that they are ready to give up. His purpose is to motivate them to action. A text's internal clues can sometimes help you fill in the rhetorical context, but often you may need to do outside research.
- **Unfamiliar genre.** You will encounter a range of genres such as textbooks, trade books, scholarly articles, scientific reports, historical documents, newspaper articles, op-ed pieces, and so forth. Each of these makes different demands on readers and requires a different reading strategy.
- **Lack of background knowledge.** Writers necessarily make assumptions about what their readers already know. For example, Pollan makes numerous references to popular culture (Al Gore's *An Inconvenient Truth*; "the Ed Begley Jr.

treatment"; "imported chops at Costco") or to general liberal arts knowledge (references to the economist Adam Smith or to the recent history of Communist Czechoslovakia and Poland). The more familiar you are with this cultural background, the more you will understand Pollan's argument on first reading.

---

**FOR WRITING AND DISCUSSION**

### Appreciating the Importance of Background Knowledge

The importance of background knowledge is easily demonstrated any time you dip into past issues of a newsmagazine or try to read articles about an unfamiliar culture. Consider the following passage from a 1986 *Newsweek* article. How much background knowledge do you need before you can fully comprehend this passage? What cultural knowledge about the United States would a student from Ethiopia or Indonesia need?

> Throughout the NATO countries last week, there were second thoughts about the prospect of a nuclear-free world. For 40 years nuclear weapons have been the backbone of the West's defense. For almost as long American presidents have ritually affirmed their desire to see the world rid of them. Then, suddenly, Ronald Reagan and Mikhail Gorbachev came close to actually doing it. Let's abolish all nuclear ballistic missiles in the next 10 years, Reagan said. Why not all nuclear weapons, countered Gorbachev. OK, the president responded, like a man agreeing to throw in the washer-dryer along with the house.
>
> What if the deal had gone through? On the one hand, Gorbachev would have returned to Moscow a hero. There is a belief in the United States that the Soviets need nuclear arms because nuclear weapons are what make them a superpower. But according to Marxist-Leninist doctrine, capitalism's nuclear capability (unforeseen by Marx and Lenin) is the only thing that can prevent the inevitable triumph of communism. Therefore, an end to nuclear arms would put the engine of history back on its track.
>
> On the other hand, Europeans fear, a nonnuclear United States would be tempted to retreat into neo-isolationism.
>
> —Robert B. Cullen*

Working in small groups or as a class, identify words and passages in this text that depend on background information or knowledge of culture for complete comprehension.

---

## Using the Reading Strategies of Experts

In Chapter 11, we describe the differences between the writing processes of experts and those of beginning college writers. There are parallel differences between the reading processes of experienced and inexperienced readers, especially when they encounter complex materials. In this strategies chart we describe some expert reading strategies for any kind of college-level material.

## Strategies for Reading Like an Expert

| Strategies | What to Do | Comments |
|---|---|---|
| Reconstruct the rhetorical context. | Ask questions about purpose, audience, genre, and motivating occasion. | If you read an article that has been anthologized (as in the readings in this textbook), note any information you are given about the author, publication, and genre. Try to reconstruct the author's original motivation for writing. |
| Take notes. | Make extensive marginal notes as you read. | Expert readers seldom use highlighters, which encourage passive, inefficient reading. |
| Get in the dictionary habit. | Look up words whose meaning you can't get from context. | If you don't want to interrupt your reading, check off words to look up when you are done. |
| Match your reading speed to your goals. | Speed up when skimming or scanning for information. Slow down for complete comprehension or detailed analysis. | Robert Sternberg, a cognitive psychologist, discovered that novice readers tend to read everything at about the same pace, no matter what their purpose. Experienced readers know when to slow down or speed up. |
| Read a complex text in a "multidraft" way. | Read a text two or three times. The first time, read quickly, skimming ahead rapidly, looking at the opening sentences of paragraphs and at any passages that sum up the writer's argument or clarify the argument's structure. Pay particular attention to the conclusion, which often ties the whole argument together. | Rapid "first-draft reading" helps you see the text's main points and structure, thus providing background for a second reading. Often, experienced readers reread a text two or three times. They hold confusing passages in mental suspension, hoping that later parts of the essay will clarify earlier parts. |

## Reading with the Grain and against the Grain

For an explanation of the believing and doubting game, see Chapter 2, Concept 2.1.

The reading and thinking strategies that we have just described enable skilled readers to interact strongly with texts. Your purpose in using these strategies is to read texts both *with the grain* and *against the grain*, a way of reading that is analogous to the believing and doubting game we introduced in Chapter 2. This concept is so important that we have chosen to highlight it separately here.

When you read with the grain of a text, you practice what psychologist Carl Rogers calls "empathic listening," in which you try to see the world through the author's eyes, role-playing as much as possible the author's intended readers by adopting their beliefs and values and acquiring their background knowledge. Reading with the grain is the main strategy you use when you summarize a text, but it comes into play also when you develop a strong response. When making with-the-grain points, you support the author's thesis with your own arguments and examples, or apply or extend the author's argument in new ways.

When you read against the grain of a text, you question and perhaps even rebut the author's ideas. You are a resistant reader who asks unanticipated questions, pushes back, and reads the text in ways unforeseen by the author. Reading against the grain is a key part of creating a strong response. When you make against-the-grain points, you challenge the author's reasoning, sources, examples, or choices of language. You present alternative lines of reasoning, deny the writer's values, or raise points or specific data that the writer has omitted. Strategies for thinking with the grain and against the grain are shown in the following chart, along with particular occasions when each is helpful.

| Strategies for Reading with and against the Grain | |
|---|---|
| **Reading with the Grain** | **Reading against the Grain** |
| • Listen to the text, follow the author's reasoning, and withhold judgment.<br>• Try to see the subject and the world from the author's perspective.<br>• Add further support to the author's thesis with your own points and examples.<br>• Apply the author's argument in new ways. | • Challenge, question, and resist the author's ideas.<br>• Point out what the author has left out or overlooked; note what the author has *not* said.<br>• Identify what assumptions, ideas, or facts seem unsupported or inaccurate.<br>• Rebut the author's ideas with counterreasoning and counterexamples. |
| **Occasions When Most Useful** | **Occasions When Most Useful** |
| • In writing summaries, you listen to a text without judgment to identify the main ideas.<br>• In writing analyses, you seek to understand a text to determine points to elaborate on and discuss.<br>• In synthesizing ideas from sources, you determine what ideas to adopt and build on.<br>• In writing arguments, you inhabit an author's viewpoint to deepen your understanding of an issue and to understand alternative views so you can represent them fairly. | • In writing an initial strong response, you determine the ways in which your beliefs, values, and views might be different from the author's.<br>• In writing analyses, you identify limitations in the author's view.<br>• In synthesizing, you determine which ideas to reject, replace, or go beyond.<br>• In writing arguments, you develop refutations and rebuttals to the author's views. |

Strong readers develop their ability to read in both ways—with the grain and against the grain. Some readers prefer to separate these approaches by first reading a text with the grain and then rereading it with more against-the-grain resistance. Throughout the rest of this chapter, we show you different ways to apply these strategies in your reading and writing.

## Understanding Summary Writing

A **summary** (often called an **abstract**) is a condensed version of a text that extracts and presents main ideas in a way that does justice to the author's intentions. As fairly and objectively as possible, a summary states the main ideas of a longer text, such as an article or even a book. Although the words "summary" and "abstract" are often used interchangeably, the term "abstract" is usually used for a stand-alone summary at the head of a published article. Scholars often present "abstracts" of their own work (that is, a summary of their argument) for publication in a conference program.

### Usefulness of Summaries

Students often report later in their academic careers how valuable summary writing skills are. Summary writing fosters a close engagement between you and the text and demonstrates your understanding of it. By forcing you to distinguish between main and subordinate points, summary writing is a valuable tool for improving your reading comprehension. Summary writing is also useful in other ways. For example, summaries at the beginning of articles, in prefaces to books, and on book jackets help readers determine if they want to read the article or book. To participate in conferences, your professors—and perhaps you also—send abstracts of proposed papers to conference committees in hopes of getting the paper accepted for presentation. Engineers and business executives place "executive summaries" at the beginning of proposals of major reports. In the "literature review" section of scientific papers, summaries of previous research are used to demonstrate gaps in knowledge that the present researchers will try to fill. Finally, writing summaries is a particularly important part of research writing, where you often present condensed views of other writers' arguments, either in support of your own view or as alternative views that you are analyzing or responding to.

### The Demands that Summary Writing Makes on Writers

Even though summaries are short, they are challenging to write. You must distinguish between the main and subordinate points in a text, and you must provide even coverage of the text. You must also convey clearly the main ideas—ideas that are often complex—in a limited number of words. Often, summaries are written to certain specifications, say, one-tenth of the original article, or 200 words, or 100 words.

One of the biggest challenges of summarizing is framing the summary so that readers can easily tell your own ideas from those of the author you are summarizing. Often, you are incorporating a summary into a piece of writing as a basis of your own analysis or argument, so this distinction is particularly important. You make this distinction by using frequent **attributive tags** (sometimes called "signal phrases") such as "Pollan claims," "according to Pollan," or "Pollan says"; by putting quotation marks around any passages that use the writer's original wording; and by citing the article using the appropriate documentation style. Typically, writers also introduce the summary with appropriate contextual information giving the author's name and perhaps also the title and genre (in research writing, this information is repeated in the "Works Cited" or "References" list). The first sentence of the summary typically presents the main idea or thesis of the entire article. Here is an example summary of the Pollan article using MLA citation and documentation style.

Chapter 14 provides additional instruction in summarizing, paraphrasing, and quoting sources. It also explains how to incorporate sources smoothly into your own writing and avoid plagiarism.

---

Summary of "Why Bother?"

In "Why Bother?" published in the *New York Times Magazine*, environmental journalist Michael Pollan asks why, given the magnitude of the climate change problem, any individual should bother to go green, and argues that an individual's actions can bring multiple rewards for individuals, society, and the environment. Explaining that "the warming and the melting" (115) are occurring much faster than earlier models had predicted, Pollan acknowledges the apparent powerlessness of individuals to make a difference. Not only are we uncertain what actions to take to preserve the planet, but we realize that whatever we do will be offset by growing carbon emissions from emerging nations. Our actions will be "too little too late" (115). He asserts that our environmental problem is a "crisis of lifestyle"—"the sum total of countless little everyday choices" (116) made possible by cheap fossil fuel, which has led to our increasingly specialized jobs. Nevertheless, to counteract our practical and moral distance from the environment caused by this specialization, Pollan urges individuals to go green. Although he concedes that "'laws and money'" (116) are necessary, he still believes that individual actions may be influential by setting off a "process of viral social change" (118). A particularly powerful act, he claims, is to convert yards into vegetable gardens. Growing your own vegetables, he argues, will help us overcome "specialization," eat locally, reduce carbon emissions, get healthy exercise, reconnect with neighbors, and restore our relationship with the earth. (227 words)

*Identification of the article, journal, and author*

*Gives overview summary of whole article*

*Attributive tag*

*Short quotations from article, MLA documentation style; number in parentheses indicates page number of original article where quotation is found*

Work Cited

Pollan, Michael. "Why Bother?" *New York Times Magazine* 20 Apr.

2008: 19+. Rpt. in *The Allyn and Bacon Guide to Writing.* John

D. Ramage, John C. Bean, and June Johnson. 7th ed. New York:

Pearson, 2015, 114–19. Print.

Note in this example how the use of attributive tags, quotation marks, and citations makes it easy to tell that the writer is summarizing Pollan's ideas rather than presenting his own. Note too the writer's attempt to remain neutral and objective and not to impose his own views. To avoid interjecting your own opinions, you need to choose your verbs in attributive tags carefully. Consider the difference between "Smith argues" and "Smith rants" or between "Brown asserts" and "Brown leaps to the conclusion that...." In each pair, the second verb, by moving beyond neutrality, reveals the writer's judgment of the author's ideas.

In an academic setting, then, think of summaries as short, tightly written pieces that retain an author's main ideas while eliminating the supporting details. In the writing projects for this chapter, we'll explain the strategies you can use to write a good summary. The following chart lists the criteria for incorporating a summary effectively into your own prose.

### CRITERIA FOR AN EFFECTIVE SUMMARY INCORPORATED INTO YOUR OWN PROSE

- Represents the original article accurately and fairly.
- Is direct and concise, using words economically.
- Remains objective and neutral, not revealing the writer's own ideas on the subject, but, rather, only the original author's points.
- Gives the original article balanced and proportional coverage.
- Uses the writer's own words to express the original author's ideas.
- Distinguishes the summary writer's ideas from the original author's ideas by using attributive tags (such as "according to Pollan" or "Pollan argues that").
- Uses quotations sparingly, if at all, to present the original author's key terms or to convey the flavor of the original.
- Is a unified, coherent piece of writing in its own right.
- Cites and documents the text the writer is summarizing and any quotations used according to an appropriate documentation system.

**FOR WRITING AND DISCUSSION**

## Determining What Is a Good Summary

This exercise asks you to work with the "Criteria for an Effective Summary Incorporated into Your Own Prose" (above) as you analyze the strengths and weaknesses of three summaries of the same article: "Protect Workers' Rights" by Bruce Raynor, published in the *Washington Post* on September 1, 2003. Imagine three student writers assigned to summarize this editorial in approximately 200 words. The first of the summaries below we have rated as excellent. Read the excellent summary first and then determine how successful the other summaries are.

### SUMMARY 1 (AN EXCELLENT SUMMARY OF THE RAYNOR ARTICLE)

In Bruce Raynor's op-ed article "Protect Workers' Rights," originally published in the *Washington Post* on September 1, 2003, union official Raynor argues that workers everywhere are threatened by the current rules of globalization that allow corporations and governments to seek out the cheapest and least regulated labor around the world. Using the example of the Pillowtex Corporation that recently shut down its plant in Kannapolis, North Carolina, he shows how ending manufacturing that has played a long and major role in the economies of towns leaves workers without severance pay, medical insurance, money to pay taxes and mortgages, and other options for employment. According to Raynor, in the last three years, millions of jobs have been lost in all branches of American manufacturing. While policymakers advise these workers to seek education to retool for white-collar jobs, Raynor points out that fields such as telemarketing and the computer industry are also losing millions of jobs. Furthermore, outsourcing has caused a drop in wages in the United States. The same dynamic of jobs moving to countries with cheaper and less stringent safety and health regulation has recently caused Mexican and Bangladeshi workers to lose their jobs to Chinese workers. Raynor concludes with a call to protect the rights of workers everywhere by rewriting the "rules for the global economy" (A25). (214 words)

Work Cited

Raynor, Bruce. "Protect Workers' Rights." *Washington Post* 1 Sept. 2003: A25. Print.

### SUMMARY 2

The closing of the Pillowtex Corporation's factories in the United States represents a loss of sixteen textile plants and about 6,500 jobs, according to Bruce Raynor, president of UNITE, a union of textile workers.

The workers left in Kannapolis, North Carolina, former home of one of the largest Pillowtex plants, are experiencing financial problems as they are unable to buy medical insurance, pay their taxes or mortgages or find other jobs.

Raynor argues that the case of the Pillowtex workers is representative of workers in other industries such as metals, papers, and electronics and that "this is the longest decline since the Great Depression" with about three million jobs gone in the last three years.

He then explains that white-collar jobs are not safe either because millions of jobs in telemarketing, claims adjusting, and even government are predicted to go overseas in the next five years. Furthermore, Raynor states that the possibility of outsourcing jobs leads to lowering of wages within the United States, as "outsourcing has forced down hourly wage rates by 10 percent to 40 percent for many U.S. computer consultants" (A25).

However, according to Raynor, the developing countries like Mexico and Bangladesh that have acquired manufacturing jobs are also threatened by countries like China who can offer employees who are willing to work for even lower wages and under worse conditions.

*(continued)*

Raynor concludes that "a prosperous economy requires that workers be able to buy the products that they produce" (A25) and that workers everywhere need to be protected. (251 words)

Work Cited

Raynor, Bruce. "Protect Workers' Rights." *Washington Post* 1 Sept. 2003: A25. Print.

### SUMMARY 3

In his article "Protect Workers' Rights," Bruce Raynor, president of UNITE, a textile workers' union, criticizes free trade and globalization for taking away workers' jobs. Using the Pillowtex Corporation's closing of its plant in Kannapolis, North Carolina, as his prime example, Raynor claims that outsourcing has destroyed the economy of this town and harmed workers across the United States. Raynor threatens that millions of white-collar jobs are also being lost and going to be lost in the next five years. Raynor complains that the whole national and global economy is falling apart and is going to get worse. He implies that the only solution is to keep jobs here in the United States. He maintains that workers around the world are also suffering when factories are moved from one developing country to another that has even more favorable conditions for the corporations. Raynor naively fails to factor in the role of consumers and the pressures on corporations into his defense of workers' rights. Clearly, Raynor loves unions and hates corporations; he probably fears that he is going to lose his own job soon. (183 words)

## Understanding Strong Response Writing

We have said that the summary or abstract is an important academic genre and that summary writing is an essential academic skill. Equally important is strong response writing in which you identify and probe points in a text, sometimes by examining how a piece is written and often by inserting your own ideas into the text's conversation. "Strong response" is an umbrella term that incorporates a wide variety of ways that you can speak back to a text. In all cases, you are called on to do your own critical thinking by generating and asserting your own responses to the text.

In this section we will explain four different genres of strong response writing:

- Rhetorical critique
- Ideas critique
- Reflection
- Blended version of all three of these

### Strong Response as Rhetorical Critique

A strong response as **rhetorical critique** analyzes a text's rhetorical strategies and evaluates how effectively the author achieves his or her intended goals. When writing a rhetorical critique, you discuss how a text is constructed, what rhetorical strategies it employs, and how effectively it appeals to *logos*, *ethos*, and *pathos*. In other words, you closely analyze the text itself, giving it the same close attention that an art critic gives a painting, a football coach gives a game video, or a biologist gives a cell formation. The close attention can be with the grain, noting the effectiveness of the text's rhetorical strategies, or against the grain, discussing what is ineffective or problematic about these strategies. Or an analysis might point out both the strengths and weaknesses of the text's rhetorical strategies.

For example, suppose that you are writing a rhetorical critique of an article from a conservative business journal advocating oil exploration in the Arctic National Wildlife Refuge (ANWR). You might analyze the article's rhetorical strategies by asking questions like these:

- How is the argument shaped to appeal to a conservative, business-oriented audience?
- How has the writer's angle of vision influenced the selection of evidence for his or her argument?
- How does the writer make himself or herself seem credible to this audience?

You would also evaluate the *logos* of the argument:

- How sound is the logic of the argument?
- Is the evidence accurate and current?
- What are the underlying assumptions and beliefs on which the argument is based?

Rhetorical critiques are usually closed-form, thesis-driven essays. The essay has a thesis that captures the writer's overall assessment of the text and maps out the specific points that the writer will develop in the analysis. When you are writing a rhetorical critique, your goal is to find a few rhetorical points that you find particularly intriguing, important, or disturbing to discuss and probe. Typically, your analysis zeroes in on some key features that you, the writer, find noteworthy. In the following strategies chart, we suggest the kinds of questions you can ask about a text to construct a rhetorical critique.

## Question-Asking Strategies for Writing a Rhetorical Critique

| Ask Questions about Any of the Following: | Examples |
| --- | --- |
| Audience and purpose: <br> • Who is the intended audience? <br> • What is the writer's purpose? <br> • How well does the text suit its particular audience and purpose? | Examine how Michael Pollan writes to the well-educated audience of the *New York Times Magazine*, who are aware of climate change debates and most likely concerned about the problems ahead. Consider how Pollan writes to move these readers beyond good intentions to action. Examine how the text's structure, language, and evidence support this purpose. |

*(continued)*

| Ask Questions about Any of the Following: | Examples |
| --- | --- |
| **Influence of genre on the shape of the text:**<br>• How has the genre affected the author's style, structure, and use of evidence? | Examine how the genre of the feature editorial for a highbrow magazine accounts for the length, structure, and depth of Pollan's argument. Examine how his references to political and intellectual figures (Al Gore, then Vice President Cheney, Adam Smith, Wendell Berry, and so forth) carry weight in this magazine's investigation of contemporary issues. |
| **Author's style:**<br>• How do the author's language choices and sentence length and complexity contribute to the impact of the text? | Examine how Pollan's casual and cordial connections with readers (use of "I," "you," and "we"), his urgency, and his use of questions contribute to the article's effect. |
| **Appeal to _logos_, the logic of the argument:**<br>• How well has the author created a reasonable, logically structured argument? | Examine how well Pollan uses logical points to support his claim and make his claim persuasive. |
| **Use of evidence:**<br>• How reputable, relevant, current, sufficient, and representative is the evidence? | Examine how Pollan uses references to scientific articles, newspaper accounts, and his own experiences to develop his points. |
| **Appeal to _ethos_ and the credibility of the author:**<br>• How well does the author persuade readers that he/she is knowledgeable, reliable, credible, and trustworthy? | Examine how Pollan conveys his knowledge of environmentalism, economics, and social trends. Examine the effects of genre and style in creating this _ethos_. Examine whether this _ethos_ is effective for readers who are not familiar with Pollan's other writing, are skeptical of climate change, or are less in tune with environmental activism. |
| **Appeal to _pathos_:**<br>• How well does the writer appeal to readers' emotions, sympathies, and values? | Examine how Pollan seeks to tap his audience's values and feelings. Consider how he conveys his familiarity with the everyday choices and decisions facing his readers. |
| **Author's angle of vision:**<br>• How much does the author's angle of vision or interpretive filter dominate the text, influencing what is emphasized or omitted? | Examine how Pollan's angle of vision shapes his perspective on climate change, his choice of activist solutions, and his development of solutions. Consider how Pollan's reputation as the author of a number of books on food system reform influences his focus in this argument. |

For a rhetorical critique, you would probably not choose all of these questions but would instead select three or four to highlight. Your goal is to make insightful observations about how a text works rhetorically and to support your points with examples and short quotations from the text.

## Strong Response as Ideas Critique

A second kind of strong response, the **ideas critique**, focuses on the ideas at stake in the text. Rather than treat the text as an artifact to analyze rhetorically (as in a rhetorical critique), you treat it as a voice in a conversation—one perspective on an issue or one solution to a problem or question. Your strong response examines how the ideas of the original author mesh or conflict with your own. Based on your own critical thinking, personal experiences, and research, to what extent do you agree or disagree with the writer's thesis? A with-the-grain reading of a text would support all or some of the text's ideas, while also supplying additional evidence or extending the argument, perhaps applying it in a new context. An against-the-grain reading would challenge the writer's ideas, point out flaws and holes in the writer's thinking, and provide counterexamples and rebuttals. You might agree with some ideas and disagree with others in the text. In any case, in an ideas critique you speak back to the text from your own experience, background, reading, and thoughtful wrestling with the writer's ideas.

As an example, let's return to the article from the conservative business journal on drilling for oil in the ANWR. For an ideas critique, you would give your own views on oil exploration in the ANWR to support or challenge the writer's views, to raise new questions, and otherwise to add your voice to the ANWR conversation.

- You might supply additional reasons and evidence for drilling.
- You might oppose drilling in the ANWR by providing counterreasoning and counterexamples.
- You might propose some kind of synthesis or middle ground, where you would allow drilling in the ANWR but only under certain conditions.

When you write an ideas critique you are thus joining an important conversation about the actual subject matter of a text. Because much academic and professional writing focuses on finding the best solution to complex problems, this kind of strong response is very common. Usually this genre requires closed-form, thesis-governed prose. The following strategies chart suggests questions you can ask about a text to enter into its conversation of ideas.

## Question-Asking Strategies for Writing an Ideas Critique

| Questions to Ask | Examples |
|---|---|
| Where do I agree with this author? (with the grain) | Consider how you might amplify or extend Pollan's ideas. Build on his ideas by discussing examples where you or acquaintances have tried to change your lifestyle to lower carbon emissions. Show how these changes might have inspired others to do so. |

*(continued)*

| Questions to Ask | Examples |
|---|---|
| What new insights has this text given me? (with the grain) | Explore Pollan's ideas that the environmental crisis is at heart a "crisis of lifestyle" or that specialization leads to a disjuncture between our everyday acts and their environmental consequences. Explore Pollan's argument that individual actions may lead to a social revolution. Think of how your eating habits or relationship to gardens has or could contribute to reform. |
| Where do I disagree with this author? (against the grain) | Challenge Pollan's assumptions about the magnitude of the problem. Challenge Pollan's idea that individuals can make a difference. Challenge his assumptions that technological solutions won't work because we still will face a crisis of lifestyle. Challenge the practicality and value of his main solution—growing gardens. |
| What points has the author overlooked or omitted? (against the grain) | Recognize that Pollan overlooks the constraints that would keep people from gardening. Consider that Pollan chooses not to focus on problems of overpopulation, water shortage, or economic disruption caused by environmentalism. |
| What new questions or problems has the text raised? (with or against the grain) | Explain how Pollan minimizes the economic impact of environmental action and downplays the role of government and business. Consider how we might need to "change the system" rather than just change ourselves. Consider his apparent lack of interest in technological solutions to the energy crisis. |
| What are the limitations or consequences of this text? (with or against the grain) | Consider ways that Pollan excludes some of his readers even while reaching out to others. Consider how Pollan, given his books on food and his passion for replacing industrial food production with local food, has written a predictable argument. Consider what new ideas he brings to his readers. |

Because critiques of ideas appear in many contexts where writers search for the best solutions to problems, this kind of thinking is essential for academic research. In writing research papers, writers typically follow the template "This other writer has argued A, but I am going to argue B." Often the writer's own view (labeled "B") results from the writer's having wrestled with the views of others. Because this kind of dialectic thinking is so important to academic and professional life, we treat it further in Chapter 6 on exploratory writing, in Chapter 8 on analysis and synthesis, and in Chapter 9 on classical argument. Each of these chapters encourages you to articulate alternative views and respond to them.

## Strong Response as Reflection

A third kind of strong response is often called a "reflection" or a "reflection paper." (An instructor might say, for example, "Read Michael Pollan's article on climate change and write a reflection about it.") Generally, a **reflection** is an introspective genre; it invites you to connect the reading to your own personal experiences, beliefs, and values. In a reflection paper, the instructor is particularly interested in how the reading has affected you personally—what memories it has triggered, what personal experiences it relates to, what values and beliefs it has challenged, what dilemmas it poses, and so forth. A **reflection paper** is often more exploratory, open-ended, musing, and tentative than a rhetorical critique or an ideas critique, which is usually closed form and thesis governed.

To illustrate, let's consider how you might write a reflection in response to the article in the conservative business journal on drilling for oil in the ANWR. One approach might be to build a reflection around a personal conflict in values by exploring how the reading creates a personal dilemma:

- You might write about your own wilderness experiences, musing about the importance of nature in your own life.
- But at the same time, you might reflect on the extent to which your own life depends on cheap oil and acknowledge your own reluctance to give up owning a car.

In short, you want pristine nature and the benefits of cheap oil at the same time. Another quite different approach might be to reflect on how this article connects to discussions you are having in your other courses, say, the economic cost of individuals' and companies' going green. Here are some strategies you can use to generate ideas for a reflective strong response:

| Question-Asking Strategies for Writing a Reflective Strong Response | |
| --- | --- |
| **Questions to Ask** | **Examples** |
| What personal memories or experiences does this text trigger? | Explore how Pollan's article evokes memories of your own frustrations about or successes with "green" living. Have you ever tried to change your habits for environmental reasons? If so, how did you go about doing it? Would your changes have met Berry's and Pollan's criteria for a change of "lifestyle"? |
| What personal values or beliefs does this text reinforce or challenge? | Explore the extent to which you can or can't identify with Pollan, Al Gore, and others who are proclaiming the seriousness of climate change and advocating changes in lifestyle. To what extent does Pollan as a person of conviction spark your admiration? |
| What questions, dilemmas, or problems does this text raise for me? | Explore how Pollan has challenged readers to take actions that may be difficult for them. For instance, you may have arrived at other solutions or know groups or organizations that are contributing positively in other ways. Perhaps Pollan's level of commitment or his particular approach to living green disturbs you in some way. |

*(continued)*

| Questions to Ask | Examples |
|---|---|
| What new insights, ideas, or thoughts of my own have been stimulated by this text? | Explore any moments of enlightenment you had while reading Pollan. For example, perhaps his focus on individual action rather than on "laws and money" seems problematic to you. Perhaps there are other causes besides the environment that spur you to concern or to action. Perhaps you are now interested in exploring what inspires people to make major changes in how they live. |

As you can tell from these questions, a reflective strong response highlights your own personal experiences and beliefs in conversation with the text. Whereas the focus of a rhetorical critique is on analyzing the way the text works rhetorically and the focus of an ideas critique is on taking a stance on the ideas at stake in the text, a reflective response focuses on the personal dimension of reading the text. Reflections call for a degree of self-disclosure or self-exploration that would be largely absent from the other kinds of strong responses.

## Strong Response as a Blend

It should be evident that the boundaries among the rhetorical critique, ideas critique, and reflection overlap and that a strong response could easily blend features of each. In trying to decide how to respond strongly to a text, you often don't have to confine yourself to a pure genre but can mix and match different kinds of responses. You can analyze and critique a text's rhetorical strategies, show how the text challenges your own personal values and beliefs, and also develop your own stance on the text's ideas. In writing a blended response, you can emphasize what is most important to you, while not limiting yourself to only one approach.

Before we turn to the writing project for this chapter, we show you an example of a student's summary/strong response that is a blend of rhetorical critique, ideas critique, and personal reflection. Note that the essay begins by conveying the writer's investment in environmental conservation. It then summarizes Pollan's article. Following the summary, the student writer states his thesis, followed by his strong response, which contains both rhetorical points and points engaging Pollan's ideas.

### Kyle Madsen (student)

## Can a Green Thumb Save the Planet?

### A Response to Michael Pollan

When I was a child, our household had one garbage can, in which my family and I would deposit all of our cardboard, plastic, glass, and paper waste. No one on my block had ever heard of recycling or using energy saving bulbs, and we never considered turning down our thermostats during the frozen winters and ice storms that swept our region from November to March. It wasn't that we didn't care about what we were doing to our environment. We just didn't know any better. However, once I got to college all that changed. My university's policies requested that students separate glass bottles and pizza boxes from plastic candy wrappers and old food containers. Thanks in large part to the chilling success of Al Gore's documentary *An Inconvenient Truth,* many of my old neighbors were starting to catch on as well, and now my home town is as devoted to its recycling as any major metropolitan area. Still, even though we as a country have come a long way in just a few years, there is a long way to go. Environmental journalist Michael Pollan in his article "Why Bother?" for the *New York Times Magazine* examines why working to slow the threat of climate change is such a daunting task.

In "Why Bother?" Michael Pollan explores how we have arrived at our current climate change crisis and argues why and how we should try to change our individual actions. Pollan sums up the recent scientific evidence for rapid climate change and then focuses on people's feeling overwhelmed in the face of this vast environmental problem. He presents his interpretation of how we have contributed to the problem and why we feel powerless. Pollan asserts that the climate-change crisis is "the sum total of countless everyday choices" made by consumers globally and that it is "at its very bottom a crisis of lifestyle—of character, even" (116). Our reliance on "cheap fossil fuel" has contributed to both the problem and to our sense of helplessness. In the final part of his article, Pollan concedes that "laws and money" (90) are necessary to create change, but he still advocates acting on our values and setting an example, which might launch a green social revolution. According to Pollan, "The idea is to find one thing to do in your life that does not involve spending or voting...that will offer its own rewards" (93). He concludes by encouraging readers to plant gardens in order to reduce carbon emissions, to lessen our "sense of dependence and dividedness" (93)— to empower ourselves to contribute positively to our environment.

Although Pollan has created an argument with strong logical, ethical, and emotional appeals, his very dominant angle of vision—seen in his assumptions, alarmist language, and exclusive focus on garden-growing—may fail to win neutral readers. I also think Pollan's argument loses impact by not discussing more realistic alternatives such as pursuing smart consumerism and better environmental education for children.

Pollan builds a forceful case in his well-argued and knowledgeable interpretation of our climate-change problem as a "crisis of lifestyle—of character, even" (116). His frank confrontation of the problem of how to motivate people is compelling, especially when he admits the contrast between "the magnitude of the problem" and the "puniness" of individual action (114). Pollan both deepens his argument and constructs a positive *ethos* by drawing on the ideas of environmental ethicist Wendell Berry and classical economist Adam Smith to explain how modern civilization has developed through the division of labor (specialization), which has brought us many advantages but also cut us off from community and environmental responsibility. In this part of his argument, Pollan helps readers understand how our dependence on cheap oil and our lifestyle choices have enhanced our roles as limited, specialized producers and ma-

*(continued)*

---

*Side annotations:*

*Introduces topic/problem and shows writer's investment in caring for the environment*

*Identifies Pollan's article and Pollan's purpose*

*Summary of Pollan's article*

*Presentation of thesis statement focused first on rhetorical points and second on ideas critique*

*With-the-grain rhetorical point focused on the logos and ethos of Pollan's argument* jor consumers. Pollan's development of his theory of the "cheap-energy mind" (117) and his reasonable support of this idea are the strongest part of his argument and the most relevant to readers like me. I have thought that we have become small cogs in an overbearing machine of consumption and only larger cogs such as the government can have enough influence on the overall system to make change happen. From time to time, I have wondered what I as one person could really do. This sense of insignificance, which Pollan theorizes, has made me wait until my regular light bulbs burned out before considering replacing them with energy-efficient ones.

Another strength of Pollan's argument is the way he builds bridges to his audience through his appeals to *pathos*. He understands how overwhelmed the average person can feel when confronted with the climate-change problem. Pollan never criticizes his readers for not being as concerned as he is. Instead he engages them in learning with him. He explores with readers the suggestion of walking to work, a task on par with light bulb changing, when he writes, even if "I decide that I am going to bother, there arises the whole vexed question of getting it right. Is eating local or walking to work really going to reduce my carbon footprint?" (114–15). By asking questions like these, he speaks as a concerned citizen who tries to create a dialogue with his audience about the problem of climate change and what individuals can do.

However, despite his outreach to readers, Pollan's angle of vision may be too dominant and intense for some readers. He assumes that his *New York Times Magazine* readers already share his agreement with the most serious views of climate change held by many scientists and environmentalists, people who are focusing on the "truly terrifying feedback loops" (115) in weather and climate. He also assumes that his readers hold similar values about local food and gardening. This intense angle of vision may leave out some readers. For example, I am left wondering why gardening is more effective than, say, converting to solar power. He also tries to shock his readers into action with his occasional alarmist or overly dramatic use of language. For example, he tries to invoke fear: "Have you looked into the eyes of a climate scientist recently? They look really scared" (115). However, how many regular people have run-ins with climate scientists?

In addition, after appearing very in tune with readers in the first part of his argument, in the final part he does not address his readers' practical concerns. He describes in great detail the joys of gardening—specifically how it will connect readers not only to the earth, but to friends and neighbors as well—yet he glosses over the amount of work necessary to grow a garden. He writes, "Photosynthesis still works so abundantly that in a thoughtfully organized vegetable garden (one planted from seed, nourished by compost from the kitchen and involving not too many drives to the gardening center), you can grow the proverbial free lunch" (118). However, not everyone has a space for a garden or access to a public one to grow tomatoes themselves, and it takes hours of backbreaking labor to grow a productive vegetable garden—hardly a free lunch. Average Americans work upwards of sixty hours per week, so it is unrealistic to expect them to spend their free time working in a garden. In not addressing readers' objections to gardening or suggesting other ways to mend our cheap oil values, I think Pollan proposes simply another situation for semi-concerned individuals to again say, "Why bother?"

Also, besides gardens, I think Pollan could emphasize other avenues of change such as sustainable consumerism. In different places in the article, he mentions that individuals can use their consumer lifestyles to achieve a more sustainable way of life, but he chooses to insist that gardening be the main means. I would have liked him to discuss how we as consumers could buy more fuel-efficient cars, avoid plastic packaging, drink tap water, and buy products from green industries. This "going green" trend has already taken root in many of America's top industries—at least in their advertising and public relations campaigns. We can't leave a Starbucks without inadvertently learning about what they are doing to offset global warming. But we consumers need to know which industries really are going green in a significant way so that we can spend our shopping dollars there. If Pollan is correct, environmentally conscientious consumers can demand a change from the corporations they rely on, so why not use the same consumerism that got us into this mess to get us out?

*Another point critiquing Pollan's ideas. Madsen proposes sustainable consumerism as an alternative to gardening.*

Besides sustainable consumerism, I think we should emphasize the promotion of better environmental education for our children. Curriculum in K–12 classrooms presented by teachers rather than information from television or newspapers will shape children's commitment to the environment. A good example is the impact of Recycle Now, an organization aimed at implementing recycling and global awareness in schools. According to Dave Lawrie, a curriculum expert featured on their Web site, "Recycling at school is a hands-on way to show pupils that every single person can help to improve the environment. Everyone in our school has played a part in making a difference." With serious education, kids will learn the habits of respecting the earth, working in gardens, and using energy-saving halogen bulbs, making sustainability and environmental stewardship a way of life.

*Another point addressing Pollan's ideas— environmental education in the schools as an alternative to gardening.*

While Pollan is correct in pushing us into action now, asking Americans to grow a garden, when changing a light bulb seems daunting, is an unrealistic and limited approach. However, Pollan persuasively addresses the underlying issues in our attitudes toward the climate crisis and works to empower readers to become responsible and involved. Whether it be through gardening, supporting green businesses, or education, I agree with Pollan that the important thing is that you learn to bother for yourself.

*Short conclusion bringing closure to the essay.*

### Works Cited

Lawrie, Dave. "Bringing the Curriculum to Life." School Success Stories. *RecycleNow* 11 Nov. 2009. Web. 28 Feb. 2010.

Pollan, Michael. "Why Bother?" *New York Times Magazine* 20 Apr. 2008: 19+. Rpt. in *The Allyn and Bacon Guide to Writing*. John D. Ramage, John C. Bean, and June Johnson. 7th ed. New York: Pearson, 2015. 114–19. Print.

*Citation of works cited in the essay using MLA format*

In the student example just shown, Kyle Madsen illustrates a blended strong response that includes both a rhetorical critique of the article and some of his own views. He analyzes Pollan's article rhetorically by pointing out both the persuasive features of the argument and the limiting angle of vision of a worried environmentalist and extremely committed gardening enthusiast. He seconds some of Pollan's points with his own examples, but he also reads Pollan against the grain by suggesting how Pollan's word choice and fixation on gardening as a solution prevent him from developing ideas that might seem more compelling to some readers.

**WRITING**

**PROJECT**

**5.2**
Write strong
responses
to texts by
interacting with
them, either by
agreeing with,
questioning,
or actively
challenging
them.

## A Summary

Write a summary of an article assigned by your instructor for an audience who has not read the article. Write the summary using attributive tags and providing an introductory context as if you were inserting it into your own longer paper (see the model on p. 89). The word count for your summary will be specified by your instructor. Try to follow all the criteria for a successful summary listed on page 90, and use MLA documentation style, including a Works Cited entry for the article that you are summarizing. (Note: Instead of an article, your instructor may ask you to summarize a longer text such as a book or a visual-verbal text such as a Web page or an advocacy brochure. We address these special cases at the end of this section.)

## Generating Ideas: Reading for Structure and Content

Once you have been assigned an article to summarize, your first task is to read it carefully a number of times to get an accurate understanding of it. Remember that summarizing involves the essential act of reading with the grain as you figure out exactly what the article is saying. In writing a summary, you must focus on both a text's structure and its content. In the following steps, we recommend a process that will help you condense a text's ideas into an accurate summary. As you become a more experienced reader and writer, you'll follow these steps without thinking about them.

***Step 1: The first time through, read the text fairly quickly for general meaning.*** If you get confused, keep going; later parts of the text might clarify earlier parts.

***Step 2: Read the text carefully paragraph by paragraph.*** As you read, write gist statements in the margins for each paragraph. A *gist statement* is a brief indication of a paragraph's function in the text or a brief summary of a paragraph's content. Sometimes it is helpful to think of these two kinds of gist statements as "what it does" statements and "what it says" statements.* A "what it does" statement specifies the paragraph's function—for example, "summarizes an opposing view," "introduces another reason," "presents a supporting example," "provides

---

*For our treatment of "what it does" and "what it says" statements, we are indebted to Kenneth A. Bruffee, *A Short Course in Writing*, 2nd ed. (Cambridge, MA: Winthrop, 1980).

statistical data in support of a point," and so on. A "what it says" statement captures the main idea of a paragraph by summarizing the paragraph's content. The "what it says" statement is the paragraph's main point, in contrast to its supporting ideas and examples.

When you first practice detailed readings of a text, you might find it helpful to write complete *does* and *says* statements on a separate sheet of paper rather than in the margins until you develop the internal habit of appreciating both the function and content of parts of an essay. Here are *does* and *says* statements for selected paragraphs of Michael Pollan's article on climate change activism.

**Paragraph 1:** ***Does:*** Introduces the need for environmental action as a current problem that readers know and care about and sets up the argument. ***Says:*** We as individuals often wonder if our small, minor actions are worth doing in light of the magnitude of the climate change problem.

**Paragraph 2:** ***Does:*** Explores another reason why individuals may doubt whether individual actions could make a difference. ***Says:*** People willing to change their lifestyles to combat climate change may be discouraged by the increase in a carbon-emissions lifestyle in other parts of the world such as China.

**Paragraph 8:** ***Does:*** Expresses an alternative view, partially concedes to it, and asserts a counterview. ***Says:*** Although big money and legislation will be important in reversing climate change, the problem at its heart is a "crisis of lifestyle—of character" (116), and therefore will require the effort of individuals.

**Paragraph 18:** ***Does:*** Presents and develops one of Pollan's main reasons that concerned individuals should take personal action to fight climate change. ***Says:*** Setting an example through our own good environmental choices could exert moral influence here and abroad, on individuals and big business.

Writing a *says* statement for a paragraph is sometimes difficult. You might have trouble, for example, deciding what the main idea of a paragraph is, especially if the paragraph doesn't begin with a closed-form topic sentence. One way to respond to this problem is to formulate the question that you think the paragraph answers. If you think of chunks of the text as answers to a logical progression of questions, you can often follow the main ideas more easily. Rather than writing *says* statements in the margins, therefore, some readers prefer writing *says* questions. *Says* questions for the Pollan text may include the following:

- What are some of the biggest obstacles that discourage people from undertaking individual actions to fight climate change?
- Despite our excuses not to act, why is individual action still necessary?
- How is the problem of climate a "crisis of lifestyle"?
- What are the reasons we should "bother"?
- Why is growing one's own vegetable garden a particularly powerful individual act?

No matter which method you use—*says* statements or *says* questions—writing gist statements in the margins is far more effective than underlining or highlighting in helping you recall the text's structure and argument.

***Step 3: Locate the article's main divisions or parts.*** In longer closed-form articles, writers often forecast the shape of their essays in their introductions or use their conclusions to sum up main points. For example, Pollan's article uses some forecasting and transitional statements to direct readers through its parts and main points. The article is divided into several main chunks as follows:

- Introductory paragraphs, which establish the problem to be addressed and describe the reasons that people don't take action to help slow climate change (paragraphs 1–5)
- Two short transitional paragraphs (a one-sentence question and a two-word answer) stating the author's intention to call for individual action in spite of the obstacles. These two paragraphs prepare the move into the second part of the article (paragraphs 6 and 7).
- A paragraph conceding to the need for action beyond the individual (laws and money) followed by a counterclaim that the climate change problem is a "crisis of lifestyle" (paragraph 8)
- Eight paragraphs developing Pollan's "crisis of lifestyle" claim, drawing on Wendell Berry and explaining the concepts of specialization and the "cheap-energy mind" that have led us into both the climate change problem and our feelings of inadequacy to tackle it (paragraphs 9–16)
- A transitional paragraph conceding that reasons against individual action are "many and compelling," but proposing better ways to answer the "why bother" question (paragraph 17)
- Two paragraphs developing Pollan's reasons for individual action—how individuals will influence each other and broader communities and lead to "viral social change" (paragraphs 18–19)
- Two paragraphs elaborating on the possibility of viral social change based on analogy to the end of Communism in Czechoslovakia and Poland and to various ways individuals might make significant changes in their lifestyles (paragraphs 20–21)
- Five paragraphs detailing Pollan's choice for the best solution for people to reduce their carbon emissions and make a significant environmental statement: grow gardens (paragraphs 22–26)

Instead of listing the sections of your article, you might prefer to make an outline or tree diagram of the article showing its main parts.

## Drafting and Revising

Once you have determined the main points and grasped the structure of the article you are summarizing, combine and condense your *says* statements into clear sentences that capture the gist of the article. These shortened versions of your *says* statements will make up most of your summary, although you might mention the structure of the article to help organize the points. For example, you might say, "[Author's name] makes four main points in this article.... The article concludes with a call to action...." Because representing an article in your own words in a greatly abbreviated form is a challenge, most writers revise their sentences to find the clearest, most concise way to express the article's ideas accurately. Choose and use your words carefully to stay within your word limit.

The procedures for summarizing articles can work for book-length texts and visual-verbal texts as well. For book-length texts, your *does* and *says* statements may cover chapters or parts of the book. Book introductions and conclusions as well as chapter titles and introductions may provide clues to the author's thesis and subthesis to help you identify the main ideas to include in a book summary. For verbal-visual texts such as a public affairs advocacy ad, product advertisement, Web page, or brochure, examine the parts to see what each contributes to the whole. In your summary, help your readers visualize the images, comprehend the parts, and understand the main points of the text's message.

Plan to create several drafts of all summaries to refine your presentation and wording of ideas. Group work may be helpful in these steps.

**FOR WRITING AND DISCUSSION**

### Finding Key Points in an Article

If the whole class or a group of students is summarizing the same article, brainstorm together and then reach consensus on the main ideas that you think a summary of that article should include to be accurate and complete. Then reread your own summary and check off each idea.

When you revise your summary, consult the criteria on page 90 in this chapter as well as the Questions for Peer Review that follow.

## Questions for Peer Review

In addition to the generic peer review questions explained in Skill 11.4, ask your peer reviewers to address these questions:

1. In what way do the opening sentences provide needed contextual information and then express the overall thesis of the text? What information could be added or more clearly stated?
2. How would you evaluate the writer's representation and coverage of the text's main ideas in terms of accuracy, balance, and proportion? What ideas have been omitted or overemphasized?
3. Has the writer treated the article fairly and neutrally? If judgments have crept in, where could the writer revise?
4. How could the summary use attributive tags more effectively to keep the focus on the original author's ideas?
5. Has the writer used quotations sparingly and cited them accurately? Has the writer translated points into his or her own words? Has the writer included a Works Cited?
6. Where might the writer's choice of words and phrasing of sentences be revised to improve the  clarity, conciseness, and coherence of the summary?

In response to a text assigned by your instructor, write a "summary/strong response" essay that incorporates a 150–250-word summary of the article. In your strong response to that reading, speak back to its author from your own critical thinking, personal experience, values, and, perhaps, further reading or research. Unless your instructor assigns a specific kind of strong response (rhetorical critique, ideas critique, or reflection), write a blended response in which you are free to consider the author's rhetorical strategies, your own agreement or disagreement with the author's ideas, and your personal response to the text. Think of your response as your analysis of how the text tries to influence its readers rhetorically and how your wrestling with the text has expanded and deepened your thinking about its ideas. As you work with ideas from the text, remember to use attributive tags, quotation marks for any quoted passages, and MLA documentation to distinguish your own points about the text from the author's ideas and language.

## Exploring Ideas for Your Strong Response

Earlier in the chapter we presented the kinds of strong responses you may be asked to write in college. We also provided examples of the questions you can ask to generate ideas for different kinds of strong response. Your goal now is to figure out what you want to say. Your first step, of course, is to read your assigned text with the grain, listening to the text so well that you can write a summary of its argument. Use the strategies described in the previous writing project to compose your summary of the assigned text.

After you have written your summary, which demonstrates your full understanding of the text, you are ready to write a strong response. Because your essay cannot discuss every feature of the text or every idea the text has evoked, you will want to focus on a small number of points that enable you to bring readers a new, enlarged, or deepened understanding of the text. You may decide to write a primarily with-the-grain response, praising, building on, or applying the text to a new context, or a primarily against-the-grain response, challenging, questioning, and refuting the text. If your strong response primarily agrees with the text, you must be sure to extend it and apply the ideas rather than simply make your essay one long summary of the article. If your strong response primarily disagrees with the text and criticizes it, you must be sure to be fair and accurate in your criticisms. Here we give you some specific rereading strategies that will stimulate ideas for your strong response, as well as an example of Kyle Madsen's marginal response notes to Pollan's article (Figure 5.1).

See Chapter 1, Concept 1.2, for a discussion of audience analysis.

## Strategies for Rereading to Stimulate Ideas for a Strong Response

| Strategies | What to Do | Comments |
|---|---|---|
| Take notes. | Make copious marginal notes while rereading, recording both with-the-grain and against-the-grain responses. | Writing a strong response requires a deep engagement with texts. For example, in Figure 5.1, observe how Kyle Madsen's notes incorporate with-the-grain and against-the-grain responses and show him truly talking back to and interacting with Pollan's text. |
| Identify "hot spots" in the text. | Mark all hot spots with marginal notes. After you've finished reading, find these hot spots and freewrite your responses to them in a reading journal. | By "hot spot" we mean a quotation or passage that you notice because you agree or disagree with it or because it triggers memories or other associations. Perhaps the hot spot strikes you as thought provoking. Perhaps it raises a problem or is confusing yet suggestive. |
| Ask questions. | Write several questions that the text caused you to think about. Then explore your responses to those questions through freewriting, which may trigger more questions. | Almost any text triggers questions as you read. A good way to begin formulating a strong response is to note these questions. |
| Articulate your difference from the intended audience. | Decide who the writer's intended audience is. If you differ significantly from this audience, use this difference to question the author's underlying assumptions, values, and beliefs. | Your gender, age, class, ethnicity, sexual orientation, political and religious beliefs, interests, values, and so forth, may cause you to feel estranged from the author's imagined audience. If the text seems written for straight people and you are gay, or for Christians and you are a Muslim or an atheist, or for environmentalists and you grew up in a small logging community, you may well resist the text. Sometimes your sense of exclusion from the intended audience makes it difficult to read a text at all. |

## Michael Pollan
# Why Bother?

*This idea is very direct and clear.*

Why bother? That really is the big question facing us as individuals hoping to do something about climate change, and it's not an easy one to answer. I don't know about you, but for me the most upsetting moment in *An Inconvenient Truth* came long after Al Gore scared the hell out of me, constructing an utterly convincing case that the very survival of life on earth as we know it is threatened by climate change. No, the really dark moment came during the closing credits, when we are asked to…change our light bulbs. That's when it got really depressing. The immense disproportion between the magnitude of the problem Gore had described and the puniness of what he was asking us to do about it was enough to sink your heart.

*Informal speech.*

*Sounds like Pollan is talking to readers.*

*How I felt when I saw this film.*

*Short sentence sounds casual.*

*Another very informal statement.*

But the drop-in-the-bucket issue is not the only problem lurking behind the "why bother" question. Let's say I do bother, big time. I turn my life upside-down, start biking to work, plant a big garden, turn down the thermostat so low I need the Jimmy Carter signature cardigan, forsake the clothes dryer for a laundry line across the yard, trade in the station wagon for a hybrid, get off the beef, go completely local. I could theoretically do all that, but what would be the point when I know full well that halfway around the world there lives my evil twin, some carbon-footprint *doppelgänger* in Shanghai or Chongqing who has just bought his first car (Chinese car ownership is where ours was back in 1918), is eager to swallow every bite of meat I forswear and who's positively itching to replace every last pound of $CO_2$ I'm struggling no longer to emit. So what exactly would I have to show for all my trouble?

*Helpful examples.*

*Look up this word.*

*Exaggerated statement?*

*Good word choice? Sounds prejudiced and alarmist.*

A sense of personal virtue, you might suggest, somewhat sheepishly. But what good is that when virtue itself is quickly becoming a term of derision? And not just on the editorial pages of the *Wall Street Journal* or on the lips of the vice president, who famously dismissed energy conservation as a "sign of personal virtue." No, even in the pages of the *New York Times* and the *New Yorker*, it seems the epithet "virtuous," when applied to an act of personal environmental responsibility, may be used only ironically. Tell me: How did it come to pass that virtue—a quality that for most of history has generally been deemed, well, a virtue—became a mark of liberal softheadedness? How peculiar, that doing the right thing by the environment—buying the hybrid, eating like a locavore—should now set you up for the Ed Begley Jr. treatment.

*This paragraph shows Pollan's liberal perspective.*

*Former Vice President Cheney?*

*What's the definition of this term?*

**FIGURE 5.1** Kyle Madsen's Marginal Response Notes

## Practicing Strong Response Reading Strategies

What follows is a short passage by writer Annie Dillard in response to a question about how she chooses to spend her time. This passage often evokes heated responses from our students.

> I don't do housework. Life is too short.... I let almost all my indoor plants die from neglect while I was writing the book. There are all kinds of ways to live. You can take your choice. You can keep a tidy house, and when St. Peter asks you what you did with your life, you can say, "I kept a tidy house, I made my own cheese balls."

**Individual task:** Read the passage and then briefly freewrite your reaction to it.

**Group task:** Working in groups or as a whole class, develop answers to the following questions:

1. What values does Dillard assume her audience holds?
2. What kinds of readers are apt to feel excluded from that audience?
3. If you are not part of the intended audience for this passage, what in the text evokes resistance?

## Articulate Your Own Purpose for Reading

Although you usually read a text because you are joining the author's conversation, you might occasionally read a text for an entirely different purpose from what the author intended. For example, you might read the writings of nineteenth-century scientists to figure out what they assumed about nature (or women, or God, or race, or capitalism). Or suppose that you examine a politician's metaphors to see what they reveal about her values, or analyze *National Geographic* for evidence of political bias. Understanding your own purpose will help you read deeply both with and against the grain.

## Writing a Thesis for a Strong Response Essay

A thesis for a strong response essay should map out for readers the points that you want to develop and discuss. These points should be risky and contestable; your thesis should surprise your readers with something new or challenging. Your thesis might focus entirely on with-the-grain points or entirely on against-the-grain points, but most likely it will include some of both. Avoid tensionless thesis statements such as "This article has both good and bad points."

Here are some thesis statements that students have written for strong responses in our classes. Note that each thesis includes at least one point about the rhetorical strategies of the text.

See Chapter 2, Concept 2.2, for a discussion of surprising thesis statements.

- In "The Beauty Myth," Naomi Wolf makes a very good case for her idea that the beauty myth prevents women from ever feeling that they are good enough; however, Wolf's argument is geared too much toward feminists to be persuasive for a general audience, and she neglects to acknowledge the strong social pressures that I and other men feel to live up to male standards of physical perfection.
- Although Naomi Wolf in "The Beauty Myth" uses rhetorical strategies persuasively to argue that the beauty industry oppresses women, I think that she overlooks women's individual resistance and responsibility.
- Although the images and figures of speech that Thoreau uses in his chapter "Where I Lived, and What I Lived For" from *Walden* wonderfully support his argument that nature is spiritually renewing, I disagree with his antitechnology stance and with his extreme emphasis on isolation as a means to self-discovery.
- In "Where I Lived, and What I Lived For" from *Walden*, Thoreau's argument that society is missing spiritual reality through its preoccupation with details and its frantic pace is convincing, especially to twenty-first century audiences; however, Thoreau weakens his message by criticizing his readers and by completely dismissing technological advances.
- Although the booklet *Compassionate Living* by People for the Ethical Treatment of Animals (PETA) uses the design features of layout, color, and image powerfully, its extreme examples, its quick dismissal of alternative views, and its failure to document the sources of its information weaken its appeal to *ethos* and its overall persuasiveness.

**FOR WRITING AND DISCUSSION**

## Examining Thesis Statements for Strong Response Critiques

Working individually or in groups, identify the points in each of the thesis statements in the preceding section and briefly state them. Think in terms of the ideas you are expecting the writers to develop in the body of the essay. As a follow-up to this exercise, you might share in your groups your own thesis statements for your strong response essays. How clearly does each thesis statement lay out points that the writer will probe? As a group, discuss what new, important perspectives each thesis statement promises to bring to readers and how each thesis suits a rhetorical critique, ideas critique, or some combination of these.

## Shaping and Drafting

A possible framework for a summary/response essay is shown in Figure 5.2. Most strong response essays call for a short contextualizing introduction to set up your analysis. In the essay on pages 98–101, student writer Kyle Madsen begins by reflecting on personal and societal changes in environmental awareness and then raises the question that Pollan will address: What challenges confront us in changing how we live?

**FIGURE 5.2** Framework for a Summary/Strong Response Essay

| | |
|---|---|
| **Introduction (usually one paragraph)** | • Introduces the topic/problem/question that the article (or book, chapter, or piece) addresses<br>• Conveys the writer's investment in the author's topic<br>• Provides rhetorical context of the article and its question, and identifies the author and the author's title and purpose |
| **Summary (one paragraph)** | • Summarizes the article, chapter, or book, giving a balanced, accurate, concise, and neutral presentation of its main points |
| **Thesis statement (forms its own paragraph or comes at the end of the summary)** | • Presents the two or more rhetorical or ideas points that the writer will analyze and discuss in the body of the essay<br>• Establishes the writer's perspective on the author's text<br>• Often maps out the analysis and critique to follow, giving readers a clear sense of the direction and scope of the essay |
| **Body section 1 (one or more paragraphs)** | • Develops the first rhetorical or ideas point with examples from the text<br>• Explains and discusses this point in a thorough critique with the writer's own perspective (and perhaps knowledge and personal experience, for an ideas critique) |
| **Body section 2 (one or more paragraphs** | • Develops the second rhetorical or ideas point with examples from the text<br>• Explains and discusses this point in a thorough critique with the writer's own perspective (and perhaps knowledge and personal experience, for an ideas critique) |
| **Body section 3, 4, etc., on additional rhetorical or ideas points (one or more paragraphs per main point)** | • Continues the critique and analysis by explaining writer's ideas with examples and elaboration until all points in the thesis statement are fleshed out |
| **Conclusion (usually a short paragraph)** | • Might briefly recap the writer's points, but summarizes these ideas only if the essay is long and complex<br>• Wraps up the critique and analysis to leave readers thinking about both the author's piece and the writer's strong response |
| **Work Cited** | • Gives an appropriate citation in MLA format for the text discussed in the paper and any other sources mentioned in the essay (often only one source to list) |

Kyle introduces the question addressed by the article he is critiquing, and he includes a short summary of the article that gives readers a foundation for the critique before he presents the points he will address in his strong response.

Each of the thesis statements in the preceding section, as well as Kyle's thesis statement, identifies and maps out two or more points that readers will expect to see developed and explained in the body of the essay. In a closed-form, thesis-driven strong response, readers will also expect the points to follow the order in which they are presented in the thesis. If your strong response is primarily a rhetorical critique, your evidence will come mainly from the text you are analyzing. If your strong response is primarily an ideas critique, your evidence is apt to come from personal knowledge of the issue or from further reading or research. If your strong response is primarily reflective, much of your evidence will be based on your own personal experiences and inner thoughts. A blended response, of course, can combine points from any of these perspectives.

Each point in your thesis calls for a lively discussion, combining general statements and specifics that will encourage readers to see this text your way. Just as you do in your summary, you must use attributive tags to distinguish between the author's ideas and your own points and responses. In addition, you must document all ideas gotten from other sources as well as place all borrowed language in quotation marks or block indentations according to MLA format and include a Works Cited in MLA format. Most strong response essays have short conclusions—just enough commentary to bring closure to the essay.

## Revising

In a summary/strong response essay, you may want to work on the summary separately before you incorporate it into your whole essay. Use the peer review questions for summaries (p. 90) for that part of your essay. You will definitely want to get feedback from readers to make your strong response as clear, thorough, and compelling as possible.

## Questions for Peer Review

In addition to the generic peer review questions explained in Skill 11.4, ask your peer reviewers to address these questions:

1. How appealingly do the title and introduction of the essay set up the topic of critique, convey the writer's interest, and lay a foundation for the summary of the article and the writer's thesis?
2. How could the writer's thesis statement be clearer in presenting several focused points about the text's rhetorical strategies and ideas?
3. How could the body of the strong response follow the thesis more closely?
4. Where do you, the reader, need more clarification or support for the writer's points? How could the writer develop with-the-grain or against-the-grain points more appropriately?
5. Where could the writer work on the effectiveness of attributive tags, quotations, and documentation?

## Multimodal or Online Options

1. **Summary/Strong Response to a Blog Post** Identify a blogger with a reputation for substantial, serious, in-depth analysis or commentary. Select a recent post from your chosen blogger (recent enough that the "comments" feature for this post is still open). Write a summary/strong response critique of your chosen post, and post your critique to the "comments" section of the blog, adapting your response to the conventions of responses on this site. Although all respondents will have read the original blog, a short summary of its argument will help frame your own response. Your goal is to contribute significantly to the conversation initiated by the blogger's original post.

2. **Online Book Review** Write a summary/strong response critique of a book and "publish" it as an online book review for a site such as Amazon or Goodread. Typically, online customer reviews are likely to be much shorter than an academic essay, so you need to plan the points you want to highlight. Writers contributing to these public online forums should be aware of their ethical responsibility. Customer reviews are a powerful marketing tool that can boost or hurt authors' sales and success. Take this responsibility seriously: Consider your *ethos* as a careful, insightful reader and insightful critic and make your review lively, interesting, and fair.

For understanding rhetorical issues connected to online and multimodal compositions, see Chapter 4, pp. 66–79.

Our first reading for this chapter is the article by Michael Pollan, which forms the basis of the examples for this chapter and is best read before you read the chapter.

# Michael Pollan
# Why Bother?

1    **Why bother?** That really is the big question facing us as individuals hoping to do something about climate change, and it's not an easy one to answer. I don't know about you, but for me the most upsetting moment in *An Inconvenient Truth* came long after Al Gore scared the hell out of me, constructing an utterly convincing case that the very survival of life on earth as we know it is threatened by climate change. No, the really dark moment came during the closing credits, when we are asked to…change our light bulbs. That's when it got really depressing. The immense disproportion between the magnitude of the problem Gore had described and the puniness of what he was asking us to do about it was enough to sink your heart.

2    But the drop-in-the-bucket issue is not the only problem lurking behind the "why bother" question. Let's say I do bother, big time. I turn my life upside-down, start biking to work, plant a big garden, turn down the thermostat so low I need the Jimmy Carter* signature cardigan, forsake the clothes dryer for a laundry line across the yard, trade in the station wagon for a hybrid, get off the beef, go completely local. I could theoretically do all that, but what would be the point when I know full well that halfway around the world there lives my evil twin, some carbon-footprint *doppelgänger* in Shanghai or Chongqing who has just bought his first car (Chinese car ownership is where ours was back in 1918), is eager to swallow every bite of meat I forswear and who's positively itching to replace every last pound of $CO_2$ I'm struggling no longer to emit. So what exactly would I have to show for all my trouble?

3    A sense of personal virtue, you might suggest, somewhat sheepishly. But what good is that when virtue itself is quickly becoming a term of derision? And not just on the editorial pages of the *Wall Street Journal* or on the lips of the vice president,* who famously dismissed energy conservation as a "sign of personal virtue." No, even in the pages of the *New York Times* and the *New Yorker,* it seems the epithet "virtuous," when applied to an act of personal environmental responsibility, may be used only ironically. Tell me: How did it come to pass that virtue—a quality that for most of history has generally been deemed, well, a virtue—became a mark of liberal softheadedness? How peculiar, that doing the right thing by the environment—buying the hybrid, eating like a locavore—should now set you up for the Ed Begley Jr.* treatment.

4    And even if in the face of this derision I decide I am going to bother, there arises the whole vexed question of getting it right. Is eating local or walking to work really

---

* Jimmy Carter was the Democratic president (1977–1981) who supported environmental policies, world peace, and human rights.
* Pollan is referring to Dick Cheney, who served as George W. Bush's vice president from 2001 to 2009.
* Ed Begley, Jr., is a prominent television star who has his own green living reality TV show, *Living with Ed.* Begley has explored such topics as tapping the energy produced by people using exercise equipment.

going to reduce my carbon footprint? According to one analysis, if walking to work increases your appetite and you consume more meat or milk as a result, walking might actually emit more carbon than driving. A handful of studies have recently suggested that in certain cases under certain conditions, produce from places as far away as New Zealand might account for less carbon than comparable domestic products. True, at least one of these studies was co-written by a representative of agribusiness interests in (surprise!) New Zealand, but even so, they make you wonder. If determining the carbon footprint of food is really this complicated, and I've got to consider not only "food miles" but also whether the food came by ship or truck and how lushly the grass grows in New Zealand, then maybe on second thought I'll just buy the imported chops at Costco, at least until the experts get their footprints sorted out.

5    There are so many stories we can tell ourselves to justify doing nothing, but perhaps the most insidious is that, whatever we do manage to do, it will be too little too late. Climate change is upon us, and it has arrived well ahead of schedule. Scientists' projections that seemed dire a decade ago turn out to have been unduly optimistic: the warming and the melting is occurring much faster than the models predicted. Now truly terrifying feedback loops threaten to boost the rate of change exponentially, as the shift from white ice to blue water in the Arctic absorbs more sunlight and warming soils everywhere become more biologically active, causing them to release their vast stores of carbon into the air. Have you looked into the eyes of a climate scientist recently? They look really scared.

6    So do you still want to talk about planting gardens?

7    I do.

8    Whatever we can do as individuals to change the way we live at this suddenly very late date does seem utterly inadequate to the challenge. It's hard to argue with Michael Specter*, in a recent *New Yorker* piece on carbon footprints, when he says:

| Egypt | 32% |
| Russia | 40% |
| China | 42% |
| Britain | 45% |
| United States | 47% |
| France | 68% |
| Japan | 78% |
| Bangladesh | 85% |
| Brazil | 88% |

**High Anxiety?**
Percentage of people by country who view global warming as a "very serious" problem.

*Michael Specter is a staff writer for the *New Yorker* and a national science reporter, who has most recently written a book, *Denialism*, about people's refusal to accept scientific evidence.

"Personal choices, no matter how virtuous [N.B.!], cannot do enough. It will also take laws and money." So it will. Yet it is no less accurate or hardheaded to say that laws and money cannot do enough, either; that it will also take profound changes in the way we live. Why? Because the climate-change crisis is at its very bottom a crisis of lifestyle—of character, even. The Big Problem is nothing more or less than the sum total of countless little everyday choices, most of them made by us (consumer spending represents 70 percent of our economy), and most of the rest of them made in the name of our needs and desires and preferences.

9        For us to wait for legislation or technology to solve the problem of how we're living our lives suggests we're not really serious about changing—something our politicians cannot fail to notice. They will not move until we do. Indeed, to look to leaders and experts, to laws and money and grand schemes, to save us from our predicament represents precisely the sort of thinking—passive, delegated, dependent for solutions on specialists—that helped get us into this mess in the first place. It's hard to believe that the same sort of thinking could now get us out of it.

10       Thirty years ago, Wendell Berry, the Kentucky farmer and writer, put forward a blunt analysis of precisely this mentality. He argued that the environmental crisis of the 1970s—an era innocent of climate change; what we would give to have back *that* environmental crisis!—was at its heart a crisis of character and would have to be addressed first at that level: at home, as it were. He was impatient with people who wrote checks to environmental organizations while thoughtlessly squandering fossil fuel in their everyday lives—the 1970s equivalent of people buying carbon offsets to atone for their Tahoes and Durangos. Nothing was likely to change until we healed the "split between what we think and what we do." For Berry, the "why bother" question came down to a moral imperative: "Once our personal connection to what is wrong becomes clear, then we have to choose: we can go on as before, recognizing our dishonesty and living with it the best we can, or we can begin the effort to change the way we think and live."

11       For Berry, the deep problem standing behind all the other problems of industrial civilization is "specialization," which he regards as the "disease of the modern character." Our society assigns us a tiny number of roles: we're producers (of one thing) at work, consumers of a great many other things the rest of the time, and then once a year or so we vote as citizens. Virtually all of our needs and desires we delegate to specialists of one kind or another—our meals to agribusiness, health to the doctor, education to the teacher, entertainment to the media, care for the environment to the environmentalist, political action to the politician.

12       As Adam Smith and many others have pointed out, this division of labor has given us many of the blessings of civilization. Specialization is what allows me to sit at a computer thinking about climate change. Yet this same division of labor obscures the lines of connection—and responsibility—linking our everyday acts to their real-world consequences, making it easy for me to overlook the coal-fired power plant that is lighting my screen, or the mountaintop in Kentucky that had to be destroyed to provide the coal to that plant, or the streams running crimson with heavy metals as a result.

13       Of course, what made this sort of specialization possible in the first place was cheap energy. Cheap fossil fuel allows us to pay distant others to process our food for us, to entertain us and to (try to) solve our problems, with the result that there is very

little we know how to accomplish for ourselves. Think for a moment of all the things you suddenly need to do for yourself when the power goes out—up to and including entertaining yourself. Think, too, about how a power failure causes your neighbors—your community—to suddenly loom so much larger in your life. Cheap energy allowed us to leapfrog community by making it possible to sell our specialty over great distances as well as summon into our lives the specialties of countless distant others.

14      Here's the point: Cheap energy, which gives us climate change, fosters precisely the mentality that makes dealing with climate change in our own lives seem impossibly difficult. Specialists ourselves, we can no longer imagine anyone but an expert, or anything but a new technology or law, solving our problems. Al Gore asks us to change the light bulbs because he probably can't imagine us doing anything much more challenging, like, say, growing some portion of our own food. We can't imagine it, either, which is probably why we prefer to cross our fingers and talk about the promise of ethanol and nuclear power—new liquids and electrons to power the same old cars and houses and lives.

15      The "cheap-energy mind," as Wendell Berry called it, is the mind that asks, "Why bother?" because it is helpless to imagine—much less attempt—a different sort of life, one less divided, less reliant. Since the cheap-energy mind translates everything into money, its proxy, it prefers to put its faith in market-based solutions—carbon taxes and pollution-trading schemes. If we could just get the incentives right, it believes, the economy will properly value everything that matters and nudge our self-interest down the proper channels. The best we can hope for is a greener version of the old invisible hand. Visible hands it has no use for.

16      But while some such grand scheme may well be necessary, it's doubtful that it will be sufficient or that it will be politically sustainable before we've demonstrated to ourselves that change is possible. Merely to give, to spend, even to vote, is not to do, and there is so much that needs to be done—without further delay. In the judgment of James Hansen, the NASA climate scientist who began sounding the alarm on global warming 20 years ago, we have only 10 years left to start cutting—not just slowing—the amount of carbon we're emitting or face a "different planet." Hansen said this more than two years ago, however; two years have gone by, and nothing of consequence has been done. So: eight years left to go and a great deal left to do.

17      Which brings us back to the "why bother" question and how we might better answer it. The reasons not to bother are many and compelling, at least to the cheap-energy mind. But let me offer a few admittedly tentative reasons that we might put on the other side of the scale:

18      If you do bother, you will set an example for other people. If enough other people bother, each one influencing yet another in a chain reaction of behavioral change, markets for all manner of green products and alternative technologies will prosper and expand. (Just look at the market for hybrid cars.) Consciousness will be raised, perhaps even changed: new moral imperatives and new taboos might take root in the culture. Driving an S.U.V. or eating a 24-ounce steak or illuminating your McMansion like an airport runway at night might come to be regarded as outrages to human conscience. Not having things might become cooler than having them. And those who did change the way they live would acquire the moral standing to demand changes in behavior from others—from other people, other corporations, even other countries.

19    All of this could, theoretically, happen. What I'm describing (imagining would probably be more accurate) is a process of viral social change, and change of this kind, which is nonlinear, is never something anyone can plan or predict or count on. Who knows, maybe the virus will reach all the way to Chongqing and infect my Chinese evil twin. Or not. Maybe going green will prove a passing fad and will lose steam after a few years, just as it did in the 1980s, when Ronald Reagan took down Jimmy Carter's solar panels from the roof of the White House.

20    Going personally green is a bet, nothing more or less, though it's one we probably all should make, even if the odds of it paying off aren't great. Sometimes you have to act as if acting will make a difference, even when you can't prove that it will. That, after all, was precisely what happened in Communist Czechoslovakia and Poland, when a handful of individuals like Václav Havel and Adam Michnik resolved that they would simply conduct their lives "as if" they lived in a free society. That improbable bet created a tiny space of liberty that, in time, expanded to take in, and then help take down, the whole of the Eastern bloc.

21    So what would be a comparable bet that the individual might make in the case of the environmental crisis? Havel himself has suggested that people begin to "conduct themselves as if they were to live on this earth forever and be answerable for its condition one day." Fair enough, but let me propose a slightly less abstract and daunting wager. The idea is to find one thing to do in your life that doesn't involve spending or voting, that may or may not virally rock the world but is real and particular (as well as symbolic) and that, come what may, will offer its own rewards. Maybe you decide to give up meat, an act that would reduce your carbon footprint by as much as a quarter. Or you could try this: determine to observe the Sabbath. For one day a week, abstain completely from economic activity: no shopping, no driving, no electronics.

22    But the act I want to talk about is growing some—even just a little—of your own food. Rip out your lawn, if you have one, and if you don't—if you live in a high-rise, or have a yard shrouded in shade—look into getting a plot in a community garden. Measured against the Problem We Face, planting a garden sounds pretty benign, I know, but in fact it's one of the most powerful things an individual can do—to reduce your carbon footprint, sure, but more important, to reduce your sense of dependence and dividedness: to change the cheap-energy mind.

23    A great many things happen when you plant a vegetable garden, some of them directly related to climate change, others indirect but related nevertheless. Growing food, we forget, comprises the original solar technology: calories produced by means of photosynthesis. Years ago the cheap-energy mind discovered that more food could be produced with less effort by replacing sunlight with fossil-fuel fertilizers and pesticides, with a result that the typical calorie of food energy in your diet now requires about 10 calories of fossil-fuel energy to produce. It's estimated that the way we feed ourselves (or rather, allow ourselves to be fed) accounts for about a fifth of the greenhouse gas for which each of us is responsible.

24    Yet the sun still shines down on your yard, and photosynthesis still works so abundantly that in a thoughtfully organized vegetable garden (one planted from seed, nourished by compost from the kitchen and involving not too many drives to the garden center), you can grow the proverbial free lunch—CO2-free and dollar-free.

This is the most-local food you can possibly eat (not to mention the freshest, tastiest and most nutritious), with a carbon footprint so faint that even the New Zealand lamb council dares not challenge it. And while we're counting carbon, consider too your compost pile, which shrinks the heap of garbage your household needs trucked away even as it feeds your vegetables and sequesters carbon in your soil. What else? Well, you will probably notice that you're getting a pretty good workout there in your garden, burning calories without having to get into the car to drive to the gym. (It is one of the absurdities of the modern division of labor that, having replaced physical labor with fossil fuel, we now have to burn even more fossil fuel to keep our unemployed bodies in shape.) Also, by engaging both body and mind, time spent in the garden is time (and energy) subtracted from electronic forms of entertainment.

25       You begin to see that growing even a little of your own food is, as Wendell Berry pointed out 30 years ago, one of those solutions that, instead of begetting a new set of problems—the way "solutions" like ethanol or nuclear power inevitably do—actually beget other solutions, and not only of the kind that save carbon. Still more valuable are the habits of mind that growing a little of your own food can yield. You quickly learn that you need not be dependent on specialists to provide for yourself—that your body is still good for something and may actually be enlisted in its own support. If the experts are right, if both oil and time are running out, these are skills and habits of mind we're all very soon going to need. We may also need the food. Could gardens provide it? Well, during World War II, victory gardens supplied as much as 40 percent of the produce Americans ate.

26       **But there are sweeter** reasons to plant that garden, to bother. At least in this one corner of your yard and life, you will have begun to heal the split between what you think and what you do, to commingle your identities as consumer and producer and citizen. Chances are, your garden will re-engage you with your neighbors, for you will have produce to give away and the need to borrow their tools. You will have reduced the power of the cheap-energy mind by personally overcoming its most debilitating weakness: its helplessness and the fact that it can't do much of anything that doesn't involve division or subtraction. The garden's season-long transit from seed to ripe fruit—*will you get a load of that zucchini?!*—suggests that the operations of addition and multiplication still obtain, that the abundance of nature is not exhausted. The single greatest lesson the garden teaches is that our relationship to the planet need not be zero-sum, and that as long as the sun still shines and people still can plan and plant, think and do, we can, if we bother to try, find ways to provide for ourselves without diminishing the world.

# 6 WRITING AN EXPLORATORY ESSAY OR ANNOTATED BIBLIOGRAPHY

## WHAT YOU WILL LEARN

**6.1** To pose a significant and problematic research question.

**6.2** To explore your problem and narrate your thinking process in an exploratory essay.

**6.3** To think about your problem dialectically, find relevant sources, and take effective research notes.

**6.4** To summarize and critique your research sources in an annotated bibliography.

In Part 1, we explained how writers wrestle with subject-matter problems. During exploration, experienced writers often redefine their problem, discover new ideas, and alter or even reverse their initial thesis. In contrast, inexperienced writers often truncate this process, closing off the period of exploratory thinking. Asserting a thesis too soon can prevent writers from acknowledging an issue's complexity, whereas dwelling with a question invites writers to contemplate multiple perspectives, entertain new ideas, and let their thinking evolve. In this chapter, we introduce two genres of writing built on exploratory thinking:

- An **exploratory essay** narrates a writer's thinking process while doing research. The essay recounts your attempt to examine your question's complexity, explore alternatives, and arrive at a solution or answer. Because an exploration often requires research, many instructors pair this project with Part 4, "A Rhetorical Guide to Research."
- An **annotated bibliography** summarizes and briefly critiques the research sources a writer used while exploring a problem. It encourages exploration and inquiry, provides a "tracing" of your work, and creates a guide for others interested in your research problem.

## Engaging Exploratory Writing

Through our work in writing centers, we often encounter students disappointed with their grades on essay exams or papers. "I worked hard on this paper," they tell us, "but I still got a lousy grade. What am I doing wrong? What do college professors want?"

To help you think about this question, read the following two essays written for a freshman placement examination in composition at the University of Pittsburgh, and then formulate your own response to the questions that follow.* The essays were written for this assignment:

Describe a time when you did something you felt to be creative. Then, on the basis of the incident you have described, go on to draw some general conclusions about "creativity."

### ESSAY A

I am very interested in music, and I try to be creative in my interpretation of music. While in high school, I was a member of a jazz ensemble. The members of the ensemble were given chances to improvise and be creative in various songs. I feel that this was a great experience for me, as well as the other members. I was proud to know that I could use my imagination and feelings to create music other than what was written.

Creativity to me means being free to express yourself in a way that is unique to you, not having to conform to certain rules and guidelines. Music is only one of the many areas in which people are given opportunities to show their creativity. Sculpting, carving, building, art, and acting are just a few more areas where people can show their creativity.

Through my music I conveyed feelings and thoughts which were important to me. Music was my means of showing creativity. In whatever form creativity takes, whether it be music, art, or science, it is an important aspect of our lives because it enables us to be individuals.

### ESSAY B

Throughout my life, I have been interested and intrigued by music. My mother has often told me of the times, before I went to school, when I would "conduct" the orchestra on her records. I continued to listen to music and eventually started to play the guitar and the clarinet. Finally, at about the age of twelve, I started to sit down and to try to write songs. Even though my instrumental skills were far from my own high standards, I would spend much of my spare time during the day with a guitar around my neck, trying to produce a piece of music.

Each of these sessions, as I remember them, had a rather set format. I would sit in my bedroom, strumming different combinations of the five or six chords I could play, until I heard a series which sounded particularly good to me. After this, I set the music to a suitable rhythm (usually dependent on my mood at the time), and ran through the tune until I could play it fairly easily. Only after this section was complete did I go on to writing lyrics, which generally followed along the lines of the current popular songs on the radio.

---

*For our discussion of the creativity assignment, we are indebted to David Bartholomae, "Inventing the University," *When Writers Can't Write: Studies in Writer's Block and Other Composing Process Problems.* Ed. Mike Rose. New York, Guilford Press, 1985: pp. 273–85.

At the time of the writing, I felt that my songs were, in themselves, an original creation of my own; that is, I, alone, made them. However, I now see that, in this sense of the word, I was not creative. The songs themselves seem to be an oversimplified form of the music I listened to at the time.

In a more fitting sense, however, I *was* being creative. Since I did not purposely copy my favorite songs, I was, effectively, originating my songs from my own "process of creativity." To achieve my goal, I needed what a composer would call "inspiration" for my piece. In this case the inspiration was the current hit on the radio. Perhaps, with my present point of view, I feel that I used too much "inspiration" in my songs, but, at the time, I did not.

Creativity, therefore, is a process which, in my case, involved a certain series of "small creations" if you like. As well, it is something the appreciation of which varies with one's point of view, that point of view being set by the person's experience, tastes, and his own personal view of creativity. The less experienced tend to allow for less originality, while the more experienced demand real originality to classify something a "creation." Either way, a term as abstract as this is perfectly correct, and open to interpretation.

**ON YOUR OWN**

Note the major differences between Essay A and Essay B. What might cause college professors to rate one essay higher than the other?

**IN CONVERSATION**

Compare your responses with those of other class members. As a group, make suggestions about what the writer of the weaker essay has to do to produce an essay more like the stronger.

## 6.1 Understanding Exploratory Writing

Pose a significant and problematic research question.

Even though academic readers usually expect thesis-driven arguments, both exploratory essays and annotated bibliographies are frequently encountered. Exploratory essays exist in embryo in the research or lab notebooks of scholars. For students, both the exploratory essay and the annotated bibliography serve as an intermediate stage in the research process. Student Kent Ansen's exploratory paper and annotated bibliography in this chapter are products of the exploratory phase of his research about mandatory public service, which later resulted in a researched argument. You can compare his exploratory essay with the final thesis-driven argument in Chapter 10 (pp. 263–272).

The essential move for exploratory thinking and writing is to keep a problem alive through consideration of multiple solutions or points of view. The thinker identifies a problem, considers a possible solution or point of view, explores its strengths and weaknesses, and then moves on to consider another possible solution or viewpoint. The thinker resists closure—that is, resists settling too soon on a thesis.

To show a mind at work examining multiple solutions, let's return to the two student essays you examined in the previous Engaging activity (pp. 121–122). The fundamental difference between Essay A and Essay B is that the writer of Essay B treats the concept of "creativity" as a true problem. Note that the writer of Essay A is satisfied with his or her initial definition:

> Creativity to me means being free to express yourself in a way that is unique to you, not having to conform to certain rules and guidelines.

The writer of Essay B, however, is *not* satisfied with his or her first answer and uses the essay to think through the problem. This writer remembers an early creative experience—composing songs as a twelve-year-old:

> At the time of the writing, I felt that my songs were, in themselves, an original creation of my own; that is, I, alone, made them. However, I now see that, in this sense of the word, I was not creative. The songs themselves seem to be an oversimplified form of the music I listened to at the time.

This writer distinguishes between two points of view: "On the one hand, I used to think *x*, but now, in retrospect, I think *y*." This move forces the writer to go beyond the initial answer to think of alternatives.

The key to effective exploratory writing is to create a tension between alternative views. When you start out, you might not know where your thinking process will end up; at the outset you might not have formulated an opposing, countering, or alternative view. Using a statement such as "I used to think…, but now I think" or "Part of me thinks this…, but another part thinks that…" forces you to find something additional to say; writing then becomes a process of inquiry and discovery.

The second writer's dissatisfaction with the initial answer initiates a dialectic process that plays one idea against another, creating a generative tension. In contrast, the writer of Essay A offers no alternative to his or her definition of creativity. This writer presents no specific illustrations of creative activity (such as the specific details in Essay B about strumming the guitar) but presents merely space-filling abstractions ("Sculpting, carving, building, art, and acting are just a few more areas where people can show their creativity"). The writer of Essay B scores a higher grade, not because the essay creates a brilliant (or even particularly clear) explanation of creativity; rather, the writer is rewarded for thinking about the problem dialectically.

We use the term **dialectic** to mean a thinking process often associated with the German philosopher Hegel, who said that each thesis ("My act was creative") gives rise to an antithesis ("My act was not creative") and that the clash of these opposing perspectives leads thinkers to develop a synthesis that incorporates some features of both theses ("My act was a series of 'small creations'"). You initiate dialectic thinking any time you play Elbow's believing and doubting game or use other strategies to place alternative possibilities side by side.

Essay B's writer uses a dialectic thinking strategy that we might characterize as follows:

1. Sees the assigned question as a genuine problem worth puzzling over.
2. Considers alternative views and plays them off against each other.

3. Looks at specific examples and illustrations.
4. Continues the thinking process in search of some sort of resolution or synthesis of the alternative views.
5. Incorporates the stages of this dialectic process into the essay.

These same dialectic thinking habits can be extended to research writing where the researcher's goals are to find alternative points of view on the research question, to read sources rhetorically, to consider all the relevant evidence, to search for a resolution or synthesis of alternative views, and to use one's own critical thinking to arrive at a thesis.

---

**FOR WRITING AND DISCUSSION**

## Keeping a Problem Open

1. Working individually, read each of the following questions and write out the first plausible answer that comes to your mind.
   - Why on average are males more attracted to video games than females? Are these games harmful to males?
   - Have online social networks such as Facebook improved or harmed the lives of participants? Why?
   - The most popular magazines sold on college campuses are women's fashion and lifestyle magazines such as *Glamour*, *Elle*, and *Cosmopolitan*. Why do women buy these magazines? Are these magazines harmful?
2. As a whole class, take a poll to determine the most common first-response answers for each of the questions. Then explore other possible answers and points of view. The goal of your class discussion is to postulate and explore answers that go against the grain of or beyond the common answers. Try to push deeply into each question so that it becomes more complex and interesting than it may at first seem.
3. How would you use library and Internet research to deepen your exploration of these questions? Specifically, what keywords might you use in a database search? What databases would you use?

---

**WRITING PROJECT**

**6.2**
Explore your problem and narrate your thinking process in an exploratory essay.

## An Exploratory Essay

Choose a question, problem, or issue that genuinely perplexes you. At the beginning of your essay, explain why you are interested in this problem, why you think it is significant, and why you have been unable to reach a satisfactory answer. Then write a first-person, chronologically organized narrative account of your thinking process as you investigate your question through research, talking with others, and doing your own reflective thinking. Your goal is to examine your question, problem, or issue from a variety of perspectives, assessing the strengths and weaknesses of different positions and points of view. Your goal is not to answer your question but to report on the process of wrestling with it.

This assignment asks you to dwell on a problem—and not necessarily to solve that problem. Your problem may shift and evolve as your thinking progresses. What matters is that you are actively engaged with your problem and demonstrate why it is problematic.

## Generating and Exploring Ideas

Your process of generating and exploring ideas is, in essence, the *subject matter* of your exploratory essay. This section will help you get started and keep going.

### Posing Your Initial Problem

If your instructor hasn't assigned a specific problem to be investigated, then your first step is to choose one that currently perplexes you. Perhaps a question is problematic for you because you haven't yet had a chance to study it (Should the United States turn to nuclear power for generating electricity?). Maybe the available data seem conflicting or inconclusive (Should women younger than fifty get annual mammograms?). Or, possibly, the problem or issue draws you into an uncomfortable conflict of values (Should we legalize the sale of organs for transplant?).

The key to this assignment is to choose a question, problem, or issue *that truly perplexes you.* (Your instructor may limit the range of topics you can choose.) Here are several exercises to help you think of ideas for this essay:

- Make a list of issues or problems that both interest and perplex you within the range of subjects specified by your instructor. Then choose two or three and freewrite about them for five minutes or so. Use as your model Kent Ansen's freewrite on pages 26–27, which marked the origin of his exploratory paper for this chapter. Share your questions and your freewrites with friends and classmates because doing so often stimulates further thinking and discovery.
- A particularly valuable kind of problem to explore for this assignment is a current public controversy. Often such issues involve disagreements about facts and values that merit open-ended exploration. This assignment invites you to explore and clarify where you stand on such public issues as gay marriage, immigration, health care reform, energy policies, government responses to terrorism, and so forth. Make a list of currently debated public controversies that you would like to explore. Share your list with classmates and friends.

### Formulating a Starting Point

After you've chosen a problem, you are ready to write a first draft of your introduction in which you identify your chosen problem and show why you are interested in it, why you find it perplexing, and why it is significant. You might start out with a sharp, clearly focused question (Should the United States build a fence between the United States and Mexico?). Often, however, formulating a focused question will turn out to be part of the *process* of writing the paper. Instead of a single, focused question, you might start with a whole cluster of related questions swimming in your head. That's fine too because you can still explain why you are interested in this cluster of questions.

The goal of your introduction is to hook your reader's interest in your chosen problem. Often the best way to do so is to show why you yourself became interested in it. For example, Kent Ansen opens his exploratory essay by recalling his experience with volunteer work and his discussion with older friends who are questioning their majors and their futures (see p. 136). He then introduces the questions he wants to investigate—how could mandatory public service benefit the country and youth and should it be installed as a requirement for all youth?

## 6.3
Think about your problem dialectically, find relevant sources, and take effective research notes.

## Taking "Double-Entry" Research Notes

After you have formulated your initial problem, you are ready to start your research. As you read, take purposeful notes. Whereas novice researchers often avoid taking notes and instead create a pile of photocopied or downloaded-and-printed articles, experienced researchers use note taking as a discipline to promote strong rhetorical reading. We recommend "double-entry" notes in which you use one column for taking notes on a source and another column for recording your own thinking about the source. When you have finished taking notes in the first column, write a "strong response" to the source in the second column, explaining how the source advanced your thinking, raised questions, or pulled you in one direction or another.

What follows is Kent Ansen's double-entry research notes for one of the articles he used in his exploratory essay. When you read both his exploratory essay in this chapter and his final researched argument in Chapter 10, you'll be able to see how he used this article at a crucial place in his research.

---

*Date of entry so you can reconstruct chronological order*

**Kent's Double-Entry Research Log Entry for the Opinion Piece in the *Chronicle of Philanthropy***

February 8

*Bibliographic citation following assigned format, in this case MLA*

Rosenman, Mark. "A Call for National Service." *Chronicle of Philanthropy* 2007: 38. *Proquest*. Web. 8 Feb. 2013.

*Rhetorical notation about genre, purpose, audience*

Editorial in the journalistic style in the opinion section of a magazine for "the nonprofit world"

---

*Reading notes in column 1 on content of the source*

*Include full quotations if you won't keep a copy of the full source*

| Reading Notes | Strong Response Notes |
|---|---|
| —Begins with the current political discussions about national service as voluntary or compulsory. Expresses Rosenman's view that compulsory national service might be good for citizen participation in public policy. Identifies a problem that as tax and fee payers only "we are reduced to little more than consumers of government services, to being government's customers." | —*Rosenman's point is a good one, but I think as voters and campaigners for candidates we also have a role as citizens. This quotation could be useful.* |

—Argues that people have to own their government and get in there and do work.

—Says that "[m]andatory national service would change the relationship of people to their government and vice versa" and would lead to greater accountability required of leaders.

*—This point makes sense and is a compelling moral argument. Makes me think of how a volunteer army keeps us from having the kind of stakes in our government's decisions as we did when we had a military draft.*

◄ *Strong response notes in column 2 show reactions to the source*

—Moves into a section on the urgency of citizen involvement in deteriorating conditions, loss of economic status for poor and middle class, money spent on wars, and so forth.

*—I wish Rosenman could have offered more examples and maybe some statistics.*

—Mentions low voter turnout.

*—Could give more details.*

—Develops the reasons supporting his main claim by discussing his points: people would make a connection between policies and their effects; observing "constituencies poorly served by government" would increase people's involvement in government; service would connect Americans across typical barriers "by race, class, ethnicity, religion, geography, perhaps even age."

*—This thinking is useful in presenting one angle on my question. In my volunteer work I often saw how government service could be improved— made me want to do something.*

—Rosenman then briefly discusses the practical dimensions of his view—how to make a mandatory national service plan work. He mentions two-year service, stipends or salary, and credit toward education. He says that schools should make service an important part of the curriculum to build character and citizens....

*—I am glad he devotes some space to practical considerations. However, I wonder if I would have found my high school volunteering as effective if the school made me do it?*

—He acknowledges that any employees who might have their jobs taken by community-service workers should be given new opportunities, maybe training the service workers.

*—Good idea to confront this objection to mandatory public service.*

[Kent's research log continued to cover the whole article.]

**Part of Kent's strong response summary:**
Very useful article, not scholarly but clear in the argument it asserts. I will use this source to represent the liberal perspective on mandatory public service. Rosenman is a public service professor at Union Institute and University and clearly has a strong background in this issue. This article provides a broad-strokes approach and overview of the pro–national service position. I will want to give more depth to this view and also examine arguments against it.

# Shaping and Drafting

Your exploratory essay records the history of your researching and thinking process (what you read or whom you talked to, how you responded, how your thinking evolved). Along the way you can make your narrative more colorful and grounded by including your strategies for tracking down sources, your conversations with friends, your late-night trips to a coffee shop, and so forth. What you will quickly discover about this exploratory assignment is that it forces you actually to do the research. Unless you conduct your research in a timely fashion, you won't have any research process to write about.

Exploratory essays can be composed in two ways—what we might call the "real-time strategy" and the "retrospective strategy."

| Strategies for Composing an Exploratory Essay | |
| --- | --- |
| **Strategies** | **Advantages** |
| **Real-time strategy.** Compose the body of the essay during the actual process of researching and thinking. | Yields genuine immediacy—like a sequence of letters or e-mails sent home during a journey. |
| **Retrospective strategy.** Look back over your completed research notes and then compose the body of the essay. | Allows for more selection and shaping of details and yields a more artistically designed essay. |

In either case, the goal when writing with an exploratory aim is to reproduce the research and thinking process, taking the readers on the same intellectual and emotional journey you have just traveled. The exploratory essay has the general organizational framework shown in Figure 6.1.

There are a number of keys to writing successful exploratory papers. As you draft, pay particular attention to the following:

- ***Show how you chose sources purposively and reflectively rather than randomly.*** As you make a transition from one source to the next, help your reader see your thought processes. Note the following examples of bridging passages that reveal the writer's purposeful selection of sources:

  At this point, I decided I should investigate more thoroughly the drawbacks of mandatory national service, so I turned to an online *Time* article that was a direct response to Stengel: Michael Kinsley's "National Service? Puh-lease" (from Kent Ansen's essay, para. 7, p. 138).

  After reading Friedman's views of how globalization was changing lives in India and China, I realized that I needed to *talk* to some students from these countries, so I grabbed my backpack and headed to the International Student Center.

- ***Give your draft both open-form and closed-form features.*** Because your exploratory paper is a narrative, it follows an unfolding, open-form structure. Many of your paragraphs should open with chronological transitions such as "I *started* by reading," "*Early the next morning*, I headed for the library to...," "On the *next* day, I decided," or "*After* finishing...I *next* looked at...." At the same time, your summaries of your sources and your strong responses to them should be framed within closed-form structures with topic sentences and logical transitions: "This article, in raising objections to genetic screening of embryos, began changing my views about new advances in reproductive technology. Whereas before I felt..., now I feel...."

**FIGURE 6.1** Framework for an Exploratory Essay

| Introduction (one or more paragraphs) | • Establishes that your question is complex, problematic, and significant<br>• Shows why you are interested in it<br>• Presents relevant background<br><br>You can begin with your question or build up to it, using it to end your introductory section. |
|---|---|
| Body section 1 on first source | • Introduces your first source and shows why you started with it<br>• Provides rhetorical context and information about the source<br>• Summarizes the source's content and argument<br>• Offers your strong response to this source, frequently including both with-the-grain and against-the-grain points<br>• Talks about what this source contributes to your understanding of your question: What did you learn? What value does this source have for you? What is missing from this source that you want to consider? Where do you want to go from here? |
| Body section 2 on second source | • Repeats the process with a new source selected to advance the inquiry<br>• Explains why you selected this source (to find an alternative view, pursue subquestions, find more data, and so forth)<br>• Summarizes the source's argument<br>• Provides a strong response<br>• Shows how your cumulative reading of sources is shaping your thinking or leading to more questions |
| Body sections 3, 4, 5, etc., on additional sources | • Continues the process |
| Conclusion | • Wraps up your intellectual journey and explains where you are now in your thinking and how your understanding of your problem has changed<br>• Presents your current answer to your question based on all that you have read and learned so far, or explains why you still can't answer your question, or explains what further research you might do |
| Works Cited or References list | • Includes a complete list of citations in MLA or APA format, depending on your assignment |

- ***Show yourself wrestling with ideas.*** Readers want to see how your research stimulates your own thinking. Throughout, your paper should show you responding strongly to your sources. Here is a good example from Kent's paper on mandatory public service.

  However, Rosenman did not offer any concrete evidence in support of his claims. Instead, his philosophical approach helped me understand some of the moral arguments—essentially, that public service can make us better people who live in better communities—but these arguments would not convince people who value small government and dislike government intrusion on personal freedom. I was particularly drawn to the idea that national service would make people feel more invested in their government. I wondered if I could locate any evidence showing that community service led people to become more personally involved in working on our country's problems.

Although you might feel that sentences that show your mind talking its way through your research will sound too informal, they actually work well in exploratory essays to create interest and capture your critical thinking.

## Revising

Because an exploratory essay describes the writer's research and thinking in chronological order, most writers have little trouble with organization. When they revise, their major concern is to improve their essay's interest level by keeping it focused and lively. Often drafts need to be pruned to remove extraneous details and keep the pace moving. Frequently, introductions can be made sharper, clearer, and more engaging. Peer reviewers can give you valuable feedback about the pace and interest level of an exploratory piece. They can also help you achieve the right balance between summarizing sources and showing the evolution of your own thinking. As you revise, make sure you use attributive tags and follow proper stylistic conventions for quotations and citations.

## Questions for Peer Review

In addition to the generic peer review questions explained in Skill 11.4, ask your peer reviewers to address these questions:

### POSING THE PROBLEM

1. In the introduction, how has the writer tried to show that the problem is interesting, significant, and problematic? How could the writer engage you more fully with the initial problem?
2. How does the writer provide cues that his/her purpose is to explore a question rather than argue a thesis? How might the opening section of the draft be improved?

### NARRATING THE EXPLORATION

3. Is the body of the paper organized chronologically so that you can see the development of the writer's thinking? Where does the writer provide chronological transitions?
4. Part of an exploratory essay involves summarizing the argument of each new research source. Where in this draft is a summary of a source particularly clear and well developed? Where are summary passages either undeveloped or unclear or too long? How could these passages be improved?
5. Another part of an exploratory paper involves the writer's strong response to each source. Where in this draft is there evidence of the writer's own critical thinking and questioning? Where are the writer's ideas particularly strong and effective? Where are the writer's own ideas undeveloped, unclear, or weak?

6. Has the writer done enough research to explore the problem? How would you describe the range and variety of sources that the writer has consulted? Where does the writer acknowledge how the kinds of sources shape his or her perspective on the subject? What additional ideas or perspectives do you think the writer should consider?

## An Annotated Bibliography

WRITING PROJECT

6.4
Summarize and critique your research sources in an annotated bibliography.

Create an annotated bibliography that lists the research sources you have used for your exploratory project. Because annotated bibliographies can vary in the number, length, and kinds of entries, follow guidelines provided by your instructor. Some instructors may also require a critical preface that explains your research question and provides details about how you selected the bibliographic sources.

## What Is an Annotated Bibliography?

**Bibliographies** are alphabetized lists of sources on a given topic, providing readers with the names of authors, titles, and publication details for each source. Unlike a plain list of sources, an **annotated bibliography** also includes the writer's "annotation" or commentary on each source. These annotations can be either *summary-only* or *evaluative*.

- A **summary-only annotation** provides a capsule of the source's contents without any additional comments from the bibliography's author.
- An **evaluative annotation** adds the author's critique or assessment of the work, including comments about the source's rhetorical context, its particular strengths or weaknesses, and its usefulness or value.

Whichever type is used, the length of the annotation is a function of its audience and purpose. Brief annotations comprise only a few sentences (one standard approach—to be described later—uses three sentences) while longer annotations can be up to 150 words. Brief annotations are most common when the annotated bibliography has numerous entries; longer annotations, which allow for fuller summaries and more detailed analyses, are often more helpful for readers but can make an annotated bibliography too long if there are many sources.

Annotated bibliographies serve several important functions. First, writing an annotated bibliography engages researchers in exploratory thinking by requiring that they read sources rhetorically like experts, entering critically into scholarly conversations. Annotated bibliographies can also be valuable time-saving tools for new researchers in a field. By providing overview information about potential sources, they help new researchers determine whether a particular source might be useful for their own purposes. Think of source annotations as analogous to short movie reviews that help you select your next film. (What's this movie about? How good is it?) Additionally, annotated bibliographies can establish the writer's *ethos* by showing the depth, breadth, and competence of the writer's research. (A good annotated bibliography proves that you have read and thought about your sources.)

## Features of Annotated Bibliography Entries

Each entry has two main parts, the bibliographic citation and the annotation. The **bibliographic citation** should follow the conventions of your assigned documentation style such as the Modern Language Association (MLA) or the American Psychological Association (APA).

An **evaluative annotation** (the most common kind) typically includes three elements. In a three-sentence evaluative annotation, each element is covered in one sentence.

- *Rhetorical information,* including the source's rhetorical context, particularly its genre and (if not implied by the genre) its purpose and audience. Is this source a scholarly article? An op-ed piece? A blog? What is the author's purpose and who is the intended audience? Are there any political biases that need to be noted?
- *A summary of the source's content.* In some cases, a writer simply lists what is covered in the source. Whenever possible, however, summarize the source's actual argument. (Note: In a *summary-only* annotation, this summary is the only element included.)
- *The writer's evaluation of the source.* What are the source's particular strengths or weaknesses? How useful is the source for specific purposes? How might the writer use the source for his or her research project? (Or, if the annotated bibliography comes at the end of the project, how did the writer use the source?)

## Examples of Annotation Entries

Here are examples of different kinds of annotations based on Kent Ansen's research notes for one of his sources (see pp. 126–127):

### SUMMARY-ONLY ANNOTATION

Rosenman, Mark. "A Call for National Service." *Chronicle of Philanthropy* 2007: 38. *Proquest.* Web. 8 Feb. 2013.

Rosenman argues that compulsory national service would engage Americans directly with the urgent problems facing our nation, shifting Americans from being passive consumers of government services to active stakeholders who demand accountability from elected officials. He suggests that compulsory service would promote empathy for the poor and marginalized, create awareness of the real world impacts of public policy, and inspire a sense of shared responsibility for the results. He also provides some practical considerations for how to make compulsory service work.

### EVALUATIVE ANNOTATION

Rosenman, Mark. "A Call for National Service." *Chronicle of Philanthropy* 2007: 38. *Proquest.* Web. 8 Feb. 2013.

The article is a call to action directed at nonprofit leaders, urging them to build bipartisan support for compulsory national service and providing tips on how to make their proposals effective. It was published in the opinion section of the *Chronicle of Philanthropy*, which provides news and information to influence philanthropic professionals who likely already support an expansion of national service. The author argues that compulsory national service would engage Americans directly with the urgent problems facing the nation, shifting a disengaged and passive public to an active, engaged citizenry capable of holding the government accountable for its response. The article provides a good overview of the basic arguments and assumptions that support mandatory service and is helpful in understanding how people who already believe in national service think about its value and impact. However, its claims lack specific evidence and therefore read mostly as assumptions, which weakens the persuasive power of the piece and its usefulness as backing for the call for national service.

### THREE-SENTENCE EVALUATIVE ANNOTATION

Rosenman, Mark. "A Call for National Service." *Chronicle of Philanthropy* 2007: 38. *Proquest.* Web. 8 Feb. 2013.

This persuasive argument aims to help nonprofit leaders make an effective public policy case for compulsory national service. Rosenman argues that by connecting Americans with real-world problems and the people negatively affected by them, compulsory service would create active, responsive citizens who hold government accountable for results. This source provides some good general suggestions for how to make compulsory national service work and asserts many of the common arguments in support of it, although its claims are mostly assumptions unsupported by evidence.

## Writing a Critical Preface for Your Annotated Bibliography

Scholars who publish annotated bibliographies typically introduce them with a critical preface that explains the scope and purpose of the bibliography. When you write a critical preface for your own annotated bibliography, you have a chance to highlight your critical thinking and show the purposeful way that you conducted your research. Typically the critical preface includes the following information:

- A contextual overview that shows the purpose of the annotated bibliography and suggests its value and significance for the reader
- The research question posed by the author
- The dates during which the bibliography was compiled
- An overview of the number of items in the bibliography and the kinds of material included

A student example of an annotated bibliography with a critical preface is found in the Readings section of this chapter (pp. 141–143).

## Shaping, Drafting, and Revising

The key to producing a good annotated bibliography is to take good research notes as you read. Compare the various versions of the above annotations with Kent Ansen's research notes (pp. 126–127). Before composing your annotated bibliography, make sure that you understand your instructor's preferences for the number of entries required and for the length and kinds of annotations. Arrange the bibliography in alphabetical order as you would in a "Works Cited" (MLA format) or "References" (APA format) list.

The specific skills needed for an annotated bibliography are taught in various places in this text. If you are having problems with aspects of an annotated bibliography, you can find further instruction as follows.

| Problems With | Where to Find Help |
| --- | --- |
| Formatting the citations. | Refer to Skill 15.1 for MLA style, and Skill 15.2 for APA style. |
| Describing the rhetorical context and genre. | Reread Chapter 1, Concept 1.2. |
| Writing a summary. | Read Chapter 5, pages 88–90, on summary writing; read also Skill 14.2. |
| Writing an evaluation. | Use the strategies for strong response in Chapter 5, pages 92–98, and also Skill 14.1. |

## Questions for Peer Review

The following questions are based on the assumption that your instructor requires evaluative annotations and a critical preface. Adjust the questions to fit a different assignment.

### CRITICAL PREFACE

1. Where does the writer explain the following: The purpose and significance of the bibliography? The research question that motivated the research? The dates of the research? The kinds of sources included?
2. How could the critical preface be improved?

### BIBLIOGRAPHIC CITATIONS

3. Does each citation follow MLA or APA conventions? Pay particular attention to the formatting of sources downloaded from a licensed database or from the Web.
4. Are the sources arranged alphabetically?

### ANNOTATIONS

5. Where does each annotation include the following: Information about genre or rhetorical context? A capsule summary of the source's contents? An evaluative comment?
6. Identify any places where the annotations are confusing or unclear or where the writer could include more information.
7. How could one or more of the annotations be improved?

## Multimodal or Online Options

**Speech with Visual Aids (Flip Chart, PowerPoint, Prezi)** Deliver your exploratory paper as a formal speech supported with visual aids. You can imagine an occasion for a short speech in which the audience is interested in your exploratory process while you wrestled with an interesting and engaging problem. If you use PowerPoint or Prezi slides to illustrate your exploration, you can include slides showing how you found sources (screen shots of search results or database abstracts). If you used any online sources such as blogs or videos, you might use hyperlinks to show these to your audience also. Pay equal attention to the construction and delivery of your speech and to the multimodal design of the visual aids. Your goal is to reproduce for your audience the narrative of your thinking process, particularly the moments that advanced or complicated your thinking.

Our first reading is an exploratory essay by student writer Kent Ansen on mandatory public service for young adults. After completing the exploratory essay, Kent continued his research, writing a proposal argument on the benefits of instigating a mandatory public service. Kent's final argument is our sample MLA student research paper and appears in Chapter 10 (pp. 263–272).

### Kent Ansen (Student)
## Should the United States Establish Mandatory Public Service for Young Adults?

1 During high school, I volunteered at an afterschool tutoring program in a poor neighborhood near my school. My guidance counselor stressed the importance of volunteer work in strong college applications, which was my primary motivation for volunteering. The more I volunteered, though, the more I began to see evidence of the two-way benefits of volunteer work. The program I volunteered with connected community members to a number of resources, such as food and healthcare benefits, and organized community cleanups and neighborhood celebrations. At the same time, I diversified my resume and had memorable experiences that gave me a different view of the community I lived in and people who were struggling with issues like poverty and hunger.

2 This experience was in the back of my mind during some recent conversations I had with friends who are college seniors. As they make plans for their lives after graduation, some of them are questioning the value of their majors as they face the competitive job market. Others are not sure what they want to do, even after four years of focused study in a particular field. I have heard a lot of buzz about volunteer programs like AmeriCorps and Jesuit Volunteer Corps, which place volunteers in needy communities for a year in exchange for a living stipend and the opportunity to gain work experience. In fact, the tutoring program I volunteered with was run by an AmeriCorps team. This type of volunteer work seems like a valuable opportunity for our generation, often referred to as the "Lost Generation" because of our struggles to settle on career paths and find direction, find jobs at all, and achieve stability in our lives. I have even heard of proposals to bring back the draft, not necessarily for military service but for national service on a broader scale. While mandatory public service would probably be controversial, it might benefit the country and youth in numerous ways. Pondering what I could gain from a mandatory year working on a national service project, I decided to pose the following question for this exploratory paper: Should the United States require a year of national service for all its young adults?

3 To begin, I wanted to familiarize myself with current national service programs in the United States. First, I wanted to have a good grasp of the range of work that AmeriCorps workers do, so I consulted the AmeriCorps website. According to this site, team-based projects focus on service in five areas: "natural and other disasters,

infrastructure improvement, environmental stewardship and conservation, energy conservation, and urban and rural development." Another part of the site spelled out this work even more concretely, explaining that participants can "tutor and mentor disadvantaged youth, fight illiteracy, improve health services, build affordable housing, teach computer skills, clean parks and streams, manage or operate after-school programs, and help communities respond to disasters...." AmeriCorps also supports the work of nonprofit organizations such as Habitat for Humanity and the Red Cross.

4    I then did several Google searches using search terms such as "national public service," "mandatory public service," and "AmeriCorps." These searches gave me a quick overview of the issues. The first lead I followed in depth was an article from a fact-checking website run by the Annenberg Corporation, which explained a proposed bill in the House and the Senate aimed at expanding national service (Robertson). Called the GIVE Act ("Generations Invigorating Volunteerism and Education") this bill expands national service organizations like AmeriCorps and funds increased participation to include 250,000 volunteers by 2014. Currently, 75,000 people participate in national service programs, so the GIVE Act represents a drastic increase in participation. Notably, the GIVE Act is not a bill for mandatory national service. It seems heavily reliant on expanding the current AmeriCorps program, which places volunteers in a variety of different volunteer settings in nonprofit and public agencies in exchange for a living stipend and an education award to pay for student loans or future educational opportunities. The GIVE Act helped me understand the scale of our current national service system. I was encouraged that the GIVE Act has strong bipartisan support. It suggests that there is public support for an expansion of national service.

5    To understand what an expanded national service program would look like, I wanted to find out if anyone had ever proposed a model. From my notes on my original Google searches, I found a 2007 article from *Time* entitled "A Time to Serve" (Stengel), which I then located in print in our library. Stengel describes a ten-point plan for creating universal national service, including a cabinet-level Department of National Service and the government purchase of a "baby bond" for each American baby (56). This bond would mature to around $19,000 by the time the baby reached young adulthood. This money could then be accessed if the person committed to a year of national service. The plan also includes ideas for a rapid response corps for disasters like Hurricane Katrina and for creating a national service academy. In addition to offering practical suggestions about how a national service program would work, Stengel argues that "a republic, to survive, [needs] not only the consent of the governed but also their active participation," asserting that "free societies do not stay free without the involvement of their citizens" (51).

6    This article made me confident that mandatory national public service was feasible, but I also began to realize why many people might object to mandatory service. It is one thing to recruit more young adults to volunteer for public service. It is another thing to require them to do so through a draft-like process. But then I noted that this article does not actually advocate *mandatory* national service. Instead it's calling for the "compelling idea that devoting a year or more to national service, whether military or civilian, should become a countrywide rite of passage" (55) or a socially perpetuated norm, not a government-mandated one. It seems like a nation powered

by a socially conscious momentum rather than a national service law would inspire more pride in and ownership of the service experience. Yet, would the people who might most benefit from doing public service actually volunteer if they weren't compelled to serve? For these people, national service could be incredibly transformative, but they might miss out on these opportunities if service were optional.

7    At this point, I decided I should investigate more thoroughly the drawbacks of mandatory national service, so I turned to an online *Time* article that was a direct response to Stengel: Michael Kinsley's "National Service? Puh-lease." (I Googled Michael Kinsley and discovered that he is a widely known conservative writer.) Kinsley uses a sarcastic tone to raise several problems with a mandatory national service plan or voluntary plans with strong incentives to participate. He argues that Stengel's proposal for a $19,000 bond that a person could access after completing a year of service would appeal to poor people more than rich people. In effect, the rich would simply buy their way out of public service. He also notes the hypocrisy of using social pressure and government incentives to encourage participation and then calling it "volunteerism." He sees Stengel's proposal as an infringement on personal freedom and on free markets. Arguing that people are willing to do any job for the right amount of money, Kinsley wonders why we would force someone to work for drastically less than a traditional employee would be paid when there is already a supply of workers in the market willing to do the same job for reasonable pay. Instead of making someone happy by providing a decently paying job, Stengel's proposal would put poor people out of work and force volunteers to work unhappily at minimum wage. For me, Kinsley's most powerful point was a reference to George Orwell's novel *1984*, which he uses to paint a picture of people forced into doing jobs that they would otherwise not take. Kinsley is also worried that volunteer work would be "make-work," meaning bureaucrats would spend time finding trivial ways to keep all the volunteers busy.

8    While I think Kinsley vastly underestimates the value of community service, I do understand his concern that forcing people to volunteer could undermine its impact. For me, though, a larger problem is putting volunteers to work on projects that require a lot of care when the volunteers themselves may not feel the intrinsic motivations and empathy required to deliver good service because they were forced into the role rather than choosing it for themselves. His article made me consider exactly how our democracy and the market do and should work together to create a socially-optimal reality. I agree that mandating service is problematic in a country that values freedom, but I also agree that many young Americans seem to take our democracy for granted. I understand Kinsley's point that mandatory service would interfere with market solutions to problems. Yet my understanding of government is that it exists to provide goods and services that the market fails to provide on its own. If the market is failing poor people, why should we rely on it to provide the solutions? Again, the conflict seems to come back to values, in this case the disagreements between those who value market solutions and those who value government intervention.

9    I decided I needed to pursue the perspective of someone who values government intervention and found Mark Rosenman's 2007 article "A Call for National Service," which I located in the journal *Chronicle of Philanthropy* using the *Proquest*

*Complete* database. Rosenman's main argument is that military or civilian national service "may be invaluable for getting Americans more involved in their government and more concerned about influencing public policy." He argues that through this direct service, citizens become more involved in government-provided services and "would more likely demand accountability from their elected leaders." Rosenman is concerned that we have become citizens whose only responsibility to government is to pay taxes and user fees, which makes us customers who passively take from government without investing effort to maintain and manage our democracy. Becoming more involved through national service will help restore citizens to being "owners" of government.

10      Overall, I found Rosenman's argument compelling, even though it did not help me resolve the conflict between those who value market solutions and those who value government intervention. His thoughts on active versus passive citizens echoed some of the points raised by "A Time to Serve" and got me excited about the idea of using national service to reinvigorate our levels of public engagement. However, Rosenman did not offer any concrete evidence in support of his claims. Instead, his philosophical approach helped me understand some of the moral arguments—essentially, that public service can make us better people who live in better communities—but these arguments would not convince people who value small government and dislike government intrusion on personal freedom. I was particularly drawn to the idea that national service would make people feel more invested in their government. I wondered if I could locate any evidence showing that community service led people to become more personally involved in working on our country's problems.

11      At this point, I realized it would be helpful to gain the perspectives of young adults who had volunteered for public service. I decided to look more closely at the AmeriCorps website and discovered a link to a page of quotations from AmeriCorps members who served with Rise, an organization in Minnesota that helps people with disabilities and other problems become self-sufficient ("Americorps Testimonials"). Several alumni noted the learning opportunities offered by AmeriCorps such as better understanding of the kinds of problems experienced by vulnerable populations and the difficulty of getting help. Several alumni noted how AmeriCorps provided opportunities for professional development and gave them work skills and leadership experiences that would transfer to future careers. Others noted how inspired they were by the people they worked with, both clients and coworkers.

12      These testimonials highlighted how impactful a year of service can be for individuals professionally and socially. I became convinced again that community service nurtures personal growth and civic engagement. Through helping others, AmeriCorps members are also able to help themselves—some even note they gain so much more than they give. This seemed like direct evidence of the two-way benefits I had experienced as a volunteer in high school and highlighted the potential value of service opportunities in light of the challenges young adults are facing today. However, I reminded myself that these testimonials did not constitute a random sample of AmeriCorps volunteers and didn't provide evidence that every volunteer (much less somebody forced to serve) would experience the same benefits.

13    The testimonials highlighted the anecdotal evidence of the benefits of national service. However, I wanted to find out whether there were any empirical studies that showed these benefits. On the "Research and Evaluation" section of the AmeriCorps website, I found a report issued by Abt Associates, an independent social policy and research firm, titled "Serving Country and Community: A Longitudinal Study of Service in AmeriCorps" (Jastrzab et al.). The study examines the impacts on participants' civic engagement, education, employment and life skills by surveying members upon entering and completing a term of service, including some follow-up three years after enrollment in AmeriCorps. This study found that participation in AmeriCorps had positive impacts on civic engagement and employment outcomes. In comparison to a control group not enrolled in service, alumni across AmeriCorps programs demonstrated statistically significant gains in basic work skills. Additionally, civic engagement behavior and attitudes were positively affected. Participation in AmeriCorps led to higher community-based activism and to a greater belief that communities could identify and solve problems. This study seemed to corroborate the AmeriCorps testimonials, providing evidence of the benefits of national service in terms of greater civic engagement.

14    Looking back over my research, I think the rewards of national service to individual volunteers and the communities they serve are clear. However, I continue to worry about the feasibility of making national service a mandatory program. As I end this exploratory paper, I still have some more research and thinking to do before I am ready to start my proposal argument. I am leaning in the direction of supporting mandatory public service. I am convinced that such service will benefit America's communities and also help the "Lost Generation" find themselves through learning more about our country's problems and developing valuable job skills. But the clincher for me—if I go in the direction I am leaning—is that mandatory public service would get Americans more involved in their government.

## Works Cited

*AmeriCorps.* 2012. Web. 9 Feb. 2013.

"AmeriCorps Testimonials." *Rise: A Partnership that Works*. Rise, 2012. Web. 9 Feb. 2013.

Jastrzab, JoAnn, et al. "Serving Country and Community: A Longitudinal Study of Service in AmeriCorps." *Corporation for National and Community Service*. Abt Associates, Apr. 2007. Web. 10 Feb. 2013.

Kinsley, Michael. "National Service? Puh-lease." *Time Lists*. Time, 30 Aug. 2007. Web. 8 Feb. 2013.

Robertson, Lori. "Mandatory Public Service." *FactCheck.org*. Annenberg Public Policy Center, 31 Mar. 2009. Web. 6 Feb. 2013.

Rosenman, Mark. "A Call for National Service." *Chronicle of Philanthropy* 2007: 38. *Proquest.* Web. 8 Feb. 2013.

Stengel, Richard. "A Time to Serve." *Time* 10 Sept. 2007: 48–67. Print.

## THINKING CRITICALLY
### about "Should the United States Establish Mandatory Public Service for Young Adults?"

1. How does Kent show that his personal experience contributed to his interest in his chosen question?

2. Earlier in this chapter, we suggested ways to organize and strengthen an exploratory essay. Where do you see Kent including the following features: (a) A blend of open-form narrative moves with closed-form focusing sentences? (b) A purposeful selection of sources? (c) A consideration of the rhetorical context of his sources—that is, an awareness of the kinds of sources he is using and how the genre of the source influences its content? (d) Reflective/critical thinking that shows his strong response to his sources? (e) His dialectical thinking and critical evaluation of his sources?

3. Trace the evolution of Kent's ideas in this paper. How does his thinking change?

4. Read Kent's argument in favor of mandatory public service for young adults on pages 263–272. What new research did he do for his final argument? How do you see the exploratory paper contributing to Kent's argument in the final paper? How do differences in purpose (exploration versus persuasion) lead to different structures for the two papers?

5. What are the strengths and weaknesses of Kent's exploration of mandatory public service?

---

Our next reading is an excerpt from Kent's annotated bibliography based on the same research he did for his exploratory paper. We have used Kent's research for both examples so that you can compare an exploratory paper with an annotated bibliography. His original annotated bibliography contained six entries. We have printed three of these, along with his critical preface. Additionally, the evaluative annotated bibliography entry for the Rosenman article is shown on pages 132–133.

## Kent Ansen (student)
# Should the United States Establish Mandatory Public Service for Young Adults?

## An Annotated Bibliography

**Critical Preface**

1     Today, national service programs like AmeriCorps seem to be gaining the attention of young adults who are facing a hostile job market and are unsure about their futures. I have also noticed some proposals to create a kind of draft that would extend

beyond military service to require terms of civil service from young adults, putting them to work on projects that meet basic needs like hunger and poverty. These plans are always controversial, especially in America, where we value freedom of choice. With this research project, I set out to explore the following questions: Should the United States require a year of national service from all its young adults? How would a plan of this scale be feasible? These questions are particularly important during a time of scarce resources, Congressional budget battles, growing social and economic divisions among our citizens, and general public mistrust of government. The country seems to be reevaluating the optimal level of citizen involvement in public life and where we should invest public resources.

2      I conducted this research over several days in early February 2013. My research included a variety of sources: a scholarly research study, two articles from a popular newsmagazine, an article from an online non-profit-sector journal, two webpages that provided program overviews and background information, a fact-checking website, and a nonprofit webpage of testimonials from national service participants. This research helped me better understand our current system of national service opportunities and see how this system could be expanded. The testimonials and the scholarly research study by Jastrzab et al. also highlighted the impacts national service has on individual participants. Several of these sources (particularly Rosenman and Kinsley) illuminated the different values, beliefs, and assumptions that drive disagreements about mandatory national service. Ultimately, these sources convinced me that our nation and young adults could greatly benefit from expanding national service, although I remain concerned about the feasibility of implementing a mandatory plan.

### Annotated Bibliography

Jastrzab, JoAnn, et al. "Serving Country and Community: A Longitudinal Study of Service in AmeriCorps." *Corporation for National and Community Service*. Abt Associates, Apr. 2007. Web. 10 Feb. 2013.
    This scholarly research report examines the impacts of AmeriCorps participation on participants' attitudes and behavior related to civic engagement, education, employment and life skills. The findings of the study were mixed. Surveys of participants initially and up to three years after enrolling in AmeriCorps revealed generally positive gains, particularly in measures of civic engagement, but the findings were not always statistically significant and revealed no impacts in educational outcomes. This study is helpful in providing statistically significant data on the positive impacts AmeriCorps participation can have on participants' future attitudes and behavior and provides some evidence of an important claim that national service increases lifelong civic engagement. However, it does not identify the impacts of mandatory service, as AmeriCorps enrollment is voluntary.

Kinsley, Michael. "National Service? Puh-lease." *Time Lists*. Time, 30 Aug. 2007. Web. 8 Feb. 2013.
    This op-ed written by a popular conservative writer offers a direct response to and critique of Stengel's proposal for universal national service. Kinsley scornfully addresses the Baby Boomer generation Stengel represents, chastising their attempts to force national service on young people from the safety of retirement. He opposes universal service on the following grounds: (1) service cannot be both universal and voluntary, which jeopardizes freedom of

choice and undermines the virtue of volunteerism, (2) capitalism and our system of voting and taxation, when functioning well, properly respond to social needs, and (3) there is not enough work to go around, so a universal corps would end up doing unimportant work. This article provides a clear, well-reasoned conservative perspective on the problems with mandatory national service.

Stengel, Richard. "A Time to Serve."*Time* 10 Sept. 2007: 48-67. Print.

This article from a popular news magazine argues that the next president and the US more broadly should take action to make national service a central part of American culture because a healthy republic requires not only the consent but the active participation of its citizens. It outlines a 10-point plan for how to institute universal national service by expanding the existing network of opportunities (like AmeriCorps) and creating new corps in education, health, environmental work, and disaster response. The article proposes using baby bonds that mature during young adulthood and increasing private investment to pay for the expansion. The proposal and 10-point plan are particularly valuable in illustrating how to make service work on a universal scale while simultaneously emphasizing why voluntary service motivated by a shared culture is superior to a mandatory plan.

## THINKING CRITICALLY
about "Should the United States Establish Mandatory Public Service for Young Adults? An Annotated Bibliography"

1. Explain how Kent includes the three common elements of an evaluative annotation (genre/rhetorical context, summary of content, evaluation) in each of his annotations.

2. Compare Kent's annotated bibliography with his exploratory essay (pp. 136–140), noting differences between the way each source is described in the bibliography versus the essay. What insights do you get from the exploratory essay that are missing from the bibliography? What information about the sources comes through more clearly in the bibliography than in the essay?

3. How might Kent use information and points in this annotated bibliography in his researched argument?

# 7 ANALYZING IMAGES

This chapter asks you to think about three major kinds of communication through images—documentary or news photos, paintings, and advertisements—to increase your visual literacy skills. By **visual literacy**, we mean your awareness of the importance of visual communication and your ability to interpret or make meaning out of images by examining their context and visual features. We focus on the ways that images influence our conceptual and emotional understanding of a phenomenon and the ways that they validate, reveal, and construct the world.

This chapter invites you to analyze images in order to understand their rhetorical and experiential effects. To **analyze** means to divide or dissolve the whole into its parts, examine these parts carefully, look at the relationships among them, and then use this understanding of the parts to better understand the whole—how it functions, what it means. As Chapter 1 explains (Concept 1.2), when you analyze, your goal is to raise interesting questions about the image or object being analyzed—questions that perhaps your reader hasn't thought to ask—and then to provide tentative answers, supported by points and details derived from your own close examination.

The ability to analyze visual texts rhetorically is important because we are surrounded by glamorous and disturbing images from photojournalism, the Internet, billboards, newspapers, television, and magazines—images that, as one critic has stated, "have designs on us," yet we may not fully understand how they affect us.

## Engaging Image Analysis

To introduce you to image analysis, we provide an exercise that asks you to interact with several news photographs on the issue of immigration reform.

Immigration reform is one of the most complex issues facing the United States today; the problem is particularly acute with respect to immigrants from Mexico and Central America, who are drawn to the United States by employment opportunities. U.S. citizens benefit from immigrants' inexpensive labor, which helps keep the prices of services and goods low. In addition to a sizable Mexican-American citizenry, more than ten million illegal immigrants currently live in the United States. All these factors give rise to a number of controversial questions: Should the United States increase border security and focus on building impassable barriers? Should it deport illegal immigrants or explore routes to making them citizens? Should it crack down on employers of illegal immigrants or should it implement a guest worker program to legitimize immigrant labor?

Public debate about immigration issues is particularly susceptible to manipulation by the rhetorical appeal of images. Examine these news photos and consider their rhetorical effects.

**FIGURE 7.1** Wall between Tijuana, Mexico, and the United States

**FIGURE 7.2** Immigrants Crossing the Border Illegally

**FIGURE 7.3** Protestors Marching for Compassionate Treatment of Immigrants

**FIGURE 7.4** Immigrants Saying Their Citizenship Pledge

**ON YOUR OWN**

1. What objects, people, or places stand out in each photo? Does the photo look candid or staged, taken close-up or from a distance? How do the angle of the photo (taken from below or above the subject) and the use of color contribute to the effect?

2. What is the dominant impression conveyed by each photo?

3. Examine how the similarities and differences among the four photos convey different rhetorical impressions of immigrants, Latino culture, or the role of immigrants and ethnic diversity in U.S. culture.

**IN CONVERSATION**

Share your responses to the photos and then speculate about how you might use these photos to enhance the persuasiveness of particular claims. Choose one or two photos to support or attack each claim below and explain what the photo could contribute to the argument.

1. The United States should install stricter border security using physical barriers, increased border patrols, and more visa checks.

2. The United States should offer amnesty and citizenship to immigrants who are currently in the United States illegally.

**7.1**

Analyze the persuasive effects of images and how these effects are created.

# Understanding Image Analysis: Documentary and News Photographs

Documentary and news photos are aimed at shaping the way we think and feel about an event or cultural/historical phenomenon. For example, consider the newspaper photos, TV news footage, or Internet videos of the billowing clouds of smoke and ash from the collapsing World Trade Center towers on September 11, 2001. Figures 7.5, 7.6, and 7.7 present three well-known documentary images of this event, taken from three different positions and at three slightly different moments as the event unfolded.

Although all three photos convey the severity of the terrorist attack, each has a different impact. Figure 7.5 records the event shortly before the north tower collapsed and just after the south tower was struck by the second plane, marked in the photo by the red flames. The sheer magnitude and horror of the moment-by-moment action unfolding before our eyes evoked shock, anger, and feelings of helplessness in Americans.

In contrast to the first image, which was taken from a distance below the towers, Figure 7.6 was taken by a police detective in a helicopter searching for survivors on the roof of the north tower before it collapsed. This photo suggests the apocalyptic explosion and implosion of a contemporary city. The destruction pictured here is too massive to be an ordinary event such as a fire in a major building, and yet the streams of ash and smoke don't reveal exactly what is happening.

Another well-publicized view of this event is that of the firefighters on the ground, seen in Figure 7.7. Here the firefighters, risking their lives while trying to rescue the people in the towers, have come to symbolize the self-sacrifice, courage, and also vulnerability of the human effort in the face of such colossal

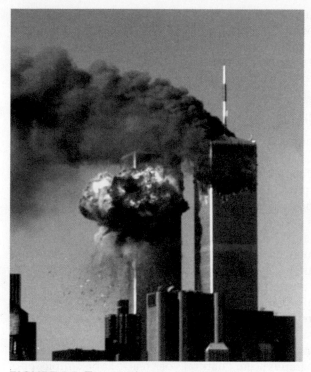

**FIGURE 7.5** Terrorist Attack on the World Trade Center

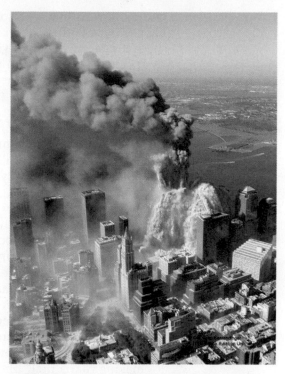

**FIGURE 7.6** World Trade Center Attack Seen from the Air

**FIGURE 7.7** Firefighters in the World Trade Center Wreckage destruction. This image also suggests the terror and suspense of a science-fiction-like conflict. All three photos, while memorializing the same event, have different specific subjects, angles of vision, and emotional and mental effects.

The rest of this section introduces you to the ways that photographers think about their use of the camera and the effects they are trying to achieve.

## Angle of Vision and Credibility of Photographs

Although the word "documentary" is associated with an objective, transparent, unmediated glimpse of reality, the relationship of documentary photography to its subject matter has always been complex. Historians are now reassessing early documentary photographs, exploring the class and race agendas of the photographers in the kinds of scenes chosen, the photographers' stance toward them, and the wording of the narratives accompanying the photographs. In other words, despite a photograph's appearance of capturing a moment of reality (whose reality?), its effect is always influenced by the photographer's rhetorical angle of vision conveyed through the framing and focusing power of the camera. Perhaps now more than ever, we are aware that the photographer's purpose and techniques actually shape the reality that viewers see. (Think of the multiple cameras tracking a football game and replaying a touchdown from different angles, often creating very different impressions of a particular play.)

The photographer's power to shape reality is enhanced by various strategies for making "unnatural" photographs seem "natural" or "real." For example, photographs can be manipulated or falsified in the following ways:

- staging images (scenes that appear spontaneous but are really posed)
- altering images (airbrushing, reshaping body parts)
- selecting images or parts of images (cropping photographs so that only certain parts are shown)
- mislabeling images (putting a caption on a photograph that misrepresents the image)
- constructing images (putting the head of one person on the body of another)

Research has revealed that many famous photographs were tampered with. As early as the Civil War, composite photos of generals were created by combining heads, bodies, and scenery and inserting figures into scenes. Today this manipulation is also conducted by amateur photographers using photo-editing software. The potential for altering images gives us additional reasons for considering the active role of the photographer and for investigating the credibility and purpose behind images.

## How to Analyze a Documentary Photograph

Photographs are always created and interpreted within a social, political, and historical context—the original context in which the photograph was made and viewed and your own context as a current viewer and interpreter. At play are the assumptions, values, and cultural knowledge of the photographer, the original viewers, and the later viewers. Also at play are the sites in which the photograph is viewed—whether in an original news story, a museum, an upscale art exhibit, an expensive coffee-table book, a documentary film, an Internet site, or a textbook. These sites invite us to respond in different ways. For example, one site may call us to social action or deepen our understanding of an event, while another aims to elicit artistic appreciation or to underscore cultural differences.

**Examining the Rhetorical Contexts of a Photo** A first step in analyzing a documentary photograph is to consider its various rhetorical contexts. The following chart will help you ask illuminating questions.

| Strategies for Analyzing the Rhetorical Contexts of Documentary Photographs | |
|---|---|
| **Context** | **Questions to Ask** |
| Photographer's purpose and context in making the photograph | • What was the photographer's original intention/purpose in making the image (to report an event, convey information, persuade viewers to think about the event or people a certain way)?<br>• What was the original historical, cultural, social, and political context in which the photograph was taken? |
| Original context for displaying the photograph | • Where was the photograph originally viewed (news story, photo essay, scientific report, public exhibit, advocacy Web site)?<br>• How does the original title or caption, if any, reflect the context and shape impressions of the image? |
| Cultural contexts for interpreting the photograph | • How does the photograph's appearance in a particular place influence your impression of it?<br>• How does your own cultural context differ from that of original viewers?<br>• What assumptions and values do you bring to the context? |

**Examining the Effects of a Photo on a Viewer** In addition to considering the contexts of photographs, we can explore how photographs achieve their effects—that is, how they move us emotionally or intellectually, how they imply arguments and cause us to see the subject in a certain way. An image might soothe us or repel us; it might evoke our sympathies, trigger our fears, or call forth a web of interconnected ideas, memories, and associations.

Before you begin a detailed analysis of a photograph, you will find it helpful to explore the photograph's immediate impact.

- What words come to mind when you view this photograph?
- What is the mood or overall feeling conveyed by the photo?
- Assuming that photographs "have designs on us," what is this photograph trying to get you to feel, think, do, or "see"?

The following chart will help you examine a photograph in detail in order to analyze how it achieves its persuasive effects.*

| Strategies for Analyzing the Persuasive Effects of Photographs and Other Images | |
|---|---|
| **What to Examine** | **Some Questions to Ask about Rhetorical Effect** |
| **Subject matter: People in portraits:** Portraits can be formal or informal and can emphasize character or social role.<br><br>The gaze of the human subjects can imply power through direct eye contact and deference or shyness through lack of eye contact. | Is the emphasis on identity, character, and personality, or representative status (wife of wealthy merchant, king, soldier, etc.), or symbolic (an image of wisdom, daring, etc.)?<br><br>What do details of clothing and setting (a room's furnishings, for example) reveal about historical period, economic status, national or ethnic identity? |
| **Subject matter: People in scenes:** Scenes can make a statement about everyday life or capture some aspect of a news event or crisis. | What is the relationship of the people to each other and the scene? Can you re-create the story behind the scene?<br><br>Does the scene look natural/realistic or staged/aesthetically attractive? |
| **Subject matter: Landscape or nature:** Scenes can focus on nature or the environment as the dominant subject. | If the setting is outdoors, what are the features of the landscape: urban or rural, mountain or desert?<br><br>What aspects of nature are shown?<br><br>If people are in the image, what is the relationship between nature and the human figures?<br><br>What vision of nature is the artist constructing—majestic, threatening, hospitable, tamed, orderly, wild? |

*We are indebted to Terry Barrett, Professor Emeritus of Art Education at Ohio State University, for his formulation of questions, "Looking at Photographs, Description and Interpretation," and to Claire Garoutte, Associate Professor of Photography at Seattle University, for informing our discussion of context in analyzing documentary photographs.

| What to Examine | Some Questions to Ask about Rhetorical Effect |
|---|---|
| **Distance from subject:** Close-ups tend to increase the intensity of the image and suggest the importance of the subject.<br><br>Long shots tend to blend the subject into the environment. | Are viewers brought close to the subject or distanced from it?<br><br>How does the distance from the subject contribute to the effect of the photo or painting? |
| **Angle and orientation:** The vantage point from which the photograph was taken and the positioning of the photographer to the subject determine the effect of images.<br><br>Low angle makes the subject look larger. High angle makes the subject look smaller. A level angle implies equality.<br><br>Front views tend to emphasize the persons in the image. Rear views often emphasize the scene or setting. | How does the angle influence what you see?<br><br>Why do you think this angle was chosen?<br><br>How would the photograph have changed if it had been taken from another angle? |
| **Framing:** Framing determines what is inside the image and what is closed off to viewers; it's a device to draw the attention of viewers. | How does the framing of the image direct your attention?<br><br>What is included and what is excluded from the image?<br><br>How does what the photo or painting allows you to see and know contribute to its effect?<br><br>Why do you think this particular frame was chosen? |
| **Light:** The direction of the light determines the shadows and affects the contrasts, which can be subtle or strong.<br><br>Lighting has different effects if it is natural or artificial, bright, soft, or harsh. | How does the light reveal details?<br><br>What does the direction of the light contribute to the presence of shadows?<br><br>How do these shadows affect the mood or feeling of the photo? |
| **Focus:** Focus refers to what is clearly in focus or in the foreground of the photo versus what is blurry.<br><br>The range between the nearest and farthest thing in focus in the photo is referred to as the depth of field. | What parts of the image are clearly in focus?<br><br>Are any parts out of focus?<br><br>What effect do these choices have on viewers' impression of the image?<br><br>How great is the depth of field and what effect does that have? |

*(continued)*

| What to Examine | Some Questions to Ask about Rhetorical Effect |
|---|---|
| **Scale, space, and shape:** Size/scale and shape affect prominence and emphasis. Size and scale can be natural, minimized, or exaggerated.<br><br>Use of space can be shallow, deep, or both.<br><br>Both positive shapes and voids can draw viewers' attention. | How do the scale, space, and shape of objects direct viewers' attention and affect a feeling or mood?<br><br>Are shapes geometric and angular or flowing and organic?<br><br>Are shapes positive such as objects, or negative such as voids? |
| **Use of repetition, variety, and balance:** Repetition of elements can create order, wholeness, and unity.<br><br>Variety can create interest.<br><br>Balance can create unity and harmony. | What elements are repeated in this image?<br><br>What variety is present, say, in shapes?<br><br>Does the visual weight of the photo seem to be distributed evenly on the sides, top, and bottom?<br><br>What roles do repetition, variety, and balance play in the impression created by the photo? |
| **Line:** Lines can be curved and flowing, straight, or disjointed and angular.<br><br>Lines can be balanced/symmetrical, stable, and harmonious, or disjointed and agitated. | Does the use of line create structure and convey movement/action or calm/stasis?<br><br>How does the use of line control how viewers look at the photo or painting? |
| **Color:** Choice of black and white can reflect the site of publication, the date of the photo, or an artistic choice.<br><br>Colors can contribute to the realism and appeal; harmonious colors can be pleasing; clashing or harsh colors can be disturbing. | How many colors are used? What is the relationship of the colors? Which colors dominate? Are the colors warm and vibrant or cool, bright, or dull?<br><br>How are light and dark used? How does the use of color direct viewers' attention and affect the impression of the image?<br><br>What emotional response do these colors evoke? |

## Sample Analysis of a Documentary Photograph

To illustrate how a documentary photograph can work on the viewer's mind and heart, we show you our own analysis of a photo titled *The Fall of the Berlin Wall* (Figure 7.8), taken by photojournalist Peter Turnley in 1989. At the time, the Berlin Wall, which separated communist East Berlin from democratic West Berlin, symbolized the oppression of communism. In 1987 President Ronald Reagan appealed to Mikhail Gorbachev, president of the Union of Soviet Socialist Republics, saying in a famous speech, "Mr. Gorbachev, tear down this wall." When the border opened in November 1989, marking the end of communist rule in Eastern Europe, East Berliners flooded into West Berlin, sparking weeks of celebration. Peter Turnley is a world-famous American photojournalist whose photos of major world events have appeared on the covers of *Newsweek* as well as international magazines. This photograph appeared in a 1996 exhibit (and

**FIGURE 7.8**  Fall of the Berlin Wall, 1989, by Peter Turnley

later a book) entitled *In Time of War and Peace* at the International Center of Photography in New York.

This documentary photograph of a celebratory scene following the opening of the Berlin Wall in 1989 uses elements of framing, orientation, focus, balance, and color to convey the dominant impression of a life-changing explosion of energy and emotion triggered by this significant event. This distance photo is divided into three horizontal bands—the sky, the wall, and the celebratory crowd—but the focal point is the yelling, triumphant German youth sitting astride the wall, wearing jeans, a studded belt, and a black jacket. The graffiti indicate that the photo was taken from the West Berlin side (East Berliners were not permitted to get close to the wall), and the light post between the two cranes was probably used to illuminate the no-man zone on the communist side.

Every aspect of the photograph suggests energy. In contrast with the mostly homogeneous sky, the wall and the crowd contain many diverse elements. The wall is heavily graffitied in many colors, and the crowd is composed of many people. The wall looks crowded, tattered, and dirty, something to be torn down rather than cleaned up. Most of the graffiti consist of tags, people's response to the ugly obstruction of the wall; West Berliners had no power to destroy the wall, but they could mark it up. The slightly blurred crowd of heads suggests that the people are in motion. At first it is hard to tell if they are angry protesters storming the wall or celebrators cheering on the German youth. The photograph captures this dual emotion—anger and joy—all at once.

At the center of the photograph is the German youth, whose dark jacket makes him stand out against the light blue sky. A few days earlier the wall had fenced him in (at that time, it would have been unthinkable even to approach the wall lest he be shot by border guards). Now he rides the wall like an American cowboy at a rodeo. He has conquered the wall. He has become transformed from prisoner to liberator. His cowboy gesture, reflecting European fascination with American cowboy movies, becomes the symbol of the ideological West, the land of freedom, now the wave of the future for these reunited countries. He holds in his hand a tool (a hammer or chisel?) used to chip away the wall symbolically, but the position of his arm and hand suggests a cowboy with a pistol.

What makes this photograph so powerful is the distance. Had Turnley used a telescopic lens to focus on the German youth up close, the photograph would have been about the youth himself, a personal story. But by placing the youth into a larger frame that includes the crowd, the long expanse of ugly wall, and the cranes and lamppost behind the wall, Turnley suggests both the enormous public and political nature of this event and the implications for individual lives. The youth appears to be the first of the energized crowd to demonstrate the conquering of the powerful barrier that had shaped so many German lives for almost three decades. Thus the composition of this photo packs many layers of meaning and symbolism into its depiction of this historic event.

---

**FOR WRITING AND DISCUSSION**

## Exploring a Photograph's Compositional Elements and Rhetorical Effect

In the last eight years, documentary photographs have played a key role in persuading audiences that climate change is a serious threat that must be addressed through stricter carbon dioxide emission limits and investments in clean energy. One recurring image shows mountains with receding or disappearing glaciers. An example is the photograph on page 275 at the beginning of Part 3.

1. Working in groups or individually, describe and interpret this photo using questions from the strategies charts for analyzing the context, composition, and rhetorical effects of photos (p. 149 and pp. 150–152). What is the dominant impression conveyed by this photograph?
2. Then using the Internet, search for another photograph that is currently being used in the public discussion of climate change (for example, a photograph employed by environmentalists to fight climate change on an advocacy Web site). Analyze its context, composition, and rhetorical effect.
3. If you were writing to underscore to young voters the seriousness of climate change, which photograph—the one on page 275, the one you found on the Internet, or another—would you choose and why?

---

**7.2**
Respond to visual images as a more informed citizen and perceptive cultural critic.

## Understanding Image Analysis: Paintings

When you analyze a painting, many of the strategies used for analyzing documentary photographs still apply. You still look carefully at the subject matter of the painting (the setting, the people or objects in the setting, the arrangement in space, the clothing, the gaze of persons, the implied narrative story, and so forth). Likewise, you consider the painter's distance from the subject, the angle of orientation, the framing, and other features that paintings share with photographs. Additionally, your analysis of paintings will be enriched if you consider, as you did with documentary photographs, the context in which the painting was originally created and originally viewed as well as your own cultural context and place of viewing.

But painters—by means of their choice of paints, their brushstrokes, their artistic vision, and their methods of representation—often do something quite different from photographers. For example, they can paint mythological or imaginary subjects and can achieve nonrepresentational effects not associated with a camera such as a medieval allegorical style or the striking distortions of Cubism. Also, the long history of painting and the ways that historical periods influence painters' choices of subject matter, medium, and style affect what viewers see and feel about paintings. Background on the artist, historical period, and style of paintings (for example, Baroque, Impressionism, Expressionism, and Cubism) can be found in sources such as the Oxford Art Online database. In analyzing paintings, art critics and historians often contrast paintings that have similar subject matter (for example, two portraits of a hero, two paintings of a biblical scene, two landscapes) but that create very different dominant impressions and effects on viewers.

## How to Analyze a Painting

Just as with photographs, you should ground your interpretation of a painting in close observation. Many of the elements introduced in the strategies chart on pages 150–152 for analyzing photographs can apply or be adapted to the analysis of paintings. In addition, you will want to examine the following elements of the paintings you are analyzing.

### Strategies for Analyzing the Particular Elements of Paintings

| Elements to Analyze | Questions to Ask about Rhetorical Effect |
| --- | --- |
| **Design and shape of the painting:** The width to height, division into parts, and proportional relationship of parts influence the impression of the painting. | What is the viewer's impression of the shape of the painting and the relationship of its parts? How does line organize the painting? Is the painting organized along diagonal, horizontal, or vertical lines? |
| **Medium, technique, and brushstrokes:** The material with which the painting is made (for example, pen and ink, tempera/ water colors, charcoal, oil paints on paper or canvas) and the thickness and style of brushstrokes determine the artistic effect. | In what medium is the artist working? How does the medium contribute to the impression of the painting? Are brushstrokes sharp and distinct or thick, layered, or fused? Are they delicate and precise or vigorous? What effect does the awareness or lack of awareness of brushstrokes have on the appearance of the painting? |

## Sample Analysis of a Painting

As an example of a visual analysis of a painting, we offer an interpretation of a famous painting by Pierre-Auguste Renoir (1841–1919), a French Impressionist painter of the late nineteenth century. The French Impressionists were recognized for their refusal to paint old themes; their embrace of scenes of modern society, especially the city and suburbs; and their experimentation with light and brush-strokes as a way to capture fleeting impressions. Figure 7.9 shows Renoir's oil painting *La Loge* (The Theater Box), which he painted as his main contribution to the first exhibit of Impressionist paintings in 1874. Impressionist paintings were considered too *avant garde* to be displayed at the conservative state-controlled Salon, which was the official arbiter and channel of the work of established French artists.

Renoir's *La Loge* depicts social life in nineteenth-century urban society as an occasion to act out social roles. This painting of a man and a woman elegantly dressed in a theater box at the opera, a popular social spot of the period, suggests that attending the theater/opera entailed displaying one's wealth, being seen, and inspecting others as much as it did watching a performance. This painting focuses intensely on two members of the audience and specifically on the woman, who catches and holds our gaze. While the man in the background is looking at some-one in the audience through his opera glasses, the woman looks directly at view-ers and invites their attention.

Renoir has compelled viewers to dwell on this woman by a number of his choices in this painting. He has chosen to paint her in a tightly framed close-up

**FIGURE 7.9** Renoir's *La Loge* (1874)

image, which the slightly off-center woman dominates. Her face and eyes convey the impression that she and the viewer are staring at each other, while in the shadows the man's eyes are blocked by his opera glasses. Thus this painting combines the woman's portrait with a scene at the opera, even though most of the setting, the theater box, is excluded from the painting. (We know we are at the opera because of the painting's title and the man's and woman's accessories.) There seems to be a story behind the scene: What is the man looking at and why is he not noticing the woman as we, the viewers, are compelled to do? This depiction of a moment seems to be less a shared experience of relationship and more a site for performance: men engaged in looking, women inviting the gaze of others.

Another choice Renoir has made to focus viewers' attention on the woman is his striking use of color. In this painting, the color palette is not large—white, black, brown/gold/sepia, with her red lips and red flowers on her bodice. The white of her face and her upper body is the brightest, suggesting light shining on her. Renoir also highlights the woman with short, thick brushstrokes, which give her shimmering, elegant dress texture and the impression of silk, velvet, and lace. As additional signs of wealth, she wears earrings, a gold bracelet, a flower in her hair, and a flower at her bosom. The stark contrast of the black and white in her dress, the white of her face, and the red of her lips—and the agitated diagonal but converging lines of the stripes of her dress that, along with her arms angled out from her body, shape her into a diamond—all work to direct viewers' eyes to her bosom and most of all to her face. Although the expression of the woman is calm, smiling in mild amusement or subtle emotion, the painting captures intensity, perhaps excitement or anticipation, through the sharp contrast of the red, white, and black. The piece is fairly still, and yet we are transfixed by this woman's eyes and lips. With the complex interaction of artistic elements in this painting, Renoir has invited viewers to experience an exciting scene of privileged nineteenth-century urban life.

---

## Contrasting the Compositional Features of Two Paintings

**FOR WRITING AND DISCUSSION**

This exercise asks you to apply the analysis strategies presented on pages 155 and 150–152 to examine the pastel painting *Carousel* by Camille Pissarro shown in Figure 7.10 and to contrast it with Renoir's painting in Figure 7.9. Camille Pissarro (1830–1903) was also a French Impressionist who regularly exhibited his works in Impressionist exhibitions. He painted *Carousel* in 1885; the medium is pastel on paper mounted on board.

**Your task**: Working individually or in groups, analyze Pissarro's painting and then find some striking points of commonality or difference with the Renoir painting that you think merit discussion.

- Begin by applying the strategies for analyzing photographic images and paintings on pages 150–152 and 155.
- After you have analyzed the visual features of the paintings, consider why Pissarro titled his painting *Carousel*.

*(continued)*

**FIGURE 7.10** *Carousel* by Camille Pissarro (1885)

- Finally, what are the thematic differences between these two paintings? How do these paintings, both Impressionistic images of well-dressed women at leisure, create similar or different effects on viewers? What view or feeling about life or about the artists' worlds is conveyed in each painting? What way of seeing or thinking are these paintings persuading you to adopt?

## Understanding Image Analysis: Advertisements

The images in advertisements are fascinating to analyze. Like other images, they employ the rhetorical strategies we described in the section on documentary photographs. Often, the ad's words (called the "copy") also contribute to its rhetorical effect. Moreover, ads make a more direct and constant demand on us than do documentary photographs and paintings. Advertising, a multibillion-dollar global industry whose business is communicating across a wide range of media to stimulate the purchase of products or services, comes to us in multiple forms: not just as slick, glamorous magazine ads, but also as direct mail, billboards, radio and television commercials, e-advertisements, banners, pop-ups, and spam. Figures 7.11 and 7.12, a billboard and a bus ad, illustrate the ordinary ubiquity of ads. Because of advertising's powerful role in shaping our culture and influencing our self-images, we have good reason to analyze the rhetorical strategies of advertisers.

**FIGURE 7.11** A Billboard Ad

**FIGURE 7.12** Ad on a City Bus

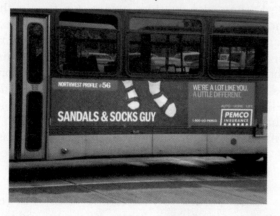

## Examining the Appeal of Ads

Think about the images and words in the two car insurance ads in Figures 7.11 and 7.12.

1. What do you notice most about the images and copy in these ads?
2. What is the appeal of these ads?
3. How are these ads designed to suit their contexts, a billboard and a bus panel? Why would they be less suitable for a magazine?

## How Advertisers Think about Advertising

Although cultural critics frequently focus on ads as manipulative messages that need to be decoded to protect unwary consumers, we confess that we actually enjoy ads, appreciate how they hold down the consumer cost of media, and admire their often-ingenious creativity. (We suspect that others secretly enjoy ads also: Think of how the Super Bowl is popular both for its football and for its ads.) In this section, we take a look at advertising from a marketer's point of view in order to deepen your awareness of an ad's context and the many behind-the-scenes decisions and negotiations that produced it. Whether marketing professionals design an individual ad or a huge marketing campaign, they typically begin by asking questions.

**Who Is Our Target Audience?** At the outset, marketers identify one or more target audiences for their product or service. They often use sophisticated psychological research to identify segments of the population who share similar values, beliefs, and aspirations and then subdivide these categories according to age, gender, region, income level, ethnicity, and so forth. Think of the different way you'd pitch a product or service to, say, Wal-Mart shoppers versus Neiman Marcus shoppers, steak eaters versus vegans, or skateboarders versus geeks.

**How Much Media Landscape Can We Afford?** While identifying their target audience, marketers also consider how much terrain they can afford to occupy on the enormous media landscape of billboards, newspapers, magazines, mailing lists, Internet pop-ups, mobile ads, TV and radio commercials, posters, naming rights for sports stadiums, T-shirts, coffee mugs, product placements in films, sandwich boards, or banners carried across the sky by propeller airplanes. Each of these sites has to be rented or purchased, with the price depending on the perceived quality of the location and the timing. For example, a thirty-second TV commercial during the 2013 Super Bowl cost $3.8 million, and a one-time, full-page ad in a nationally circulated popular magazine can cost up to $500,000 or more. Overall, advertisers hope to attain the best possible positioning and timing within the media landscape at a price they can afford.

**What Are the Best Media for Reaching Our Target Audience?** A marketer's goal is to reach the target audience efficiently and with a minimum of overflow—that is, messages sent to people who are not likely buyers. Marketers are keenly aware of both media and timing: Note, for example, how daytime TV is dominated by ads for payday loans, exercise equipment, or technical colleges, while billboards around airports advertise rental cars. Women's fashion magazines advertise lingerie and perfume but not computers or life insurance, while dating services advertise primarily through Internet ads.

**Is Our Goal to Stimulate Direct Sales or to Develop Long-Term Branding and Image?** Some ads are intended to stimulate retail sales directly: "Buy two, get one free." In some cases, advertisements use information and argument to show how their product or service is superior to that of their competitors. Most advertisements, however, involve parity products such as soft drinks, deodorants, breakfast cereals, or toothpaste. (*Parity products* are roughly equal in quality among competitors and so can't be promoted through any rational or scientific proof of superiority.) In such cases, advertisers' goal is to build brand loyalty based on a long-lasting relationship with consumers. Advertisers, best thought of as creative teams of writers and artists, try to convert a brand name appearing on a cereal box or a pair of jeans to a field of qualities, values, and imagery that lives inside the heads of its targeted consumers. Advertisers don't just want you to buy Nikes rather than Reeboks but also to see yourself as a Nike kind of person, who identifies with the lifestyle or values conveyed in Nike ads.

## Mirrors and Windows: The Strategy of an Effective Advertisement

A final behind-the-scenes concept that will help you analyze ads is the marketers' principle of *"mirrors and windows,"* a psychological and motivational strategy to associate a product with a target audience's dreams, hopes, fears, desires, and wishes (often subconscious).

- ***The mirror effect*** refers to the way in which the ad mirrors the target audience's self-image, promoting identification with the ad's message. The target audience has to say, "I am part of the world that this ad speaks to. I have this problem (pimples, boring hair, dandelions, cell phone service without enough bars)."
- ***The window effect*** provides visions of the future, promises of who we will become or what will happen if we align ourselves with this brand. The ad implies a brief narrative, taking you from your ordinary self (mirror) to your new, aspirational self (window).

For example, the acne product Proactiv Solutions uses a very common mirrors/windows strategy. Proactiv infomercials create the mirror effect by featuring regular-looking teenagers with pimples and the window effect by using a gorgeous actress as endorsing spokesperson: If I use Proactiv Solutions, ordinary "me" will look beautiful like Jessica Simpson.

But the mirrors and windows principle can be used in much more subtle and creative ways. Consider the brilliance of the Geico insurance gecko ads promoting what advertisers call "a resentful purchase"—that is, something you need to have but that doesn't give you material pleasure like a new pair of shoes or money in a savings account. Insurance, a hassle to buy, is also associated with fear—fear of needing it, fear of not having it, fear of not being able to get it again if you ever use it. In this light, think of the Geico campaign featuring the humorous, big-eyed gecko (friendly, cute) with the distinctive cockney voice (working-class swagger). When this chapter was being written, Geico billboards were sprouting up all over the country (see Figure 7.13), while large-print ads were appearing in popular magazines along with numerous TV and radio commercials. Here are some of the particular advantages of the gecko for Geico's layered advertising campaign across many media:

- ***"Gecko" sounds like "Geico."*** In fact, this sound-alike feature was the inspiration for the campaign.
- ***The gecko is identifiable by both sight and sound.*** If you see a print ad or a billboard, you remember what the voice sounds like; if you hear a radio ad, you remember what the gecko looks like; on TV or YouTube, you get both sight and sound.
- ***The gecko is cheap.*** The cost of the computer simulations that produce the gecko is minimal in comparison to the royalties paid to celebrities for an advertising endorsement.

**FIGURE 7.13** Geico Gecko Billboard Ad

- ***The gecko is ethnically/racially neutral.*** Marketers didn't have to decide whether to choose a white versus black versus Asian spokesperson, yet a person of any race or nationality can identify with the little lizard. (Think Kermit the Frog on *Sesame Street*.) Feminist critics, however, might rightly ask why the gecko has to be male.

- ***The gecko is scandal-proof.*** When in 2010 the Tiger Woods imbroglio ruined the golfer's public image, the huge insurance company Accenture, along with TagHauer watches and other companies, had to drop his endorsement ads, forcing them at great expense to create new advertising campaigns and to lose media visibility in the interim.

Yet we must still ask why the gecko is a good advertising device for an insurance company. How does the gecko campaign incorporate mirrors and windows? Let's start with the mirror effect. It is easy to identify with the Geico ads because everyone has to buy insurance and because everyone wants to save money. (The gecko's main sales pitch is that Geico will save you 15 percent.) Moreover, our long cultural history of identifying with animated characters (*Sesame Street, ET*) makes it easy to project our own identities onto the gecko. Additionally, the cockney voice makes the gecko a bit of an outsider, someone breaking into corporate culture through sheer bravado. (Many people think of the gecko's accent as Australian more than cockney, giving the lizard a bit of sexy, macho Crocodile Dundee appeal.)

The ads also create a window effect, which comes from the way the gecko humanizes the insurance company, removing some of the fear and anxiety of buying insurance. You don't think of the gecko as *selling* you the insurance so much as *buying* it for you as your agent, hopping right up on the corporate desk and demanding your rights. Geico becomes a fun company, and you as consumer picture yourself going away with a pile of saved money. Recent ads have added another symbolic feature to the gecko—a pair of glasses—which makes him seem intellectual and responsible, more serious and grown-up. Meanwhile, another Geico campaign, the talking-money ad (see the billboard ad in Figure 7.11), extends the concept of a humorous, friendly creature, like the gecko, that turns Geico insurance into a savings, not an expense.

---

### Designing Ads

This exercise asks you to apply these marketing concepts to designing your own ad. Imagine you are an advertising professional assigned to the Gloopers account. Gloopers is a seaweed (kelp)-based snack treat (a fiction, but pretend it is real) that is very popular under another name in Japan. It was introduced earlier in the American market and failed miserably—what sort of a treat is seaweed? But now, you have laboratory evidence that Gloopers provides crucial nutritional benefits for growing bodies and that it is a healthy alternative to junk food. Many food companies would kill for the endorsement of nutritious content that you now have to work with, but the product is still made out of gunky seaweed. Working in groups or individually, develop a campaign for this product by working out your answers to the following questions:

- Who is your target audience? (Will you seek to appeal to parents as well as children?)
- What is your core message or campaign concept? (Think of a visual approach, including a mirror and window appeal, and perhaps a tagline slogan.)
- What is the best positioning in the media landscape for this campaign?
- How will you build a brand image and brand loyalty?

---

## How to Analyze an Advertisement

In addition to thinking about the decision making behind an ad, when you analyze a print ad you need to ask three overarching questions:

1. How does the ad draw in the target audience by helping them identify with the ad's problematic situation or story (mirror effect)?
2. How does the ad create a field of values, beliefs, and aspirations that serve as windows into a more fulfilled life?
3. How do the ad's images and words work together to create the desired persuasive effects?

For the images in an ad, all the strategies we have already described for documentary photographs and for paintings continue to apply—for example, angle of vision, framing, and so forth. (Review the strategies chart on pp. 150–152.) With many ads you also have to factor in the creative use of words—puns, connotations, and intertextual references to other ads or cultural artifacts. Note that in professionally created ads, every word, every punctuation mark, and every visual detail down to the props in the photograph or the placement of a model's hands are consciously chosen.

The following strategies chart focuses on questions particularly relevant to print ads.

## Strategies for Analyzing the Compositional Features of Print Ads

| What to Do | Some Questions to Ask |
|---|---|
| **Examine the settings, furnishings, and all other details.** | • Is the room formal or informal; neat, lived-in, or messy?<br>• How is the room furnished and decorated?<br>• If the setting is outdoors, what are the features of the landscape: urban or rural, mountain or meadow?<br>• Why are particular animals or birds included? (Think of the differences between using a crow, a hummingbird, or a parrot.) |
| **Consider the social meaning of objects.** | • What is the emotional effect of the objects in a den: for example, duck decoys and fishing rods versus computers and high-tech printers?<br>• What is the social significance (class, economic status, lifestyle, values) of the objects in the ad? (Think of the meaning of a groomed poodle versus a mutt or a single rose versus a fuchsia in a pot.) |
| **Consider the characters, roles, and actions.** | • Who are these people and what are they doing? What story line could you construct behind the image?<br>• Are the models regular-looking people, "beautiful people," or celebrities?<br>• In product advertisements, are female models used instrumentally (depicted as mechanics working on cars or as consumers buying cars) or are they used decoratively (bikini-clad and lounging on the hood of the latest truck)? |

| What to Do | Some Questions to Ask |
|---|---|
| **Observe how models are dressed, posed, and accessorized.** | • What are the models' facial expressions?<br>• What are their hairstyles and what cultural and social significance do they have?<br>• How well are they dressed and posed? |
| **Observe the relationships among actors and among actors and objects.** | • How does the position of the models signal importance and dominance?<br>• Who is looking at whom?<br>• Who is above or below, in the foreground or background? |
| **Consider what social roles are being played out and what values appealed to.** | • Are the gender roles traditional or nontraditional?<br>• Are the relationships romantic, erotic, friendly, formal, uncertain?<br>• What are the power relationships among characters? |
| **Consider how document design functions and how the words and images work together.** | • What features of document design (variations of font style and size, placement on the page, formal or playful lettering) stand out?<br>• How much of the copy is devoted to product information or argument about superiority of the product or service?<br>• How much of the copy helps create a field of values, beliefs, aspirations?<br>• How do the words contribute to the "story" implied in the visual images?<br>• What is the style of the language (for example, connotations, double entendres, puns)? |

## Sample Analysis of an Advertisement

With an understanding of possible photographic effects and the compositional features of ads, you now have the background knowledge needed to begin doing your own analysis of ads. Many of the most dramatic and effective ads now come to us in the form of billboards and television commercials. To show you how such ads can be analyzed, let's examine the acclaimed General Electric Cloud commercial that first aired in 2008. Most people think of General Electric as a company that produces consumer electronics and appliances (refrigerators, dishwaters, etc.); however, GE, one of the largest multinational corporations in the world, actually has divisions focused on energy, technology infrastructure, and consumer industrial products as well. In 2005, in a push to be recognized as a green company, GE initiated its Ecoimagination campaign and has since increased its presence in wind power, solar panels, desalination, and water purification technology. GE's positioning of itself as a green company invested in water reuse solutions is the back story as well as the subtext of the GE Cloud commercial. You can see the forty-eight second commercial on YouTube.

From its first frame, this ad plays on imagination and pulls viewers into a highly romanticized industrial fantasy of the water cycle in which workers in the clouds perform the purification processes of nature. In the first several frames, white buckets sail through the air above green fields to the clouds, where they are received by male and female workers dressed in perfectly white uniforms, wearing white gloves, white hair coverings, and white hardhats. The sequence of frames that follows depicts the synchronized process of these workers feeding the water from earth through enormous bellows, which vaporize it and then condense it through a giant wringer, like those once used for laundry. Then a scientist-technician examines a test tube of this water and pronounces it pure so that the brigade of workers in an assembly line in the clouds can pass buckets of the water to other technicians, who pour it into a vast watering can structure. As thunder crashes, the watering can tips and the purified water falls to earth as rain. In the final few seconds of the commercial, a voice-over interprets the action of the narrative: "Just as nature reuses water, GE water technologies turn billions of gallons into clean water every year. Rain or shine." The final frame shows a glimpse of these actual industrial processes, and the ad ends with the "Ecoimagination" logo.

Our students in film studies noticed how this ad exemplifies the intense dynamism of commercials with the camera constantly moving, zooming in and out, and panning left or right. These movements reflect the time constraints and attention spans commercials must accommodate. The rapidly moving images are tied together by the color palette—mostly whites and grays—and the consistent pace of rapidly changing frames.

Our students also noted that this ad affects viewers first through its multiple, fantastical, and powerful appeals to *pathos*, which arouse viewers' curiosity with a narrative that does not directly declare its product or its purpose. Why is the setting for this ad the clouds? Why are the characters in the ad dressed in technicians' uniforms that are scrupulously white? What exactly are these workers producing? One curiosity-arousing appeal to *pathos* derives from the "heavenly" associations conveyed through the gorgeous images of billowing clouds and radiant sun beams outlining and shining through them and the predominance of white, the color of purity. These images conjure up paintings of heaven in which the figures in the sky are angels or good souls entering the afterlife. These associations suggest that there is something supernatural and divine about this scene, a message underscored by the Creedence Clearwater Revival song "Have You Ever Seen the Rain?" sung by the winsome voice of Julu Stulbach. In this case, a familiar classic song, charged with personal associations and emotional power, is rendered in a new arrangement, making it particularly evocative. The song with its lyrics about "the calm before the storm" adds a seriousness and builds on the audience's fascination with weather—what causes it and how could we control it? A second, more playful appeal to *pathos* is generated by the white-uniformed workers who tap viewers' familiarity with science fiction and children's fantasy stories in their resemblance to the uniformed Umpa-Lumpa factory workers in the film *Willy Wonka and the Chocolate Factory*. These workers signal, as do their counterparts in fiction and film, that readers are in an imagined world but one that comments on the real world. A third appeal to *pathos* carries the mirror effect of the commercial. In depicting these workers as purposeful, industrious, coordinated, and effective, the ad prompts viewers to admire the hard work and indirectly see themselves as dedicated team players engaged in a project to accomplish some important task.

This analysis of the ad's appeals to *pathos* reveals why GE chose to romanticize and fantasize rather than be realistic and direct. If we ask, "Why not take viewers on a tour of a wastewater treatment plant?", the answer dawns on us. A wastewater treatment plant with its giant steel rakes and grates, with scraps of toilet paper and even condoms caught in the prongs, and its various holding tanks for different stages of processing sewage, would interest only a small portion of the audience—and perhaps disgust others—while limiting water technologies to one process. Similarly, the actual technology and plants for industrial cleanup might bore many viewers, who are more interested in product than in process. Instead, the fantastical and associational appeals of the ad can deliver a larger hopeful message while shaping a positive and memorable image of the company.

All these appeals to *pathos* build the company's *ethos* and brand recognition and prepare viewers to absorb the subtly conveyed core message of the ad: Not only is GE good for the environment in the care it takes with resources like water, but GE also possesses the power of nature, and equipped with human ingenuity, knowledge, and ecoimagination, GE's water technologies can solve the world's water problems. The ad, through its window effect, comforts viewers with a sense of the world in which tough problems such as available clean water are faced and solved by the wonders of technology. The dirty process of recycling is now connected with cleanliness, purity, and ample supply of water. The ad inspires appreciation and confidence in GE's know-how and technological capabilities that are as good as, if not better than, nature itself. After all, GE can process billions of gallons of water a year and can do it whether it is raining or sunny.

## Analyzing an Ad from Different Perspectives

**FOR WRITING AND DISCUSSION**

The Axe Apollo men's cologne ad that aired during the 2013 Super Bowl is part of a recent campaign that features traditional culture heroes—lifeguards and firefighters—in competition with another culture hero, the astronaut. Go to YouTube to see the ad with its story line of a shark-endangered, bikini-clad woman rescued by a handsome, buff lifeguard. The audience's expected narrative—rescued girl falls in love with lifeguard—is thwarted, strangely and humorously, by the out-of-nowhere appearance of the geeky, uniformed astronaut. What makes this strange ad effective? You may want to watch the entire ad several times to aid you in your analysis.

*(continued)*

1. ***Campaign and analysis***. After watching this ad, analyze its rhetorical effect and appeal by using the strategies suggested in the chart on pages 164–165 as well as ideas presented throughout this section (target audience, choice of medium, brand building, mirror-and-window strategy, and compositional features).

2. ***Focus on camera techniques***. Think especially in terms of camera shifts and framing, angle and orientation, distance from the subject, and focus. How do these visual techniques contribute to the narrative and the overall impact of the ad?

3. ***Cultural criticism***. Reexamine the ad from the perspective of gender, class, ethnicity, and historical moment. Think about the relationships among the characters and focus on the gender roles. To what extent does this ad break or reinforce traditional notions of gender, race, and class? Consider also our particular historical moment. India and China are strengthening their educational systems in math, science, and technology as they look to the development of their space programs; meanwhile funding for the U.S. space program has not kept pace with its robust start in the 1960s and 1970s. Speculate on the cultural relevance of this campaign at this historical moment.

4. ***Cultural criticism continued.*** Compare the view of heroism and gender in the Axe Apollo ad with that of the Air Force recruitment poster on page 81. To what extent does the woman as expert, solo pilot in the Air Force poster reverse the stereotype of the bikini-clad woman in the Axe Apollo ad? What strategies do advertisers use to appeal simultaneously to both power and femininity in their portrayals of female leaders?

| | |
|---|---|
| **WRITING PROJECT** **7.3** Write a comparative analysis of two visual texts. | **Analysis of Two Visual Texts** Choose two documentary/news photographs, two paintings, or two advertisements to analyze in a closed-form essay. Your two visual texts should have enough in common to facilitate meaningful comparisons. Show these images in your essay (if you are analyzing videos, you'll need to show screen captures), but also describe your two visual texts in detail to highlight what you want viewers to see and to provide a foundation for your analysis. For this closed-form analysis, choose several key points of contrast as the focus. Your thesis statement should make a claim about key differences in the way that your chosen visual texts establish their purposes and achieve their persuasive effects. |

# Exploring and Generating Ideas for Your Analysis

For the subject of your analysis, your instructor may allow you to choose your own images or may provide them for you. If you choose your own, be sure to follow your instructor's guidelines. In choosing your visual texts, look for some important commonality that will enable you to concentrate on similarities and differences in your analysis:

- *Documentary or news photographs.* Analyze two photographs of an event from magazines with different political biases; two news photographs from articles addressing the same story from different angles of vision; or two images on Web sites presenting different perspectives on a recent controversial issue such as industrial farming or the war against terrorists.
- *Paintings.* Find two paintings with similar subject matter but different dominant impressions or emotional impacts.
- *Print ads or television (YouTube) ads.* Look for two ads for the same product (for example, cars, perfume, watches, shampoo) that are aimed at different target audiences or that make appeals to noticeably different value systems.

No matter what type of visual texts you are using, we suggest that you generate ideas and material for your analysis by using the question-asking strategies presented earlier in this chapter (see the strategies charts on pp. 149, 150–152, 155, and 164–165).

To help you generate more ideas, go detail by detail through your images, asking how the rhetorical effect would be different if some detail were changed:

- How would this documentary photo have a different effect if the homeless man were lying on the sidewalk instead of leaning against the doorway?
- Why did the artist blur images in the background rather than make them more distinct?
- What if the advertisers had decided the model should wear jogging shorts and a tank top instead of a bikini? What if the model were a person of color rather than white?

# Shaping and Drafting Your Analysis

Your closed-form essay should be fairly easy to organize at the big-picture level, but each part will require its own organic organization depending on the main points of your analysis. At the big-picture level, you can generally follow a structure like the one shown in Figure 7.14.

If you get stuck, we recommend that you write your rough draft rapidly, without worrying about gracefulness or correctness, merely trying to capture your initial ideas. Many people like to begin with the description of the two visual texts and then write the analysis before writing the introduction and conclusion. After you have written your draft, put it aside for a while before you begin revising.

FIGURE 7.14 Framework for an Analysis of Two Visuals

| Introduction | • Hooks readers' interest;<br>• Gives background on the two visual texts you are analyzing;<br>• Sets up the similarities;<br>• Poses the question your paper will address;<br>• Ends with initial mapping in the form of a purpose or thesis statement. |
| --- | --- |
| General description of your two visual texts (ads, photographs, paintings) | • Describes each visual text in turn. |
| Analysis of the two visual texts | • Analyzes and contrasts each text in turn, using the ideas you generated from your observations, question asking, and close examination. |
| Conclusion | • Returns to the big picture for a sense of closure;<br>• Makes final comments about the significance of your analysis. |

## Revising

Most experienced writers make global changes in their drafts when they revise, especially when they are doing analytical writing. The act of writing a rough draft generally leads to the discovery of more ideas. You may also realize that some of your original ideas aren't clearly developed or that the draft feels scattered or disorganized.

We recommend that you ask your classmates for a peer review of your draft early in the revising process to help you enhance the clarity and depth of your analysis.

## Questions for Peer Review

In addition to the generic peer review questions explained in Skill 11.4, ask your peer reviewers to address these questions:

1. How well do the title, introduction, and thesis set up an academic analysis?
2. Where does the writer capture your interest and provide necessary background information? How might the writer more clearly pose the question to be addressed and map out the analysis?
3. Where could the writer describe the visual texts more clearly so that readers can "see" them?
4. How has the writer established the complexity of the texts and their commonalities and differences?
5. How well has the writer used the questions about angle of vision, artistic techniques, and compositional features presented in this chapter to achieve a detailed and insightful analysis of the texts? Where could the writer add more

specific details about settings, props, posing of characters, facial expressions, manners of dress, story line, and so forth?

6. In what ways could the writer improve this analysis by clarifying, deepening, expanding, or reorganizing the analysis? How has the writer helped you understand something new about these two texts?

## Multimodal or Online Options

1. **Museum Audioguide Podcast** Many art museums feature portable audioguide recorders that prompt viewers to pause in front of exhibits to hear an analysis of the painting or photograph. Assume that your chosen images (if you have selected two paintings or two documentary photographs) are exhibited side by side at a museum as part of a featured display. Create a podcast describing and analyzing the exhibits. You can assume that your audience will be looking at the exhibit as you talk. For advice on preparing a podcast, see Skill 13.3.

2. **Lecture with Visual Aids** Assume that for a global outreach program you have been invited to present an analysis of two ad campaigns for the same product or company as this product or company is marketed in different cultures. For example, how are Coca Cola products advertised in China? How is MacDonald's advertised in Central America? Prepare a lecture with PowerPoint or Prezi slides that you can record on video and upload to YouTube. Your slides can hone in on certain features of the ads as you talk. For advice on preparing oral presentations with visual aids, see Skill 13.3.

Lydia Wheeler wrote the following analytical essay for the writing project in this chapter. It analyzes two documentary photos focused on economic hardship and displacement. One photo, taken by photographer Stephen Crowley, accompanied a *New York Times* story about a mother and her daughters in the 2008 recession caused by the collapse of the housing bubble in the United States. The subject, Isabel Bermudez, was subsisting on food stamps unable to find a job; previously she had supported her daughters with a six-figure salary. Then the market collapsed, she lost her job, and shortly afterward she lost her house. The second photo is a famous image taken in 1936 in Nipoma, California, during the Great Depression. The photo is part of the *Migrant Mother* series by photographer Dorothea Lange. Lydia decided to examine the original newspaper contexts for these photographs and to approach them as depictions of women's experiences of economic crisis.

## Lydia Wheeler (student)
## Two Photographs Capture Women's Economic Misery

1     During economic crises, the hardship of individuals is often presented to us as statistics and facts: number of bankruptcies, percentage of the population living below the poverty line, and foreclosures or unemployment rates. Although this numerical data can be shocking, it usually remains abstract and impersonal. In contrast, photographers such as Stephen Crowley and Dorothea Lange help us visualize the human suffering involved in the economic conditions, skillfully evoking the emotional, as well as the physical, reality of their subjects. Crowley's color photograph, first published January 2, 2010, in a *New York Times* article titled "Living on Nothing but Food Stamps," is captioned "Isabel Bermudez, who has two daughters and no cash income." Lange's black and white photograph was commissioned by the Resettlement Agency to document Americans living in the Great Depression; she originally captioned it *Destitute pea pickers in California; a 32 year old mother of seven children. February 1936.* However, in March of the same year, the *San Francisco Times* published Lange's photograph in an article demanding aid for workers like Florence Owens Thompson, the central subject of the picture. Once published, the photograph became famous and was nicknamed *Migrant Mother*. A close look at these two photos shows that through their skillful use of photographic elements such as focus, framing, orientation, and shape, Stephen Crowley and Dorothea Lange capture the unique emotional and physical realities of their subjects, eliciting compassion and admiration, respectively.

2     Stephen Crowley's photograph of a mother sitting in a room, perhaps the dining room of her house, and her young daughter standing and reaching out to comfort her sets up contrasts and tensions that underscore loss and convey grief. The accompanying article explains that Isabel Bermudez, whose income from real estate once amply supported her family, now has no income or prospect for employment and relies entirely on food stamps. A careful examination of Crowley's photograph implies this loss by hinting that Bermudez's wealth is insecure.

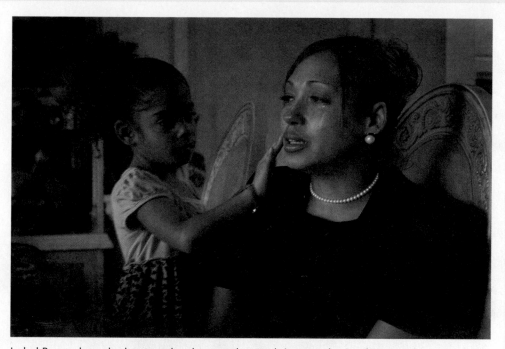

Isabel Bermudez, who has two daughters and no cash income, by Stephen Crowley

3    The framing, distance, and focus of Crowley's photograph emphasize this vanished wealth and the emotional pain. The image is a medium close up with its human subjects to the side, surrounding them with empty space and hints of expensive furnishings. While part of the foreground is sharply focused, the background is blurry and unfocused. There is a suggestion that the room is spacious. Further, the high, decorative backs of the room's chairs, the repetitive design decorating the bookshelf on the frame's left, and the houseplant next to the bookshelf show that the room is well furnished, even luxurious. Bermudez and her daughter match their surroundings in being elegantly dressed. Bermudez looks across the room as if absorbed in her troubles; her daughter looks intently at her. Viewers' eyes are drawn to Bermudez's dark dress and her pearl necklace and earrings. However, the ostensible comfort of Bermudez and her surroundings starkly contrasts with her grief.

4    Crowley heightens this contrast and tension through the subjects' orientation and the space between them. The space between Bermudez and her daughter is one of the photograph's dominant features, but it contains only out-of-focus objects in the background. Neither figure is centered in the photo; neither looks at the camera. Consequently, the viewers' attention moves back and forth between them, creating a sense of uneasiness. The meaning of this photo is focused not on what Bermudez has but on what she has lost.

5    Crowley also evokes sympathy and compassion for his subjects with his choice of angle, scale, and detail. The photograph's slightly high angle makes viewers look

Destitute pea pickers in California; a 32 year old mother of seven children
[*Migrant Mother*] by Dorothea Lange

down—literally—on Bermudez, making her appear vulnerable and powerless and reinforcing the pathos. The most striking bid for compassion is the tears streaming down Bermudez's well made-up face. The contrast between her tidy appearance and the tear tracks on her face suggest overwhelming sadness. The poignancy of her apparent breakdown is heightened by her somber daughter's attempt to wipe away the tears on her mother's face. Crowley's decisions regarding *Isabel's* composition create an image that is highly disturbing.

6    In contrast to Crowley's photograph, Lange's *Migrant Mother*—through its content, focus, frame, rhythm, and angle—conveys long-standing poverty. Yet through this image of inescapable poverty pressing upon its subjects, it evokes admiration for this mother.

7    Lange's frame and focus generate much of the intensity of *Migrant Mother.* This photo is also a medium close up, but Lange's frame is tight with no open space. The lack of this openness cramps Lange's subjects and creates a claustrophobic feel intensified by the number of subjects shown—four to *Isabel's* two. There is almost no background. The subjects filling the foreground are crowded and sharply focused. The contrast between crowded foreground and empty background exaggerates the former and adds a touch of loneliness to *Migrant Mother;* this mother has no resources besides herself. Additionally, the subjects of *Migrant Mother* almost epitomize poverty: Their hair is messy and uncombed, their skin dirt-stained. Even their clothes are worn—from the hem of Thompson's frayed sleeve to the smudges on her baby's blanket, Lange's photograph shows that Thompson can barely afford functional items.

8    *Migrant Mother's* circular lines also create a sense of sameness, stagnation, and hopelessness. Thompson's face draws viewers' eyes as the dominant feature, and Lange has ringed it with several arcs. The parentheses of her standing children's bodies, the angle of her baby in its blanket, and the arc of her dark hair form a ring that hems Thompson in and creates a circular path for the eyes of viewers. Seen with the obvious destitution of Lange's subjects, this repetition is threatening and grimly promises that it will be difficult, if not impossible, for this family to escape its poverty.

9    Like Crowley's *Isabel*, the impact of Lange's *Migrant Mother* derives from both the tragedy of her subjects' situation and their reactions. Lange uses angle and scale to generate sympathy and admiration for Thompson's strength. Once again we see a slightly high angle highlighting the subjects' vulnerability, which Lange reinforces with the slender necks of Thompson's children and a glimpse of her brassiere. However, Lange then contrasts this vulnerability with Thompson's strength, fostering viewers' admiration rather than compassion. *Migrant Mother's* scale, for example, exaggerates rather than diminishes Thompson's size: the photograph's frame focuses viewers' attention on the mother, who looks large, compared to her children. Additionally, Lange's subject literally supports the bodies of the children surrounding her. Unlike Bermudez, Thompson sits tall as a pillar of strength for her vulnerable children. Even her expression—worried but dry eyed—fosters admiration and respect in viewers. By juxtaposing Thompson's vulnerability with her strength, Lange creates a photograph that conveys both its subjects' poverty and their stoicism in facing the Great Depression.

10    Lange and Crowley guide viewer's reactions to their photographs through careful control of the elements that influence our emotional responses to their work. Though they both show women in economic crises, these artists are able to convey the distinct realities of their subjects' situations and consequently send viewers away in different

emotional states: one of compassion, one of admiration. The fame and veneration of Lange's *Migrant Mother* is a testament to her ability to evoke desired emotions. The photograph was exhibited at the Museum of Modern Art in 1941 and again in 1955, and was co-opted by countless movements since it was first published. Whether Crowley's *Isabel* will achieve similar fame for epitomizing this generation's economic crisis remains to be seen, but both photographs certainly succeed in delivering strong, lasting emotional statements.

## THINKING CRITICALLY
about "Two Photographs Capture Women's Economic Misery"

1. What photographic elements has Lydia chosen to emphasize in her analysis of each of these photos?

2. What parts of Lydia's analysis help you see and understand these photos with greater insight? Do you agree with her choice of important elements and her analysis of their effects?

3. If you were analyzing these photos, what features would you choose to compare and stress?

# ANALYZING AND SYNTHESIZING IDEAS

8

**WHAT YOU WILL LEARN**

**8.1** To explain the thinking moves involved in writing analysis and synthesis essays.

**8.2** To analyze texts with different perspectives and synthesize their ideas to present a new perspective of your own.

Many college courses require synthesis essays in which you will be asked to explore connections and contradictions among groups of texts and to work your way to your own perspective through a series of essential thinking and writing moves. You will need first to formulate a synthesis question that connects your chosen or assigned texts. You will then need to summarize the texts accurately, analyze the main commonalities and disagreements among them, and, through your own critical thinking, arrive at your own perspective on the synthesis question.

## Engaging Analysis and Synthesis

This exercise introduces you to the main thinking moves required for analysis and synthesis. The subject for the short articles that follow—"boomerang kids," the new social phenomenon of young adults in their twenties and thirties who live with parents while they are looking for jobs or starting their careers—is also explored by the student writing in this chapter. The first reading, "Ground Rules for Boomerang Kids" by John Miley*, appeared in the June 2012 edition of *Kiplinger's Personal Finance*. The second reading is a review of Katherine Newman's book *The Accordian Family: Boomerang Kids, Anxious Parents, and the Private Toll of Global Competition*, which appeared in *Publishers Weekly* on August 29, 2011. After reading these short pieces, develop answers to the questions that follow.

## John Miley
# Ground Rules for Boomerang Kids

### It's Okay to Help, but Don't Coddle

Suzanne Bernier is one of the lucky ones. Just before graduating from Brandeis University in 2010, she landed a job at a medical software company. Yet after graduation, the frugal 24-year-old moved back in with her parents. "I wanted to save as much money as possible," she says. More than one-fifth of people ages 25 to 34 live in multi-generational homes, the highest level since the 1950s, reports Pew Research. The hospitality helps boomerangers stay positive in tough times. More than three-fourths of people ages 25 to 34 who have lived at home are upbeat about their future finances, according to Pew. Laying ground rules can help prevent a clash of the generations. "Put a game plan together with expectations," says Linda Leitz, a certified financial planner in Colorado. Parents who open their homes should establish a time limit for the stay and get regular progress reports. The child should pay rent, save money or pay off debt. Don't subsidize a lavish lifestyle. If kids can't contribute money, consider requiring household chores instead. Parents should gradually turn up the heat, Leitz says. Raise the cost of rent by a certain date, for example, even if your plan is to make a gift of the money when your child departs. The comfort of home shouldn't be cushy enough to erode financial independence.

## Publishers Weekly
# Book Review

### Review of *The Accordion Family* by Katherine Newman

Newman examines the proliferation of "accordion families," in which children continue to live with their parents late into their 20s and 30s. It's a phenomenon that spans cultures and continents, and Newman's inquiry takes her around the world to examine how family structures are responding to societal changes. She examines how high unemployment rates, the rise of short-term employment, staggered birth rates, longer life expectancies, and the high cost of living have affected the younger generation's transition to adulthood. While in Spain and Italy the new family dynamics mark a change from the past, they are more easily accepted than they are in Japan, where expectations for maturity and developmental milestones are more socially fixed. Newman's interviews with parents and their cohabitating children reveal how the definition of "adulthood" is changing, from the possession of external markers (a marriage, a home) to a psychological state, an understanding of one's place in the world and one's responsibilities. While the book fails to provide a prescription to the accordion family, it does provide an alternative when Newman looks north to strong welfare states like Sweden and Denmark, where the government subsidizes housing and provides grants to help young adults transition more easily, a place that the U.S. can look "to see what can be done, and at what cost, to insure the orderly transition of the generations."

**ON YOUR OWN**

Jot down responses to the following questions:

1. How would you summarize the main points of each piece in one or two sentences?
2. What rhetorical features (about audience, purpose, genre, angle of vision) stand out for you in each piece?
3. List ideas that the two pieces have in common.
4. List any contradictions or disagreements you see in these pieces' views of boomerang kids.
5. Freewrite your own responses to these readings, exploring what questions they raise for you or personal experiences or views you have about this subject.

**IN CONVERSATION**

In groups or as a class, share your responses, looking for points in the readings that many people found important.

# Understanding Analysis and Synthesis

Synthesis, which is a way of seeing and coming to terms with complexities, is an extension of and counterpart to analysis. When you **analyze** something, you break it down into its parts to see the relationships among them. When you **synthesize**, you take one more step, putting parts together in some new fashion. The cognitive researcher Benjamin Bloom schematized "synthesis" as the fifth of six levels of thinking processes, ranked in order of complexity and challenge: knowledge, comprehension, application, analysis, synthesis, and evaluation. Bloom defined *synthesis* as the "putting together of constituent elements or parts to form a whole requiring original creative thinking." Recent educational theorists have revised Bloom's hierarchy to place synthesis at the top, relabeling it "creating" rather than synthesizing: remembering, understanding, applying, analyzing, evaluating, and creating.* This revision emphasizes the creative aspect of synthesis through which you arrive at your own revelations ("Aha!" moments) based on new ways of seeing something or on your creating a new idea or product.

A second useful way to look at synthesis is as a dialectical critical thinking process. Throughout this text, we have explained that college writing involves posing a significant question that often forces you to encounter clashing or contradictory ideas. Such conflicts intrigued the German philosopher Hegel, who posited that thinking proceeds dialectically when a thesis clashes against an antithesis, leading the thinker to formulate a synthesis encompassing dimensions of both the original thesis and the antithesis. When you write to synthesize ideas, your thinking exemplifies this dialectical process.

Synthesis is an especially important component of academic research writing, where you use synthesis to carve out your own thinking space on a question while sifting through the writings of others. Synthesis, then, is the skill of wrestling with ideas from different texts and sources and creatively forging a new

**8.1**
Explain the thinking moves involved in writing analysis and synthesis essays.

*Benjamin Bloom, *Taxonomy of Educational Objectives: Handbook I: Cognitive Domain* (New York: David McKay, 1956).

whole out of potentially confusing parts. It is the principal way you enter into a conversation on a social, civic, or scholarly issue.

## Posing a Significant Synthesis Question

As we have shown throughout this text, most academic and professional writing begins with the posing of a problem. Writing a synthesis essay follows the same principle. The need to synthesize ideas usually begins when you are given or pose a problematic question that sends you off on an intellectual journey through a group of texts. The synthesis question focuses your attention by directing you to look for ways that a group of texts are connected and ways that they differ in their approaches to a particular problem or issue. A synthesis question helps you zero in on a problem that these texts address or that you are trying to solve through exploring these texts. Your goal is to achieve your own informed view on that question, a view that reflects your intellectual wrestling with the ideas in your sources and in some way integrates ideas from these sources with your own independent thinking.

Although synthesis writing appears in college courses across the curriculum, the set-up of these assignments varies. Sometimes instructors will specify the question and the texts that you are to explore whereas at other times you will be asked to articulate your own synthesis question and choose your texts. The following examples show typical synthesis assignments that you might encounter in different disciplines, with both the synthesis questions and the texts provided in each case.

| Texts to Be Analyzed | Possible Synthesis Questions |
| --- | --- |
| **Environmental Studies Course** | |
| A chapter from Gary Chamberlain's *Troubled Waters: Religion, Ethics, and the Global Water Crisis* (2008) | • Who owns our water? Should water be a human right or a commodity? |
| A chapter from Charles Fishman's *The Big Thirst: The Secret Life and Turbulent Future of Water* (2011) | • Who should have control of water sources and management—corporations or governments representing citizens? |
| "College Issues" video "Student Activism 101" on the Bottled Water Matters Web site | • What are the best solutions to providing safe drinking water in water-stressed areas of the world? |
| Maude Barlow, "Address to the UN General Assembly on Need to Conserve Water" (2009) | • What are the main points of disagreement in the bottled water controversy? |
| **Introductory Sociology Course on Global Culture** | |
| Samuel P. Huntington's article "The Clash of Civilizations?" *Foreign Affairs* (1993) | • What are the power dynamics of cultural globalization? |
| Jan Nederveen Pieterse's "Globalization and Culture: Three Paradigms" in *Readings in Globalization: Key Concepts and Major Debates* edited by George Ritzer and Zeynep Atalay (2010) | • Can cultural exchange be an instrument for promoting global understanding, cooperation, and peace? |
| Helena Norberg-Hodge's *Ancient Futures: Learning from Ladakh* (1991) | • How is increasing global cultural contact affecting cultural diversity? |
| Tony Karon, "What Soccer Means to the World" *Time* (2004) | |

## Synthesis Writing as an Extension of Summary/Strong Response Writing

Chapter 5 introduced you to writing summaries of texts and responding strongly to them through critique of their rhetorical strategies and ideas. These skills are the basis of synthesis writing as well. In writing a synthesis essay, you use both with-the-grain and against-the-grain thinking. You listen carefully to texts as you summarize them to determine their main points. You also conduct—at least informally in your exploratory stages—a critique of both the rhetorical features and the ideas of these texts. This analysis builds the platform from which you create a synthesis of ideas—that is, from which you begin your own independent thinking based on the synthesis question that ties your texts together.

A synthesis essay differs from a summary/strong response essay in that a synthesis essay extends the process to more texts with the aim of bringing them into conversation with each other. A synthesis essay shows how you have taken apart, made sense of, assessed, and recombined the ideas of these texts in an integration of ideas all your own that creates a new vision of the subject. A synthesis essay most likely incorporates the following features:

### TYPICAL FEATURES OF A SYNTHESIS ESSAY

- A statement of the synthesis question that shows your interest in the texts and presents this question as problematic and significant
- Short summaries of these texts to give your readers a sense of the readings you are working with
- A thesis that indicates how you have analyzed and synthesized the readings to arrive at a new perspective
- Your analysis of key points in these texts, determined in part by the synthesis question
- Your new view, which combines ideas gathered from readings with your own independent ideas

The student example of a synthesis essay by Rosie Evans at the end of this chapter shows you how these parts are developed in a complete essay (pp. 198–201).

## A Synthesis Essay

Write a synthesis essay that meets the following criteria:

- Addresses a synthesis question that your instructor provides or that you formulate for yourself
- Summarizes and analyzes the views of at least two writers on this question
- Shows how you have wrestled with different perspectives on the question and have synthesized these ideas to arrive at your own new view of the question

**WRITING**

**PROJECT**

**8.2**
Analyze texts with different perspectives and synthesize their ideas to present a new perspective of your own.

## Ideas for Synthesis Questions and Readings

Readings and Images Options for This Assignment

| Synthesis Questions | Possible Readings and Images |
|---|---|
| What contemporary social and economic conditions are complicating young people's transition to adulthood?<br><br>What actions can families take to help young adults with this transition? | • John Miley, "Ground Rules for Boomerang Kids: It's Okay to Help but Don't Coddle," p. 178<br>• Publishers' Weekly, "Review of *The Accordion Family: Boomerang Kids, Anxious Parents, and the Private Tool of Global Competition* by Katherine Newman," p. 178 |
| Should women be accepted as equals in military combat? | • Air Force Recruitment, "Women of the Air Force," (poster) p. 81 |
| Should the United States increase, curb, or more stringently regulate oil companies' practice of hydraulic fracturing (fracking) to obtain natural gas? | • Josh Fox, *Gasland,* (photos), p. 341<br>• Web page for Energy from Shale: Arkansas, p. 347<br>• Web page for Americans Against Fracking, p. 347 |

## Understanding the Components of Synthesis Thinking and Writing

A synthesis essay involves summarizing, analyzing, and synthesizing. A productive way to move through these stages is to break your process into a series of incremental thinking and writing steps in order to show how your wrestling with the ideas in the texts has influenced your own thinking. Consider these strategies as your toolkit to use when you are asked to write essays involving analysis and synthesis.

In the sections that follow, we explain each of these thinking and writing steps in more detail, show you examples, and give you strategies to do them. Our examples come from the idea-generating strategies used by student writer Rosie Evans, whose final synthesis essay is shown on pages 198–201. Her essay, written for this assignment, asks the question, "What are the causes of the delayed-adulthood trends we see within Generation Y and how should society respond?" Rosie analyzed and synthesized two texts:

• Robin Marantz Henig, "What Is It about 20- Somethings?" from the *New York Times Magazine*, August 18, 2010
• A blog post by ScammedHard! "What's Wrong with 20-Somethings?" posted on the Web on August 20, 2010

Although we have not reprinted these two texts, Rosie's summaries and exploratory pieces will familiarize you with their content. (You can also look them up on the Web yourself.)

# Summarizing Your Texts to Explore Their Ideas

Depending on your instructor's specific assignment, the texts you are working with will most likely be magazine articles, op-ed pieces, blogs, scholarly articles, or book chapters. As a starting point for grappling with each author's ideas, we recommend that you compose careful summaries of each text. Writing summaries prompts you to read each text with the grain, adopting each text's perspective and walking in each author's shoes. When you summarize a text, you try to achieve an accurate, thorough understanding of it by stating its main ideas in a tightly distilled format. It is often a good idea to create a full paragraph summary of each reading to give you space to cover the main ideas of the article or chapter. Later, for your essay itself, your instructor may give you a word limit for your summaries and may ask you to shorten them to make more room in your essay for your analysis and synthesis.

Instructions on how to write a summary are found on pp. 89–90.

What follows are student Rosie Evans's summaries of the two readings she used in her synthesis essay. Notice how she uses attributive tags to show that she is representing the authors' ideas, not her own, and notice the neutral, nonjudgmental approach she takes.

Instructions on how to use attributive tags are found in Skill 14.3.

## Rosie Evans's Summary of Robin Marantz Henig's Article

In her *New York Times Magazine* article "What Is It about 20-Somethings?" Robin Marantz Henig explores psychology professor Jeffrey Arnett's claim that twentysomethings are experiencing a new life stage called "emerging adulthood." For Arnett, this is a time for twentysomethings to explore their possibilities and identities, but this exploration also brings uncertainty, instability, and fear. He argues that these experiences are meaningful even though twentysomethings can seem lazy and directionless. Arnett thinks we should devote more resources to supporting them during this time. Henig links Arnett's claims to scientific findings that brains are not fully developed until the mid-twenties and suggests that Millennials' transition to adulthood may be limited because their brains haven't fully matured. She also wonders if changing cultural norms about traditional signs of adulthood, like marriage and financial independence, have removed pressure on twentysomething brains to assume adult functioning earlier in life. If brain development or emerging adulthood are really causing Millennials to delay adulthood, then Henig thinks some of our social institutions, like education and health care, should change to offer better support. She imagines expanding programs like AmeriCorps to help young people explore their interests and options before choosing a career. She acknowledges some drawbacks to providing more time for twentysomething to become self-supporting adults such as the drain on their parents' long-term financial security. Although she never firmly settles on a cause of Generation Y's delayed adulthood, she ultimately seems drawn to the idea of Arnett's emerging adults who use their twenties to become better-prepared adults.

## Rosie Evans's Summary of Scammed Hard!'s Blog Post

In response to Henig, blogger Scammed Hard! argues in "What's Wrong with 20-Somethings?" that the economy is to blame for Generation Y's struggles. While agreeing that the brain is constantly changing, he characterizes Arnett's theory of emerging adulthood as a psychology professor's attempt to gain professional distinction by inventing a new theory. Referencing twentysomethings like Alexander the Great and Winston Churchill, he argues that our ancestors would not have achieved the success they did if emerging adulthood were a real life stage. Instead, he blames Baby Boomers for creating the conditions that killed the ambition and creativity of Generation Y. According to Scammed Hard!, the Boomers promoted the comfort of a middle-class lifestyle, encouraged dangerous levels of student debt, and then wrecked the economy. By setting high expectations and then limiting the possibility of meeting those expectations, they have destroyed this generation's incentives for hard work and sacrifice needed to succeed in America today. Scammed Hard! believes that although drifting through the twenties may provide Generation Y with a fun distraction, it does not prepare them with the skills and motivation to respond to our serious economic problems. Scammed Hard! notes that this reality endangers our shared welfare by failing to create a new generation of productive workers contributing to tax revenue. Most dangerous of all in the eyes of this blogger is characterizing Generation Y's shared strife as a positive new life stage, diverting attention from the urgent economic problems that drive this generation's reality.

**FOR WRITING AND DISCUSSION**

### Summarizing Your Texts

Begin by writing a 200-250 word summary of each of your texts. Then confirm your decisions about main ideas by working in small groups or as a whole class to list the ideas that must be included in a summary of each piece for the summary to be accurate and complete. What points do you agree are secondary and can be left out?

## Analyzing Your Texts

After writing summaries to achieve a solid grasp of the content of your texts, the next key thinking step is to analyze your texts. When you analyze a text, you examine its parts and features, what it says and how it says it. This examination, unlike a more neutral summary, involves your own pondering, questioning, weighing, and wrestling with ideas in the texts. Now your independent observations and sense of what is important come into play. In the process of analyzing your texts, you should consider what rhetorical features are important in each text, how these texts relate to your synthesis question, and how these texts express similar and different views.

## Analyzing the Rhetorical Features of Your Texts

In order to understand how your texts work rhetorically, you should analyze the rhetorical strategies. What do you observe and think is important about the way your texts handle purpose, audience, genre, angle of vision, the use of appeals to *logos, ethos*, and *pathos*, and the use of evidence? Seek out background information on the author of a text and on the publication and genre (for instance, whether it's a scholarly book, journal, popular magazine, or a blog). Applying the following questions in your analysis of each text will help you reach a deeper understanding of how the text conveys its ideas.

These rhetorical terms are explained in Chapter 1 (Concept 1.2) and Chapter 3, (Concept 3.2)

Instructions on how to write a rhetorical critique of a text are found in Chapter 5 on pp. 92–95.

### QUESTIONS TO ASK TO EXAMINE RHETORICAL FEATURES IN EACH TEXT

- Who is the author? To whom is the author writing and why? What is the motivating occasion?
- How do the publication and genre of the text influence the author's choices about structure and language?
- What angle of vision shapes the text and accounts for what is included, emphasized, and excluded?
- How logically developed and consistent is this text? Is the author's argument well supported with relevant evidence?
- How fair, reliable, knowledgeable, and authoritative does the author appear to be?
- How well does the author appeal to readers' emotions, imaginations, and values?
- Do you share the values of the author or of his or her intended audience?

Rosie Evans's informal rhetorical analyses of her texts show her exploratory thinking.

## Rosie Evans's Rhetorical Analysis of Henig's Article

Henig's article poses a set of related questions about Millennials and then tries to answer them by exploring psychological studies, neuroscience research, case studies, and survey data. The piece is written for a general audience; the

*Writer comments on the author's purpose.*

*Writer comments on the audience and publication.*

*Writer discusses the author's purpose.*

*Writer shares background information about the author.*

readership of *The New York Times Magazine* is typically educated and liberal. However, the article is not directed at the Millennials themselves. Instead, it addresses their parents and society at large, who may feel responsible for causing and even solving the generation's problems. Henig aims to raise awareness about the twentysomething experience, explore the possible causes, and convince readers about the importance of the questions she raises and the solutions we choose. In my research, I discovered that the popularity of this article led her to write a book on the topic with her twentysomething daughter. I thought this suggested her investment in the topic as a mother witnessing her daughter or her daughter's friends adrift in their twenties.

*Writer discusses the author's use of evidence.*

Henig is a science writer, so she discusses the science and psychology of emerging adulthood in a balanced, reasoned way and uses survey data as evidence. For example, she explains a Purdue University survey that provides information about how much parents help their twentysomething children. Then, she uses the survey findings to suggest that the gap between the resources of low-income and high-income emerging adults probably grows during this time. Henig also carefully examines Arnett's claims and points out his contradictions. She questions how emerging adulthood could be a new life stage when not every twentysomething experiences it. She is concerned that Arnett uses one case study to represent all low-income Millennials and wants more evidence of their experiences. Henig's use of evidence and the problems she identifies with some of the information she finds help build trust with her readers.

*Writer identifies gaps in the author's article, commenting on the limitations of the angle of vision and raising her own question.*

However, what her article lacks is the voice of the twentysomethings themselves. The details of the twentysomething experience are revealed by academics' studies and experts' observations. When we finally meet a Millennial at the end of the article, her words and experiences are interpreted for us by her caregivers at a mental-health treatment facility. As the talking heads fret over the experiences of Generation Y, I wonder how the so-called emerging adults feel about all of this? In examining the Millennials' problems, I think Henig should have included them in the conversation.

## Rosie Evans's Rhetorical Analysis of Scammed Hard!'s Blog Post

*Writer identifies the angle of vision and tone of the blog author.*

In contrast, Scammed Hard! is writing as a Millennial, and he is angry! In his post, he identifies as an "older (young) curmudgeon," and the tagline of his blog, "Sold down the river for a law school dream," hints that he is a disillusioned law student or graduate. He is probably writing from the "scam blog" movement, a loose band of law school students and graduates who feel cheated by the high cost of school and the limited availability of jobs. The blog post reads as more of a stream-of-consciousness rant than a carefully-reasoned argument, but the writer's anger itself is convincing. You can feel his outrage at the economic realities crippling his generation and at Henig's willingness to consider a psychological explanation for their problems.

*Writer shares her specula-tions about the author's background.*

     Posting anonymously on a blog, with its typical informal format, gives Scammed Hard! greater freedom of expression. For example, he uses sarcasm to show his dis-gust with Arnett and Henig, whom he calls "academic puffs and their pals at the *NYT.*" But this sarcasm is also an example of his failure to build trust with his readers. Readers from the older generations whom he blames for the current state of affairs would probably be offended by his tone and aggression. He also sometimes treats Henig unfairly, assigning meaning to her work that I do not think she intended. He rarely supports his claims, and when he does, he uses underdeveloped anecdotes (like name-dropping Alexander the Great). The unbalanced nature of his work, com-bined with his sarcastic tone, is unlikely to convince readers who do not already agree with his views, no matter how large a role the economy plays in delaying adulthood for Millennials.

*Writer discusses how the blog genre influences the depth and shape of this argument.*

*Writer points out the weak-nesses of this blog post as persuasive writing and the blog au-thor's limited audience appeal.*

## Analyzing the Rhetorical Strategies in Your Texts

**FOR WRITING AND DISCUSSION**

Use the list of questions on page 185 to analyze the rhetorical features of your selected texts. You may choose to list the features as bullet points or write out paragraph descriptions. In small groups or as the whole class, discuss the features that you listed. Which features particularly give you a deeper under-standing of the texts?

## Analyzing the Main Themes and  Similarities and Differences in Your  Texts' Ideas

After you understand how your texts work rhetorically, you are ready to analyze closely how each text addresses your synthesis question and to envision these texts in conversation. At this stage in your thinking, your main task is to identify main issues, ideas, or themes that surface in your texts. Then from closely exam-ining the ideas in each individual text, you can move to looking for similarities and differences among your texts. This process of thinking—using comparison and contrast—will help you clarify your understanding of each reading, but it will also help you see the texts in relationship to your synthesis question and in relationship to each other. As you consider the ideas and underlying values and assumptions of each author, think about how each text offers answers to your synthesis question and where these answers coincide and where they clash. The following questions can guide your thinking and help you generate ideas for the analysis part of your synthesis essay.

### QUESTIONS TO ASK TO HELP YOU EXPLORE SIMILARITIES AND DIFFERENCES IN YOUR TEXTS

- What main ideas or themes related to your synthesis question do you see in each text?
- What similarities and differences do you see in the way the authors choose to frame the issues they are writing about? How do their theses (either implied or stated) differ?
- What are the main similarities and differences in their angles of vision?
- What commonalities and intersections related to your synthesis question do you see in their ideas? What contradictions and clashes do you see in their ideas?
- What similarities and differences do you see in the authors' underlying values and assumptions?
- What overlap, if any, is there in these authors' examples and uses of terms?
- On the subject of your synthesis question, how would Author A respond to Author B?

In the following example of Rosie Evans's exploratory analysis of ideas in her texts, note that she has restated her synthesis question and identified similarities among her texts. Note also how she begins to organize comparisons by points, to make analytical connections among them, and to push herself to think out exactly where these authors agree and differ.

**Synthesis Question**: What are the causes of the delayed-adulthood trends we see within Generation Y and how should society respond?

### SIMILARITIES BETWEEN THE TWO ARTICLES:

- Both authors acknowledge that Generation Y's problems are not unique to their generation, and both use Baby Boomer experiences in the 60s and 70s as evidence.
- Despite the similarities between Generation Y and the Baby Boomers, both authors seem to think that Generation Y's problems are worse.
- Both authors find Arnett's theory limited by the fact that the emerging adult experience is more common among the privileged and therefore not universal.

- Both authors accept the evidence that brains continue to develop into the mid- and late-twenties.

Rosie has also articulated what she considers to be important differences between the ideas in her two texts.

**Differences between the Two Articles**

| Henig | Scammed Hard! |
|---|---|
| • Henig explores in-depth how psychology and brain science offer explanations for the Millennials' unsettled condition. | • Scammed Hard! does not accept psychological or neurological explanations and finds that these theories divert attention from the true causes. |
| • Henig believes the economy exacerbated trends already present in Millennials and would point to evidence of Generation Y's trends beginning before the Great Recession. | • Scammed Hard! believes the economy is the primary cause of the Millennials' drifting and blames the Baby Boomers for wrecking economic opportunity for Millennials. |
| • Henig suggests that if emerging adulthood is a new life stage, then social services should adapt to expand opportunities for Millennials to support themselves while simultaneously exploring their identities. | • Scammed Hard! implies that if the economy is the problem, then fixing it will address the Millennials' problems. He would be frustrated if resources were diverted from fixing the economy to encouraging Millennial self-exploration. |
| • Henig agrees with Arnett that Millennials may appear lazy and directionless and suggests that experiences in their twenties might help them make better choices later in life. | • Scammed Hard! thinks the Baby Boomers have ruined Millennials' work ethic with high expectations that reality cannot match. He seems to find Millennials lazy, but does not blame them. |
| • Henig finds evidence of parental support among both low-income and privileged Millennials, but also finds that privileged Millennials receive more benefits. These findings show how emerging adulthood, if it exists, is problematic because it widens the resource gap. | • Scammed Hard! believes that the lack of evidence of emerging adulthood in low-income Millennials falsifies Arnett's theory. |

## Generating Points about Themes, Shared Ideas, and Differences

**FOR WRITING AND DISCUSSION**

Working on your own, identify main issues or themes in your assigned or chosen texts. Then explore the similarities and differences in their ideas. You may find that using bullets for your points helps you picture your points clearly, or you may want to write out your ideas in a draft form. Then working in small groups or as a whole class, review the accuracy and importance of these similarities and differences. To deepen your analysis, discuss this question: How do each author's purposes, assumptions, and values account for the similarities and differences you have identified?

# Synthesizing Ideas From Your Texts

One of your biggest challenges in writing a synthesis essay is to move beyond summary and analysis to synthesis. A successful synthesis essay incorporates ideas from your texts and yet represents your own independent, creative thinking, showing evidence of the dialectic process.

## Generating Ideas of Your Own

As you synthesize ideas, you put ideas together in new combinations and you demonstrate how the texts you have analyzed have informed and influenced the development of your own views. To move to synthesis, you need to think about how the differing perspectives of each text have led you to new realizations that you want to contribute to the conversation of these texts. As you begin to formulate your synthesis views, you will also need to reassert your personal/intellectual investment in the conversation of the texts. You will need to take ownership of the ideas and to emerge with a clearer sense of your own views. You may also want to consider which text—in your mind—makes the most significant contribution to the question you are exploring. You may want to evaluate the texts to determine which has influenced your thinking the most and why. The following questions can help you generate your own views.

QUESTIONS TO HELP YOU DEVELOP YOUR OWN VIEWS

- Do I have any knowledge from my personal experiences that is influencing my response to these texts?
- What do I agree with and disagree with in the texts I have analyzed?
- If I find one author's perspective more valid, accurate, interesting, or useful than another's, why is that?
- How have these texts changed my perception and understanding of an issue, question, or problem? (You might want to use these prompts: "I used to think _____, but now I think _____." "Although these texts have persuaded me that _____, I still have doubts about _____.")
- What is my current view on the synthesis question that connects my texts and that all my texts explore?
- Related to my synthesis question, what new, significant questions do these texts raise for me? What do I now see as the main controversies?
- How would I position myself in the conversation of the texts?

To illustrate this step in writing a synthesis essay, we show you Rosie Evans's wrestling with the ideas in both texts and with her own experiences as she begins to work out her position. You may find that several of these questions resonate more with you than others, and you may choose to probe your responses to those particular questions.

# Rosie Evans's Exploration of Her Personal Connections to Her Texts and the Synthesis Question

My older sister always seemed to succeed easily. She was high school valedictorian and mastered a long list of academic and leadership achievements in college. After she graduated, though, she seemed to drift. After several years of volunteer work and traveling, she returned home during the height of the Great Recession to live with our parents and work a retail job. My parents and other adults who expected success and greatness from her were baffled. I saw her frustration and even signs of depression as she worked a job she was overqualified for and struggled to afford health insurance while averaging 25 hours per week at $10 per hour. At the time, I felt sorry for her and suspected that she just didn't know what she was supposed to do without the structure of school and a clear definition of success to strive for. I sympathized with my parents, who were frustrated by her moping around the house and staying out late with friends while they footed her grocery bills and paid for her car insurance.

Both Henig's and ScammedHard!'s articles caused me to consider other causes of my sister's struggles. I related to Scammed Hard!'s piece because I could hear my sister's voice in his angry exclamations. She definitely feels cheated by our parents, who raised us to believe if we studied hard and earned a Bachelor's degree, professionals would be begging us to work for them. It seems clear that the Great Recession changed the economic reality Millennials face once they graduate, perhaps permanently, and that they feel underprepared for the uncertain future. However, I had never considered that brain development had anything to do with it. Although I am not totally persuaded that "emerging adulthood" exists, Henig's article convinced me that the state of the economy alone cannot have caused Millennials' delayed adulthood. Like Henig, I wonder how changing cultural norms impact the pathways our brains choose for us. Henig at one point mentions that the Baby Boomer generation of "helicopter parents" might actually be pleased to be so needed by their children this late in life. Other articles I've skimmed offer deeper studies on the psychology of emerging adults, isolating variables like Millennials' relationships with their parents and their social support structures to understand their experiences as emerging adults. I wonder how much parents' willingness and capacity to help their children enables Millennials to postpone the traditional markers of adulthood? If my sister hadn't had the option to spend three years traveling and volunteer teaching and then return home to my parents' couch, would she have harnessed her talents and grown up earlier?

*Writer chooses to explore the personal experience that led to her interest in the synthesis question.*

*Writer shows how the texts have influenced her thinking.*

*She discusses her attraction to one of her text's ideas.*

*She discusses how the texts opened up new avenues of thought for her.*

*She shows how the texts have moved her to an enlarged view of the synthesis question and to ask more questions.*

## Taking Your Position in the Conversation: Your Synthesis

After you have discovered what you think about the texts you have analyzed—what ideas you accept and reject, what new questions you have formulated, how your ideas have been modified and transformed through your analysis of your texts—you need to find a way to pull your ideas together. How do you want to enter the conversation of your synthesis question and your texts? What two or three main synthesis points would you like to develop? How will you respond to the ideas you have presented in your analysis and build on them in your own independent way? Your synthesis view should be the fruit of your intellectual work, a perspective that you have come to after analyzing the ideas of other authors and pondering them reflectively and keenly. Here are some questions that can help you articulate the points that you want to develop in your essay.

### QUESTIONS TO HELP YOU FORMULATE AND DEVELOP YOUR SYNTHESIS VIEWS

- What discoveries have I made after much thought?
- What are the most important insights I have gotten from these readings?
- What is my intellectual or personal investment with the synthesis question at this point?
- Where can I step out on my own, even take a risk, in my thinking about the ideas discussed in these texts?
- What new perspective do I want to share with my readers?

In the following passage, we show you Rosie Evans's step toward integrating her own ideas with ideas from her texts as she inserts her voice into the conversation about Millennials.

*Writer tenta-tively offers two main synthesis points.*

*First synthesis point: no simple or single cause of Millennials' problems.*

I think both authors make strong cases for what they think is causing Millennials to delay adulthood, Scammed Hard! with his impassioned experiential case and Henig with her willingness to seek out and carefully examine evidence. They have convinced me that the unsettled state of Millennials is far too complex to have one isolated cause. Rather, it is the result of numerous factors: a shift in cultural expectations and parent-child relationships, economic realities created by the previous generation, and even twentysomethings' brains' responses to these changing circumstances. This high level of complexity is the very reason why identifying problems and agreeing on solutions are so difficult. What is the relationship between individuals and their parents? What role does the economic damage of decades of irresponsible policies play? How should social services respond to the increasingly accepted idea that young adulthood experiences dramatic brain development? Rather than grapple with all these factors, I think many people fret over Millennials' mental health and argue over who deserves blame. Society at large seems guilty of the same inaction they see in the Millennials.

*Second synthesis point: Writer stresses need to examine who Millennials really are before gener-alizing about them.*

*These points incorporate writer's personal knowl-edge with ideas from the texts.*

However, I don't think the Millennials are as inert as adults—and even these authors—seem to think they are. My sister worked very hard to survive on a retail salary while trying to navigate a home life she had left many years earlier. What she gave up on, though, was seeking out other opportunities, instead channeling her energy into surviving her immediate situation. When she faced the job market for a second time after earning a graduate degree, she submitted over fifty job applications, participated in multiple rounds of interviews for a total of eight positions, and was finally offered a part-time job she probably could have done without her graduate degree. She had gone from living a life where hard work led to success to a life where hard work led to a cycle of rejection and more hard work. Because of this, she feels powerless and trapped. How can we expect Millennials to stay motivated under such circumstances? It seems as though everyone needs to adjust their expectations, adults and Millennials alike.

## Generating and Developing Your Synthesis Points

In light of the ideas you have developed through your exploratory analysis of your texts, explore your own views of your synthesis question by freewriting in response to the questions on page 192. What do you want to say in your own voice to show the connections you have made and the new insights you now have? What risky, surprising, or new views could you bring to your readers? Share your ideas with a writing partner or a group and explain why these points interest you.

## Shaping and Drafting

Your main project in shaping and drafting your synthesis essay is to move from the kernels of good ideas that you generated in your thinking and early writing stages to a focused, fully developed, and logically organized discussion of these ideas. Focusing and organizing your ideas for a synthesis essay are both challenging writing tasks. We offer some strategies for developing the analysis and synthesis sections of your essay and then for formulating a thesis that will direct and hold together your essay.

| Strategies for Shaping the Analytical Section of Your Essay | |
| --- | --- |
| **What to Consider in Planning the Analysis Section of Your Essay** | **Questions and Decisions** |
| • Your analysis section, usually one-half to two-thirds of your essay, lays the foundation for your synthesis.<br>• This section discusses several ways that your texts relate to your synthesis question. | • How many analytical points do you want to develop?<br>• What are these points? |
| • Your analysis section should show that you have wallowed in the complexity of your texts.<br>• It may include points about the rhetorical features of your texts (as in a rhetorical critique), and it may include points about the ideas (as in an ideas critique).<br>• It should map out and explain a number of important similarities and differences in your texts. | Consider developing answers to these questions:<br>• How do your texts frame the problem? How do they present different angles of vision? Where do they intersect in their perspectives and approaches? How do they argue and support their views with evidence?<br>• How rhetorically effective are these texts?<br>• What do the authors do to make their readers think? |

## Strategies for Shaping the Synthesis Section of Your Essay

| What to Consider in Planning the Synthesis Section of Your Essay | Questions and Decisions |
|---|---|
| • Your essay should build to your synthesis section, typically one-third to one-half of your essay. | • How can you best show where the texts and their authors promote your own independent thinking?<br>• What synthesis points do you want to explore and discuss? |
| • The synthesis section of your essay should show your informed, independent thinking.<br>• It should show how you have worked your way to a new understanding and created your own view. | • What new insights have you developed through studying these texts?<br>• What new perspectives have you gained through the contrast and/or clash of different ideas?<br>• How much or how little have these texts changed your views and why? |

## Writing a Thesis for a Synthesis Essay

In a synthesis essay, your thesis statement is particularly important and challenging to write. It sets up your readers' expectations, promising an illuminating view of the texts you have worked with. It should reflect earnest intellectual work, promise insights achieved through serious reflection, present your own original connection of ideas, and contain some element of risk and newness. Avoid bland, noncontestable thesis statements such as "These articles have both good and bad points."

You will probably want to work back and forth between formulating your thesis statement and drafting the analysis and synthesis sections of your essay. We recommend that you map out a rough thesis, draft your essay, and then revise and sharpen your thesis. For a synthesis essay, it is sometimes difficult to write a one-sentence, high-level thesis statement that encompasses both your analysis and your synthesis points. In such cases, you can write two lower-level, more specific thesis statements—one for your analysis section and one for your synthesis section—and simply join them together. What is important is that your thesis forecasts your main analysis and synthesis points and creates a map for your readers. The following examples illustrate these different options.

### LOW-LEVEL, TWO-SENTENCE THESIS

Although both authors identify the negative impacts of Generation Y's delayed adulthood and call for society's urgent attention and action, Henig highlights the positive opportunities while Scammed Hard! focuses on the economic dangers. Both articles helped me understand why it is complicated to identify causes and propose solutions and nurtured my conviction that any workable solution must offer Millennials an active role in crafting society's response.

### HIGH-LEVEL, ONE-SENTENCE THESIS

Both Henig's more psychological approach to the problems of Millennials and Scammed Hard!'s economic critique and their suggestions for solutions have led me to examine more closely the causes of Millennials' problems and to endorse a more complex explanation and a solution that involves active participation of Millennials themselves.

## Organizing a Synthesis Essay

The biggest organizational decision you have to make in writing a synthesis essay is how much to summarize your texts and how to incorporate these summaries into your essay. Your decision should be guided by your audience's familiarity with the texts you are discussing and the complexity of the points you are making. Two ways of organizing a synthesis essay are shown in Figure 8.1.

**FIGURE 8.1** Two Frameworks for a Synthesis Essay

**Framework 1**

| Introduction and summary of both texts (several paragraphs) | • Presents the synthesis question and hooks readers<br>• Summarizes the texts (unless your instructor posits that readers have already read the texts, in which case you can omit the summaries or reduce them to one or two sentences each)<br>• Presents your thesis, which maps out your main analytical and synthesis points (Your thesis might come at the end of the paragraphs with your summaries or in a mini-paragraph of its own.) |
|---|---|
| Analytical section | • Includes paragraphs discussing and developing your analytical points |
| Synthesis section | • Includes paragraphs discussing and developing your synthesis points |
| Concluding paragraph | • Reiterates the values and limitations of the texts you have analyzed<br>• Pulls together your new insights<br>• Leaves readers thinking about your views |

**Framework 2**

| Introduction | • Presents the synthesis question and hooks readers<br>• Presents your thesis, which maps out your main analytical and synthesis points |
|---|---|
| Summary/analysis of first text | • Summarizes the first text<br>• Analyzes the first text |
| Summary/analysis of second text | • Summarizes the second text<br>• Analyzes the second text, perhaps with connections and differences with the first text |
| Synthesis section | • Develops several main synthesis points |
| Concluding paragraph | • Reiterates values and limitations of the texts you have analyzed<br>• Pulls together your new insights<br>• Leaves readers thinking about your views |

# Revising

As you revise your synthesis essay, make sure that you have set up the synthesis question effectively. Then work on clarifying and developing your analytical points while striving for an engaging style. Also consider how to make your synthesis views more clearly reflect your own wrestling with the texts' ideas. Think about finding the most interesting ways to show how these texts have enlarged and deepened your own views.

# Questions for Peer Review

In addition to the generic peer review questions explained in Skill 11.4, ask your peer reviewers to address these questions:

### INTRODUCTION, SUMMARIES OF THE TEXTS, AND THESIS

1. What works well about the writer's presentation of the synthesis question that connects the texts under examination? How could the writer better show this question's significance and problematic nature?
2. Where could the writer's summaries of the texts be expanded, condensed, or clarified? Where would the summaries be better located in the essay to help readers?
3. How could the thesis be made more focused, risky, and clear in setting up the writer's analytical and synthesis points?

### ANALYTICAL SECTION OF THE ESSAY

1. How could the writer's analytical points more clearly compare and contrast the authors' values, assumptions, angles of vision, or rhetorical strategies in addressing the synthesis question?
2. What further textual evidence could the writer add to develop these analytical points and make them more interesting or comprehensive?

### SYNTHESIS SECTION OF THE ESSAY

1. How could the writer's synthesis points more clearly demonstrate the writer's thoughtful interaction with these texts?
2. What examples or other specifics could the writer include to develop these synthesis points more effectively?
3. How could the writer conclude this essay more effectively to leave readers with a new perspective on the texts and on the underlying question?

## Multimodal or Online Options

**Online Discussion** On a class discussion board, class blog, or wiki space, post your own summaries of several readings your class has done and then include your own synthesis of these readings, exploring several points of similarity and difference. Share your own perspective of the way these readings have shaped your thinking. You may also want to respond to the synthesis discussions that others have posted.

**Reading**

The reading for this chapter is Rosie Evans's final synthesis essay, which developed out of the exploratory writing and thinking steps described earlier. The specifics of Rosie's assignment are provided on page 182.

## Rosie Evans (student)

## Boomerang Kids: What Are the Causes of Generation Y's Growing Pains?

*Opens with writer's investment and introduces the context for the issue, showing why it is problematic, and leads into the synthesis question.*

My older sister always seemed to succeed easily—that is, until she graduated from college. She went from high school valedictorian and university academic leader to perpetual volunteer and wandering world traveler. When the economy collapsed during the Great Recession, she returned home to live with our parents and work a retail job, confounding the many adults who expected great accomplishments from her. As it turns out, my sister's experience is not isolated but rather represents the experience of a larger cohort, those born roughly between 1980 and 2000. This generation is delaying life choices that traditionally signaled adulthood—like marriage, parenthood, or establishing a career—choosing instead to travel and experiment with different jobs. Many from this generation end up returning to live at home and/or relying on their parents for financial support, putting stress on their family relationships and their own mental health. The numerous labels attached to this generation—Millennials, Generation Y, the Lost Generation, boomerang kids, the Peter Pan generation, emerging adults, accordion families—show that our society is struggling to name and define exactly what is happening and what to do about it. What are the

*States the synthesis question.*

causes of the delayed-adulthood trends we see within Generation Y and how should society respond?

*Introduces the first text and summarizes it.*

One point of view on this question comes from Robin Marantz Henig's 2010 *New York Times Magazine* article "What Is It About 20-Somethings?" Henig, a science writer, explores possible psychological and neurological explanations for Generation Y's delayed adulthood. She examines psychology professor Jeffrey Arnett's claim that twentysomethings are experiencing a new life stage called "emerging adulthood" in which they explore their possibilities and identities while also dealing with the instability, uncertainty, and fear that exploration brings. Rather than seeing Millennials as lazy and directionless, Arnett sees them as having meaningful experiences leading to better decisions about the kinds of lives they want to lead as adults. Henig links Arnett's claims to scientific findings that brains are not fully developed until the mid-twenties and suggests that immature brains might contribute to Millennials' delaying of adulthood. She also wonders if changing cultural norms about traditional signs of adulthood have removed pressure on twentysomething brains to achieve adult functioning earlier in life. If these claims are true, Henig suggests that our social institutions, like education and health care, should change to offer better support to Millennials as they transition to adulthood.

*Introduces the second text and summarizes it.*

In response to Henig's article, blogger Scammed Hard! argues in his post "What's Wrong with 20-Somethings?" that the economy is to blame for Generation Y's struggles. While agreeing that the brain is constantly changing, he dismisses Arnett's theory of emerging adulthood as a bogus psychological theory designed to give its inventor professional distinction. Instead, Scammed Hard! blames Generation Y's struggles on Baby Boomers' destruction of the economy combined with their promotion of dangerous levels of student debt and their encouragement of a comfortable middle-class lifestyle. By setting high expectations and then making those expectations impossible to fulfill, Boomers have destroyed Generation Y's incentives for hard work and sacrifice. Scammed Hard! believes that although drifting toward adulthood may provide Millennials with a fun distraction, it does not prepare them with the skills and motivation needed to find success in a destroyed economy.

Although both authors identify the negative impacts of GenerationY's delayed adulthood and call for society's urgent attention and action, Henig highlights the positive opportunities while Scammed Hard! focuses on the economic dangers. Both articles helped me understand why it is complicated to identify causes and propose solutions and nurtured my conviction that any workable solution must offer Millennials an active role in crafting society's response.

*Thesis statement with analytical points and synthesis points.*

Both Henig and Scammed Hard! acknowledge that the current trends among Millennials are not unique to this generation (after all, the Baby Boomers themselves went through a hippie period). Nevertheless, they acknowledge that the problem of delayed adulthood is more widespread and troubling today. Using survey data, Henig compares the average age of marriage and the percentage of twentysomethings living at home in the 70s and today to show that delayed adulthood is more prevalent now. Scammed Hard! argues that even hippies eventually had to settle down and make productive contributions to society. Both authors worry about the long-term impacts to our society as Millennials take longer to reach adulthood and become innovative, industrious, taxpaying members of society.

*Analysis: compares and contrasts ideas in both texts and develops similarities in ideas.*

While both authors accept the science on brain development, they disagree on the role it plays in causing the Millennials' problems. Henig uses the psychological research to suggest that it might be time for society to enact policies that enrich "the cognitive environment of people in their 20s" in order to better shape their brains for the demands of adulthood. As a science writer and parent of a Millennial, Henig constructs a balanced, reasoned discussion that builds trust with her readers—other parents and the larger society who may feel responsible for causing and solving the Millennials' problems. In contrast, Scammed Hard's refuses to "write off the problems my generation faces as merely 'normal stages of development.'" He thinks that focusing on a new "life stage" diverts attention from the urgent economic problems that drive this generation's reality and account for Millennials' anger, depression, and humiliating inability to support themselves. Writing as a Millennial from the "scam blog" movement, a loose band of law school students and graduates who feel cheated by the high cost of education and the limited availability of jobs, Scammed Hard! effectively employs his outrage to make a compelling argument for economic causes of Generation Y's problems. He believes that the Boomers' decision to outsource jobs, lend irresponsibly, and encourage student debt led to the catastrophic economic collapse that has limited Millennials' financial independence, whereas Henig thinks the economy has merely accelerated trends that already existed among Millennials before the Great Recession.

*Continuation of analysis section: writer analyzes differences in views.*

*Writer brings in rhetorical points to explain the differences.*

*Analyzes and elaborates on differences.*

*Continuation of analysis section focusing on the differences in the ideas in the two texts.*

*Writer brings in rhetorical points to explain the differences.*

The differences in how each author views the causes of Generation Y's problems affect their proposed solutions. Henig thinks we should devote our resources to modifying and expanding social services that support Millennials of all income levels as their brains and identities develop. In contrast, Scammed Hard! urges Baby Boomers to fix the economy and calls on everyone to mobilize to create better incentives for hard work and innovation among the younger generation.

Henig's discussion of emerging adulthood raised some important questions for me. She mentions that the Boomer generation of "helicopter parents" might actually be pleased to be so involved in their children's lives. I wonder how much parents' willingness and capacity to help their children enables Millennials to delay adulthood. If my sister hadn't had the parent-subsidized option to spend three years volunteering and traveling and then return home to our parents' couch, would she have harnessed her talents and grown up earlier? And if mostly privileged Millennials are the ones choosing to delay adulthood, does it make sense to devote even more resources to this already well-supported group? Or should the social support systems be expanded to provide low-income Millennials similar opportunities for financial security and self-exploration?

After reading these articles, I am convinced that Generation Y's delayed adulthood is the result of many complex causes, not just one. These factors include shifts in cultural expectations for young adults, evolving parent-child relationships, collapse of the job market, and other economic realities created by the previous generation, and maybe also the effects of not-yet-mature twentysomething brains. The factors also likely reinforce each other, strengthening their collective impact. For example, perhaps Baby Boomer parents are subconsciously trying to cover up their guilt over the state of the economy by lifting their children's financial burdens. Also, because it is more culturally acceptable to marry later in life and medically possible to have kids during middle age, perhaps Millennials don't worry about a career because they do not yet need financial security for starting a family. Rather than tackle the complex causes of the problems, I sense that established adults find it easier to fret over Millennials' mental health and argue over who is to blame, making society at large guilty of the same inaction they accuse Millennials of.

However, when I think about my sister, I can't agree that Millennials are as inert as adults seem to think they are. What concerns me about the perspectives on Millennials is how often older generations view them as passive actors in their own lives. I think Millennials work a lot harder and more courageously than people realize and make active, intentional choices as best they can under the circumstances. Henig's piece, for all its measured evidence in its ten pages, fails to offer the authentic perspective of a Millennial voice. She should have talked to my sister, who worked very hard to survive on a retail salary while trying to navigate a home life she had left behind years earlier. However, as my sister devoted most of her energy to survival, she gave up on seeking other opportunities for herself. I think this happened because of her disappointment as she transitioned between life where hard work led to success and life where hard work led to a cycle of rejection and more hard work. When she faced the job market for a second time after earning a graduate degree, she submitted over fifty job applications, participated in multiple rounds of interviews for a total of eight positions, and was finally offered a part-time job she probably could have done without her graduate degree. This situation—certainly not unique among Millennials—made her feel powerless and trapped, because she wants to be making successful, valuable contributions to society.

Writer integrates personal experience with ideas from the two texts.

I believe a real solution to Millennials' problems must be multifaceted if it is going to significantly impact the numerous interrelated causes. But more importantly, an effective solution will be one that creates a partnership with Millennials, listens to *them*, and offers them an active role in the response. It is a challenge I think all of their experiences and self-reflection have prepared them for. And it will align with their desires to participate, rather than watch, as the economy, and maybe even adulthood, pass them by.

Synthesis point discusses the writer's own view.

Henig and Scammed Hard! offer differing perspectives on the causes and solutions to Generation Y's delayed adulthood. I encourage them, and anyone else who is serious about making changes to the systems and social structures that have created an America in which it is difficult to grow up, to begin by connecting with the Millennials themselves. They might find that Generation Y is full of ideas, creativity, and possibility waiting to be unleashed.

Conclusion with final connections.

## Works Cited

Henig, Robin Marantz. "What Is It About 20-Somethings?" *The New York Times Magazine*, 18 Aug. 2010. Web. 15 Dec. 2013.

"What's Wrong with 20-Somethings?" *Scammed Hard!*, 20 Aug. 2010. Web. 15 Dec. 2013.

Complete citation of texts in MLA format.

# 9 WRITING A CLASSICAL ARGUMENT

**9.1** To explain the theory and rhetorical principles underlying effective arguments.

**9.2** To write a classical argument that offers reasons and evidence in support of your position while also summarizing and responding to opposing views.

On many occasions in your academic or civic life you will be asked to take a stand on an issue, to support your stand persuasively with reasons and evidence, and to respond ethically to opposing or alternative views. The need for argument arises whenever members of a community disagree about the best solution to a problem or the best answer to a question. Classical rhetoricians believed that the art of arguing is essential for good citizenship. If disputes can be resolved through exchange of perspectives, negotiation of differences, and flexible seeking of the best solutions to a problem, then nations won't have to resort to war or individuals to fisticuffs.

## Engaging Classical Argument

The following thought exercise, which involves ethical treatment of animals, introduces you to an issue that invites classical argument. References to this thought exercise will recur as the chapter progresses. Your initial position may reflect what social scientists call your personal *ideology*—that is, a network of basic values, beliefs, and assumptions that tend to guide a person's view of the world. However, if you adopt an open-minded, truth-seeking attitude, your initial position may evolve as the argumentative conversation progresses. In fact, the conversation may even cause changes in some of your basic beliefs, since ideologies aren't set in stone and since many of us have unresolved allegiances to competing ideologies that may be logically inconsistent (for example, a belief in freedom of speech combined with a belief that hate speech should be banned). In this thought exercise we ask you to record your initial views and then to keep track of how your views may change during further reflection or ensuing class discussions.

**Situation**
A bunch of starlings build nests in the attic of a family's house, gaining access to the attic through a torn vent screen. Soon the eggs hatch, and every morning at sunrise the family is awakened by the sound of birds squawking and wings beating against rafters as the starlings fly in and out of the house to feed the hatchlings. After losing considerable early morning sleep, the family repairs the screen. Unable to get in and out, the parent birds are unable to feed their young. The birds die within a day.

**Question at issue**
Was the family's action an instance of cruelty to animals (that is, was their decision to repair the screen ethically justifiable or not)?

**ON YOUR OWN**

1. Freewrite your initial response to this question. Explain why you think the family's act was or was not ethical.
2. We initially framed this issue as an after-the-fact yes/no question: Is the family guilty of cruelty to animals? But we can also frame it as an open-ended, before-the-fact question: "What should the family have done about the starlings in the attic?" Suppose you are a family member discussing the starlings at dinner, prior to the decision to fix the vent screen. Make a list of your family's other options and try to determine whether one of these options would have been better than fixing the vent screen. Why?

**IN CONVERSATION**

1. Working in small groups or as a whole class, share your individual responses to these questions and then try to reach a group consensus on the issues: Was fixing the screen an instance of cruelty to animals? What other alternatives, if any, might have been ethically preferable?
2. If class discussion caused some students' views to evolve or change, how and why?

# Understanding Classical Argument

## What Is Argument?

The study of argumentation involves two components: truth seeking and persuasion:

- By *truth seeking,* we mean a diligent, open-minded, and responsible search for the best course of action or solution to a problem, taking into account all the available information and alternative points of view.
- By *persuasion,* we mean the art of making a claim* on an issue and justifying it convincingly so that the audience's initial resistance to your position is overcome and they are moved toward your position.

*By long-standing tradition, the thesis statement of an argument is often called its "claim."

**9.1**
Explain the theory and rhetorical principles underlying effective arguments.

These two components of argument seem paradoxically at odds: Truth seeking asks us to relax our certainties and be willing to change our views; persuasion asks us to be certain, to be committed to our claims, and to get others to change their views. We can overcome this paradox if we dispel two common but misleading views of argument. The most common view is that argument is a fight as in "I just got into a horrible argument with my roommate." This view of argument as a fist-waving, shouting match in which you ridicule anyone who disagrees with you (popularized by radio and television talk shows and the Internet) entirely disregards argument as truth seeking, but it also misrepresents argument as persuasion because it polarizes people, rather than promoting understanding, new ways of seeing, and change.

Another common but misleading view is that argument is a pro/con debate modeled after high school or college debate matches. Although debating can be an excellent way to develop critical thinking skills, it misrepresents argument as a two-sided contest with winners and losers. Because controversial issues involve many different points of view, not just two, reducing an issue to pro/con positions distorts the complexity of the disagreement. Instead of thinking of *both* sides of an issue, we need to think of *all* sides. Equally troublesome, the debate image invites us to ask, "Who won the debate?" rather than "What is the best solution to the question that divides us?" The best solution might be a compromise between the two debaters or an undiscovered third position. The debate image tends to privilege the confident extremes in a controversy rather than the complex and muddled middle.

From our perspective, the best image for understanding argument is neither "fight" nor "debate" but the deliberations of a committee representing a wide spectrum of community voices charged with finding the best solution to a problem. From this perspective, argument is both a *process* and a *product*. As a process, argument is an act of inquiry characterized by fact-finding, information gathering, and consideration of alternative points of view. As a product, it is someone's contribution to the conversation at any one moment—a turn taking in a conversation, a formal speech, or a written position paper such as the one you will write for this chapter. The goal of argument as process is truth seeking; the goal of argument as product is persuasion. When members of a diverse committee are willing to argue persuasively for their respective points of view but are simultaneously willing to listen to other points of view and to change or modify their positions in light of new information or better arguments, then both components of argument are fully in play.

We cannot overemphasize the importance of both truth seeking and persuasion to your professional and civic life. Truth seeking makes you an informed and judicious employee and a citizen who delays decisions until a full range of evidence and alternative views are aired and examined. Persuasion gives you the power to influence the world around you, whether through letters to the editor or blogs on political issues or through convincing position papers for professional life. Whenever an organization needs to make a major decision, those who can think flexibly and write persuasively can wield great influence.

Having introduced you to argument as both process and product, we now turn to the details of effective argumentation. To help orient you, we begin by describing the typical stages that mark students' growth as arguers.

## Stages of Development: Your Growth as an Arguer

We have found that when we teach argument in our classes, students typically proceed through identifiable stages as their argumentative skills increase. While these stages may or may not describe your own development, they suggest the skills you should strive to acquire.

- ***Stage 1: Argument as personal opinion.*** At the beginning of instruction in argument, students typically express strong personal opinions but have trouble justifying their opinions with reasons and evidence and often create short, undeveloped arguments that are circular, lacking in evidence, and insulting to those who disagree. The following freewrite, written by a student first confronting the starling case, illustrates this stage:

  > The family shouldn't have killed the starlings because that is really wrong! I mean that act was disgusting. It makes me sick to think how so many people are just willing to kill something for no reason at all. How are these parents going to teach their children values if they just go out and kill little birds for no good reason?!! This whole family is what's wrong with America!

  This writer's opinion is passionate and heartfelt, but it provides neither reasons nor evidence why someone else should hold the same opinion.

- ***Stage 2: Argument structured as claim supported by one or more reasons.*** This stage represents a quantum leap in argumentative skill because the writer can now produce a rational plan containing point sentences (the reasons) and particulars (the evidence). The writer who produced the previous freewrite later developed a structure like this:

  The family's act constituted cruelty to animals

  - because the starlings were doing minimal harm.
  - because other options were available.
  - because the way they killed the birds caused needless suffering.

- ***Stage 3: Increased attention to truth seeking.*** In Stage 3 students become increasingly engaged with the complexity of the issue as they listen to their classmates' views, conduct research, and evaluate alternative perspectives and stances. They are often willing to change their positions when they see the power of other arguments.

- ***Stage 4: Ability to articulate the unstated assumptions underlying their arguments.*** As we show later in this chapter, each reason in a writer's argument is based on an assumption, value, or belief (often unstated) that the audience must accept if the argument is to be persuasive. Often the writer needs to state these assumptions explicitly and support them. At this stage students identify and analyze their own assumptions and those of their intended audiences. Students gain increased skill at accommodating alternative views through refutation or concession.

- ***Stage 5: Ability to link an argument to the values and beliefs of the intended audience.*** In this stage students are increasingly able to link their arguments to their audience's values and beliefs and to adapt structure and tone to the resistance level of their audience. Students also appreciate how delayed-thesis arguments or other psychological strategies can be more effective than closed-form arguments when addressing hostile audiences.

The rest of this chapter helps you progress through these stages. Although you can read the remainder in one sitting, we recommend that you break your reading into sections, going over the material slowly and applying it to your own ideas in progress. Let the chapter's concepts and explanations sink in gradually, and return to them periodically for review. This section on "Understanding Classical Argument" comprises a compact but comprehensive course in argumentation.

## Creating an Argument Frame: A Claim with Reasons

Somewhere in the writing process, whether early or late, you need to create a frame for your argument. This frame includes a clear question that focuses the argument, your claim, and one or more supporting reasons. Often your reasons, stated as *because* clauses, can be attached to your claim to provide a working thesis statement.

**Finding an Arguable Issue**    At the heart of any argument is an **issue,** which we can define as a question that invites more than one reasonable answer and thus leads to perplexity or disagreement. This requirement excludes disagreements based on personal tastes, where no shared criteria can be developed ("Baseball is more fun than soccer"). It also excludes purely private questions because issues arise out of disagreements in communities.

Issue questions are often framed as yes/no choices, especially when they appear on ballots or in courtrooms: Should gay marriage be legalized? Should the federal government place a substantial tax on gasoline to elevate its price? Is this defendant guilty of armed robbery? Just as frequently, they can be framed openly, inviting many different possible answers: What should our city do about skateboarders in downtown pedestrian areas? How can we best solve the energy crisis?

It is important to remember that framing an issue as a yes/no question does not mean that all points of view fall neatly into pro/con categories. Although citizens may be forced to vote yes or no on a proposed ballot initiative, they can support or oppose the initiative for a variety of reasons. Some may vote happily for the initiative, others vote for it only by holding their noses, and still others oppose it vehemently but for entirely different reasons. To argue effectively, you need to appreciate the wide range of perspectives from which people approach the yes/no choice.

How you frame your question necessarily affects the scope and shape of your argument itself. In our exploratory exercise we framed the starling question in two ways: (1) Was the family guilty of cruelty to animals? and (2) What should the family have done about the starlings? Framed in the first way, your argument would have to develop criteria for "cruelty to animals" and then argue whether the family's actions met those criteria. Framed in the second way, you could argue for your own solution to the problem, ranging from doing nothing (waiting for the birds to grow up and leave, then fixing the screen) to climbing into the attic and drowning the birds so that their deaths are quick and painless. Or you could word the question in a broader, more philosophical way: When are humans justified in killing animals? Or you could focus on a subissue: When can an animal be labeled a "pest"?

---

**FOR WRITING AND DISCUSSION**

## Identifying Arguable Issues

1. Working individually, make a list of several communities that you belong to and then identify one or more questions currently being contested within those communities. (If you have trouble, check your local campus and city newspapers or an organizational newsletter; you'll quickly discover a wealth of contested issues.) Then share your list with classmates.
2. Pick two or three issues of particular interest to you, and try framing them in different ways: as broad or narrow questions, as open-ended or yes/no questions. Place several examples on the chalkboard for class discussion.

---

**Stating a Claim**  Your **claim** is the position you want to take on the issue. It is your brief, one-sentence answer to your issue question:

> The family was not ethically justified in killing the starlings.
> The city should build skateboarding areas with ramps in all city parks.
> The federal government should substantially increase its taxes on gasoline.

You will appreciate argument as truth seeking if you find that your claim evolves as you think more deeply about your issue and listen to alternative views. Be willing to rephrase your claim to soften it or refocus it or even to reverse it as you progress through the writing process.

## Articulating Reasons

Your claim, which is the position you take on an issue, needs to be supported by reasons and evidence. A **reason** (sometimes called a "premise") is a subclaim that supports your main claim. In speaking or writing, a reason is usually linked to the claim with such connecting words as *because, therefore, so, consequently,* and *thus.* In planning your argument, a powerful strategy for developing reasons is to harness the grammatical power of the conjunction *because;* think of your reasons as *because* clauses attached to your claim. Formulating your reasons in this way allows you to create a thesis statement that breaks your argument into smaller parts, each part devoted to one of the reasons.

For advice on how much of your supporting argument you should summarize in your thesis statement, see Skill 12.3 on effective introductions.

Suppose, for example, that you are examining the issue "Should the government legalize hard drugs such as heroin and cocaine?" Here are several different points of view on this issue, each expressed as a claim with *because* clauses:

**ONE VIEW**

Cocaine and heroin should be legalized
- because legalizing drugs will keep the government out of people's private lives.
- because keeping these drugs illegal has the same negative effects on our society that alcohol prohibition did in the 1920s.

**ANOTHER VIEW**

Cocaine and heroin should be legalized
- because taking drug sales out of the hands of drug dealers would reduce street violence.
- because decriminalization would cut down on prison overcrowding and free police to concentrate on dangerous crime rather than on finding drug dealers.
- because elimination of underworld profits would change the economic structure of the underclass and promote shifts to socially productive jobs and careers.

**STILL ANOTHER VIEW**

The government should not legalize heroin and cocaine
- because doing so will lead to an increase in drug users and addicts.
- because doing so will send the message that it is okay to use hard drugs.

Although the yes/no framing of this question seems to reduce the issue to a two-position debate, many different value systems are at work here. The first pro-legalization argument, libertarian in perspective, values maximum individual freedom. The second argument—although it too supports legalization—takes a community perspective valuing the social benefits of eliminating the black market drug-dealing culture. In the same way, individuals could oppose legalization for a variety of reasons.

---

**FOR WRITING AND DISCUSSION**

## Generating *Because* Clauses

Working in small groups or as a whole class, generate a list of reasons for and against one or more of the following yes/no claims. State your reasons as *because* clauses. Think of as many *because* clauses as possible by imagining a wide variety of perspectives on the issue.

1. The school year for grades 1 through 12 should be lengthened to eleven months.
2. The federal government should place a substantial tax on gasoline.
3. The United States should adopt a single-payer, government-financed healthcare system like that of Canada.
4. Playing violent video games is a harmful influence on teenage boys. [or] Women's fashion and style magazines (such as *Glamour* or *Seventeen*) are harmful influences on teenage girls.
5. The war on terror requires occasional use of "enhanced interrogation techniques" on some detainees.

---

## Articulating Underlying Assumptions

So far, we have focused on the frame of an argument as a claim supported with one or more reasons. Shortly, we will proceed to the flesh and muscle of an argument, which is the evidence you use to support your reasons. But before turning to evidence, we need to look at another crucial part of an argument's frame: its *underlying assumptions*.

**What Do We Mean by an Underlying Assumption?** Every time you link a claim with a reason, you make a silent assumption that may need to be articulated and examined. Consider this argument:

> The family was justified in killing the starlings because starlings are pests.

To support this argument, the writer would first need to provide evidence that starlings are pests (examples of the damage they do and so forth). But the persuasiveness of the argument rests on the underlying assumption that it is okay to kill pests. If an audience doesn't agree with that assumption, then the argument flounders unless the writer articulates the assumption and defends it. The complete frame of the argument must therefore include the underlying assumption.

> ***Claim:*** The family was justified in killing the starlings.
>
> ***Reason:*** Because starlings are pests.
>
> ***Underlying assumption:*** It is ethically justifiable to kill pests.

It is important to examine the underlying assumption that connects any reason to its claim *because you must determine whether your audience will accept that assumption. If not, you need to make it explicit and support it.* Think of the underlying assumption as a general principle, rule, belief, or value that connects the reason to the claim. It answers your reader's question, "Why, if I accept your reason, should I accept your claim?"*

Here are a few more examples:

> ***Claim with reason:*** Women should be allowed to join combat units because the image of women as combat soldiers would help society overcome gender stereotyping.
>
> ***Underlying assumption:*** It is good to overcome gender stereotyping.

> ***Claim with reason:*** The government should not legalize heroin and cocaine because doing so will lead to an increase in drug users.
>
> ***Underlying assumption:*** It is bad to increase the number of drug users.

> ***Claim with reason:*** The family was guilty of cruelty to animals in the starling case because less drastic means of solving the problem were available.
>
> ***Underlying assumption:*** A person should choose the least drastic means to solve a problem.

---

*Our explanation of argument structure is influenced by the work of philosopher Stephen Toulmin, who viewed argument as a dynamic courtroom drama where opposing attorneys exchange arguments and cross-examinations before a judge and jury. Although we use Toulmin's strategies for analyzing an argument structure, we have chosen not to use his specialized terms, which include *warrant* (the underlying assumption connecting a reason to a claim), *grounds* (the evidence that supports the claim), *backing* (the evidence and subarguments that support the warrant), *conditions of rebuttal* (all the ways that skeptics could attack an argument or all the conditions under which the argument wouldn't hold), and finally *qualifier* (an indication of the strength of the claim). However, your instructor may prefer to use these terms and in that case may provide you with more explanation and examples.

## Identifying Underlying Assumptions

Identify the underlying assumptions in each of the following claims with reasons.

1. Cocaine and heroin should be legalized because legalizing drugs will keep the government out of people's private lives.
2. The government should raise gasoline taxes because the higher price would substantially reduce gasoline consumption.
3. The government should not raise gasoline taxes because the higher price would place undue hardship on low-income people.
4. The government should not raise gasoline taxes because other means of reducing gasoline consumption would be more effective.
5. The government is justified in detaining suspected terrorists indefinitely without charging them with a crime because doing so may prevent another terrorist attack.

## Using Evidence Effectively

Inside your arguments, each of your reasons (as well as any underlying assumptions that you decide to state explicitly and defend) needs to be supported either by subarguments or by evidence. By "evidence" we mean facts, examples, summaries of research articles, statistics, testimony, or other relevant data that will persuade your readers to accept your reasons. Note that evidence always exists within a rhetorical context; as a writer you select and shape the evidence that will best support your position, knowing that skeptics may point to evidence that you did not select. Evidence is thus not the same as "proof"; used ethically, evidence presents the best case for your claim without purporting to be the whole truth.

Evidence can sometimes come from personal experience, but in most cases it comes from your own field or library research. The kinds of evidence most often used in argument are the following:

**Factual Data** Factual data can provide persuasive support for your arguments. (Keep in mind that writers always select their facts through an angle of vision, so the use of facts doesn't preclude skeptics from bringing in counterfacts.) Here is how evolutionary biologist Olivia Judson used factual data to support her point that malaria-carrying mosquitoes cause unacceptable harm to human lives and wealth.

> Each year, malaria kills at least one million people and causes more than 300 million cases of acute illness. For children worldwide, it's one of the leading causes of death. The economic burden is significant too: malaria costs Africa more than $12 billion in lost growth each year. In the United States, hundreds of millions of dollars are spent every year on mosquito control.

**Examples** An example from personal experience can often be used to support a reason. Here is how student writer Ross Taylor used personal experience to argue that paintball is safe even though accidents can happen. (You can read his complete essay on pp. 230–233.)

I admit that paintball can be dangerous and that accidents do happen. I personally had a friend lose an eye after inadvertently shooting himself in the eye from a very close range. The fact of the matter is that he made a mistake by looking down the barrel of a loaded gun and the trigger malfunctioned. Had he been more careful or worn the proper equipment, he most likely would have been fine. During my first organized paintball experience I was hit in the goggles by a very powerful gun and felt no pain. The only discomfort came from having to clean all the paint off my goggles after the game. When played properly, paintball is an incredibly safe sport.

Besides specific examples like this, writers sometimes invent hypothetical examples, or *scenarios,* to illustrate an issue or hypothesize about the consequences of an event. (Of course, you must tell your reader that the example or scenario is hypothetical.)

**Summaries of Research**    Another common way to support an argument is to summarize research articles. Here is how a student writer, investigating whether menopausal women should use hormone replacement therapy to combat menopausal symptoms, used one of several research articles in her paper. The student began by summarizing research studies showing possible dangers of hormone replacement therapy. She then made the following argument:

Another reason not to use hormone replacement therapy is that other means are available to ease menopausal symptoms such as hot flashes, irritability, mood changes, and sleep disturbance. One possible alternative treatment is acupuncture. One study (Cohen, Rousseau, and Carey) revealed that a randomly selected group of menopausal women receiving specially designed acupuncture treatment showed substantial decreases in menopausal symptoms as compared to a control group. What was particularly persuasive about this study was that both the experimental group and the control group received acupuncture, but the needle insertion sites for the experimental group were specifically targeted to relieve menopausal symptoms whereas the control group received acupuncture at sites used to promote general well-being. The researchers concluded that "acupuncture may be recommended as a safe and effective therapy for reducing menopausal hot flushes as well as contributing to the reduction in sleep disruptions" (299).*

**Statistics**    Another common form of evidence is statistics. Here is how one writer used statistics to argue that the federal government should raise fuel-efficiency standards placed on auto manufacturers:

There is very little need for most Americans to drive huge SUVs. One recent survey found that 87 percent of four-wheel-drive SUV owners had never taken their SUVs off-road (Yacobucci)... . By raising fuel-efficiency standards, the government would force vehicle manufacturers to find a way to create more earth-friendly vehicles that would lower vehicle emissions and pollution. An article entitled "Update:

*The examples in this section use the MLA (Modern Language Association) style for documenting sources. See Chapter 15 for full explanations of how to use both the MLA and APA (American Psychological Association) systems for citing and documenting sources. The complete bibliographic information for this article would be found in the "Works Cited" pages alphabetized under "Cohen."

What You Should Know Before Purchasing a New Vehicle" states that for every gallon of gasoline used by a vehicle, 20 to 28 pounds of carbon dioxide are released into the environment. This article further states that carbon dioxide emissions from automobiles are responsible for 20 percent of all carbon dioxide released into the atmosphere from human causes.

Just as writers select facts, examples, and research studies according to their angle of vision, so do they select and shape numerical data. In the above example, the writer focuses on the environmental harm caused by vehicles, especially SUVs. But you must always read statistics rhetorically. For example, the same statistical "fact" can be framed in different ways. There is a difference in focus and feel between these two ways of using the same data:

- "20 percent of human-caused $CO_2$ emissions come from automobiles" [puts automobiles in the foreground]
- "Although cars do cause some pollution, a full 80 percent of human-caused $CO_2$ emissions come from sources other than cars." [puts automobiles in the background]

**Testimony**   Writers can also use expert testimony to bolster a case. The following passage from a student essay arguing in favor of therapeutic cloning uses testimony from a prominent physician and medical researcher. Part of the paragraph quotes this expert directly; another part paraphrases the expert's argument.

> As Dr. Gerald Fischbach, Executive Vice President for Health and Biomedical Sciences and Dean of Medicine at Columbia University, said in front of a United States Senate subcommittee: "New embryonic stem cell procedures could be vital in solving the persistent problem of a lack of genetically matched, qualified donors of organs and tissues that we face today." Fischbach goes on to say that this type of cloning could also lead to the discovery of cures for diseases such as ALS, Parkinson's disease, Alzheimer's disease, diabetes, heart disease, cancer, and possibly others.

Rather than provide direct research evidence that stem cell cloning might one day lead to cures for diseases, the writer draws on testimony from the dean of a prestigious medical school. Opponents of stem cell research might draw on other experts, selecting those who are skeptical of this claim.

**Subarguments**   Sometimes writers support reasons not directly through data but through sequences of subarguments. Sometimes these subarguments develop a persuasive analogy, hypothesize about consequences, or simply advance the argument through a chain of connected points. In the following passage, taken from a philosophic article justifying torture under certain conditions, the author uses a subargument to support one of his main points—that a terrorist holding victims hostage has no "rights":

> There is an important difference between terrorists and their victims that should mute talk of the terrorist's "rights." The terrorist's victims are at risk unintentionally, not having asked to be endangered. But the terrorist knowingly initiated his actions. Unlike his victims, he volunteered for the risks of his deed. By threatening to kill for profit or idealism, he renounces civilized standards, and he can have no complaint if civilization tries to thwart him by whatever means necessary.

Rather than using direct empirical evidence, the author supports his point with a subargument showing how terrorists differ from victims and thus relinquish their claim to rights.

## Evaluating Evidence: The STAR Criteria

To make your arguments as persuasive as possible, apply to your evidence what rhetorician Richard Fulkerson calls the STAR criteria (**S**ufficiency, **T**ypicality, **A**ccuracy, and **R**elevance),* as shown in the chart on this page.

It is often difficult to create arguments in which all your evidence fully meets the STAR criteria. Sometimes you need to proceed on evidence that might not be typical, verifiable, or as up-to-date as you would like. In such cases, you can often increase the effectiveness of your argument by qualifying your claim. Consider the difference between these two claims:

- ***Strong claim:*** Watching violent TV cartoons increases aggressive behavior in boys.
- ***Qualified claim:*** Watching violent TV cartoons can increase aggressive play behavior in some boys.

To be made persuasive, the strong claim requires substantial evidence meeting the STAR criteria. In contrast, the qualified claim requires less rigorous evidence, perhaps only an example or two combined with the results of one study.

### The STAR Criteria for Evaluating Evidence

| STAR Criteria | Implied Question | Comments |
|---|---|---|
| **S**ufficiency | Is there enough evidence? | If you don't provide enough evidence, skeptical audiences can dismiss your claim as a "hasty generalization." To argue that marijuana is not a harmful drug, you would probably need more evidence than the results of one study or the testimony of a healthy pot smoker. |
| **T**ypicality | Are the chosen data representative and typical? | If you choose extreme or rare-case examples, rather than typical and representative ones, your audience might accuse you of cherry-picking your data. Testimony from persons whose back pain was cured by yoga may not support the general claim that yoga is good for back pain. |
| **A**ccuracy | Are the data accurate and up-to-date? | Providing recent, accurate data is essential for your own *ethos* as a writer. Data from 1998 on homelessness or inaccurately gathered data may be ineffective for a current policy argument. |
| **R**elevance | Are the data relevant to the claim? | Even though your evidence is accurate, up-to-date, and representative, if it's not pertinent to the claim, it will be ineffective. For example, evidence that nuclear waste is dangerous is not relevant to the issue of whether it can be stored securely in Yucca Mountain. |

*Richard Fulkerson, *Teaching the Argument in Writing*, Urbana: National Council of Teachers of English, 1996, pp. 44–53. In this section we are indebted to Fulkerson's discussion.

See Skill 14.1 for advice on evaluating sources for reliability and bias.

As you gather evidence, consider also its source and the extent to which your audience will trust that source. While all data must be interpreted and hence are never completely impartial, careful readers are aware of how easily data can be skewed. Newspapers, magazines, blogs, and journals often have political biases and different levels of respectability. Generally, evidence from peer-reviewed scholarly journals is more highly regarded than evidence from secondhand sources. Particularly problematic is information gathered from Internet Web sites, which can vary widely in reliability and degree of bias.

## Addressing Objections and Counterarguments

Having looked at the frame of an argument (claim, reasons, and underlying assumptions) and at the kinds of evidence used to flesh out the frame, let's turn now to the important concern of anticipating and responding to objections and counterarguments. In this section, we show you an extended example of a student's anticipating and responding to a reader's objection. We then describe a planning schema that can help you anticipate objections and show you how to respond to counterarguments, either through refutation or concession. Finally, we show how your active imagining of alternative views can lead you to qualify your claim.

**Anticipating Objections: An Extended Example** In our earlier discussions of the starling case, we saw how readers might object to the argument "The family was justified in killing the starlings because starlings are pests." What rankles these readers is the underlying assumption that it is okay to kill pests. Imagine an objecting reader saying something like this:

It is *not* okay to get annoyed with a living creature, label it a "pest," and then kill it. This whole use of the term *pest* suggests that humans have the right to dominate nature. We need to have more reverence for nature. The ease with which the family solved their problem by killing living things sets a bad example for children. The family could have waited until fall and then fixed the screen.

Imagining such an objection might lead a writer to modify his or her claim. But if the writer remains committed to that claim, then he or she must develop a response. In the following example in which a student writer argues that it is okay to kill the starlings, note (1) how the writer uses evidence to show that starlings are pests; (2) how he summarizes a possible objection to his underlying assumption that killing pests is morally justified; and (3) how he supports his assumption with further arguments.

STUDENT ARGUMENT DEFENDING REASON AND UNDERLYING ASSUMPTION

*Claim with reason*

*Evidence that starlings are pests*

The family was justified in killing the starlings because starlings are pests. Starlings are nonindigenous birds that drive out native species and multiply rapidly. When I searched "starlings pests" on Google, I discovered thousands of Web sites dealing with starlings as pests. Starlings are hated by farmers and gardeners because huge flocks of them devour newly planted seeds in spring as well as fruits and berries at harvest. A flock of starlings can devastate a cherry orchard in a few days. As invasive nesters, starlings can also damage attics by tearing up insulation and defecating on stored items. Many of the Web site articles focused on ways to kill off starling populations. In killing the starlings, the family was protecting its own property and reducing the population of these pests.

Many readers might object to my argument, saying that humans should have a reverence for nature and not quickly try to kill off any creature they label a pest. Further, these readers might say that even if starlings are pests, the family could have waited until fall to repair the attic or found some other means of protecting their property without having to kill the baby starlings. I too would have waited until fall if the birds in the attic had been swallows or some other native species without starlings' destructiveness and propensity for unchecked population growth. But starlings should be compared to rats or mice. We set traps for rodents because we know the damage they cause when they nest in walls and attics. We don't get sentimental trying to save the orphaned rat babies. In the same way, we are justified in eliminating starlings as soon as they begin infesting our houses.

*Summary of a possible objection*

*Response to the objection*

In the preceding example, we see how the writer uses evidence to support his reason and then, anticipating readers' objection to his underlying assumption, summarizes that objection and provides a response to it. One might not be convinced by the argument, but the writer has done a good job of trying to support both his reason (starlings are pests) and his underlying assumption (it is morally justifiable to kill at least some pests).

**Using a Planning Schema to Anticipate Objections**  In the previous example, the student's arguing strategy was triggered by his anticipation of reader objections. Note that a skeptical audience can attack an argument by attacking either a writer's reasons or a writer's underlying assumptions. This knowledge allows us to create a planning schema that can help writers develop a persuasive argument. This schema encourages writers to articulate their argument frame (claim, reason, and underlying assumption) and then to imagine what kinds of evidence or arguments could be used to support both the reason and the underlying assumption. Equally important, the schema encourages writers to anticipate counterarguments by imagining how skeptical readers might object to the writer's reason or underlying assumption or both. To create the schema, simply make a chart with slots for each of these elements. Here is how another student writer used this schema to plan an argument on the starling case:

### CLAIM WITH REASON

The family showed cruelty to animals because the way they killed the birds caused needless suffering.

### UNDERLYING ASSUMPTION

If it is necessary to kill an animal, then the killing should be done in the least painful way possible.

### EVIDENCE TO SUPPORT REASON

First I've got to show how the way of killing the birds (starving them slowly) caused the birds to suffer. I've also got to show that this way of killing was needless since other means were available such as calling an exterminator who would remove the birds and either relocate them or kill them painlessly. If no other alternative was available, someone should have crawled into the attic and found a painless way to kill the birds.

### EVIDENCE/ARGUMENTS TO SUPPORT UNDERLYING ASSUMPTIONS

I've got to convince readers it is wrong to make an animal suffer if you don't have to. Humans have a natural antipathy to needless suffering—our feeling of unease if we imagine cattle or chickens caused to suffer for our food rather than being cleanly and quickly killed. If a horse is incurably wounded, we put it to sleep rather then let it suffer. We are morally obligated to cause the least pain possible.

### WAYS SKEPTICS MIGHT OBJECT

*How could a reader object to my reason?* A reader might say that the starlings didn't suffer much (baby birds don't feel pain). A reader might also object to my claim that other means were available: They might say there was no other way to kill the starlings. Poison may cause just as much suffering. Cost of exterminator is prohibitive.

*How could a reader object to my underlying assumption?* Perhaps the reader would say that my rule to cause the least pain possible does not apply to animal pests. In class, someone said that we shouldn't worry about the baby starlings any more than we would worry about killing baby rats. Laws of nature condemn millions of animals each year to death by starvation or by being eaten alive by other animals. Humans occasionally have to take their place within this tooth-and-claw natural system.

How many of the ideas from this schema would the writer use in her actual paper? That is a judgment call based on the writer's analysis of the audience. If this student's target audience includes classmates who think it is morally okay to kill pests by the most efficient means possible, then she should summarize her classmates' argument fairly and then try to convince them that humans are ethically called to rise above tooth-and-claw nature.

---

**FOR WRITING AND DISCUSSION**

### Creating Argument Schemas

Working individually or in small groups, create a planning schema for the following arguments. For each claim with reason: (a) imagine the kinds of evidence needed to support the reason; (b) identify the underlying assumption; (c) imagine a strategy for supporting the assumption; and (d) anticipate possible objections to the reason and to the assumption.

1. ***Claim with reason:*** We should buy a hybrid car rather than an SUV with a HEMI engine because doing so will help the world save gasoline. (Imagine this argument aimed at your significant other, who has his or her heart set on a huge HEMI-powered SUV.)
2. ***Claim with reason:*** Gay marriage should be legalized because doing so will promote faithful, monogamous relationships among lesbians and gay men. (Aim this argument at supporters of traditional marriage.)
3. ***Claim with reason:*** The war in Iraq was justified because it rid the world of a hideous and brutal dictator. (Aim this argument at a critic of the war.)

# Responding to Objections, Counterarguments, and Alternative Views

We have seen how a writer needs to anticipate alternative views that give rise to objections and counterarguments. Surprisingly, one of the best ways to approach counterarguments is to summarize them fairly. Make your imagined reader's best case against your argument. By resisting the temptation to distort a counterargument, you demonstrate a willingness to consider the issue from all sides. Moreover, summarizing a counterargument reduces your reader's tendency to say, "Yes, but have you thought of...?" After you have summarized an objection or counterargument fairly and charitably, you must then decide how to respond to it. Your two main choices are to rebut it or concede to it.

**Rebutting Opposing Views** When rebutting or refuting an argument, you can question the argument's reasons and supporting evidence or the underlying assumptions or both. In the following student example, the writer summarizes her classmates' objections to abstract art and then analyzes shortcomings in their argument.

> Some of my classmates object to abstract art because it apparently takes no technical drawing talent. They feel that historically artists turned to abstract art because they lacked the technical drafting skills exhibited by Remington, Russell, and Rockwell. Therefore these abstract artists created an art form that anyone was capable of and that was less time consuming, and then they paraded it as artistic progress. But I object to the notion that these artists turned to abstraction because they could not do representative drawing. Many abstract artists, such as Picasso, were excellent draftsmen, and their early pieces show very realistic drawing skill. As his work matured, Picasso became more abstract in order to increase the expressive quality of his work. *Guernica* was meant as a protest against the bombing of that city by the Germans. To express the terror and suffering of the victims more vividly, he distorted the figures and presented them in a black and white journalistic manner. If he had used representational images and color—which he had the skill to do—much of the emotional content would have been lost and the piece probably would not have caused the demand for justice that it did.

**Conceding to Opposing Views** In some cases, an alternative view can be very strong. If so, don't hide that view from your readers; summarize it and concede to it.

Making concessions to opposing views is not necessarily a sign of weakness; in many cases, a concession simply acknowledges that the issue is complex and that your position is tentative. In turn, a concession can enhance a reader's respect for you and invite the reader to follow your example and weigh the strengths of your own argument charitably. Writers typically concede to opposing views with transitional expressions such as the following:

| | | | |
|---|---|---|---|
| admittedly | I must admit that | I agree that | granted |
| even though | I concede that | while it is true that | |

After conceding to an opposing view, you should shift to a different field of values where your position is strong and then argue for those new values. For example, adversaries of drug legalization argue plausibly that legalizing drugs would increase the number of users and addicts. If you support legalization, here is how you might deal with this point without fatally damaging your own argument:

> Opponents of legalization claim—and rightly so—that legalization will lead to an increase in drug users and addicts. I wish this weren't so, but it is. Nevertheless, the other benefits of legalizing drugs—eliminating the black market, reducing street crime, and freeing up thousands of police from fighting the war on drugs—more than outweigh the social costs of increased drug use and addiction, especially if tax revenues from drug sales are plowed back into drug education and rehabilitation programs.

The writer concedes that legalization will increase addiction (one reason for opposing legalization) and that drug addiction is bad (the underlying assumption for that reason). But then the writer redeems the case for legalization by shifting the argument to another field of values (the benefits of eliminating the black market, reducing crime, and so forth).

**Qualifying Your Claim**    The need to summarize and respond to alternative views lets the writer see an issue's complexity and appreciate that no one position has a total monopoly on the truth. Consequently, writers often need to qualify their claims—that is, limit the scope or force of a claim to make it less sweeping and therefore less vulnerable. Consider the difference between the sentences "After-school jobs are bad for teenagers" and "After-school jobs are often bad for teenagers." The first claim can be refuted by one counterexample of a teenager who benefited from an after-school job. Because the second claim admits exceptions, it is much harder to refute. Unless your argument is airtight, you will want to limit your claim with qualifiers such as the following:

| | |
|---|---|
| perhaps | maybe |
| in many cases | generally |
| tentatively | sometimes |
| often | usually |
| probably | likely |
| may *or* might (*rather than* is) | |

You can also qualify a claim with an opening *unless* clause ("*Unless* your apartment is well soundproofed, you should not buy such a powerful stereo system").

## Seeking Audience-Based Reasons

Much of the advice that we have presented so far can be consolidated into a single principle: Seek "audience-based reasons." By **audience-based reasons**, we mean reasons that depend on underlying assumptions, values, or beliefs that your targeted audience already holds. In such cases, you won't need to state and defend your underlying assumptions because the audience already accepts them. A good illustration comes from civil engineer David Rockwood's argument against wind power that we used in Chapter 1, page 15. Rockwood's targeted readers are environmentalists who have high hopes for wind-generated electricity. Rockwood's final reason opposing wind power is that constructing thousands of wind towers will damage the pristine mountain environment. To environmentalists, this reason is powerful because its underlying assumption ("Preserving the environment is good") appeals to their values.

When you plan your argument, seek audience-based reasons whenever possible. Suppose, for example, that you are advocating the legalization of heroin and cocaine. If you know that your audience is concerned about street crime, then you can argue that legalization of drugs will make the streets safer.

| | |
|---|---|
| We should legalize drugs *because doing so will make our streets safer:* It will cut down radically on street criminals seeking drug money, and it will free up narcotics police to focus on other kinds of crime. | Audience-based reason: Underlying assumption is that making our streets safer is a good thing—a value the audience already holds. |

For another group of readers—those concerned about improving the quality of life for youths in inner cities—you might argue that legalization of drugs will lead to better lives for people in poor neighborhoods.

| | |
|---|---|
| We should legalize drugs *because doing so will improve the lives of inner-city youth* by eliminating the lure of drug trafficking that tempts so many inner-city youth into crime. | Audience-based reason: Its underlying assumption is that it is good to improve the lives of inner-city youth. |

Or if your audience is concerned about high taxes and government debt, you might say:

| | |
|---|---|
| We should legalize drugs *because doing so will help us balance federal and state budgets:* It will decrease police and prison costs by decriminalizing narcotics; and it will eliminate the black market in drugs, allowing us to collect taxes on drug sales. | Audience-based reason: Assumes that it is a good thing to balance federal and state budgets. |

In contrast, if you oppose legalizing drugs, you could appeal to those concerned about drug addiction and public health by using the following audience-based reason:

| | |
|---|---|
| We should not legalize drugs *because doing so will increase the number of drug addicts and make drug use seem socially acceptable.* | Audience-based reason: Appeals to the underlying assumption that increasing the number of drug addicts and making drugs socially acceptable are bad things. |

In each case, you move people toward your position by connecting your argument to their beliefs and values.

## Appealing to *Ethos* and *Pathos*

When the classical rhetoricians examined ways that orators could persuade listeners, they focused on three kinds of proofs: *logos,* the appeal to reason; *ethos,* the appeal to the speaker's character; and *pathos,* the appeal to the emotions and the sympathetic imagination. We introduced you to these appeals in Chapter 3, Concept 3.2, because they are important rhetorical considerations in any kind of writing. Understanding how arguments persuade through *logos, ethos,* and *pathos* is particularly helpful when your aim is persuasion. So far in this chapter we have focused on *logos.* In this section we examine *ethos* and *pathos.*

**Appeals to Ethos**  A powerful way to increase the persuasiveness of an argument is to gain your readers' trust. You appeal to *ethos* whenever you present yourself as credible and trustworthy. For most readers to accept your argument, they must perceive you as knowledgeable, trustworthy, and fair. In the following chart, we suggest ways to enhance your argument's *ethos:*

## Strategies for Enhancing Your Argument's *Ethos*

| What to Do | Explanation |
|---|---|
| Be knowledgeable by doing your homework. | Your credibility is enhanced when readers are convinced that you know your subject thoroughly. |
| Use evidence responsibly. | If you cherry-pick your evidence, you may be perceived as a propagandist rather than as a thoughtful arguer who recognizes complexity. |
| Be fair to alternative views. | If you scorn or misrepresent opposing views, you will win favor only with those who already agree with you. If you are a good listener to others, they will be more apt to listen to you. |
| Search for values and assumptions you can share with your audience. | You will build bridges toward skeptical readers, rather than alienate them, if you can highlight shared assumptions or values. Use audience-based reasons where possible. |
| Show that you care about your issue; show also why your readers should care about it. | By showing why the issue matters both to you and your readers, you portray yourself as a person of integrity rather than as someone playing an argumentative game. |

**Appeals to Pathos**  Besides appealing to *logos* and *ethos,* you might also appeal to what the Greeks called *pathos.* Sometimes *pathos* is interpreted narrowly as an appeal to the emotions and is therefore devalued on the grounds that arguments should be rational rather than emotional. Although appeals to *pathos* can sometimes be irrational and irrelevant ("If you don't give me at least a B in this course, I will lose my scholarship and break my ill grandmother's heart"), they can also arouse audience interest and deepen understanding of an argument's human dimensions. The following chart suggests ways to increase *pathos* in your arguments:

| Strategies for Enhancing Your Argument's *Pathos* | | |
| --- | --- | --- |
| **What to Do** | **Explanation** | **Example** |
| Include storylike anecdotes. | Specific stories often create more emotional appeal than abstract statistics or generalizations. | In promoting health care reform, President Obama often told stories of persons made bankrupt by an illness or deprived of care because of a preexisting condition. On many occasions, he spoke of his own mother's fight with insurance companies as she lay dying of cancer. |
| Choose words with emotional or values-laden connotations. | Connotations of words often carry heavy emotional impact. | Opponents of health care reform talked about the Democrats' bill as "being jammed down people's throats"; supporters used words like "safety net," "compassion," or "care for children in poverty." |
| Where appropriate, use vivid language low on the ladder of abstraction. | Specific words paint pictures that have emotional appeal. | "The homeless man is huddled over the sewer grate, his feet wrapped in newspapers. He blows on his hands, then tucks them under his armpits and lies down on the sidewalk with his shoulders over the grate, his bed for the night." [*creates sympathy for the homeless*] "Several ratty derelicts drinking wine from a shared sack caused shoppers to avoid going into the store." [*creates sympathy for shoppers rather than the homeless*] |
| If the genre permits, include visuals with emotional impact. | Photographs or other visuals, including dramatic graphs or charts, can have a strong emotional appeal. | Articles promoting the environment often include photographs of smoke-belching factories or of endangered animals (often emphasizing their beauty or cuteness); often charts can have emotional appeals—such as a graph portraying dramatic increases in coal-fired electricity plants. |

## A Brief Primer on Informal Fallacies

We'll conclude our explanation of classical argument with a brief overview of the most common informal fallacies. Informal fallacies are instances of murky reasoning that can cloud an argument and lead to unsound conclusions. Because they can crop up unintentionally in anyone's writing, and because advertisers and hucksters often use them intentionally to deceive, it is a good idea to learn to recognize the more common fallacies.

### Post Hoc, Ergo Propter Hoc (*"After This, Therefore Because of This"*)

This fallacy involves mistaking sequence for cause. Just because one event happens before another event doesn't mean the first event caused the second. The connection may be coincidental, or some unknown third event may have caused both of these events.

**Example**    When the New York police department changed its policing tactics in the early 1990s, the crime rate plummeted. But did the new police tactics cause the decline in crime? (Many experts attributed the decline to other causes.) Persons lauding the police tactics ("Crime declined because the NYPD adopted new tactics") were accused of the *post hoc* fallacy.

**Hasty Generalization** Closely related to the *post hoc* fallacy is the hasty generalization, which refers to claims based on insufficient or unrepresentative data. Generally, persuasive evidence should meet the STAR criteria that we explained on pages 213–214. Because the amount of evidence needed in a given case can vary with the audience's degree of skepticism, it is difficult to draw an exact line between hasty and justified generalizations.

**Example**    The news frequently carries stories about vicious pit bulls. Therefore all pit bills must be vicious. [or] This experimental drug has been demonstrated safe in numerous clinical trials [based on tests using adult subjects]. Therefore this drug is safe for children.

**False Analogy** Arguers often use analogies to support a claim. (We shouldn't go to war in Iraq because doing so will lead us into a Vietnam-like quagmire.) However, analogical arguments are tricky because there are usually significant differences between the two things being compared as well as similarities. (Supporters of the war in Iraq argued that the situation in Iraq in 2002 was very different from that in Vietnam in 1964.) Although it is hard to draw an exact line between a false analogy and an acceptable one, charges of false analogy are frequent when skeptical opponents try to refute arguments based on analogies.

**Example**    Gun control will work in the United States because it works in England. [or] It's a mistake to force little Johnnie to take piano lessons because you can't turn a reluctant child into a musician any more than you can turn a tulip into a rose.

**Either/Or Reasoning** This fallacy occurs when a complex, multisided issue is reduced to two positions without acknowledging the possibility of other alternatives.

> **Example**    Either you are pro-choice on abortion or you are against the advancement of women in our culture.

**Ad Hominem** (*"Against the Person"*) When people can't find fault with an argument, they sometimes attack the arguer, substituting irrelevant assertions about that person's character for an analysis of the argument itself.

> **Example**    We should discount Senator Jones's argument against nuclear power because she has huge holdings in oil stock.

**Appeals to False Authority and Bandwagon Appeals** These fallacies offer as support the fact that a famous person or "many people" already support it. Unless the supporters are themselves authorities in the field, their support is irrelevant.

> **Example**    Buy Freeble oil because Joe Quarterback always uses it in his fleet of cars. [or] How can abortion be wrong if millions of people support a woman's right to choose?

**Non Sequitur** (*"It Does Not Follow"*) This fallacy occurs when there is no evident connection between a claim and its reason. Sometimes a *non sequitur* can be repaired by filling in gaps in the reasoning; at other times, the reasoning is simply fallacious.

> **Example**    I don't deserve a B for this course because I am a straight-A student.

**Circular Reasoning** This fallacy occurs when you state your claim and then, usually after rewording it, you state it again as your reason.

> **Example**    Marijuana is injurious to your health because it harms your body.

**Red Herring** This fallacy refers to the practice of raising an unrelated or irrelevant point deliberately to throw an audience offtrack. Politicians often employ this fallacy when they field questions from the public or press.

> **Example**    You raise a good question about my support of companies' outsourcing jobs to find cheaper labor. Let me tell you about my admiration for the productivity of the American worker.

**Slippery Slope** The slippery slope fallacy is based on the fear that one step in a direction we don't like inevitably leads to the next step with no stopping place.

> **Example**    If we allow embryonic stem cells to be used for medical research, we will open the door for full-scale reproductive cloning.

## A Classical Argument

Write a position paper that takes a stand on a controversial issue. Your introduction should present your issue, provide background, and state the claim you intend to support. In constructing your claim, strive to develop audience-based reasons. The body of your argument should summarize and respond to opposing views as well as present reasons and evidence in support of your own position. You will need to choose whether to summarize and refute opposing views before or after you have made your own case. Try to end your essay with your strongest arguments. Try also to include appeals to *pathos* and to create a positive, credible *ethos*.

We call this assignment a "classical" argument because it is patterned after the persuasive speeches of ancient Greek and Roman orators. A framework chart showing the generic structure of a classical argument is shown in Figure 9.1. Although there are many other ways to persuade audiences, the classical approach is a particularly effective introduction to persuasive writing.

**FIGURE 9.1** Framework for a Classical Argument

| | |
|---|---|
| **INTRODUCTION** | • Attention-grabber (often a memorable scene)<br>• Explanation of issue and needed background<br>• Writer's thesis (claim)<br>• Forecasting passage |
| **PRESENTATION OF WRITER'S POSITION** | • Main body of essay<br>• Presents and supports each reason in turn<br>• Each reason is tied to a value or belief held by the audience |
| **SUMMARY OF OPPOSING VIEWS** | • Summary of views differing from writer's (should be fair and complete) |
| **RESPONSE TO OPPOSING VIEWS** | • Refutes or concedes to opposing views<br>• Shows weaknesses in opposing views<br>• May concede to some strengths |
| **CONCLUSION** | • Brings essay to closure<br>• Often sums up argument<br>• Leaves strong, lasting impression<br>• Often calls for action or relates topic to a larger context of issues |

# Generating and Exploring Ideas

The tasks that follow are intended to help you generate ideas for your argument. Our goal is to help you build up a storehouse of possible issues, explore several of these possibilities, and then choose one for deeper exploration before you write your initial draft.

**Finding an Issue**   If you are having trouble finding an arguable issue for this writing project, consider the following strategies:

| Strategies for Finding an Arguable Issue | |
|---|---|
| **What to Do** | **Explanation** |
| Make an inventory of various communities you belong to. | See the exercise on page 226. Communities can range from the local (family, dorm, campus) to the state, nation, and world. |
| Brainstorm contested issues in these communities. | Start off with a fairly large list and then narrow it down according to your personal interest, current knowledge level, and degree of engagement. |
| On a few of these issues, explore the causes of disagreement. | Ask questions like these: What is at the heart of the disagreement? Disagreement about facts? About beliefs and values? About benefits versus costs? |
| Then explore your own point of view. | Ask: What is my position on the issue and why? What are alternative points of view? What is at stake? |
| Determine how much research you'll need to do. | If your issue requires research (check with your instructor), do a bibliographic search and enough skim reading to determine the kinds of arguments surrounding your issue, the kinds of evidence available, and the alternative views that people have taken. |
| Choose your issue and begin your research. | Your goal is to "wallow in complexity" in order to earn your thesis and create a knowledgeable *ethos*. Note: Some issues allow you to argue from personal experience (see Ross Taylor's argument on paintball, pp. 230–233). Again, check with your instructor. |
| Brainstorm claims and reasons on various sides of the issue. | State your own claim and possible *because* clause reasons in support of your claim. Do the same thing for one or more opposing or alternative claims. |

## Conduct an In-Depth Exploration Prior to Drafting

The following set of tasks is designed to help you explore your issue in depth. Most students take one or two hours to complete these tasks; the time will pay off, however, because most of the ideas that you need for your rough draft will be on paper.

See the discussion of issue questions on pp. 206–207.

1. Write out the issue your argument will address. Try phrasing your issue in several different ways, perhaps as a yes/no question and as an open-ended question. Try making the question broader, then narrower. Finally, frame the question in the way that most appeals to you.
2. Now write out your tentative answer to the question. This will be your beginning thesis statement or claim. Put a box around this answer. Next, write out one or more different answers to your question. These will be alternative claims that a neutral audience might consider.
3. Why is this a controversial issue? Is there insufficient evidence to resolve the issue, or is the evidence ambiguous or contradictory? Are definitions in dispute? Do the parties disagree about basic values, assumptions, or beliefs?
4. What personal interest do you have in this issue? How does the issue affect you? Why do you care about it? (Knowing why you care about it might help you get your audience to care about it.)
5. What reasons and evidence support your position on this issue? Freewrite everything that comes to mind that might help you support your case. This freewrite will eventually provide the bulk of your argument. For now, freewrite rapidly without worrying whether your argument makes sense. Just get ideas on paper.
6. Imagine all the counterarguments your audience might make. Summarize the main arguments against your position and then freewrite your response to each of the counterarguments. What are the flaws in the alternative points of view?
7. What kinds of appeals to *ethos* and *pathos* might you use to support your argument? How can you increase your audience's perception of your credibility and trustworthiness? How can you tie your argument to your audience's beliefs and values?
8. Why is this an important issue? What are the broader implications and consequences? What other issues does it relate to? Thinking of possible answers to these questions may prove useful when you write your introduction or conclusion.

## Shaping and Drafting

Once you have explored your ideas, create a plan. Here is a suggested procedure:

Begin your planning by analyzing your intended audience. You could imagine an audience deeply resistant to your views or a more neutral, undecided audience acting like a jury. In some cases, your audience might be a single person, as when you petition your department chair to waive a requirement in your major. At other times, your audience might be the general readership of a newspaper, church bulletin, or magazine. When the audience is a general readership, you need to imagine from the start the kinds of readers you particularly want to sway. Here are some questions you can ask:

- ***How much does your audience know or care about your issue?*** Will you need to provide background? Will you need to convince them that your issue is important? Do you need to hook their interest? Your answers to these questions will particularly influence your introduction and conclusion.
- ***What is your audience's current attitude toward your issue?*** Are they deeply opposed to your position? If so, why? Are they neutral and undecided? If so, what other views will they be listening to?
- ***How do your audience's values, assumptions, and beliefs differ from your own?*** What aspects of your position will be threatening to your audience? Why? How does your position on the issue challenge your imagined reader's worldview or identity? What objections will your audience raise toward your argument? Your answers to these questions will help determine the content of your argument and alert you to the extra research you may have to do to respond to audience objections.
- ***What values, beliefs, or assumptions about the world do you and your audience share?*** Despite your differences with your audience, where can you find common links? How might you use these links to build bridges to your audience?

Your next step is to plan an audience-based argument by seeking audience-based reasons or reasons whose underlying assumptions you can defend. Here is a process you can use:

1. Create a skeleton, tree diagram, outline, or flowchart for your argument by stating your reasons as one or more *because* clauses attached to your claim. Each *because* clause will become the head of a main section or *line of reasoning* in your argument.
2. Use the planning schema on pages 215–217 to plan each line of reasoning. If your audience accepts your underlying assumption, you can concentrate on supporting your reason with evidence. However, if your audience is apt to reject the underlying assumption for one of your lines of reasoning, then you'll need to state it directly and argue for it. Try to anticipate audience objections by exploring ways that an audience might question either your reasons or your underlying assumptions.
3. Using the skeleton you created, finish developing an outline or tree diagram for your argument. Although the organization of each part of your argument will grow organically from its content, the main parts of your classical argument should match the framework chart shown on page 224 (Figure 9.1).

This classical model can be modified in numerous ways. A question that often arises is where to summarize and respond to objections and counterarguments. Writers generally have three choices: One option is to handle opposing positions before you present your own argument. The rationale for this approach is that skeptical audiences may be more inclined to listen attentively to your argument if they have been assured that you understand their point of view. A second option is to place this material after you have presented your argument. This approach is effective for neutral audiences who don't start off with strong opposing views. A final option is to intersperse opposing views throughout your argument at appropriate moments. Any of these possibilities, or a combination of all of them, can be effective.

Another question often asked is, "What is the best way to order one's reasons?" A general rule of thumb when ordering your own argument is to put your strongest reason last and your second-strongest reason first. The idea here is to start and end with your most powerful arguments. If you imagine a quite skeptical audience, build bridges to your audience by summarizing alternative views early in the paper and concede to those that are especially strong. If your audience is neutral or undecided, you can summarize and respond to possible objections after you have presented your own case.

## Revising

As you revise your argument, you need to attend both to the clarity of your writing (all the principles of closed-form prose described in Chapter 12) and also to the persuasiveness of your argument. As always, peer reviews are valuable, and especially so in argumentation if you ask your peer reviewers to role-play an opposing audience.

## Questions for Peer Review

In addition to the generic peer review questions explained in Skill 16.4, ask your peer reviewers to address these questions:

### INTRODUCTION

1. How could the title be improved so that it announces the issue, reveals the writer's claim, or otherwise focuses your expectations and piques interest?
2. What strategies does the writer use to introduce the issue, engage your interest, and convince you that the issue is significant and problematic? What would add clarity and appeal?
3. How could the introduction more effectively forecast the argument and present the writer's claim? What would make the statement of the claim more focused, clear, or risky?

### ARGUING FOR THE CLAIM

1. Consider the overall structure: What strategies does the writer use to make the structure of the paper clear and easy to follow? How could the structure of the argument be improved?
2. Consider the support for the reasons: Where could the writer provide better evidence or support for each line of reasoning? Look for the kinds of evidence

for each line of reasoning by noting the writer's use of facts, examples, statistics, testimony, or other evidence. Where could the writer supply more evidence or use existing evidence more effectively?

3. Consider the support for the underlying assumptions: For each line of reasoning, determine the assumptions that the audience needs to grant for the argument to be effective. Are there places where these assumptions need to be stated directly and supported with arguments? How could support for the assumptions be improved?

4. Consider the writer's summary of and response to alternative viewpoints: Where does the writer treat alternative views? Are there additional alternative views that the writer should consider? What strategies does the writer use to respond to alternative views? How could the writer's treatment of alternative views be improved?

### CONCLUSION

1. How might the conclusion more effectively bring completeness or closure to the argument?

---

## Multimodal or Online Options

**WRITING PROJECT**

1. **Speech with Visual Aids (Flip Chart, PowerPoint, Prezi)** Deliver your classical argument as a formal speech supported with visual aids. You can imagine an occasion for a short speech limited to 3–5 minutes (modeled, say, after public hearings) or a longer presentation such as a TED talk. Pay equal attention to the construction and delivery of your speech and to the multimodal design of the visual aids.

2. **Persuasive Poster or Advocacy Ad** Create a one-page poster or advocacy ad that captures your argument in a highly condensed verbal/visual form. Consider how you will use all the features of visual argument—type sizes and fonts, layout, color, and images and graphics—to grab the attention of your audience and drive home your claim.

3. **Video** Create a short video aimed at moving neutral or opposing audiences toward your point of view. Use the resources of music, voice, words, and images to reach audiences who might not be expected to read your print argument. Conversely, create a video aimed at increasing the enthusiasm of people who already support your position. Your goal is to call them to action in some way (donate funds, vote, participate in a rally or strike).

4. **T-shirt or Bumper Sticker as Part of a Campaign Plan** Imagine a full-fledged campaign advocating your position on an issue. Design a T-shirt or bumper sticker in support of your claim.

For advice on producing multimedia compositions see Chapter 13. For an example of a student speech with PowerPoint slides, see Chapter 10, pp. 260–262

Our first reading, by student writer Ross Taylor, aims to increase appreciation of paintball as a healthy sport. An avid paintballer, Ross was frustrated by how many of his friends and acquaintances didn't appreciate paintball and had numerous misconceptions about it. The following argument is aimed at those who don't understand the sport or those who condemn it for being dangerous and violent.

## Ross Taylor (student)
# Paintball:
### Promoter of Violence or Healthy Fun?

1    Glancing out from behind some cover, I see an enemy soldier on the move. I level my gun and start pinching off rounds. Hearing the incoming fire, he turns and starts to fire, but it is far too late. His entire body flinches when I land two torso shots, and he falls when I hit his leg. I duck back satisfied with another good kill on my record. I pop up again, this time to scan for more enemy forces. Out of the corner of my eye I see some movement and turn to see two soldiers peeking out from behind a sewer pipe. I move to take cover again, but it's futile. I feel the hits come one by one hitting me three times in the chest and once on the right bicep before I fall behind the cover. I'm hit. It's all over—for me at least. The paintball battle rages on as I carefully leave the field to nurse my welts, which are already showing. Luckily, I watch my three remaining teammates trample the two enemy soldiers who shot me to win the game. This is paintball in all its splendor and glory.

2    Paintball is one of the most misunderstood and generally looked down upon recreational activities. People see it as rewarding violence and lacking the true characteristics of a healthy team sport like ultimate Frisbee, soccer, or pickup basketball. Largely the accusations directed at paintball are false because it is a positive recreational activity. Paintball is a fun, athletic, mentally challenging recreational activity that builds teamwork and releases tension.

3    Paintball was invented in the early 1980s as a casual activity for survival enthusiasts, but it has grown into a several hundred million dollar industry. It is, quite simply, an expanded version of tag. Players use a range of $CO_2$ powered guns that fire small biodegradable marbles of paint at approximately 250–300 feet per second. The result of a hit is a small splatter of oily paint and a nice dark bruise. Paintball is now played nationwide in indoor and outdoor arenas. Quite often variants are played such as "Capture the Flag" or "Assassination." In "Capture the Flag" the point is to retrieve the heavily guarded flag from the other team and return it to your base. The game of "Assassination" pits one team of "assassins" against the "secret service." The secret service men guard an unarmed player dubbed the "president." Their goal is get from point A to point B without the president's getting tagged. Contrary to popular belief, the games are highly officiated and organized. There is always a referee present. Barrel

plugs are required until just before a game begins and must be reinserted as soon as the game ends. No hostages may be taken. A player catching another off guard at close range must first give the player the opportunity to surrender. Most importantly there is no physical contact between players. Punching, pushing, or butt-ending with the gun is strictly prohibited. The result is an intense game that is relatively safe for all involved.

4   The activity of paintball is athletically challenging. There are numerous sprint and dives to avoid being hit. At the end of a game, typically lasting around 20 minutes, all the players are winded, sweaty, and ultimately exhilarated. The beginning of the game includes a mad dash for cover by both teams with heavy amounts of fire being exchanged. During the game, players execute numerous strategic moves to gain a tactical advantage, often including quick jumps, dives, rolls, and runs. While undercover, players crawl across broad stretches of playing field often still feeling their bruises from previous games. These physical feats culminate in an invigorating and physically challenging activity good for building muscles and coordination.

5   In addition to the athletic challenge, paintball provides strong mental challenge, mainly the need for constant strategizing. There are many strategic positioning methods. For example, the classic pincer move involves your team's outflanking an opponent from each side to eliminate his or her mobility and shelter. In the more sophisticated ladder technique, teammates take turns covering each other as the others move onward from cover to cover. Throughout the game, players' minds are constantly reeling as they calculate their positions and cover, their teammates' positions and cover, and their opponents' positions and strength. Finally, there is the strong competitive pull of the individual. It never fails to amaze me how much thought goes into one game.

6   Teamwork is also involved. Paintball takes a lot of cooperation. You need special hand signals to communicate with your teammates, and you have to coordinate, under rapidly changing situations, who is going to flank left or right, who is going to charge, and who is going to stay back to guard the flag station. The importance of teamwork in paintball explains why more and more businesses are taking their employees for a day of action with the intent of creating a closer knit and smooth-functioning workplace. The value of teamwork is highlighted on the Web site of a British Columbia facility, Action and Adventure Paintball, Ltd, which says that in paintball,

> as in any team sport, the team that communicates best usually wins. It's about thinking, not shooting. This is why Fortune 500 companies around the world take their employees to play paintball together.

An advantage of paintball for building company team spirit is that paintball teams, unlike teams in many other recreational sports, can blend very skilled and totally unskilled players. Women like paintball as much as men, and the game is open to people of any size, body type, and strength level. Since a game usually takes no more than seven to ten minutes, teams can run a series of different games with different players to have lots of different match-ups. Also families like to play paintball together.

7    People who object to paintball criticize its danger and violence. The game's supposed danger gets mentioned a lot. The public seems to have received the impression that paintball guns are simply eye-removing hardware. It is true that paintball can lead to eye injuries. An article by medical writer Cheryl Guttman in a trade magazine for ophthalmologists warns that eye injuries from paintball are on the rise. But the fact is that Guttman's article says that only 102 cases of eye injuries from paintballs were reported from 1985 to 2000 and that 85 percent of those injured were not wearing the required safety goggles. This is not to say that accidents don't happen. I personally had a friend lose an eye after inadvertently shooting himself in the eye from a very close range. The fact of the matter is that he made a mistake by looking down the barrel of a loaded gun and the trigger malfunctioned. Had he been more careful or worn the proper equipment, he most likely would have been fine. During my first organized paintball experience I was hit in the goggles by a very powerful gun and felt no pain. The only discomfort came from having to clean all the paint off my goggles after the game. When played properly, paintball is an incredibly safe sport.

8    The most powerful argument against paintball is that it is inherently violent and thus unhealthy. Critics claim paintball is simply an accepted form of promoting violence against other people. I have anti-war friends who think that paintball glorifies war. Many new parents today try to keep their kids from playing cops and robbers and won't buy them toy guns. These people see paintball as an upgraded and more violent version of the same antisocial games they don't want their children to play. Some people also point to the connections between paintball and violent video games where participants get their fun from "killing" other people. They link paintball to all the other violent activities that they think lead to such things as gangs or school shootings. But there is no connection between school shootings and paintball. As seen in Michael Moore's *Bowling for Columbine*, the killers involved there went bowling before the massacre; they didn't practice their aim by playing paintball.

9    What I am trying to say is that, yes, paintball is violent to a degree. After all, its whole point is to "kill" each other with guns. But I object to paintball's being considered a promotion of violence. Rather, I feel that it is a healthy release of tension. From my own personal experience, when playing the game, the players aren't focused on hurting the other players; they are focused on winning the game. At the end of the day, players are not full of violent urges, but just the opposite. They want to celebrate together as a team, just as do softball or soccer teams after a game. Therefore I don't think paintball is an unhealthy activity for adults. (The only reason I wouldn't include children is because I believe the pain is too intense for them. I have seen some younger players cry after being shot.) Paintball is simply a game,

a sport, that produces intense exhilaration and fun. Admittedly, paintball guns can be used in irresponsible manners. Recently there have been some drive-by paint-ballings, suggesting that paintball players are irresponsible and violent. However, the percentage of people who do this sort of prank is very small and those are the bad apples of the group. There will always be those who misuse equipment. For example, baseball bats have been used in atrocious beatings, but that doesn't make baseball a violent sport. So despite the bad apples, paintball is still a worthwhile activity when properly practiced.

10     Athletic and mentally challenging, team-building and fun—the game of paintball seems perfectly legitimate to me. It is admittedly violent, but it is not the evil activity that critics portray. Injuries can occur, but usually only when the proper safety equipment is not being used and proper precautions are ignored. As a great recreational activity, paintball deserves the same respect as other sports. It is a great way to get physical exercise, make friends, and have fun.

## THINKING CRITICALLY
### about "Paintball: Promoter of Violence or Healthy Fun?"

1. Before reading this essay, what was your own view of paintball? To what extent did this argument create for you a more positive view of paintball? What aspects of the argument did you find particularly effective or ineffective?

2. How effective are Ross's appeals to *ethos* in this argument? Does he create a persona that you find trustworthy and compelling? How does he do so or fail to do so?

3. How effective are Ross's appeals to *pathos*? How does he appeal to his readers' values, interests, and emotions in trying to make paintball seem like an exhilarating team sport? To what extent does he show empathy with readers when he summarizes objections to paintball?

4. How effective are Ross's appeals to *logos*? How effective are Ross's reasons and evidence in support of his claim? How effective are Ross's responses to opposing views?

5. What are the main strengths and weaknesses of Ross's argument?

Our next reading is by student writer Claire Giordano, who wrote this paper for an argument assignment like the one in this chapter. In challenging the national enthusiasm for the expansion of online courses, Claire Giordano draws on her research and her experience and knowledge as an Environmental Studies major. We present her argument as an illustration of a student research paper written and formatted in APA style. For a compete explanation of APA style, see Chapter 15.

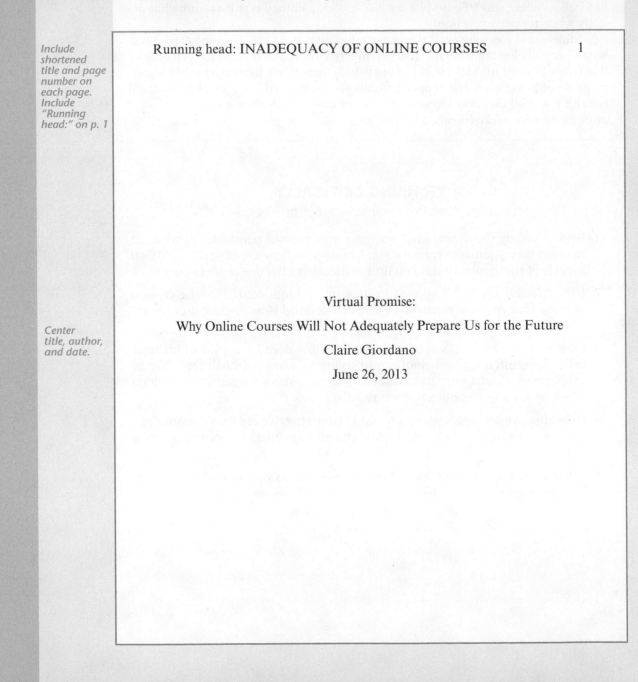

*Include shortened title and page number on each page. Include "Running head:" on p. 1*

Running head: INADEQUACY OF ONLINE COURSES                    1

*Center title, author, and date.*

Virtual Promise:

Why Online Courses Will Not Adequately Prepare Us for the Future

Claire Giordano

June 26, 2013

Virtual Promise:  Why Online Courses Will Not Adequately

Prepare Us for the Future

In 2012 more than 6.7 million students took at least one online course (Sloan Consortium, 2013). Proponents of online education hope that such courses will improve the current educational system, but this potential is undermined by the problems of reliance on technology. A 2013 Kaiser Family Foundation Survey found that children and teens spend more than 53 hours using digital media every week (as cited in Toppo, 2010). Educational programs that place more people behind more computers may not be the best way to improve education for the future, and we as a country seem to be at a critical decision-making point of whether to increase technology's role in our lives. At this historical moment, I, as an Environmental Studies major concerned about my education and the well-being of the environment around me, believe the costs and consequences of online education must be evaluated based on how well it prepares students for future engagement with the world. Although many people have great expectations for the possibilities of online courses, their negative repercussions ultimately outweigh the supposed benefits. Online courses are not the best way to educate students because these virtual classes are more expensive,  promote inequality by requiring technology that is inaccessible to many of our fellow citizens, inhibit the full development of our critical thinking skills, and further entrench our reliance on technology.

The optimism surrounding online courses arises from the belief that they will make higher education less expensive and more accessible and thus alleviate education inequality. From this perspective, the opportunities, flexibility, and lower costs of online courses outweigh their potential drawbacks. For example, H. H. Freidman, a business professor at Brooklyn College, who with L. W. Friedman  is widely published on the use of

*Repeat title before body of paper.*

*Use parenthetical in-text citations.*

*Double-space all text.*

technology and media in education, supports the expansion of online education. They state that online courses ease the financial burden on both the student and the university and provide flexible schedules which allow students to engage in other activities (2011).

However, while these ideas sound good, they have fundamental problems with cost and accreditation. For example, one of the most common arguments in favor of virtual courses cites the cost effectiveness. The problem with this claim, though, is that it oversimplifies the issue. There are currently many models for online education that students could choose, from Massive Open Online Courses (MOOCS) that don't provide credit to programs that do grant credit. Within this range of possibilities, the programs that offer accreditation are the only ones students could use in the job market and in reality do not save us substantial amounts of money. A study by Battaglino, Haldeman, and Laurans sponsored by the Fordham Institute found that the average per pupil cost to a university for a full online education ranges from $6,400 to $10,200, which translates into a higher cost to students that is in some cases close to the rates of a traditional education (2013, p. 4). With these figures in mind, I cannot see why we would advocate for a course of education that is not only unacceptable in most of the job market but that also does not substantially reduce costs to make the classes more accessible.

Proponents who mistakenly believe that online education is cheaper also believe that its widespread accessibility will alleviate education inequalities. Thomas Friedman (2013), who is a Pulitzer Prize winning journalist for *The New York Times*, believes that online courses will reduce poverty by granting all citizens equal access to the best education possible. This hope for accessibility nurtures a vision of universities "as central informational hubs that offer learning and knowledge and skills

*Use italics for periodical titles.*

APA Style

for anyone around the globe willing to absorb them" (Lagos, 2012). This image is quite compelling, and I will admit that arguments like Friedman's are appealing, especially when I consider students in similar situations like that of my sister, who has recently been overwhelmed with health problems and has missed a semester of high school and is still struggling to catch up in her classes. For students like her, online courses could be a godsend, giving them equal access to material and classes otherwise inaccessible.

However, the problem with believing that online courses create equality is that credit-bearing courses are too expensive and require technology that is simply not available to everyone. Many people struggling with poverty are not computer and Web users. Technology and business writer Jon Brodkin drew attention to the FCC's Broadband Access Report, which found that 119 million Americans do not have access to broadband internet as a result of poverty or deficient wireless infrastructure. This problem was especially pronounced in rural areas, where 25% lacked access (2012). The implications of this exclusion are explained clearly by C. L. Selfe (1999), who is a Distinguished Professor of the Humanities at The Ohio State University and the first female English teacher to receive the EDUCOM Medal for innovative computer use. She explains that the push for technological literacy by the government and businesses "disguises the fact that technology is not available to everyone in this country or to every student in our schools...and directs our attention from the realization that, in America, technology supports social divisions along race, class, and gender" (p. xxi). In light of this statement, it is clear to me that online courses are not the solution to education inequality because they require technology that perpetuates social inequality—the very problem they strive to address.

*When available, cite page number of quotations.*

INADEQUACY OF ONLINE COURSES                                          5

Supporters also claim online courses are the best way to transform current educational practices. From this point of view, advocates like H. H. Friedman  and L. W. Friedman (2011) believe that online courses can produce deeper level thinking because they appeal to different learning styles and enhance creativity by using "numerous teaching tools that include animations, videos, wikis, and virtual labs" (p. 160). According to this argument, online courses provide an atmosphere conducive to the development of critical thinking skills just as effectively as conventional courses do.

While I cannot deny that online courses employ innovative tools with the potential to engage students, the virtual nature of the classes simply cannot recreate the environment of intellectual and interpersonal challenge that is necessary for fully developing critical thinking skills. The importance of critical thinking has been emphasized by many people such as the great American philosopher John Dewey, who, according to  M. S. Roth (2012), introduced much that we now call critical thinking such as attention to experience and flexibility in thinking. Roth emphasizes Dewey's words on the need for integration of life and learning: "The inclination to learn from life itself and to make the conditions of life such that all will learn in the process of living is the finest product of schooling" (as quoted in M. S. Roth, 2012, p. A23). I would add that critical thinking is also crucial if we are going to creatively and successfully address the wicked problems that face our world, from poverty, to water shortages, to toxic environments, to global climate change.

*Cite Dewey quotation using source infomation for the source in which he is quoted (M. S. Roth).*

In light of this importance, I believe that critical thinking skills are too vital to entrust to a purely virtual environment. The weaknesses of online courses in promoting critical thinking are highlighted by R. Roth (2012), who has worked as an academic adviser for over twenty-four years and taught at the University of Washington and Skidmore College. Roth

INADEQUACY OF ONLINE COURSES                    6

argues that online education is in fact detrimental to the growth of our
critical thinking skills. He states that virtual learning through online classes
strips education of its context and interdisciplinary nature: "[B]y demanding
answers every few minutes in the form of quizzes, . . . they can't provide
enough reflective time or space for those all-important 'it all depends on
what you mean by' realizations" (2012). Furthermore, he explains that
online courses deprive us of the learning that occurs when we become stuck
and have to use reason and creativity to find a solution. Roth believes that
"profoundly challenging learning needs the oxygen of uncertainty and
ambiguity" which arises from the challenges posed by our professors and
peers (2012). This direct interaction is critical to engaging with the world
and simply cannot be facilitated in a virtual environment where the ability
to respond with a right or wrong answer is reinforced through repetitive
quizzes and evaluations. This impersonal and simplistic way of learning
lacks the challenging interactions that develop our ability to reason, to
think creatively, and to work collaboratively--important skills we need in
order to address the social and environmental problems we face as a global
community.

Finally, advocates of virtual learning claim that online courses
prepare students for the future by developing technological proficiency,
which is needed in most occupations and even to apply to many jobs. The
problem with this point of view, however, is that it ignores the many other
skills that we need to succeed in the world, and does not acknowledge the
consequences of relying on technology. I am not saying that all technology
is bad and should be abandoned, but that the modern reliance on computers
and superfluous gadgets may be more detrimental than helpful. This
concept is captured nicely by the Dutch social critic Michiel Schwarz,
who believes that "technology has become our environment as well as our

*Use ellipses for omitted words in quotation.*

ideology...we no longer use technology, we live it" (as cited in Glendinning, 1995, p. 45). These views suggest that the proliferation of technology (including online courses) may have far reaching negative effects on our lives and the entire global community.

Additionally, the dependence on technology in virtual classes merely supports and further promotes, in the words of ecopsychologists A. D. Kanner and M. E. Gomes (1995), "an almost religious belief among Americans in the ultimate good of all technological progress, through its claim that there is a product to solve each of life's problems" (p. 84). From the perspective of Kanner and Gomes, however, these hopes are merely part of the larger misplaced faith in the power of technology to cure all of the world's social and environmental ills. This misguided faith in technology encourages misunderstanding of pressing environmental problems, something which especially troubles me because I believe we should devote our resources and brain power to collaboratively solving our problems now rather than hoping that future generations will invent new technologies to solve the crises we are creating by living beyond the limits of our planet. Rather than blindly looking to future technology as a savior, we must act now to slow the environmental degradation while we still can.

Furthermore, attachment to technology not only affects our physical, social, and cultural futures, but also has huge repercussions for the health of the earth we depend on and must preserve for our own health as well as the well being of future generations. Recent international research is finding that as the use of technology increases, we are slowly losing our ability to interact with the world through all of our senses because current technology overemphasizes visual information (Sewall, 1995, p. 202). Thus, the rise of technology (such as online courses) means that we are interacting with the world through screens rather than enjoying the simple beauty and life that surrounds us, from the movement of clouds on a windy day to the smell of the first spring daffodil. This change also has direct impacts on our physical, mental, and emotional health, as R. Louv (2006) explains in his work *Last Child in the Woods*. He cites studies that link a lack of play in nature with higher rates of ADHD, depression, and other mental disorders, especially pronounced in children. But these same patterns are also seen in adults in study after study (pp. 107–110). For everyone's health, we need nature. We must spend time outside, whether it is watching a sunset from a high-rise or helping kids plant seeds and get their hands dirty in rich soil. Online courses may help us become more technologically adept, but they will also keep us more isolated behind computer screens. This gain is not worth the cost of becoming further alienated from the endangered natural world and from other people who need our compassion and understanding.

While I admit that online courses have many strong advocates and some potential to make positive change in the world, these changes simply come at too high a price. Credit-bearing virtual courses are expensive and require a technology not everyone can access. They also create an environment devoid of the necessary challenges and interactions that foster complex critical thinking. The online courses also entrench our dangerous reliance on technology and perpetuate unsustainable attitudes about how we should interact with the natural world. Amidst the current intense societal pressure to develop and employ ever more technology in every aspect of life, we must decide whether this is a direction our education should also follow. At a time when the polar ice is melting at unprecedented rates, species are becoming extinct every day, and the very air we breathe is toxic from the pollution of industrialization, entrusting our education to technology is not the answer.

INADEQUACY OF ONLINE COURSES                                    9

## References

Battaglino, T. B., Haldeman, M., & Laurans, E. (2013, February 11). The costs of online learning: Creating sound policy for digital learning. Working Paper Series, Thomas B. Fordham Institute. Retrieved from ERIC database. (ED528948)

Brodkin, J. (2012, August 21). 119 million Americans lack broadband Internet, FCC reports. *ArsTechnica*. Retrieved from http://arstechnica.com

Friedman, H. H., & Friedman, L. W. (2011). Crises in education: Online learning as a solution. *Creative Education* 2(3) 156-63. doi:10.4236/ce.2011.23022

Friedman, T. L. (2013, January 27). Revolution hits the universities. *The New York Times*. Retrieved from http://www.nytimes.com

Glendinning, C. (1995). Technology, trauma, and the wild. In T. Roszak, M. E. Gomes, & A. D. Kanner (Eds.), *Ecopsychology: Restoring the earth, healing the mind* (pp. 41-54). San Francisco, CA: Sierra Club Books.

Kanner, A. D., & Gomes, M. E. (1995). The all-consuming self. In T. Roszak, M. E. Gomes, & A. D. Kanner (Eds.), *Ecopsychology: Restoring the earth, healing the mind* (pp. 77-91). San Francisco, CA: Sierra Club Books.

Lagos, T. (2012, August 18). Pro: Are online courses good for higher education? *The Seattle Times*. Retrieved from http://seattletimes.com

Louv, R. (2006). *Last child in the woods: Saving our children from nature-deficit disorder.* Chapel Hill, NC: Algonquin Books.

Roth, M. S. (2012, September 6). Learning as freedom. *The New York Times*, p. A23.

Roth, R. (2012, August 19). Con: Assembly-line approach could end up killing nation's research engine. *The Seattle Times*. Retrieved from http://seattletimes.com

*Start References on a new page, and center heading.*

*Italicize periodical titles.*

*Use initial cap for article title and subtitle.*

*When source has a DOI, include it.*

*Provide home page URL for publications*

*Italicize book titles. Use initial cap for title and subtitle.*

*Use initials for first and middle names, and place date after authors' names.*

INADEQUACY OF ONLINE COURSES                                    10

Selfe, C. L. (1999). *Technology and literacy in the twenty-first century:*

   *The importance of paying attention.* Chicago, IL: Southern Illinois

   University Press.

Sewall, L. (1995). The skill of ecological perception. In T. Roszak, M. E.

   Gomes, & A. D. Kanner (Eds.), *Ecopsychology: Restoring the earth,*

   *healing the mind* (pp. 201-215). San Francisco, CA: Sierra Club Books.

The Sloan Consortium. (2013, January). Changing course: Ten years of tracking

   online education in the United States. In *Sloan-C.* Retrieved from http://

   sloanconsortium.org/publications/survey/changing_course_2012

Toppo, G. (2010, January 20). Kids' electronic media use jumps to 53 hours a

   week. *USA Today.* Retrieved from http://www.usatoday.com

*Break URLs after // or before other marks of punctuation*

*Check that everything cited in the paper is in the References, except personal communications*

## THINKING CRITICALLY
### about "Virtual Promise: Why Online Courses Will Not Adequately Prepare Us for the Future"

1. What is Claire Giordano's main claim and what are her reasons for opposing online courses?

2. While some classical arguments group alternative views after the writer's development of the reasons, others structure the whole argument as a rebuttal with the writer's reasons in effect answering the opposing views. What choice has Claire made? Why do you think she chose to organize her argument this way? What alternative or opposing views does she address?

3. What audience do you think Claire is trying to reach with this argument? How well does she use appeals to *pathos* to connect with readers' values, beliefs, and emotions?

4. How effectively does Claire create appeals to *ethos* in this argument? Where does her evidence draw on her experience and knowledge as an Environmental Studies major?

5. How would you assess the appeals to *logos* in this argument? Consider the range, quality, and depth of her supporting evidence.

6. What do you see as the major strengths and weaknesses of this argument?

# 10 PROPOSING A SOLUTION

## WHAT YOU WILL LEARN

**10.1** To convince your audience that a problem exists and to propose a solution to the problem.

**10.2** To use multimodal strategies to create effective proposal arguments.

**10.3** To persuade your audience by writing an effective proposal argument.

Proposal arguments call an audience to action. They make a claim that some action should or ought to be taken. Sometimes referred to informally as *should arguments*, proposals are among the most common kinds of arguments that you will write or read.

**Practical proposals** focus on local, practical problems and generally target a specific audience (usually the person with the power to act on the proposal). For example, Lucy Morsen's proposal in this chapter advocates banning laptops and cell phones in classrooms (pp. 256–259). In the work world, many individuals and businesses generate new revenues by writing competitive proposals to solve a prospective client's practical problem.

Another kind of proposal, a **policy proposal**, addresses public policy issues with the aim of swaying public support toward the writer's proposed solution. Student writer Kent Ansen's proposal to institute mandatory public service for young adults illustrates a researched policy proposal (pp. 263–207).

The power of proposal arguments is often enhanced with images, which can appeal to both *logos* and *pathos*. In fact, proposal arguments sometimes take the form of striking multimodal texts such as **posters** or **advocacy advertisements** calling an audience to action. Additionally, proposal arguments can be delivered as **oral presentations** when, for example, a citizen presents a proposal at an open-mike public hearing.

## Engaging Proposal Writing

This activity introduces you to the thinking processes involved in writing a proposal argument.

### ON YOUR OWN

Identify and list several major problems facing students in your college or university. Then decide which problems are most important and rank them in order of importance.

**IN CONVERSATION**

Working in groups, share your lists and decide on your group's number-one problem.

1. Use that problem to explore answers to the following questions. Group recorders should be prepared to present answers to the class as a whole.
   a. Why is the problem a problem?
   b. For whom is the problem a problem?
   c. How will these people suffer if the problem is not solved? Give specific examples.
   d. Who has the power to solve the problem?
   e. Why hasn't the problem been solved up to this point?
   f. How can the problem be solved? Create a proposal for a solution.
   g. What are the probable benefits of acting on your proposal?
   h. What costs are associated with your proposal?
   i. Who will bear these costs?
   j. Why should this proposal be enacted?
   k. What makes this proposal better than alternative proposals?
2. As a group, draft an outline for a proposal argument in which you:
   a. Describe the problem and its significance.
   b. Propose your solution to the problem.
   c. Justify your proposal by showing how the benefits outweigh the costs.
3. Recorders for each group should write the group's outline on the board and be prepared to present the group's argument orally to the class.

# Understanding Proposal Writing

**10.1**
Convince your audience that a problem exists and propose a solution to the problem.

All proposals have one feature in common—they offer a solution to a problem. For every proposed solution, there are always alternative solutions, including doing nothing. Your task therefore is to convince readers that the problem is worth solving, that your proposed solution will actually work, and that the benefits outweigh the costs. Accordingly, a proposal argument typically has three main parts:

1. ***Description of the problem.*** You must first demonstrate that a significant problem exists. Your goal is to make the problem vivid and real for your readers. Who is affected by the problem? What are its causes? Why hasn't it been solved before? What are the negative consequences of not solving the problem?
2. ***Proposal for a solution.*** This section describes your solution with enough detail to show how it would work and what it would cost. If you don't have a solution, you may choose to generate a planning proposal calling for a committee to propose solutions at a later date.
3. ***Justification.*** Here you persuade your audience that your proposal should be enacted. Typically you show that the benefits of your proposal outweigh the costs. You also need to show why your proposed solution is better than alternative solutions. Point out why other possible approaches would not solve the problem, would provide fewer benefits, or would cost significantly more than your proposed solution.

In the following sections, we examine the special challenges of proposal arguments and then show you a powerful strategy for developing the justification section of a proposal.

## Special Challenges of Proposal Arguments

To get your readers to take action—the ultimate purpose of a proposal—you must overcome some difficult challenges. In the following chart, we examine the special difficulties people encounter when writing proposal arguments and offer strategies for overcoming them.

## Strategies for Overcoming the Special Challenges of Proposal Arguments

| Challenge | Explanation | What to Do |
|---|---|---|
| **Giving the problem presence** | To convince readers that a problem exists, you must make them *see* and *feel* the problem—give the problem *presence*. | • Use anecdotes or examples of people suffering from the problem.<br>• Provide startling facts or statistics to dramatize the problem.<br>• Include a photograph or other image that conveys the problem.<br>• Use other appeals to *pathos*. |
| **Appealing to the interests and values of decision makers** | A proposal that benefits one group often creates costs for others. Decision makers may not share the sufferers' perspective on a problem. Solving your problem may simply cause more problems for the decision maker. | • Show decision makers how acting on your proposal will benefit *them* directly.<br>• Use audience-based reasons.<br>• If appropriate, appeal to idealism and principle (do the right thing, even if it will cause temporary grief).<br>• Show how benefits to the sufferers outweigh costs to others. |
| **Overcoming inherent conservatism** | People are inherently resistant to change, often willing to live with a flawed but bearable situation rather than risk change that could make the situation worse. "Better the devil you know than the one you don't know." | • Emphasize the seriousness of the problem (give it *presence*).<br>• Stress the benefits of solving the problem.<br>• Emphasize the lost potential in not acting.<br>• Show that the risks are minimal.<br>• Show that negative consequences are unlikely. |

| Challenge | Explanation | What to Do |
|---|---|---|
| **Predicting consequences** | Often readers distrust the proposal writer's rosy scenario. They doubt that the predicted benefits will occur, or they fear negative consequences. | • Take care not to overpromise benefits.<br>• Persuade readers that your predictions are realistic—show how the links in the chain lead directly from the solution to the benefits.<br>• Cite cases where a similar proposal led to real benefits. |
| **Evaluating consequences** | Any solution that benefits one group may bring costs to another group. It is difficult to establish a common principle of measurement for weighing costs against benefits. | • In some cases, you can use money as measurement—the savings from this proposal will be more than the initial costs.<br>• In other cases, emphasize that the benefits of increased happiness, less suffering, or saved time outweigh the initial dollar costs.<br>• Emphasize the greatest good for the greatest number (more people will have benefits; fewer will bear costs).<br>• Emphasize idealism and principle (this is the right thing to do despite the cost). |

With these particular challenges in mind, we now set forth some strategies for making proposals as effective as possible.

## Developing an Effective Justification Section

The distinctions between proposals and other kinds of arguments invite particular kinds of support for proposals. Writers often develop support for their proposals by using the three-strategy approach, which focuses sequentially on principles, consequences, and precedents or analogies, as explained here.

### Strategies for Developing a Justification Section

| Strategies | What to Do | Templates and Comments | Examples |
|---|---|---|---|
| Argument from principle | Argue that an action should (should not) be taken because it is right (wrong) according to some value, assumption, principle, or belief you share with your audience. | We should (should not) do (this action) because (this action) is _____.<br>Fill in the blank with a belief or value that the audience holds: *good, honest, fair,* and so on. | "We should create publicly financed jobs for poor people because doing so is both charitable and just." |

*(continued)*

| Strategies | What to Do | Templates and Comments | Examples |
|---|---|---|---|
| Argument from consequence | Argue that an action should (should not) be taken because doing so will lead to consequences that you and your audience think are good (bad). | We should (should not) do (this action) because (this action) will lead to these good (bad) consequences: _____, _____, and _____. <br><br>Use consequences that your audience will agree are good or bad, as needed. | "We should create publicly financed jobs for poor people because doing so will provide them with money for food and housing, promote a work ethic, and produce needed goods and services." |
| Argument from precedent or analogy | Argue that an action should (should not) be taken because doing so is similar to what was done in another case, which turned out well (badly). | We should (should not) do (this action) because doing (this action) is like _____, which turned out to be good (bad). <br><br>Use precedents or analogies that are similar to your proposed action and that will have good (bad) associations for your audience. | *Precedent:* "We should create publicly financed jobs for poor people because doing so will alleviate poverty just as a similar program has helped the poor in Upper Magnesia." <br><br>*Analogy:* "... because doing so is like teaching the poor how to fish rather than giving them fish." |

Each of these argumentation strategies was clearly evident in a public debate in Seattle, Washington, over a proposal to raise county sales taxes to build a new baseball stadium. Those favoring the stadium put forth arguments such as these:

> We should build the new stadium because preserving our national pastime for our children is important (*argument from principle*), because building the stadium will create new jobs and revitalize the adjacent Pioneer Square district (*argument from consequence*), and because building the stadium will have the same beneficial effects on the city that building Camden Yards had in Baltimore (*argument from precedent*).

Those opposing the stadium created arguments using the same strategies:

> We should not build the stadium because it is wrong to subsidize rich owners and players with tax dollars (*argument from principle*), because building a stadium diverts tax money from more important concerns such as low-income housing (*argument from consequence*), and because Toronto's experience with Skydome shows that once the novelty of a new stadium wears off, attendance declines dramatically (*argument from precedent*).

## Using Different Strategies to Develop Support

Working individually or in small groups, use the strategies of principle, consequence, and precedent/analogy to create *because* clauses that support (or oppose) the following proposals. Try to have at least one *because* clause from each of the strategies, but generate as many reasons as possible. Here is an example:

| | |
|---|---|
| **Claim** | Spanking children should be made illegal. |
| **Principle** | Because it is wrong to cause bodily pain to children. |
| **Consequence** | Because it teaches children that it is okay to hit someone out of anger; because it causes children to obey rules out of fear rather than respect; because it can lead children to be abusive parents. |
| **Precedent/analogy** | Because spanking a child is like throwing dishes or banging your fists against a wall—it relieves your anger but turns the child into an object. |

1. The school year for grades K–12 should/should not be extended to eleven months.
2. Our city should/should not require all restaurants to post the calorie content of every menu item.
3. Federal law should/should not ban assault weapons and large ammunition clips.
4. The federal government should/should not legalize marijuana.
5. The federal government should/should not enact a substantially increased tax on gasoline.

## Multimodal Proposal Arguments

**10.2**
Use multimodal strategies to create effective proposal arguments.

Proposal arguments can be particularly powerful in multimodal forms. In nonmotion or print formats, verbal text can be enhanced by photographs, drawings, graphs, or other images. Frequently we encounter multimodal proposal arguments in the form of posters or flyers, paid advertisements in newspapers or magazines, brochures, or Web pages in advocacy Web sites. Their creators know the arguments must work fast to capture our attention, give presence to a problem, advocate a solution, and enlist our support. These multimodal proposals frequently use photographs, images, or icons that are arresting or in some way memorable and that appeal to a reader's emotions and imagination. Such arguments can be enhanced further in digital environments where videos or podcasts can employ the narrative power of sound and motion. Multimodal arguments can also be presented orally as speeches, often supplemented with presentation slides in PowerPoint or Prezi.

Advice for creating effective multimodal arguments is provided in Chapter 13.

As an example of a one-page advocacy ad, consider Figure 10.1, which is sponsored by the organization Common Sense for Drug Policy. Note how the advocacy advertisement makes its view of the problem real and urgent to readers

# WHITE KIDS ARE MUCH MORE LIKELY TO BE USING (AND SELLING) DRUGS!

**CAN YOU FIND ANYTHING WRONG WITH THESE PICTURES??**

According to the federal Centers for Disease Control, he's 4 times more likely than his African-American classmate to be a regular cocaine user.

According to the Justice Department, if he's arrested on drug charges, he's 1-1/2 times more likely than his white classmate to be sent to prison.

White high-school students who are current users of cocaine: 4.1%[1]

African-American high-school students who are current users of cocaine: 1.1%[1]

Chance of a white person ever trying an illicit drug in their lifetime: 42%[2]

Chance of an African-American person ever trying an illicit drug in their lifetime: 37.7%[2]

Percent of felony drug defendants in state courts who are white: 37%[3]

Percent of felony drug defendants in state courts who are black: 61%[3]

Percent of white drug felons given probation or nonincarceration sentence by state courts: 32%[4]

Percent of black drug felons given probation or nonincarceration sentence by state courts: 25%[4]

Percent of white drug felons sentenced to prison by state courts each year: 27%[5]

Percent of black drug felons sentenced to prison by state courts each year: 43%[5]

## BLACK KIDS ARE MORE LIKELY TO GO TO PRISON!

**Note:**
According to the US Justice Department and the Office of National Drug Control Policy, drug users typically buy their drugs from sellers of their own racial or ethnic background. Research of Ethnicity & Race of Drug Sellers and Users: US Dept. of Justice National Institute of Justice & the Office of National Drug Control Policy, "Crack, Powder Cocaine, and Heroin: Drug Purchase and Use Patterns in Six U.S. Cities, " December 1997, p.1, 16, and p. 15, Table 16.
**Sources:**
[1] Data on drug use by high-school students: Youth Risk Behavior Survey 1999, Centers for Disease Control, reported in Morbidity and Mortality Weekly Report, Vol. 49, No. SS-5, p. 66, Table 24.
[2] Data on lifetime prevalence of drug use: US Dept. of HHS Substance Abuse and Mental Health Services Administration, "Summary of Findings from the 1999 National Household Survey on Drug Abuse," August 2000, p. G-13, Table G-13.
[3] Demographic data on felony drug defendants in state courts: US Dept. of Justice Bureau of Justice Statistics. "Felony Defendants in Large Urban Counties, 1996," October 1999, p.4, Table 3
[4] Demographic data on felony drug defendants in state courts: US Dept. of Justice Bureau of Justice Statistics, "State Court Sentencing of Convicted Felons, 1996," February 2000, p. 13, Table 2.5
[5] Demographic data on felony drug defendants in state courts: US Dept. of Justice Bureau of Justice Statistics, "State Court Sentencing of Convicted Felons, 1996," February 2000, p. 13, Table 2.5

**Kevin B. Zeese, President, Common Sense for Drug Policy**
3220 "N" Street, NW, #141, Washington, D.C. 20007 * 703-354-9050 * fax 703-354-5695 * info@csdp.org
For more information, visit www.csdp.org and www.drugwarfacts.org

**FIGURE 10.1**  A One-Page Advocacy Advertisement from a Magazine by using disturbing black-and-white drawings, varied type sizes and fonts, and powerful lists of evidence. It also gains credibility through its documentation of sources, presented at the bottom of the page. For a multimodal argument with a stronger visceral impact, consider the image shown on page 326. This poster, "BEWARE...Drink Only Approved Water" produced by the United States War Department in 1944, employs a visual shock technique through its horrific image of a reflected skull to warn against dinking infected water.

Further discussion of this image is found in Chapter 13, pp. 326–327.

To show how a student writer can use multimodal strategies to enhance a proposal argument, consider Joyce Keeley's PowerPoint slide on African refugee camps (Chapter 13, page 330). Early in her speech, she wants to give "presence" to her problem—the transient and unstable life of African refugees who must flee their homeland either to urban slums without any humanitarian support or to refugee camps where they have support but no economic opportunity or freedom of movement. To dramatize this problem visually, Joyce selected three Web images—a photograph of refugees on the road carrying their life's possessions on their backs, an aerial photograph of an urban slum, and a photograph of a refugee camp. Each image appeals to *pathos* through its heartbreaking connotations of disrupted life, poverty, and hopelessness.

For further discussion of Joyce's PowerPoint slide, see Chapter 13, page 327–330.

## A Proposal Argument

**WRITING PROJECT**

**10.3**
Persuade your audience by writing an effective proposal argument.

Call your audience's attention to a problem, propose a solution to that problem, and present a justification for your solution. You have two choices (or your instructor may limit you to just one): (a) create a practical proposal, with a letter of transmittal, proposing a nuts-and-bolts solution to a local problem; or (b) write a more general policy proposal, addressing a public issue, in the form of a feature editorial for a particular (state, local, or college) newspaper. If you choose (b), your instructor might ask you to do research and model your proposal after a magazine or journal article.

## Generating and Exploring Ideas

If you have trouble thinking of a proposal topic, try making an idea map of local problems you would like to see solved. Consider some of the following starting points:

### Finding a Proposal Issue

*Problems at your university:* parking, registration system, absence of recycling options, hours of cafeterias and eating facilities, too many activities on campus during the week, poor school spirit, problems with residence halls, availability of internships

***Problems in your city or town:*** lack of bike paths, inadequate lighting, unattractive public parks or lack of public parks, zoning problems, inadequate support for public education, need for public transportation, conservation of water

***Problems at your place of work:*** flow of customer traffic, inadequate staffing during peak times, unclear division of responsibilities, no policies for raises or training new employees, health care coverage, safety issues

***Social problems and problems related to other aspects of your life:*** problems with credit card debt, need for financial literacy, physical fitness in the public schools, aid for victims of disasters, employment opportunities for college students, media consumption and awareness of current events

Another approach is to freewrite your response to these trigger statements:

I would really like to solve the problem of _____.

I believe that X should_____. (Substitute for X words such as *my instructor, the president, the school administration, Congress, my boss,* and so forth.)

Note that the problem you pose for this paper can be personal, but shouldn't be private; that is, others should be able to benefit from a solution to your personal problem. For example, your inability to find child care for your daughter is a private problem. But if you focus your proposal on how zoning laws discourage development of in-home day care—and propose a change in those zoning laws to permit more in-home day care centers—then your proposal will benefit others.

## Using Stock Issues to Explore Your Problem

Once you have decided on a proposal issue, explore it by freewriting your responses to the following questions. These questions are often called *stock issues,* since they represent generic, or stock, questions that apply to almost any kind of proposal.

1. Is there a problem here that has to be solved?
2. Will the proposed solution really solve this problem?
3. Can the problem be solved in a simpler way without disturbing the status quo?
4. Is the proposed solution practical enough that it really stands a chance of being implemented?
5. What will be the positive and negative consequences of the proposal?

You might also try freewriting your responses to the questions in the "In Conversation" exercise on page 245. Although these questions cover much the same territory as the stock issues, their different presentation might stimulate additional thought.

Finally, try thinking of justifications for your solution by using the principles/consequences/precedents or analogies strategy described on pages 247–248.

## Avoiding Presupposing Your Solution in Your Problem Statement

A common mistake of inexperienced proposal writers is to write problem statements that presuppose their solutions. As a restaurant server, suppose you notice that customers want coffee refills faster than servers can provide them. To solve this problem, you propose placing carafes of hot coffee at each table. When describing your problem, don't presuppose your solution: "The problem is that we don't have carafes of hot coffee at the tables." Rather, describe the problematic situation itself: annoyed customers clamoring for coffee and harassed servers trying to bring around refills. Only by giving presence to the original problem can you interest readers in your proposed solution, which readers will compare to other possible approaches (including doing nothing).

Here is another example:

> **Weak:** The problem is that the Student Union doesn't stay open late enough at night.

> **Better:** The problem is that students who study late at night don't have an attractive, convenient place to socialize or study; off-campus coffee houses are too far to walk to at night; dorm lounges aren't attractive or conducive to studying; late-nighters make noise in the dorms instead of going to a convenient place.

## Shaping and Drafting

In Figure 10.2, we show a typical organizational plan for a proposal argument that you might use if you get stuck while composing the first draft of your essay.

**FIGURE 10.2** Framework of a Proposal Argument

| | |
|---|---|
| Introduction | • Presents and describes a problem that needs solving, giving it presence<br>• Gives background including previous attempts to solve the problem<br>• Argues that the problem is solvable (optional) |
| Presentation of the proposed solution | • States the solution succinctly<br>• Explains the specifics of the solution |
| Justification | • Persuades readers that the proposal should be implemented<br>• Presents and develops Reasons 1, 2, and so forth (Reasons to support the proposed solution may be arguments from principle, consequence, and precedent or analogy) |
| Summary and rebuttal of opposing views | *Policy proposal:*<br>• Presents opposing view(s)<br>• Rebuts opposing view(s)<br>*Practical proposal:*<br>• Presents alternative solution(s)<br>• Explains why alternative solution(s) are inferior |
| Conclusion | • Asks readers to act (sometimes incorporated into the last sentences of the final supporting reason) |

# Revising

After you have completed your first draft and begun to clarify your argument for yourself, you are ready to start making your argument clear and persuasive for your readers. Use the strategies for clear closed-form prose outlined in Chapter 12. At this stage, feedback from peer readers can be very helpful.

## Questions for Peer Review

In addition to the generic peer review questions explained in Skill 11.4, ask your peer reviewers to address these questions:

### INTRODUCTION AND STATEMENT OF PROBLEM:

1. How could the title more effectively focus the paper and pique your interest?
2. Where does the writer convince you that a problem exists and that it is significant (worth solving) and solvable? Where does the writer give the problem presence? How could the writer improve the presentation of the problem?

### PROPOSED SOLUTION:

3. Does the writer's thesis clearly propose a solution to the problem? Could the thesis be made more precise?
4. Could the writer give you more details about the solution so that you can understand it and see how it works? How could the writer make the solution clearer?

### JUSTIFICATION:

5. In the justification section, how could the writer provide stronger reasons for acting on the proposal? Where could the reasons be better supported with more details and evidence? How could the reasons appeal more to the values and beliefs of the audience?
6. Can you help the writer think of additional justifying arguments (arguments from principle, from consequences, from precedent or analogy)? How else could the writer improve support for the proposal?
7. Where does the writer anticipate and address opposing views or alternative solutions? How does the writer convince you that the proposed solution is superior to alternative solutions?
8. Has the writer persuaded you that the benefits of this proposal will outweigh the costs? Who will pay the costs and who will get the benefits? What do you think the gut reaction of a typical decision maker would be to the writer's proposal?
9. Can you think of other, unforeseen costs that the writer should acknowledge and address? What unforeseen benefits could the writer mention?
10. How might the writer improve the structure and clarity of the argument? Where might the writer better apply the principles of clarity from Chapter 12?

## Multimodal or Online Options

1. ***Advocacy Ad or Poster*** Create a one-page advocacy ad or poster that presents a controversial public problem and calls for action and support. Consider how you will use all the features of visual arguments—type sizes and fonts, layout, color, and images and graphics—to grab the attention of your audience, construct a compelling sketch of the problem, and inform your audience what course of action you want them to take. In this advocacy piece, you need to capture your proposal argument in a highly condensed form, while making it visually clear and memorable. Your instructor might ask you instead to create a longer brochure-length handout or a Web page. Advice on creating advocacy posters is found in Chapter 13, pages 331–332.

2. ***Proposal Speech with Visual Aids*** Deliver a proposal argument as a prepared but extemporaneous speech of approximately five to eight minutes supported with visual aids created on presentation software such as PowerPoint or Prezi. Your speech should present a problem, propose a solution, justify the solution with reasons and evidence, and defend it against objections or alternative solutions. As you deliver your speech, use appropriate visual aids to give presence to the problem, highlight points, provide memorable data or evidence, or otherwise enhance appeals to *logos, ethos,* and *pathos.* Although presentation software is commonly used in oral presentations, low-tech visual aids (for example, overhead transparencies or flip charts) can also be effective. Follow the guidelines provided by your instructor. As you contemplate this project, consider its three different components: creating the speech itself, designing the visuals, and delivering the speech. Advice on giving oral presentations and designing presentation slides is provided in Chapter 13, pages 332–336.

**Readings**    Our first reading, by student writer Lucy Morsen, is a practical proposal entitled "A Proposal to Improve the Campus Learning Environment by Banning Laptops and Cell Phones from Class." Because practical proposals are aimed at a specific audience, they are often accompanied by a letter of transmittal that introduces the writer, sets the context, and summarizes the proposal. We reproduce here Lucy's transmittal letter followed by her proposal. We also show you the appearance of her title page.

April 26, 2010

Professor Ralph Sorento
Chair, Faculty Senate
_____ University
Street
City, State, Zip

Dear Professor Sorento:

1      Enclosed is a proposal that I hope you will present to the Faculty Senate. It asks the university to ban all laptops and cell phones from classes in consideration of those many students like myself whose educational experience is diminished by classmates who surf the Web or send text messages during lectures or class discussion. As I try to show in this proposal, the effect of laptops and cell phones in class is distracting to many students and may hurt the academic performance of students who think they can multitask without any negative effects. I use both personal experience and recent research reports on multitasking as support for my argument.

2      Banning laptops and cell phones from class would deepen students' engagement with course material and make for more lively and energetic class discussions. I argue that an outright campus ban would be more effective than leaving the decision up to individual instructors.

3      Thank you for considering my proposal. I am happy that this university has a Faculty Senate that welcomes ideas from students on how to make teaching and learning more effective.

Sincerely,
Lucy Morsen,
First-Year Student

A PROPOSAL TO IMPROVE THE CAMPUS LEARNING ENVIRONMENT BY
BANNING LAPTOPS AND CELL PHONES FROM CLASS

Submitted to Professor Ralph Sorento
Chair of the Faculty Senate

Lucy Morsen
First-Year Student, Williamson Hall

If this were the actual proposal, it would begin on a new page following the cover page.

1    Although I am generally happy as a first-year student at this university, I wish to call the Faculty Senate's attention to a distracting problem: classmates' frequent use of laptops and cell phones during class. In many classes more than half the students have open laptops on their desks or are openly text-messaging on cell phones. Inevitably, laptop users multitask between taking notes and checking email, perusing Facebook, surfing the Web, looking at YouTube videos, playing a game, or working on an assignment for another class. (I have yet to see a student use his or her laptop solely for note-taking.) Even though I try to focus on class lectures and discussion, I find myself missing key points and ideas as my eyes are drawn to the animations and flashing colors on neighboring laptop screens. Other distractions come from the clicking of cell phone keypads—or the momentary vibration of a phone on a desktop—which can seem surprisingly loud in an otherwise quiet environment. When the person next to me continually picks up and sets down her phone to send and receive text messages, she not only distracts me from the lecture but also lets me know that she is not engaged in class, and seemingly has no interest in being so. My annoyance at my classmates and my frustration at not being able to focus undercut my enjoyment of class.

2    Given the extensive use of laptops and cell phones in class, I question the academic motivation of my classmates. As a student, I most enjoy classes when I and my classmates are actively interested and engaged in class lecture and discussion. Collective interest has a way of feeding on itself. I mean, we as students do not operate in isolation from one another, but instead we affect and influence one another in gross and subtle ways. Together with our professor we create a collective environment in the classroom, and just as we as individuals affect this collective environment, this collective environment influences us as individuals. The broad effects and consequences of this dynamic interplay should not be underestimated. Humans are highly social beings; we have the power to influence each other in both positive and negative ways. I believe that the distracting nature of laptops and cell phones is negatively affecting classroom environments. Any steps we can take collectively to help each other learn and succeed should be considered.

3    To address this problem, I propose a campus-wide ban on laptops and cell phones during class. I believe a campus-wide ban would be more effective than more limited measures some institutions have adopted, such as blocking wireless access from classrooms or allowing each professor to choose whether or not to ban laptops in his or her classroom. Blocking wireless access does not address the problem of cell phones or non-Web-based laptop distractions (such as computer games or other class work). Leaving the decision up to professors creates an added difficulty for them. I can imagine that professors, fearing resentment and poor evaluations from their students, would be reluctant to enforce a ban in their classrooms, even if they feel it would improve the classroom experience.

4    A campus-wide ban, on the other hand, would be easy to enforce, and students would more easily establish new habits—namely, not using laptops and cell phones during class. Over time, this could become the new campus norm.

5    Although many students might at first object to a ban, the decision to ban all laptops and cell phones in class would bring benefits not only to distracted students like me but also to current users of laptops and cell phones as well as to professors.

6    For one thing, the banning of laptops and cell phones would improve the learning atmosphere of a classroom. These technologies simply create too many distractions for students, and the negative consequences of these distractions are significant enough to call for institutional intervention. While some of my classmates may begrudge the ban, I believe they would quickly get used to it and notice improvements in their own classroom interest and performance. Many of my classmates may actually welcome the ban because they—like myself—are aware of the negative distractions laptops and cell phones create. In fact, an informal survey by a Georgetown University law professor who bans laptops in his classroom indicated that 70% of his students welcomed the ban (Cole, 2008).

7    Second, a ban might directly improve academic performance of current users of laptops and cell phones. A recent study at the University of Winona (Fried, 2008) found that laptop use in the classroom had a significant negative effect on class performance. In Fried's study, students who brought laptops to class received lower grades than their classmates who did not bring laptops to class. Moreover, those who brought laptops to class reported using their laptops for non-class purposes for nearly a quarter of class time.

8    Many of my classmates will likely argue that this study doesn't apply to them. They believe that they are skilled multitaskers who can continue to pay attention to a lecture while also engaging in these other activities. There is empirical evidence that they are in fact mistaken about their ability to multitask. A study by three Stanford University researchers found that persons who self-reported being heavy multitaskers were *more* easily distracted from a primary task than those who reported themselves as light multitaskers (Ophir, Nass, & Wagner, 2009). The researchers conducted this study in a lab by giving multitasking tasks to a group of self-identified heavy multitaskers and then to a group of light multitaskers. This study suggests that a person's own perception of how well he or she multitasks may not be reliable. Moreover it suggests that large amounts of daily multitasking may actually decrease a person's ability to concentrate on a single task and suppress irrelevant information.

9    A handful of students will likely argue that they only use their laptops for class-related purposes, and that an outright ban on laptops in the classroom would be unfair because they would be prohibited from using them for note-taking. However, I am skeptical of any claims that students make of only using laptops for class-related purposes. I personally have never seen any evidence of this, and research is indicating that multitasking is overwhelmingly the common norm among laptop users in the classroom. In a study by Benbunan-Fich and Truman (2009), student laptop use was monitored for 28 classroom sessions of 80 minutes (with students' permission). The researchers analyzed how often the students toggled between screens, and whether the screens were class-related or non-class-related. They found that 76% of the time students toggled between screens that were non-class-related. On average, students toggled between computer-based activities 37.5 times per 80-minute session. This research suggests that the temptations of non-class-related activities are simply too

great for students *not* to engage in multitasking in class—it is just too easy to do a brief check of email or a quick Facebook scan with a swift click of a mouse.

10    University institutions may feel reluctant to propose a campus-wide ban on laptops and cell phones in the classroom for fear of seeming overly authoritative and unnecessarily limiting student freedom. After all, students might rightly claim that they have a right to do whatever they want in the classroom as long as they aren't harming anyone else. (I have already shown they actually are harming others.) While I believe that individual rights are an important concern—in general I believe university institutions should allow for a great amount of autonomy for their students—I think that laptop use has too many negative consequences to be allowed simply in the name of student freedom. (Of course, a professor can always allow laptop use for students with special needs.)

11    For these reasons, I propose that a campus-wide ban on laptops and cell phones in the classroom should be considered. A campus-wide ban would help to create more positive, cohesive classroom experiences, and it would provide a reprieve for students from the myriad of distractions this modern technological age presents us. A campus-wide ban would be easier on professors to enforce, and it would help to establish a new (and improved) norm.

References

Benbunan-Fich, R., & Truman, G. E. (2009). Multitasking with laptops during meetings. *Communications of the ACM, 52*(2), 139–141. doi:10.1145/1461928.1461963

Cole, D. (2008, October 23). Why I ban laptops in my classroom [Web log post]. Retrieved from http://www.britannica.com/blogs/2008/10/why-i-ban-laptops-in-my-classroom

Fried, C. B. (2008). In-class laptop use and its effects on student learning. *Computers and Education, 50,* 906–914. Retrieved from www.elsevier.com

Ophir, E., Nass, C., & Wagner, A. D. (2009). Cognitive control in media multitaskers. *Proceedings of the National Academy of Sciences.* PNAS Early Edition. Retrieved from www.pnas.org

## THINKING CRITICALLY

about "A Proposal to Improve the Campus Learning Environment by Banning Laptops and Cell Phones from Class"

1. What strategies does Lucy Morsen use to convince the Faculty Senate that a problem exists?

2. What strategies does Lucy employ to persuade the Faculty Senate that her proposal is worth enacting and that it is more effective than alternative solutions?

3. How does Lucy tie her proposal to the values and beliefs of her audience—college professors who are members of the Faculty Senate?

4. How effective is Lucy's use of research evidence to support her proposal?

5. If you were a faculty member, how effective would you find Lucy's proposal? How effective do you find it as a student? What are its chief strengths and weaknesses?

Our second reading, by student writer Sam Rothchild, illustrates a multimodal argument—a speech supported with visual aids. We have reproduced Sam's outline for his speech along with six of his PowerPoint slides. His final slide was a bibliography of the sources used in the speech and the slides. Note how Sam has constructed the slides as visual arguments to support specific points in the speech as opposed to using his slides to reproduce his speech outline. In Chapter 13, we offer advice on preparing and delivering speeches and creating presentation slides.

Sam Rothchild (Student)

# Reward Work Not Wealth:

## A Proposal to Increase Income Tax Rates for the Richest 1 Percent of Americans

### Problem

1. Since 1980 the gap between rich and poor has increased enormously.
   a. Statistical evidence demonstrates the gap.
      (i)   The rich have gotten richer.
      (ii)  The poor have gotten poorer.
      (iii) The middle class are treading water.
   b. A primary cause of the income gap is the Bush-era tax cuts that benefited the rich more than the poor.
   c. Income gap leads to an unhealthy middle class and increased poverty, hurting all Americans.

### Solution

2. The solution is to raise the income tax rates on the ultra-rich back to 1980 levels.

### Reasons to Support this Proposal

3. A more progressive income tax structure promotes a more just society.
   a. Sales taxes and payroll taxes (Social Security, Medicare) take a high-percentage chunk out of low-income salaries and a tiny percentage out of high-income salaries.
   b. Progressive income tax balances the regressive effect of sales taxes and payroll taxes.
4. Reducing the gap between rich and poor creates a stronger middle class and reduces poverty.
5. Increasing tax rates on the very rich will not hurt the incentive to work or the entrepreneurial spirit.
6. The ultra-rich will still be ultra-rich.

**FIGURE 10.3** Sam's Title Slide Using an Image for *Pathos*

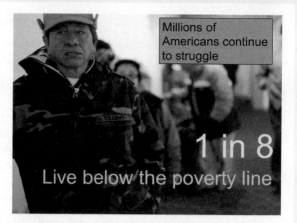

**FIGURE 10.4** Slide Using an Image for Pathos

**FIGURE 10.5** First of a Two-Slide Sequence Using Images to Illustrate Income Gap

**FIGURE 10.6** Second Slide in Sequence, Designed by Sam to Dramatize Wealth

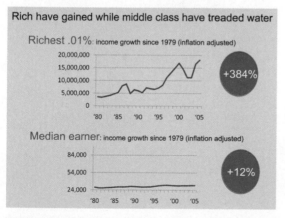

**FIGURE 10.7** Slide with Point Title and Graphics for Evidence

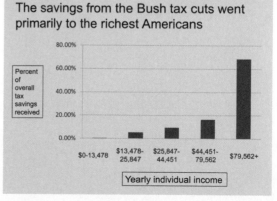

**FIGURE 10.8** Another Slide with Point Title and Graphics for Evidence

### THINKING CRITICALLY ABOUT
"Reward Work Not Wealth: A Proposal to Increase Income Tax Rates for the Richest 1 Percent of Americans"

1. Although it is common to design PowerPoint slides using topics and bullets to reproduce the speaker's outline, many media specialists prefer the approach Sam uses here in which the titles of slides are complete sentences that make a point. (See our explanation of "assertion/evidence" slides in Chapter 13, pp. 332–335). Sam's intention is to use the slide title to make a point and then use photographs, drawings, or graphics to support the point through immediate appeals to *logos* and *pathos*. How does each of Sam's slides make a point? How does the image on each slide support the point?

2. Sam was particularly proud of the way he constructed his two Ferrari slides. He wanted to create a startling way to show his audience the extreme wealth of the super-rich: "Not only can they afford a Ferrari. They can afford five Ferraris ever day of the year!" Do you find these Ferrari slides effective? What other ways might he have shown visually the wealth of the super-rich?

3. Overall, how effective do you find Sam's argument? How effectively has he used slides to support his argument? What suggestions do you have either to improve his speech or improve his visual aids?

---

Our final reading is by student writer Kent Ansen, who proposes that the United States institute mandatory national service for young adults. Kent's process in producing this paper has been discussed in various places throughout the text. Particularly see Kent's freewrite on pages 26–27, his research notes on pages 126–127, his exploratory paper and annotated bibliography, pages 136–141 and 141–143, and his outlines, "nutshell," and tree diagram on pages 295–298. We present his proposal as an illustration of a student research paper written and formatted in MLA style. For a compete explanation of MLA style, see Chapter 15.

Ansen 1

Kent Ansen

Professor Johnson

Writing Seminar

15 Mar. 2013

Engaging Young Adults to Meet America's Challenges:

A Proposal for Mandatory National Service

In high school, I volunteered at an afterschool program for elementary

school students located in one of the poorest, most dangerous neighborhoods

in town, known for high crime and gang activity. I spent a couple hours per

week helping kids complete homework and crafts, reading stories, supervising

field games, and serving snacks. The kids' snacks—usually a piece of fruit,

some crackers, and a carton of milk—often filled in for dinner because there

was no food for them at home. The program was run by a team of AmeriCorps

members, who also ran a summer program so the kids had supervision,

learning opportunities, and food during the long months of summer. In

addition to providing tutoring and food, AmeriCorps connected students

and their families to resources like clothing, healthcare, and school supplies.

They partnered with Habitat for Humanity to repair dilapidated homes, haul

trash to garbage pickup sites, and landscape overgrown yards. Over time,

the AmeriCorps program gained so much trust and respect that its program

expanded to other neighborhoods like this one, mobilizing an even greater

number of volunteers and resources to fight poverty and injustice in our town.

The successes I witnessed in AmeriCorps suggest that volunteer

programs can help address problems in our communities. But it is possible

that they can also address problems faced by young people, whose job choices

are limited by the slow economic recovery, the reduced number of entry-level

jobs, and the crushing burden of student loans. A 2012 Pew Research study

found that only 54 percent of Americans aged 18-24 were currently employed

*Put last name and page number in header on each page.*

*Place name, course information, and date on first page.*

*Center title.*

*Indent paragraphs ½ inch.*

*Use one-inch margins at top, bottom, and both sides.*

*Double-space all parts of the text (no single spacing anywhere).*

Ansen 2

(the lowest rate since the government began tracking this data in 1948) and that these young adults experienced the greatest drop in earnings of any age group in the last four years ("Young, Underemployed and Optimistic"). Young Americans have been classified as a "Lost Generation" struggling to overcome these obstacles and find the path to success and achievement.

*Parenthetical citation—for full citation, see entry under "Young..." in Works Cited.*

Problems like these present us with a unique opportunity for creative problem solving. I propose instituting a mandatory year of national service for Americans ages 18-25. A mandatory service program would engage today's underemployed Lost Generation in helping America's vulnerable communities become stable, healthy, vibrant, and self-sufficient. It would also help young adults by nurturing their personal growth and professional development, and it would help our nation by promoting democracy through increased civic engagement.

What would this year of mandatory service look like? It would require all citizens between the ages of 18 and 25 to spend a year in national service. (Alternatively, persons could volunteer for military service.) Some students might choose to serve immediately after high school as a gap year before starting college or a job. Others might take a gap year during college or wait until they graduate. Mandated national service could be built upon the model of AmeriCorps. It would allow volunteers to choose placements in a variety of nonprofit, public, faith-based, and educational organizations including work in schools and after-school programs, employment training organizations, environmental restoration and stewardship, food banks, shelters, and emergency response. It would pay minimum wage, provide health benefits, defer student loan payments, and offer a financial incentive tuition award at the end of service, which could also be taken as a cash stipend. (For an example of how a national mandatory service program might be organized and funded, see Stengel.)

*An entry beginning with "Stengel" appears in Works Cited.*

Ansen 3

Although there will be costs associated with mandatory public service, these will be far outweighed by the benefits. First, a program of mandatory national service would be an investment in communities by attacking poverty and building social capital. A national service program would build on the documented success of AmeriCorps, which in 2010 received $480 million in donations and mobilized and managed 3.4 million volunteers (*AmeriCorps Impact Guide*). By helping the poor become self-sufficient, mandatory service could help reduce the needs for future expenditures on poverty. According to an Urban Institute research study on childhood poverty (Ratcliffe and McKernan 14), childhood poverty costs $550 billion annually. Whereas current poverty spending largely aims to provide food, clothing, and housing for the poor, projects like AmeriCorps provide people-to-people contact that can help address the root causes of poverty. Particularly, service programs can help communities build social capital to enhance their capacity to solve their own problems. Social capital is the idea that the number of social connections within a community—things like civic participation, organizational membership, degree of trust in neighbors, educational achievement—determine its ability to solve shared problems. According to Lew Feldstein, a United Way director, communities with high social capital tend to have better outcomes in areas like crime, health, and education than do communities with low social capital. Expanding national service will increase people-to-people contact, creating more opportunities to form the connections that build social capital. The power of volunteers to bring people together shines through the testimonial pages of the AmeriCorps Web site, where volunteers explain why they think AmeriCorps is valuable. In the following testimonial, alumna Sarah shows how AmeriCorps volunteers help marginalized people learn the social-interaction skills needed to live successfully in their community.

*Use italics for titles of books or Web sites.*

*"14" indicates page number in pdf document.*

Ansen 4

*Use brackets to summarize material.*

> The year I served as an AmeriCorps member I lived and
> learned [in a community] of immigrants, refugees, and
> people trying to support their families. My job description
> was to help welfare recipients, people with disabilities, and
> refugees find and maintain employment; this meant mock
> interviews, anger-management, helping clients to use public
> transportation, and arranging interviews.... Through
> this experience, my clients' challenges became real and
> experiencing the same circumstances we could work on
> solutions to problems such as transportation and housing.
> ("AmeriCorps Testimonials")

*Indent longer quotations 1 inch.*

*Do not use quotation marks with block quotation. Citation comes after the period.*

Sarah's testimonial focuses on the one-on-one interactions that build
social capital to help communities solve their own problems. The skills
contributed by people like Sarah will remain in the community, reflecting
the lasting effects national service can have on a community's long-term
well-being.

Not only can a national service program benefit impoverished
communities, but it also benefits the volunteers themselves by fostering their
personal growth and professional development. For example, a volunteer
named Maia, in her testimonial on the AmeriCorps Web site, calls her
volunteer experience "invaluable." She says, "I now have experience with case
management and writing curriculums. 1 am much more confident in my skills
and abilities especially concerning the professional world." Another volunteer,
Mari, says, "I want to build a career working in social services with immigrant
communities." She praises her AmeriCorps experience for giving her the skills
she needs for this career. "I was able to work closely with Somali refugees to
assess their skills and help them find jobs.... After AmeriCorps, I plan to look

Ansen 5

for a similar job in the nonprofit sector." Another volunteer, Anjanette, goes
into more depth to show how volunteer service creates career skills:

> AmeriCorps is a good learning experience because the people
> in it are often placed in positions within fields where they don't
> have any previous experience, and yet they are able to achieve
> great progress in a short period of time. It's a great opportunity
> to expand knowledge and horizons in ways that few other jobs
> or opportunities allow.... I hoped to gain relevant experience
> for my future profession, which is being a clinical social worker,
> before going to graduate school. It was a great opportunity for
> me to see if working in the field of mental health in general
> would be a good fit. I plan on going to school to get a Master's
> degree in social work with a goal of working primarily with
> GLBTQ youth. ("AmeriCorps Testimonials")

As these testimonials suggest, public service provides hands-on experience
that can't be duplicated by academic study. According to AmeriCorps
alumnus Ben, "AmeriCorps gives you the experience that you can't find in a
textbook" ("AmeriCorps Testimonials").

    Of course, these non-random testimonials do not mean that every
AmeriCorps volunteer gains these benefits. But they ring true to my own
experience as a high school volunteer working within an AmeriCorps
program. Further support for the claim that volunteer community service
increases career skills comes from a 2007 longitudinal study where
researchers found that AmeriCorps alumni experienced statistically
significant gains in employment outcomes and job skills compared to peers
not enrolled in AmeriCorps (Jastrzab et al. 45).

    The benefits that 1 have previously mentioned could largely be
achieved simply by expanding volunteerism without making national

Ansen 6

service mandatory. But mandatory national service would bring a vital third benefit: increased civic engagement. When the United States eliminated the draft and moved to an all-volunteer army, it ended the specter of unwanted military service, but it also undermined citizens' sense of being stakeholders in America by allowing citizens to hire volunteers to fight their wars. This vital sense of personal investment in our nation—lost when the draft was eliminated—could be restored through mandatory national service, but in a context of helping our neighbor rather than fighting wars. Currently, low voter turnout and political apathy, especially among young people, suggests that our citizenry is disengaged from government (Bipartisan Policy Center). According to Mark Rosenman, an applied researcher on anti-poverty programs and an opinion writer for the *Chronicle of Philanthropy,* Americans are becoming increasingly passive citizens whose "only obligation is to pay taxes, [reducing Americans to being] little more than consumers of government services, to being government's customers." To form a healthy democracy, Rosenman argues, citizens need to be "more directly and personally involved in working on the problems facing the country and the world." They need to be more "involved in their government and more concerned about public policy."

*Use brackets to indicate alteration of quotation to fit grammar of sentence.*

For citizens to engage with government on the level advocated by Rosenman, they must first be able to identify community problems, feel a sense of responsibility for those problems, and be compelled to hold elected officials accountable for contributing to solutions. Currently service in AmeriCorps builds these civic skills because volunteers experience first-hand the impact of government failure to serve specific constituencies. For some AmeriCorps teams, a civic engagement project is built into the service experience. Teams follow a six-module civic engagement curriculum in which they work together to identify community needs, prioritize a need,

Ansen 7

and develop and implement a corresponding service project. The 2007 AmeriCorps alumni study found statistically significant gains in markers of civic engagement among alumni, including increased community-based activism, increased confidence in the ability of communities to identify and solve problems, and increased connection to the community (Jastrzab et al. 45). These markers were present eight years after service was completed, evidence that the impact of mandatory national service will extend far beyond the service year to create a generation of responsive citizens and strengthen the foundation of our democracy.

Of course, there are many objections to mandatory national service. Some fear that mandating a year of national service would harm our democracy by limiting individual freedom. These critics cite the unpopular military draft during the Vietnam War as evidence of public hostility to mandatory service. However, I argue that the unpopularity of the draft reflected the unpopularity of the Vietnam War rather than an objection to serving one's country. Moreover, the personal sacrifice of risking one's life in war is far greater than the sacrifice required for a year of service work on our own soil. Furthermore, individuals will have a greater degree of choice in terms of where, when and how they serve—choices that were not available during the draft. And while freedom is certainly a central American value, it does not mean that our freedom is without limits or that those limits are without benefits. By creating a national culture of service in this country, mandatory national service will engage young people in solving our communities' pressing problems, create bonds of friendship, and link youth to older citizens, thus creating a powerful cross-generational force of people working together.

One powerful critique of national service comes from Michael Kinsley, a consultant for the conservative think tank Heritage Foundation, in a *Time* magazine online article entitled "National Service? Puh-lease." Kinsley objects to government bureaucrats drawing on a huge labor pool of minimum wage workers to create largely useless jobs that interfere with market forces and waste taxpayer money. Arguing that people are willing to do any job for a decent enough wage, Kinsley wonders why we would force conscripted laborers to work for minimum wage when there is already a supply of workers in the market willing to do the same job for reasonable pay. Kinsley uses George Orwell's novel *1984* to paint a picture of workers forced to do jobs that they would otherwise not take. Furthermore, Kinsley believes that most of these jobs would be "make-work" activities, meaning that bureaucrats would have to spend their time finding trivial ways to keep all the volunteers busy.

Kinsley's argument is provocative, but it fails to recognize the documented valuable work already provided by AmeriCorps—work that could be scaled up nationally without leading to "make-work" jobs. Kinsley fails to acknowledge that the kind of work provided by AmeriCorps does not compete with market forces. AmeriCorps jobs supplement the work of the nonprofit sector; they do not displace market-sector jobs such as garbage haulers or carpenters. The best response to Kinsley's fear of make-work jobs created by bureaucrats is to recognize that the organizational structures for a national service program are already in place through AmeriCorps. Relying on AmeriCorps would ease the transition to mandatory national service by providing a foundational, established program from which to grow and model additional partnerships. An expansion of national service is already underway through 2009's Generations Invigorating Volunteerism and Education (GIVE) Act (Robertson). This legislation is intended to expand participation in national service from 75,000 to 250,000 by 2014 and diversifies the focus of programs

Ansen 9

to include disaster relief, urban and rural development, infrastructure improvement, and energy conservation. Building on GIVE Act's public and congressional support could boost momentum for the transition to mandatory national service.

The point to emphasize, then, is that the money used to fund mandatory national service is money directly reinvested in our communities. Our country is currently facing numerous challenges: increasing inequality, expansive poverty, slow economic recovery, environmental and educational crises, and a disengaged citizenry. But we also have a remarkable opportunity to involve our young adults in meeting these challenges. By taking bold action to create a system of mandatory national service built on the AmeriCorps model, we have the chance to fulfill our potential as a nation.

Ansen 10

Works Cited

*AmeriCorps Impact Guide.* Corporation for National and Community
Service, n.d. Web. 23 Feb. 2013.

"AmeriCorps Testimonials." *Rise: A Partnership that Works.* Rise, 2012. Web.
24 Feb. 2013.

Bipartisan Policy Center. "2012 Voter Turnout." *Bipartisan Policy Center.*
8 Nov. 2012. Web. 23 Feb. 2013.

Feldstein, Lew. "The Importance of Strengthening Social Capital in
Communities." United Way of King County, Seattle, WA.
18 Dec. 2012. Guest Lecture.

Jastrzab, JoAnn et al. "Serving Country and Community: A Longitudinal
Study of Service in AmeriCorps." *Corporation for National and
Community Service.* Abt Associates, Apr. 2007. Web.
23 Feb. 2013.

Kinsley, Michael. "National Service? Puh-lease." *Time Lists.* Time, 30 Aug.
2007. Web. 8 Feb.2013.

Ratcliffe, Caroline E. and Signe-Mary McKernan. "Childhood Poverty and
Its Lasting Consequences." Paper 21. *Low-Income Working Families.*
The Urban Institute, Sept. 2012. Web. 23 Feb. 2013.

Robertson, Lori. "Mandatory Public Service." *FactCheck.org.* Annenberg
Public Policy Center, 31 Mar. 2009. Web. 6 Feb. 2013.

Rosenman, Mark. "A Call for National Service." *Chronicle of Philanthropy*
20.1 (18 Oct. 2007). *Academic Search Complete.* Web. 12 Feb. 2013.

Stengel, Richard. "A Time to Serve." *Time* 10 Sept. 2007: 48-67. Print.

"Young, Underemployed and Optimistic." *Pew Research Social &
Demographic Trends.* Pew Research Center, 9 Feb. 2012. Web.
12 Feb. 2013.

*Start Works Cited on a new page.*

*List sources alpha-betically by author's last name or by title if there is no named author.*

*Use hanging indentation.*

*Double space throughout.*

*Use day-month-year format for dates.*

*Use quota-tion marks for article titles.*

*Use italics for book, periodical, and Web site titles.*

## THINKING CRITICALLY

about "Engaging Young Adults to Meet America's Challenges: A Proposal for Mandatory National Service"

1. Proposal arguments typically begin with the problem that the proposed solution is intended to address. How effectively does Ansen introduce the problems that mandatory national service might solve? What are these problems?

2. Where does Ansen present his solution to the problem? How effective is he at explaining the details of the solution and convincing the audience that the solution is doable?

3. Where does Ansen justify his solution by presenting reasons for enacting it? What are his primary reasons in favor of the proposal? Which of these reasons do you find particularly strong or particularly weak?

4. Where does Ansen summarize objections to his proposal? If you have objections to his proposal, are your reservations or doubts adequately summarized and addressed? Why or why not?

5. How effective is Ansen's attempt to rebut the objections?

6. Overall, how would you evaluate the *logos* of Ansen's argument? How effectively does he use reasons and evidence to move his audience toward his views? How effective are Ansen's appeals to *ethos* and *pathos*? Does he project a credible and trustworthy persona? To what extent does he connect his argument to the values or beliefs of his audience or otherwise appeal to their emotions?

# A GUIDE TO COMPOSING AND REVISING

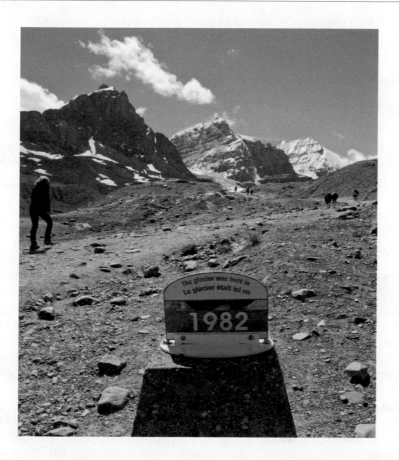

This recent photo depicts the receding Athabasca Glacier in Alberta, Canada, in the Canadian Rockies. A multimodel text, this photo uses words and image to convey its appeals to *logos, ethos,* and *pathos.* The sign informs visitors of the change in the glacier in the last thirty years. The visual impact of the photo with the people hiking up the mountain to get to the glacier, once much closer to the road, dramatically confirms the message of change and loss. You might contrast this photo with the image of the vast iceberg on page 58. Which photo do you think would be more effective in conveying the extent and urgency of global warming?

# 11 WRITING AS A PROBLEM-SOLVING PROCESS

## WHAT YOU WILL LEARN

**11.1** To follow the experts' practice of using multiple drafts.

**11.2** To revise globally as well as locally.

**11.3** To develop ten expert habits to improve your writing processes.

**11.4** To use peer reviews to help you think like an expert.

Throughout this text, we have emphasized writing as a critical thinking process requiring writers to "wallow in complexity." This opening chapter of Part 3 explains how experienced writers use multiple drafts to manage the complexities of writing.

**11.1**
Follow the experts's practice of using multiple drafts.

## SKILL 11.1 **Follow the experts' practice of using multiple drafts.**

We begin this chapter with a close look at why expert writers use multiple drafts to move from an initial exploration of ideas to a finished product. As composition theorist Peter Elbow has asserted about the writing process, "meaning is not what you start out with" but "what you end up with." In the early stages of writing, experienced writers typically discover, deepen, and complicate their ideas before they can clarify them and arrange them effectively. Only in the last drafts will expert writers be in sufficient control of their ideas to shape them elegantly for readers.

What most distinguishes expert from novice writers is the experts' willingness to keep revising their work until they feel it is ready to go public. They typically work much harder at drafting and revising than do novice writers, taking more runs at their subject. Expert writers also make more substantial alterations in their drafts during revision—what we call "global" rather than "local" revision. This difference between expert and novice writers might seem counterintuitive. One might think that novices would need to revise more than experts. But decades of research on the writing process of experts reveals how extensively experts revise. The experienced writer crosses out pages and starts over while the inexperienced writer crosses out a word or two. The experienced writer feels cognitive overload while drafting, having to attend to many different "levels and agendas" at once.

First Draft with Revisions

sticks of our favorite flavors in the bottom of the bag. That discovery was, by far, the best discovery that could ever be made, week after week. So, as you can probably guess, my opinion of farmer's markets has always been very high as they were what fulfilled my sugar fix.

~~However, another important point can come out of that story. That point being about~~ the man who sold us our precious honey sticks. He was kind, patient, and genuinely happy to have our business. *In contrast to* ~~Not quite the same vibe that one would expect to get from~~ the supermarket employee who _often_ doesn't ~~even really~~ know what isle you need in order to find the peanut butter. *Another* A huge selling point of farmer's markets, for me, is that you can go and talk to people who know about the food they are selling. It is so refreshing to go

Revised Draft

sticks of our favorite flavors in the bottom of the bag.

Another huge selling point of farmer's markets, for me, is that you can go and talk to people who know about the food they are selling. The man who sold us our *precious* honey sticks was kind, patient, and genuinely happy to have our business, in contrast to the supermarket employee who _often_ doesn't ~~even really~~ know what aisle you need in order to find the peanut butter.

**FIGURE 11.1** A First-Year Student's Substantial Revisions

In contrast, the inexperienced writer seems to think only of replacing words or adding an occasional transition. Learning to revise extensively is thus a hallmark of a maturing writer.

Figure 11.1 shows how a first-year college student demonstrates expert writing behavior when she makes a substantial revision of an early draft. Note that she crosses out several sentences at the end of one paragraph, creates a new topic sentence for the next paragraph, and moves a detail sentence so that it follows the topic sentence.

## Why Expert Writers Revise So Extensively

Our emphasis on experts' substantial revision might have surprised you. If the experts are such good writers, why do they need multiple drafts? Why don't they get it right the first time? Our answer is simply this: Expert writers use multiple drafts to break a complex task into manageable subtasks. Let's look more closely at some of the functions that drafting and revising can perform for writers.

- *Multiple drafts help writers overcome the limits of short-term memory.* Cognitive psychologists have shown that working memory—often called short-term memory—has remarkably little storage space. You can picture short-term memory as a small tabletop surrounded by filing cabinets (long-term memory). As you write, you can place on your tabletop (working memory) only a few chunks of material at any given moment—a few sentences of a draft or several ideas in an outline. The remaining portions of your draft-in-progress fall off the table without getting stored in long-term memory. (Think of your horror when your computer eats your draft—proof that you can't rely on long-term memory to restore what you wrote.) Writing a draft captures and stores your ideas as your working memory develops them. When you reread these stored ideas, you can then see your evolving ideas whole, note problem areas, develop more ideas, see material that doesn't fit, recall additional information, and begin extending or improving the draft.
- *Multiple drafts help accommodate shifts and changes in the writer's ideas.* Early in the writing process, expert writers often are unsure of where their ideas are leading; they find that their ideas shift and evolve as their drafts progress. An expert writer's finished product often is radically different from the first draft—not simply in form and style but also in actual content.
- *Multiple drafts help writers clarify audience and purpose.* While thinking about their subject matter, experienced writers also ask questions about audience and purpose: What do my readers already know and believe about my subject? How am I trying to change their views? In the process of drafting and revising, the answers to these questions may evolve so that each new draft reflects a deeper or clearer understanding of audience and purpose.
- *Multiple drafts help writers improve structure and coherence for readers.* Whereas the ideas in early drafts often follow the order in which writers conceived them, later drafts are often restructured—sometimes radically—to meet readers' needs. Writing teachers sometimes call this transformation a movement from writer-based to reader-based prose.* The composing and revising skills taught in Chapter 12 will help you learn how to revise your drafts from a reader's perspective.
- *Multiple drafts let writers postpone worrying about correctness.* Late in the revision process, experienced writers turn their energy toward fixing errors and revising sentences for increased cohesion, conciseness, and clarity. Focusing on correctness too soon can shut down the creative process.

*The terms "writer-based" and "reader-based" prose come from Linda Flower, "Writer-Based Prose: A Cognitive Basis for Problems in Writing." *College English*, 1979, 41.1, 19–37.

## An Expert's Writing Processes Are Recursive

Given this background on why expert writers revise, we can see that for experts, the writing process is recursive rather than linear. Writers continually cycle back to earlier stages as their thinking evolves. Sometimes writers develop a thesis statement early in the writing process. But just as frequently, they formulate a thesis during an "aha!" moment of discovery later in the process, perhaps after several drafts. ("So *this* is my point! Here is my argument in a nutshell!") Even very late in the process, while checking usage and punctuation, experienced writers are apt to think of new ideas, thus triggering more revision.

## SKILL 11.2   **Revise globally as well as locally.**

To think like an expert writer, you need to appreciate the difference between "global" and "local" revision. You revise **locally** whenever you make changes to a text that affect only the one or two sentences that you are currently working on. In contrast, you revise **globally** when a change in one part of your draft drives changes in other parts of the draft. Global revision focuses on the big-picture concerns of ideas, structure, purpose, audience, and genre. It often involves substantial rewriting, even starting over in places with a newly conceived plan. For example, your revising part of the middle of your essay might cause you to rewrite the whole introduction or to change the tone or point of view throughout the essay.

**11.2**
Revise globally as well as locally.

What follows are some on-the-page strategies that you can adopt to practice the global and local revision strategies of experts:*

| On-the-Page Strategies for Doing Global and Local Revision | |
|---|---|
| **Strategies to Use on the Page** | **Reasons** |
| Throw out the whole draft and start again. | • Original draft helped writer discover ideas and see the whole territory.<br>• New draft needs to be substantially refocused and restructured. |
| Cross out large chunks and rewrite from scratch. | • Original passage was unfocused; ideas have changed.<br>• New sense of purpose or point meant that the whole passage needed reshaping.<br>• Original passage was too confused or jumbled for mere editing. |

*(continued)*

---

*We have chosen to say "on the page" rather than "on the screen" because global revision is often facilitated by a writer's working off double-spaced hard copy rather than a computer screen. See page 282 for our advice on using hard copy for revision.

| Strategies to Use on the Page | Reasons |
|---|---|
| Cut and paste; move parts around; (then write new transitions, mapping statements, and topic sentences). | • Parts didn't follow in logical order.<br>• Parts occurred in the order writer thought of them rather than the order needed by readers.<br>• Conclusion was clearer than introduction; part of conclusion had to be moved to introduction.<br>• Revised thesis statement required different order for parts. |
| Add/revise topic sentences of paragraphs; insert transitions. | • Reader needs signposts to see how parts connect to previous parts and to whole.<br>• Revision of topic sentences often requires global revision of paragraph. |
| Make insertions; add new material. | • Supporting particulars needed to be added: examples, facts, illustrations, statistics, other evidence (usually added to bodies of paragraphs).<br>• New section was needed or more explanation was needed for a point.<br>• Gaps in argument needed to be filled in. |
| Delete material. | • Material is no longer needed or is irrelevant.<br>• Deleted material may have been good but went off on a tangent. |
| Recast sentences (cross out and rewrite portions; combine sentences; rephrase sentences; start sentences with a different grammatical structure). | • Passage violated old/new contract (see Skill 12.6).<br>• Passage was wordy/choppy or lacked rhythm or voice.<br>• Grammar was tangled, diction odd, or meaning confused.<br>• Passage lost focus of topic sentence of paragraph. |
| Edit sentences to correct mistakes. | • Writer found comma splices, fragments, dangling modifiers, nonparallel constructions, or other problems of grammar and usage.<br>• Writer found spelling errors, typos, repeated or omitted words. |

**FOR WRITING AND DISCUSSION**

## Revising a Paragraph Globally

Choose an important paragraph in the body of a draft you are currently working on. Then write your answers to these questions about that paragraph.

1. Why is this an important paragraph?
2. What is its main point?
3. Where is that main point stated?

Now—as an exercise only—write the main point at the top of a blank sheet of paper, put away your original draft, and, without looking at the original, write a new paragraph with the sole purpose of developing the point you wrote at the top of the page.

When you are finished, compare your new paragraph to the original. What have you learned that might help you revise your original?

Here are some typical responses of writers who have tried this exercise:

> I recognized that my original paragraph was unfocused. I couldn't find a main point.
>
> I recognized that my original paragraph was underdeveloped. I had a main point but not enough details supporting it.
>
> I began to see that my draft was scattered and that I had too many short paragraphs.
>
> I recognized that I was making a couple of different points in my original paragraph and that I needed to break it into separate paragraphs.
>
> I recognized that I hadn't stated my main point (or that I had buried it in the middle of the paragraph).
>
> I recognized that there was a big difference in style between my two versions and that I had to choose which version I liked best. (It's not always the "new" version!)

## SKILL 11.3   **Develop ten expert habits to improve your writing processes.**

11.3
Develop ten
expert habits
to improve
your writing
processes.

Now that you understand why experts revise more extensively than novices and what they do on the page, we describe in Skill 11.3 the habitual ways of thinking and acting that experts use when they write. Our hope is that this description will help you develop these same habits for yourself. Because one of the best ways to improve your writing process is to do what the experts do, we offer you the following ten habits of experienced writers, expressed as advice:

1. ***Use exploratory writing and talking to discover and clarify ideas.*** Don't let your first draft be the first occasion when you put your ideas into writing. Use exploratory strategies such as freewriting and idea mapping to generate ideas (see Chapter 2, Concept 2.1). Also seek out opportunities to talk about your ideas with classmates or friends in order to clarify your own thinking and appreciate alternative points of view.

2. ***Schedule your time.*** Don't begin your paper the night before it is due. Plan sufficient time for exploration, drafting, revision, and editing. Recognize that your ideas will shift, branch out, and even turn around as you write. Allow some time off between writing the first draft and beginning revision. For many writers, revision takes considerably longer than

writing the first draft. If your institution has a writing center, consider scheduling a visit.

3. ***Discover what methods of drafting work best for you.*** Some people compose rough drafts directly on the computer; others write longhand. Some make outlines first; others plunge directly into drafting and make outlines later. Some revise extensively on the computer as they are drafting; others plough ahead until they have a complete draft before they start revising. Some people sit at their desk for hours at a time; others need to get up and walk around every couple of minutes. Some people need a quiet room; others work best in a coffee shop. Discover the methods that work best for you.

4. ***Think about audience and purpose from the start.*** Early on, think about the effect you want your writing to have on readers. In formulating a thesis, look to change your readers' view of your subject. ("Before reading my paper, my readers will think X. But after reading my paper, my readers will think Y.")

5. ***For the first draft, reduce your expectations.*** Many novice writers get blocked by trying to make their first draft perfect. In contrast, expert writers expect the first draft to be an unreadable mess. (They often call it a "zero draft" or a "garbage draft" because they don't expect it to be good.) They use the first draft merely to get their ideas flowing, knowing they will revise later. If you get blocked, just keep writing. Get some ideas on paper.

6. ***Revise on double- or triple-spaced hard copy.*** Although many experienced writers revise on the screen without going through paper drafts, there are powerful advantages in printing occasional paper drafts. Research suggests that writers are more apt to make global changes in a draft if they work from hard copy because they can see more easily how the parts connect to the whole. They can refer quickly to page two while revising page six without having to scroll back and forth. We suggest that you occasionally print out a double- or triple-spaced hard copy of your draft and then mark it up aggressively. (See again Figure 11.1, which shows how a first-year student learned the benefits of revising off hard copy.) When your draft gets too messy, keyboard your changes into your computer and begin another round of revision.

7. ***As you revise, think increasingly about the needs of your readers.*** Experts use first drafts to help them clarify their ideas for themselves but not necessarily for readers. In many respects, writers of first drafts are talking to themselves. Through global revision, however, writers gradually convert "writer-based prose" to "reader-based prose." Writers begin to employ consciously the skills of reader-expectation theory that we explain in detail in Chapter 12.

8. ***Exchange drafts with others.*** Get other people's reactions to your work in exchange for your reactions to theirs. Experienced writers regularly seek critiques of their drafts from trusted readers. Later in this chapter we explain procedures for peer review of drafts.

9. ***Save correctness for last.*** To revise productively, concentrate first on the big questions: Do I have good ideas in this draft? Am I responding appropriately to the assignment? Are my ideas adequately organized and developed? Save questions about exact wording, grammar, mechanics, and documentation style for later. These concerns are important, but they cannot be efficiently attended to until after higher-order concerns are met. Your first goal is to create a thoughtful, richly developed draft.

10. ***To meet deadlines and bring the process to a close, learn how to satisfice.*** Our description of the writing process may seem formidable. Technically, it seems, you could go on revising forever. How can you ever know when to stop? There is no ready answer to that question, which is more a psychological than a technical problem. Expert writers have generally learned how to **satisfice**, a term coined by influential social scientist Herbert Simon from two root words, *suffice* and *satisfy*. It means to do the best job you can under the circumstances considering your time constraints, the pressures of other demands on you, and the difficulty of the task. Expert writers begin the writing process early and get as far as they can before their deadline looms. Then they let the deadline give them the energy for intensive revision. From lawyers preparing briefs for court to engineers developing design proposals, writers have used deadlines to help them put aside doubts and anxieties and to conclude their work, as every writer must. "Okay, it's not perfect, but it's the best I can do for now."

## Analyzing Your Own Writing Process

FOR WRITING AND DISCUSSION

When you write, do you follow a process resembling the one we just described? Have you ever

- had a writing project grow out of your engagement with a problem or question?
- explored ideas by talking with others or by doing exploratory writing?
- made major changes to a draft because you changed your mind or otherwise discovered new ideas?
- revised a draft from a reader's perspective by consciously trying to imagine and respond to a reader's questions, confusions, and other reactions?
- road tested a draft by trying it out on readers and then revising it as a result of what they told you?

Working in groups or as a whole class, share stories about previous writing experiences that match or do not match the description of experienced writers' processes. To the extent that your present process differs, what strategies of experienced writers might you like to try?

**11.4**
Use peer reviews
to help you think
like an expert.

## 11.4  SKILL II.4  Use peer reviews to help you think like an expert.

One of the best ways to become a better reviser is to see your draft from a *reader's* rather than a *writer's* perspective. As a writer, you know what you mean; you are already inside your own head. But you need to see what your draft looks like to readers—that is, to people who are not inside your head.

A good way to learn this skill is to practice reading your classmates' drafts and have them read yours. In this section we offer advice on how to respond candidly to your classmates' drafts and how to participate in peer reviews.

### Becoming a Helpful Reader of Classmates' Drafts

When you respond to a writer's draft, learn to make *readerly* rather than *writerly* comments. For example, instead of saying, "Your draft is disorganized," say, "I got lost when...." Instead of saying, "This paragraph needs a topic sentence," say, "I had trouble seeing the point of this paragraph." In other words, describe your mental experience in trying to understand the draft rather than use technical terms to point out problem areas or to identify errors.

When you help a writer with a draft, your goal is both to point out where the draft needs more work and to brainstorm with the writer possible ways to improve the draft. Begin by reading the draft all the way through at a normal reading speed. As you read, make mental notes to help focus your feedback. We recommend that you also mark passages that you find confusing. Write "G!" for "Good" next to parts that you like. Write "?" next to places where you want to ask questions.

After you have read the draft, use the following strategies for making helpful responses, either in writing or in direct conversation with the writer.

| Strategies for Responding Helpfully to a Classmate's Draft | |
| --- | --- |
| **Kinds of Problems Noted** | **Helpful Responses** |
| If the ideas in the draft seem thin or undeveloped, or if the draft is too short | • Help the writer brainstorm for more ideas. <br> • Help the writer add more examples, better details, more supporting data or arguments. |
| If you get confused or lost in some parts of the draft | • Show the writer where you got confused or miscued in reading the draft ("I started getting lost here because I couldn't see why you were giving me this information" or <br> "I thought you were going to say X, but then you said Y"). <br> • Have the writer talk through ideas to clear up confusing spots. |

| Kinds of Problems Noted | Helpful Responses |
|---|---|
| If you get confused or lost at the "big-picture" level | • Help the writer sharpen the thesis: suggest that the writer view the thesis as the answer to a controversial or problematic question; ask the writer to articulate the question that the thesis answers.<br>• Help the writer create an outline, tree diagram, or flowchart (see Skill 12.2).<br>• Help the writer clarify the focus by asking him or her to complete these statements about purpose:<br>  • The purpose of this paper is _____.<br>  • The purpose of this section (paragraph) is _____.<br>  • Before reading my paper, my reader will think X. But after reading my paper, my reader will think Y. |
| If you can understand the sentences but can't see the point | • Help the writer articulate the meaning by asking "So what?" questions, making the writer bring the point to the surface. ("I can understand what you are saying here but I don't quite understand why you are saying it. What do these details have to do with the topic sentence of the paragraph? Or what does this paragraph have to do with your thesis?")<br>• Help the writer create transitions, new topic sentences, or other means of making points clear. |
| If you disagree with the ideas or think the writer has avoided alternative points of view | • Play devil's advocate to help the writer deepen and complicate ideas.<br>• Show the writer specific places where you had queries or doubts. |

## Using a Generic Peer Review Guide

When participating in peer reviews, writers and reviewers often appreciate a list of guiding questions or checkpoints. What follows is a list of generic questions that can be used for peer-reviewing many different kinds of drafts. In each assignment chapter for Part 2 of this text, we have created additional peer review questions tailored specifically to that chapter's rhetorical aim and genres. For any given peer review session, your instructor may specify which generic or assignment-specific questions you are to use for the peer review.

## Generic Peer Review Guide

*For the writer*

Give your peer reviewer two or three questions to address while responding to your draft. The questions can focus on some aspect of your draft that you are uncertain about, on one or more sections where you particularly seek help or advice, on some feature that you particularly like about your draft, or on some part you especially wrestled with.

*For the reviewer*

**Basic overview:** As you read at normal speed do the following:

- Mark a "?" next to any passages that you find confusing, that somehow slow down your reading, or that raise questions in your mind.
- Mark a "G" next to any passages where you think the writing is particularly good, strong, or interesting.

**Going into more depth:** Prior to discussion with the writer, complete the following tasks:

- Identify at least one place in the draft where you got confused. Note why you got confused, using readerly rather than writely comments.
- Identify one place in the draft where you think the ideas are thin or need more development. Make discussion notes.
- Identify one place where you might write "So what?" after the passage. These are places where you don't understand the significance or importance of the writer's points. These are also places where you can't see how certain sentences connect to a topic sentence or how certain paragraphs or sections connect to the thesis statement.
- Identify at least one place where you could play devil's advocate or otherwise object to the writer's ideas. Make notes on the objections or alternative views that you will raise with the writer.

**Evaluating the writer's argument:** Look at the draft's effectiveness from the perspective of the classical rhetorical appeals:

- *Logos:* How effectively does the writer use reasons and evidence to support his or her claim? How effectively does the writer use details, particulars, examples, and other means as evidence to support points? How logical are the points and how clearly are they connected?
- *Ethos:* What image does the writer project? How effective is the tone? How trustworthy, reliable, knowledgeable, and fair does this writer seem?
- *Pathos:* How effectively does the writer engage the audience's interest? How effectively does the writer tie into the audience's beliefs and values? To what extent does the writer make the reader care about the topic?

**Noting problems of grammar and editing:** Mark problems in grammar, spelling, punctuation, documentation, or other issues of mechanics.

**Summing up:** Create a consolidated summary of your review:

- Sum up the strengths of the draft.
- Identify two or three main weaknesses or problem areas.
- Make two or three suggestions for revision.

## Practicing a Peer Review

**Background:** In the following exercise, we invite you to practice a peer review by responding to a student's draft ("Should the University Carpet the Dorm Rooms?" below) or to another draft provided by your instructor. The "Carpets" assignment asked students to take a stand on a local campus issue. Imagine that you have exchanged drafts with this student and that your task is to help this student improve the draft through both global and local revision.

**Individual task:** Read the draft carefully following the instructions in the "Generic Peer Review Guide." Write out your responses to the bulleted items under "Going into more depth," "Evaluating the writer's argument," and "Summing up."

**Small group or whole class:** Share your responses. Then turn to the following additional tasks:

1. With the instructor serving as a guide, practice explaining to the writer where or how you got confused while reading the draft. Readers often have difficulty explaining their reading experience to a writer. Let several class members role-play being the reader. Practice using language such as "I like the way this draft started because...." "I got confused when...." "I had to back up and reread when...." "I saw your point here, but then I got lost again because...." Writing theorist Peter Elbow calls such language a "movie of your mind."

2. Have several class members role-play being devil's advocates by arguing against the writer's thesis. Where are the ideas thin or weak?

### SHOULD THE UNIVERSITY CARPET THE DORM ROOMS?

Tricia, a university student, came home exhausted from her work-study job. She took a blueberry pie from the refrigerator to satisfy her hunger and a tall glass of milk to quench her thirst. While trying to get comfortable on her bed, she tipped her snack over onto the floor. She cleaned the mess, but the blueberry and milk stains on her brand-new carpet could not be removed.

Tricia didn't realize how hard it was to clean up stains on a carpet. Luckily this was her own carpet.

A lot of students don't want carpets. Students constantly change rooms. The next person may not want carpet.

Some students say that since they pay to live on campus, the rooms should reflect a comfortable home atmosphere. Carpets will make the dorm more comfortable. The carpet will act as insulation and as a soundproofing system.

Paint stains cannot be removed from carpets. If the university carpets the rooms, the students will lose the privilege they have of painting their rooms any color. This would limit students' self-expression.

The carpets would be an institutional brown or gray. This would be ugly. With tile floors, the students can choose and purchase their own carpets to match their taste. You can't be an individual if you can't decorate your room to fit your personality.

*(continued)*

According to Rachel Jones, Assistant Director of Housing Services, the cost will be $300 per room for the carpet and installation. Also the university will have to buy more vacuum cleaners. But will vacuum cleaners be all that is necessary to keep the carpets clean? We'll need shampoo machines too.

What about those stains that won't come off even with a shampoo machine? That's where the student will have to pay damage deposit costs.

There will be many stains on the carpet due to shaving cream fights, food fights, beverage parties, and smoking, all of which can damage the carpets.

Students don't take care of the dorms now. They don't follow the rules of maintaining their rooms. They drill holes into the walls, break mirrors, beds, and closet doors, and leave their food trays all over the floor.

If the university buys carpets our room rates will skyrocket. In conclusion, it is a bad idea for the university to buy carpets.

## Participating in Peer Review Workshops

If you are willing to respond candidly to a classmate's draft—in a readerly rather than a writerly way—you will be a valuable participant in peer review workshops. In a typical workshop, classmates work in groups of two to six to respond to each other's rough drafts and offer suggestions for revisions. These workshops are most helpful when group members have developed sufficient levels of professionalism and trust to exchange candid responses. A frequent problem in peer review workshops is that classmates try so hard to avoid hurting each other's feelings that they provide vague, meaningless feedback. Saying, "Your paper's great. I really liked it. Maybe you could make it flow a little better" is much less helpful than saying, "Your issue about environmental pollution in the Antarctic is well defined in the first paragraph, but I got lost in the second paragraph when you began discussing penguin coloration."

### Responsibilities of Peer Reviewers and Writers

Learning to respond conscientiously and carefully to others' work may be the single most important thing you can do to improve your own writing. When you review a classmate's draft, you are not acting as a teacher, but simply as a fresh reader. You can help the writer appreciate what it's like to encounter his or her text for the first time. Your primary responsibility is to articulate your understanding of what the writer's words say to you and to identify places where you get confused, where you need more details, where you have doubts or queries, and so on.

When you play the role of writer during a workshop session, your responsibilities parallel those of your peer reviewers. You need to provide a legible rough draft, preferably typed and double-spaced, that doesn't baffle the reader with hard-to-follow corrections and confusing pagination. Your instructor may ask you to bring copies of your draft for all group members. During the workshop, your primary responsibility is to *listen*, taking in how others respond to your draft without becoming defensive. Many instructors also ask writers to formulate two or three specific questions about their drafts—questions they particularly want their reviewers to address. These questions might focus on something writers particularly like about their drafts or on specific problem areas or concerns.

## Responding to Peer Reviews

After you and your classmates have gone over each other's papers and walked each other through the responses, everyone should identify two or three things about his or her draft that particularly need work. Before you leave the session, you should have some notion about how you want to revise your paper.

You may get mixed or contradictory responses from different reviewers. One reviewer may praise a passage that another finds confusing or illogical. Conflicting advice is a frustrating fact of life for all writers, whether students or professionals. Such disagreements reveal how readers cocreate a text with a writer: Each brings to the text a different background, set of values, and way of reading.

It is important to remember that you are in charge of your own writing. If several readers offer the same critique of a passage, then no matter how much you love that passage, you probably need to follow their advice. But when readers disagree, you have to make your own best judgment about whom to heed.

Once you have received advice from others, reread your draft again slowly and then develop a revision plan, allowing yourself time to make sweeping, global changes if needed. You also need to remember that you can never make your draft perfect. Plan when you will bring the process to a close so that you can turn in a finished product on time and get on with your other classes and your life.

# 12

# STRATEGIES FOR WRITING CLOSED-FORM PROSE

**WHAT YOU WILL LEARN**

**12.1** To satisfy reader expectations by linking new material to old material.

**12.2** To nutshell your argument and visualize its structure.

**12.3** To start and end with the "big picture" through effective titles, introductions, and conclusions.

**12.4** To keep readers on track through the use of effective topic sentences.

**12.5** To guide readers with transitions.

**12.6** To link sentences by placing old information before new.

**12.7** To present numerical data effectively through tables, graphs, and charts.

This chapter gives nuts-and-bolts advice for writing effective closed-form prose. As explained in Part 1 of this text, **closed-form prose** has an explicit thesis statement that is supported with points, subpoints, and details. Its features include unified and coherent paragraphs headed by topic sentences, good transitions between sentences and paragraphs, and forecasting of the whole before presentation of the parts. The strategies explained in this chapter are organized into ten self-contained lessons, each of which can be read comfortably in twenty minutes or less. The first lesson (Skill 12.1) provides a theoretical overview to the rest of the chapter. The remaining lessons can then be assigned and read in any order your instructor desires. Together these lessons will teach you transferable skills—useful in any academic discipline or professional setting—for producing clear, reader-friendly, and persuasive closed-form prose.

See Chapter 1, Concept 1.3, for a detailed explanation of closed-form versus open-form prose.

**12.1**
Satisfy reader expectations by linking new material to old material.

## SKILL 12.1 Satisfy reader expectations by linking new material to old material.

In this opening lesson, we ask you to imagine how readers make sense of a verbal text and what they do when they get confused. Imagine for a moment that your readers have only so much *reader energy*, which they can use either to follow your ideas or to puzzle over confusing passages.* In order to follow your ideas, readers must see how each new sentence in your essay connects to what has come before. Your goal is to keep your readers' energy focused on your meaning rather than on problems in your structure.

## The Principle of Old Before New

What makes closed-form prose "closed" is the way it consistently follows the principle of old before new. Rhetoricians sometimes calls this principle the "**old/ new contract**," which refers to the writer's obligation to help readers connect each new sentence in an essay to the previous sentences they have already read. As readers read, they don't memorize your text as if they were memorizing a list of facts. Rather they construct in their heads a big picture of your unfolding meaning, usually organized by points and subpoints. If a new sentence doesn't meaningfully connect to that big picture, they divert their reader energy from following your ideas into puzzling over your structure. "Whoa, you lost me on the turn," your reader might say. "I can't see how this part relates to what you just said."

This principle of old before new is grounded in brain research that investigates the way that the human brain makes sense of new information. For example, the old/new contract can explain the left-to-right order of business names and room or location numbers in a building directory. Suppose that you are meeting a friend at Carol's Coffee Clatch in a newly opened mall, but you don't know its exact location. To use the mall map, you begin with old information (Carol's Coffee Clatch) and seek new information (its location in the mall). Because we read English from left to right, we expect to find the business names in the left column (arranged alphabetically) and the corresponding map location indicators in the right column. If the location indicators were in the left column and the business names in the right, we would have to read backwards, slowing us down.

The principle of old-before-new is equally important when we listen as when we read. Suppose you are a passenger on a flight into Chicago and need to transfer to a flight to Memphis. As you descend into Chicago, the flight attendant announces transfer gates. Which of the following formats is easier for you to process? Why?

| Announcement A | | Announcement B | |
| --- | --- | --- | --- |
| Atlanta | Gate C12 | Gate C12 | Atlanta |
| Dallas | Gate C25 | Gate C25 | Dallas |
| Memphis | Gate B20 | Gate B20 | Memphis |
| St. Louis | Gate D15 | Gate D15 | St. Louis |

*For the useful term *reader energy*, we are indebted to George Gopen and Judith Swan, "The Science of Scientific Writing," *American Scientist* 78 (1990): 550–559. In addition, much of our discussion of writing in this chapter is indebted to the work of Joseph Williams, George Gopen, and Gregory Colomb. See especially Gregory G. Colomb and Joseph M. Williams, "Perceiving Structure in Professional Prose: A Multiply Determined Experience," in Lee Odell and Dixie Goswamie (eds.), *Writing in Nonacademic Settings* (New York: The Guilford Press, 1985), pp. 87–128.

If you are like most listeners, you prefer Announcement A, which puts old information before new. In this case, the old/known information is our destination (Memphis), while the new/unknown information is the gate number—in this case, Gate B20. Announcement B causes us to expend more *listener energy* than does A because it forces us to hold each gate number in memory until we hear its corresponding city. (The number of the gate is meaningless until it is linked to the crucial old information, "Memphis.") Whereas A allows us to relax until we hear the word "Memphis," B forces us to concentrate intensely on each gate number until we find the meaningful one.

## How the Principle of Old Before New Creates Unified and Coherent Paragraphs

This principle of old-before-new also applies to the way readers make sense of verbal texts. To keep readers on track, writers should begin their sentences with old information that hooks back to the previous material that the reader has already read. The last part of the sentence then contains the new information that drives the argument forward. When writers follow this principle, the result is tightly organized closed-form prose. Such prose is said to have both unity and coherence—two defining features of closed-form prose:

- **Unity** refers to the relationship between each part of an essay and the larger whole.
- **Coherence** refers to the relationship between adjacent sentences and paragraphs.

As an illustration of these terms, consider the differences in the following three passages, each of which begins with the same sentence about the father's role in childrearing. However, the first two of these passages thwart the principle of old before new while the third fulfills it.

### PASSAGE 1: EXHIBITS NEITHER UNITY NOR COHERENCE

Recent research has given us much deeper—and more surprising—insights into the father's role in childrearing. My family is typical of the east side in that we never had much money. Their tongues became black and hung out of their mouths. The back-to-basics movement got a lot of press, fueled as it was by fears of growing illiteracy and cultural demise.

### PASSAGE 2: EXHIBITS COHERENCE BUT NOT UNITY

Recent research has given us much deeper—and more surprising—insights into the father's role in childrearing. Childrearing is a complex process that is frequently investigated by psychologists. Psychologists have also investigated sleep patterns and dreams. When we are dreaming, psychologists have shown, we are often reviewing recent events in our lives.

### PASSAGE 3: EXHIBITS BOTH UNITY AND COHERENCE

Recent research has given us much deeper—and more surprising—insights into the father's role in childrearing. It shows that in almost all of their interactions with children, fathers do things a little differently from mothers. What fathers do—their special parenting style—is not only highly complementary to what mothers do but is by all indications important in its own right. [The passage continues by showing the special ways that fathers contribute to childrearing.]

If you are like most readers, Passage 1 comically frustrates your reader energy because it is a string of random sentences without connections to any point. Passage 2 also frustrates your reader energy but in a more subtle way. If you aren't paying attention, Passage 2 may seem to make sense because each sentence is linked to the one before it. But the individual sentences don't develop a larger whole: The topics switch from a father's role in childrearing to psychology to sleep patterns to the function of dreams. This passage has coherence (links between sentences) but not unity (links to a larger point). In contrast, Passage 3 exhibits both coherence and unity. The passage is unified because it makes a consistent point—that fathers have an important role in childrearing. It is also coherent because the opening of sentences 2 and 3 include words that refer to previous information: The pronoun "it" in sentence 2 refers to "research" in sentence 1. In sentence 3 the word "fathers" links to "fathers" in both sentences 1 and 2. We'll have more to say about the old/new contract at the sentence level in Skill 12.6.

## The Explanatory Power of the Principle of Old before New

As we will see throughout this chapter, the principle of old before new has important explanatory power for writers. At the level of the whole essay, this principle helps writers understand why they need to lay out the "big picture" of an essay before presenting the parts (Skill 12.2) or why they need to determine their audience's initial view of a topic (old information) before they can plan an argument strategy to change the audience's view. It also helps writers craft effective transitions and topic sentences for paragraphs (Skills 12.3–12.5). Most importantly, it helps writers understand why clear organization of an essay is so important to readers. The rhetorician Kenneth Burke describes "form" as "arousing and fulfillment of desires." The principle of old before new explains how closed-form prose creates this kind of pleasurable form. When a reader starts a new essay, the reader has no specific expectations: Everything in the essay is "new information." However, once the reader reads the title, the title becomes "old information." If the title is effective, it forecasts what will be new in the essay, arousing the reader's anticipation of what will follow and propelling the reader's desire to continue reading. The first part of the introduction further arouses reader desire by explaining a problem or question or knowledge gap (tying backwards into the reader's interest in the question or problem), while the last part presents the thesis (what's new). Once read, the thesis then becomes old information. Because the thesis summarizes the essay's "big picture," it leads readers to anticipate what is coming in the body of the essay. If the essay does what the thesis forecasts, the reader experiences form as a gratifying sequence of anticipation and fulfillment.

What readers need from a closed-form text, then, is an ability to predict what is coming as well as regular fulfillment of those predictions. The rest of this chapter will give you more specific advice on how to keep your reader on track throughout your essay.

**FOR
WRITING
AND
DISCUSSION**

### Explaining Old before New in a Closed-Form Essay

Reread engineer David Rockwood's letter to the editor on page 15 and analyze its structure in terms of old/new contract, unity and coherence, and forecasting and fulfillment.

1. How does the opening sentence refer to old information while forecasting new information?
2. How do the opening and concluding paragraphs create a "big picture" of the writer's argument?
3. How do the body paragraphs relate to the thesis? How does each paragraph reveal unity and coherence?
4. How does the writer use transitions to keep the reader on track?

**12.2**
Nutshell your
argument and
visualize its
structure.

## SKILL 12.2 Nutshell your argument and visualize its structure.

The previous lesson showed you how the principle of old before new creates unified and coherent paragraphs and also encourages writers to lay out the "big picture" of an essay before presenting its parts. In this lesson, we provide tips for organizing these parts into a unified and coherent whole that is easy for the reader to follow. Particularly we'll show you the value of nutshelling your argument and then visualizing its structure. A chief take-away insight from this lesson is that points need to be stated as complete sentences rather than as topic phrases. A topic phrase by itself—let's say "peanut butter"—invites you to picture (in this case) a tasty substance but not to conceptualize a meaningful point within an argument. To make a point about peanut butter you need to add a predicate (verb): "Peanut butter is surprisingly nutritious." Now you have a point—one that you can support through details about the nutritional content of peanut butter. As we'll show later in this lesson, creating an effective outline for your paper helps you organize *meanings*, not topics, and meanings require complete sentences.

### Making a List of "Chunks" and a Scratch Outline Early in the Writing Process

Early in the writing process, while you are still searching for meanings, you probably won't know how to organize your paper. But you may know that you have certain ideas, sections, parts, or "chunks" that you want to include somewhere in your paper. Although you don't yet know where they will go or how long they will be, just listing these chunks will help you get thinking about structure—like placing the pieces of a jigsaw puzzle onto a table top. Here is student writer Kent Ansen's list of chunks early in his process of writing a researched argument on mandatory public service for young adults.

Kent Ansen's final
proposal argument
is shown on
pp. 263–272

### KENT'S LIST OF CHUNKS TO INCLUDE

- Section on my own high school experience as a volunteer (perhaps in introduction)
- Testimonies of AmeriCorps volunteers on the value of their experience (from the AmeriCorps Web site)
- Rosenman's argument that national public service would make Americans feel more engaged with their country and be better citizens
- Kinsley's conservative argument against national public service (I'll need to summarize this and refute it)
- A section where I argue that experience with public service would help the "lost generation" improve their resumes and find better jobs

Once you make a list of chunks, you can begin thinking about which of them are high-level points and which are details in support of a point. Before writing a rough draft, many writers like to make a brief scratch outline to help with planning. Here is Kent's initial scratch outline.

### KENT'S INITIAL SCRATCH OUTLINE

- Introduction
  - Attention grabber (my volunteer experience—show that it benefited me)
  - Problems with Lost Generation (maybe national service would help them)
  - Thesis—we should institute national public service
- Explain my idea, show what my plan would look like
- Show the benefits of public service
  - Help people in poverty
  - Help people who serve
  - Promote civic engagement
- Summarize Kinsley's opposition
- Try to refute Kinsley

## To Achieve Focus, "Nutshell" Your Argument and Create a Working Thesis Statement

As you begin drafting, you will find your ideas gradually becoming clearer and more focused. At this point, doing the following "nutshell exercise" will ensure that your paper has a *problem-thesis* structure rather than an *and then* or *all about* structure. The six prompts in this exercise will help you focus on the "big picture" of your argument—its main high-level point and purpose. We recommend that you write your responses to each prompt as a way of seeing the "whole" of your paper.

Often writers have to go through several drafts to figure out the point of certain sections. See Skills 11.1 and 11.2.

### EXERCISE FOR NUTSHELLING YOUR ARGUMENT

1. What puzzle or problem initiated your thinking about X? _____
2. *Template: Many people think X, but I am going to argue Y.*

   Before reading my paper, my readers will think X: _____. But after reading my paper, my readers will think Y: _____.
3. The purpose of my paper is: _____.
4. My paper addresses the following question: _____.

5. My one-sentence summary answer to this question is this [my thesis statement]:

_____ .

6. A tentative title for my paper is: _____ .

Here are Kent Ansen's responses to these prompts:

1. I was initially puzzled about the value of volunteer work and then wondered if these same values would be obtained if national public service was made mandatory.
2. Before reading my paper, my readers will think that mandatory public service is a bad idea. But after reading my paper my readers will see the benefits of making public service mandatory for young adults.
3. The purpose of my paper is to show the benefits of mandatory public service for young adults.
4. Should the United States institute mandatory public service for young adults?
5. The United States should institute mandatory public service for young adults because such service would help fight poverty, help the young adults themselves, and promote civic engagement.
6. Engaging Young Adults to Meet America's Challenges: A Proposal for Mandatory National Service

Once you have nutshelled your argument, you are ready to create a working thesis statement that includes main supporting points. These supporting points help you visualize an emerging structure. Here is Kent's working thesis statement.

### KENT'S WORKING THESIS STATEMENT

The United States should institute mandatory public service for young adults because such service would help impoverished neighborhoods, would nurture the professional growth of young adults, and would promote democracy through increased civic engagement.

## Visualize Your Structure

Once you have nutshelled your argument and created a working thesis statement, you can sketch your structure to show how points, subpoints, and details can be arranged hierarchically to support your thesis. We offer you three different ways to visualize your argument: a traditional outline, a verbal/visual tree diagram, or some other kind of visual flowchart that includes both words and images. Use whichever strategy best fits your way of thinking and perceiving.

An effective outline or diagram helps you organize *meanings*, not topics. Note that in the examples that follow, Kent uses *complete sentences* in the high-level slots in order to state meanings rather than identify topics. As we explained in our earlier peanut butter example ("Peanut butter is surprisingly nutritious"), points require both subjects and verbs. Any point—whether a thesis, a main point, or a subpoint—is an assertion that requires elaboration and supporting details. By using complete sentences rather than phrases in an outline, the writer is forced to articulate the point of each section of the emerging argument.

See Skill 12.2, p. 294, for the peanut butter example.

**Outlines** The most common way of visualizing structure is the traditional outline, which uses numbers and letters to indicate levels of points, subpoints, and details. If this traditional method works for you, we recommend that you use the outlining feature of your word processing program, which allows you to move and insert material and change heading levels with great flexibility. (You can also use bullets and other symbols rather than letters and numbers if you prefer.)

Figure 12.1 shows the first half of Kent's outline for his argument. Note how the outline uses complete sentences in the high-level slots.

**Tree Diagrams** A tree diagram displays a hierarchical structure visually, using horizontal and vertical space instead of letters and numbers. Figure 12.2 shows how selected points from Kent's argument could be displayed in a tree diagram. His thesis sits at the top of the tree. The main points of his argument appear as branches beneath his claim. Supporting evidence and arguments are subbranches beneath each main point. Unlike outlines, tree diagrams allow us

Thesis: Despite arguments against the value of public service or against government attempts to mandate "volunteerism," The United States should institute mandatory public service for young adults because such service would help America's vulnerable communities become healthier, would nurture the personal growth and professional development of young adults, and would promote democracy through increased civic engagement

I.   Introduction
    A.  Attenion grabber (My high school volunteer experience showed me the value of public service.)
    B.  Public service might also address problems faced by young people
    C.  Thesis paragraph

II.  Mandatory public service would have certain features based on the model of AmeriCorps.

III. A mandatory program would invest in communities by attacking poverty and building social captial.
    A.  Based on AmeriCorps model of success, national public service would fight poverty by helping the poor become self-sufficient
        1.  Data from Ratcliffe and McKernan show social costs of poverty.
        2.  Public service provides people-to-people contact, which is better than simply providing money or food.
    B.  Testimony from AmeriCorps volunteers also shows how mandatory public service would build social capital.

IV.  A national service program would also benefit the volunteers by fostering personal growth and professional development.
    A.  Testimony from AmeriCorps volunteers shows these personal benefits.
    B.  These testimonies ring true to my own experience.
    C.  Study by Jastrzab provides empirical support for these personal benefits.

**FIGURE 12.1** Kent Ansen's Outline for First Half of Paper

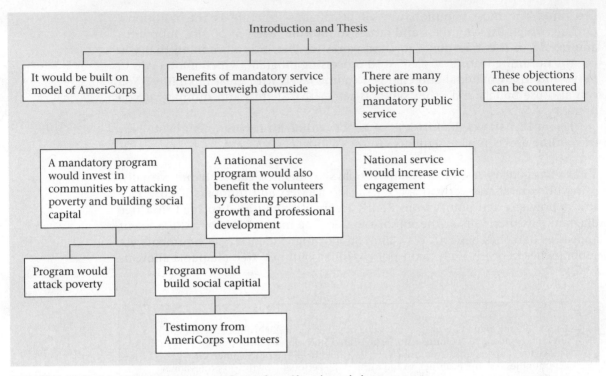

**FIGURE 12.2** Tree Diagram of Selected Points from Kent Ansen's Argument

to *see* the hierarchical relationship of points and details. When you develop a point with details, you move vertically down the tree. When you switch to a new point, you move horizontally to make a new branch. Our own teaching experience suggests that for many writers, this visual/spatial technique often produces fuller, more detailed, and more logical arguments than does a traditional outline.

**Your Own Methods of Visualizing Structure** Many writers develop their own personal ways of visualizing structure. Some create flowcharts with big boxes to represent major parts of the paper and arrows and smaller boxes to show the various parts of the big box. Others use the branching methods of a tree diagram but arrange the parts as spokes on a wheel. Still others combine outlines and flow charts in visual ways that work for them. In all cases, the key to organizing meanings is to use complete sentences to state points.

Once you have sketched out an initial outline or structural diagram, you can use it to generate additional ideas. Use question marks on the outline or diagram to "hold open" spots for new points or supporting details. Think of your structural diagrams as evolving sketches rather than rigid blueprints. As your ideas grow and change, revise your outline or diagram, adding or removing points, consolidating and refocusing sections, moving parts around, or filling in details.

# SKILL 12.3   Start and end with the "big picture" through effective titles, introductions, and conclusions.

**12.3**
Start and end
with the "big
picture" through
effective titles,
introductions,
and conclusions.

In Skill 12.1, we explained the principle of old before new and showed how this principle creates a closed approach to the pleasurable form that Kenneth Burke describes as an "arousing and fulfillment of desires." What readers need from closed-form prose is an ability to predict what is coming as well as regular fulfillment of those predictions. As we will show in this section, writers lay out the "big picture" of their essay with their title and introduction and then often return to the big picture in the conclusion.

Because our advice might differ somewhat from what you learned in high school, we'll begin with what not to do.

## What Not to Do: "Topic Title" and "Funnel Introduction"

Some students have been taught an opening strategy, sometimes called the "funnel," that encourages them to start with broad generalizations and then narrow down to their topics. This strategy often leads to a "topic title" (which names the topic area but doesn't forecast the problem being addressed) and vapid generalizations in the opening of the introduction, as the following example shows:

### B. F. SKINNER

Since time immemorial people have pondered the question of freedom. The great philosophers of Greece and Rome asked what it means to be free, and the question has echoed through the ages up until the present day. One modern psychologist who asked this question was B. F. Skinner, who wanted to study whether humans had free will or were programmed by their environment to act the way they did....

Here the writer eventually gets to his subject, B. F. Skinner, but so far presents no sense of what point the essay will make or why the reader should be interested. A better approach is to hook your readers immediately with an effective title and a problem-posing introduction.

## Creating Effective Titles

Good titles follow the principle of old before new information that we introduced in Skill 12.1. A good title needs to have something old (a word or phrase that hooks into a reader's existing interests) and something new (a word or phrase that forecasts the writer's problematic question, thesis, or purpose). Here are examples of effective titles from two student essays in this textbook:

"Boomerang Kids: What Are the Causes of Generation Y's Growing Pains?"
"Paintball: Promoter of Violence or Healthy Fun?"

Readers will be attracted to these titles if they already have some background interest in the growing pains of boomerang kids or in controversies about paintball ("old information"). But the titles also promise something "new"—arguments that promise to expand or challenge the readers' views. The first writer will explain what she sees as the causes of these growing pains; the second writer will explore the problem of violence versus fun in paintball.

As these examples show, your title should link your readers' already existing interests with the promise of something new or challenging in your essay. Academic titles are typically longer and more detailed than are titles in popular media. There are three basic approaches that academic writers take, as shown in the following strategies chart.

| Strategies for Writing Titles of Academic Papers | |
| --- | --- |
| **What to Do** | **Examples** |
| State or imply the question that your essay addresses. | • How Clean and Green Are Hydrogen Fuel Cell Cars?<br>• The Impact of Cell Phones on Motor Vehicle Fatalities (Implied question: What is the impact of...?) |
| State or imply, often in abbreviated form, your essay's thesis. | • Reward Work, Not Wealth<br>• How Foreign Aid Can Foster Democratization in Authoritarian Regimes (Implied thesis: Foreign aid can foster democratization...) |
| Use a two-part title separated by a colon:<br>• On the left, present key words from your essay's issue or problem or a "mystery phrase" that arouses interest.<br>• On the right, place the essay's question, thesis, or summary of purpose. | • Engaging Young Adults to Meet America's Challenges: A Proposal for Mandatory National Service<br>• Coping with Hurricane Katrina: Psychological Stress and Resilience among African-American Evacuees |

Such titles might seem overly formal to you, but they indicate how much the reader of an academic article appreciates a preview of its big picture. Although the titles in popular magazines may be more informal, they often use these same strategies. Here are some titles from popular magazines such as *Redbook* and *Forbes*:

"Is the Coffee Bar Trend About to Peak?" (question)
"A Man *Can* Take Maternity Leave—And Love It" (abbreviated thesis)
"Feed Your Face: Why Your Complexion Needs Vitamins" (two parts linked by colon)

Composing a title for your essay can help you find your focus when you get bogged down in the middle of a draft. Thinking about your title forces you to *nutshell* your ideas by seeing your project's big picture. It causes you to reconsider your purpose and to think about what's old and what's new for your audience.

## Writing Good Closed-Form Introductions

Just as effective titles present something old and something new, so do dynamic and powerful introductions. Old information is something your readers already know and find interesting before they start reading your essay. New information is the surprise of your argument, the unfamiliar material that you add to your readers' understanding.

Because the writer's thesis statement forecasts the new information the paper will present, a thesis statement for a closed-form essay typically comes *at the end of the introduction.* What precedes the thesis is typically the problem or question that the thesis addresses—the old information that the reader needs in order to understand the conversation that the thesis joins. A typical closed-form introduction has the following shape:

The length and complexity of your introduction is a function of how much your reader already knows and cares about the question or problem your paper addresses. The function of an introduction is to capture the reader's interest in the first few sentences, to identify and explain the question or problem that the essay addresses, to provide any needed background information, and to present the thesis. You can leave out any of the first three elements if the reader is already hooked on your topic and already knows the question you are addressing. For example, in an essay exam you can usually start with your thesis statement because you can assume the instructor already knows the question and finds it interesting.

To illustrate how an effective closed-form introduction takes the reader from the question to the thesis, consider how the following student writer revised his introduction to a paper on Napster.com, one of the earliest music file-sharing sites:

### ORIGINAL INTRODUCTION (CONFUSING)

Napster is all about sharing, not stealing, as record companies and some musicians would like us to think. Napster is an online program that was released in October of '99. Napster lets users easily search for and trade mp3s—compressed, high-quality music files that can be produced from a CD. Napster is the leading file sharing community; it allows users to locate and share music. It also provides instant messaging, chat rooms, an outlet for fans to identify new artists, and a forum to communicate their interests.

*Thesis statement*

*Background on Napster*

Most readers find this introduction confusing. The writer begins with his thesis statement before the reader is introduced to the question that the thesis addresses. He seems to assume that his reader is already a part of the Napster conversation, and yet in the next sentences, he gives background on Napster. If the reader needs background on Napster, then the reader also needs background on the Napster controversy. In rethinking his assumptions about old-versus-new information for his audience, this writer decided he wants to reach general newspaper readers who

*In this section, we elaborate on the rhetorical concept introduced in Chapter 2, Concept 2.3: "In closed-form prose, an introduction starts with the problem, not the thesis."*

may have heard about a lawsuit against Napster and are interested in the issue but aren't sure of what Napster is or how it works. Here is his revised introduction:

**REVISED INTRODUCTION (CLEARER)**

*Triggers readers' memory of lawsuit*

*Background on Napster*

*Clarification of problem (Implied question: Should Napster be shut down?)*

*Thesis*

Several months ago the rock band Metallica filed a lawsuit against Napster.com, an online program that lets users easily search for and trade mp3s—compressed, high-quality music files that can be produced from a CD. Napster.com has been wildly popular among music lovers because it creates a virtual community where users can locate and share music. It also provides instant messaging, chat rooms, an outlet for fans to identify new artists, and a forum to communicate their interests. But big-name bands like Metallica, alarmed at what they see as lost revenues, claim that Napster.com is stealing their royalties. However, Napster is all about sharing, not stealing, as some musicians would like us to think.

This revised introduction fills in the old information the reader needs in order to recall and understand the problem; then it presents the thesis.

### Typical Elements of a Closed-Form Introduction

Now that you understand the general principle of closed-form introductions, let's look more closely at its four typical features or elements:

1. ***An opening attention-grabber.*** If you aren't sure that your reader is already interested in your problem, you can begin with an attention-grabber (what journalists call the "hook" or "lead"), which is typically a dramatic vignette, a startling fact or statistic, an arresting quotation, an interesting scene, or something else that taps into your reader's interests. Attention-grabbers are uncommon in academic prose (where you assume your reader will be initially engaged by the problem itself) but frequently used in popular prose.

2. ***Explanation of the question to be investigated.*** If your reader already knows about the problem and cares about it, then you need merely to summarize it. This problem or question is the starting point of your argument. If you aren't sure whether your audience fully understands the question or fully cares about it, then you need to explain it in more detail, showing why it is both problematic and significant.

3. ***Background information.*** In order to understand the conversation you are joining, readers sometimes need background information such as a definition of key terms, a summary of events leading up to the problem, factual details needed for explaining the context of the problem, and so forth. In academic papers, this background often includes a review of what other scholars have said about the problem.

4. ***A preview of where your paper is heading.*** The final element of a closed-form introduction sketches the big picture of your essay by previewing the kind of surprise or challenge readers can expect and giving them a sense of the whole. This preview is initially new information for your readers (this is why it comes at the end of the introduction). Once stated, however, it becomes old information that readers will use to create a map for their journey through your argument. By predicting what's coming, this preview initiates the pleasurable process of forecasting/fulfillment that we discussed in

Skill 12.1. Writers typically forecast the whole by stating their thesis, but they can also use a purpose statement or a blueprint statement to accomplish the same end. These strategies are the subject of the next section.

**Forecasting the Whole with a Thesis Statement, Purpose Statement, or Blueprint Statement** The most succinct way to forecast the whole is to state your thesis directly. Student writers often ask how detailed their thesis statements should be and whether it is permissible, sometimes, to delay revealing the thesis until the conclusion—an open-form move that gives papers a more exploratory, mystery-novel feel. It is useful, then, to outline briefly some of your choices as a writer. To illustrate a writer's options for forecasting the whole, we use Kent Ansen's researched proposal argument on mandatory public service.

To see the choice that Ansen actually made, see his paper on pp. 263–272.

## Strategies for Forecasting the Whole Paper

| Options | What to Do | Examples |
|---|---|---|
| **Short thesis** | State claim without summarizing your supporting argument or forecasting your structure. | The United States should institute a mandatory year of national service for Americans ages 18 to 25. |
| **Detailed thesis** | Summarize whole argument; may begin with an *although* clause that summarizes the view you are trying to change. | Despite arguments against the value of public service, the United States should institute mandatory public service for young adults because such service would help America's vulnerable communities become healthier, would nurture the personal growth and professional development of young adults, and would promote democracy through increased civic engagement. |
| **Purpose statement** | State your purpose or intention without summarizing the argument. A purpose statement typically begins with a phrase such as "My purpose is to…" or "In the following paragraphs I wish to…" | My purpose is to show the benefits to American society of mandatory public service for young adults. |
| **Blueprint or mapping statement** | Describe the structure of your essay by announcing the number of main parts and describing the function or purpose of each one. | First I will explain how mandatory public service could be modeled on the present-day success of AmeriCorps. I will then show the benefits of mandatory public service. Finally, I will summarize the arguments against mandatory public service and respond to them. |

*(continued)*

| Options | What to Do | Examples |
|---------|-----------|----------|
| **Combination of elements** | Include two or more of these elements. In long essays, academic writers sometimes have a purpose statement followed by a detailed thesis and blueprint statement. | [Kent's essay is not long enough nor complex enough to need an extensive overview that includes a purpose or blueprint statement along with a thesis.] |
| **Thesis question only** [*Implies an exploratory or delayed thesis paper*] | State the question only, without initially implying your answer. This open-form strategy invites the reader to join the writer in a mutual search. | Although volunteer programs like AmeriCorps have been remarkably successful, I wonder if such programs would still work if people were coerced to participate. Would the benefits of a mandatory program outweigh the risks? |

Which of these options should a writer choose? There are no firm rules to help you answer this question. How much you forecast in the introduction and where you reveal your thesis is a function of your purpose, audience, and genre. The more you forecast, the clearer your argument is and the easier it is to read quickly. You minimize the demands on readers' time by giving them the gist of your argument in the introduction, making it easier to skim your essay if they don't have time for a thorough reading. The less you forecast, the more demands you make on readers' time: You invite them, in effect, to accompany you through the twists and turns of your own thinking process, and you risk losing them if they become confused, lost, or bored. For these reasons, academic writing is generally closed form and aims at maximum clarity. In many rhetorical contexts, however, more open forms are appropriate.

If you choose a closed-form structure, we can offer some advice on how much to forecast. Readers sometimes feel insulted by too much forecasting, so include only what is needed for clarity. For short papers, readers usually don't need to have the complete supporting argument forecast in the introduction. In longer papers, however, or in especially complex ones, readers appreciate having the whole argument forecast at the outset. Academic writing in particular tends to favor explicit and often detailed forecasting.

**FOR WRITING AND DISCUSSION**

## Revising a Title and Introduction

**Individual task:** Choose an essay you are currently working on or have recently completed and examine your title and introduction. Ask yourself these questions:

- What audience am I imagining? What do I assume are my readers' initial interests that will lead them to read my essay (the old information I must hook into)? What is new in my essay?
- Do I have an attention-grabber? Why or why not?

- Where do I state or imply the question or problem that my essay addresses?
- Do I explain why the question is problematic and significant? Why or why not?
- For my audience to understand the problem, do I provide too much background information, not enough, or just the right amount?
- What strategies do I use to forecast the whole?

Based on your analysis of your present title and introduction, revise as appropriate.

**Group task:** Working with a partner or in small groups, share the changes you made in your title or introduction and explain why you made the changes.

## Writing Effective Conclusions

Conclusions can best be understood as complements to introductions. In both the introduction and the conclusion, writers are concerned with the essay as a whole more than with any given part. In a conclusion, the writer is particularly concerned with helping the reader move from the parts back to the big picture and to understand the importance or significance of the essay.

Because many writers find conclusions challenging to write, we offer six possible strategies for ending an essay.

| Strategies for Concluding an Essay | | |
| --- | --- | --- |
| **Strategies** | **What to Do** | **Comments** |
| *Simple summary conclusion* | Recap what you have said. | This approach is useful in a long or complex essay or in an instructional text that focuses on concepts. However, in a short, easy-to-follow essay, a summary conclusion can be dull and even annoying to readers. A brief summary followed by a more artful concluding strategy can sometimes be effective. |
| *Larger significance conclusion* | Draw the reader's attention to the importance or the applications of your argument. | The conclusion is a good place to elaborate on the significance of your problem by showing how your proposed solution to a question leads to understanding a larger, more significant question or brings practical benefits to individuals or society. If you posed a question about values or about the interpretation of a confusing text or phenomenon, you might show how your argument could be applied to related questions, texts, or phenomena. |

*(continued)*

| Strategies | What to Do | Comments |
|---|---|---|
| ***Proposal* conclusion** | Call for action. | Often used in analyses and arguments, a *proposal* conclusion states the action that needs to be taken and briefly explains its advantages over alternative actions or describes its beneficial consequences. If your paper analyzes the negative consequences of shifting from a graduated to a flat-rate income tax, your conclusion may recommend an action such as modifying or opposing the flat tax. |
| | Call for future study. | A *call-for-future-study* conclusion indicates what else needs to be known or resolved before a proposal can be offered. Such conclusions are especially common in scientific writing. |
| ***Scenic* or *anecdotal* conclusion** | Use a scene or brief story to illustrate the theme without stating it explicitly. | Often used in popular writing, a scene or anecdote can help the reader experience the emotional significance of the topic. For example, a paper favoring public housing for the homeless may end by describing an itinerant homeless person collecting bottles in a park. |
| ***Hook and return* conclusion** | Return to something mentioned at the beginning of the essay. | If the essay begins with a vivid illustration of a problem, the conclusion can return to the same scene or story but with some variation to indicate the significance of the essay. |
| ***Delayed-thesis* conclusion** | State the thesis for the first time at the end of the essay. | This strategy is effective when you are writing about complex or divisive issues and you don't want to take a stand until you have presented all sides. The introduction of the essay merely states the problem, giving the essay an exploratory feel. |

**FOR WRITING AND DISCUSSION**

### Writing Conclusions

Choose a paper you have just written and write an alternative conclusion using one of the strategies discussed in this lesson. Then share your original and revised conclusions in groups. Have group members discuss which one they consider most effective and why.

**12.4**
Keep readers on track through the use of effective topic sentences.

## SKILL 12.4  Create effective topic sentences for paragraphs.

In our lesson on outlining (Skill 12.2) we suggested that you write complete sentences rather than phrases for the high-level slots of the outline in order to articulate the *meaning* or *point* of each section of your argument. In this lesson we show you how to place these points where readers expect them: near the beginning of the sections or paragraphs they govern.

When you place points before particulars, you follow the same principle illustrated in our old-before-new exercise (Skill 12.1) with the flight attendant announcing the name of the city before the departure gate (the city is the old information, the departure gate the new information). When you first state the point, it is the new information that the current paragraph or section will develop. Once you have stated it, it becomes old information that helps readers understand the meaning of the details that follow. If you withhold the point until later, the reader has to keep all the particulars in short-term memory until you finally reveal the point that the particulars are supposed to support or develop.

## Placing Topic Sentences at the Beginning of Paragraphs

Readers of closed-form prose need to have point sentences (usually called "topic sentences") at the beginnings of paragraphs. However, writers of rough drafts often don't fulfill this need because, as we explained in Chapter 11, drafting is an exploratory process in which writers are often still searching for their points as they compose. Consequently, in their rough drafts writers often omit topic sentences entirely or place them at the ends of paragraphs, or they write topic sentences that misrepresent what the paragraphs actually say. During revision, then, you should check your body paragraphs carefully to be sure you have placed accurate topic sentences near the beginning.

What follow are examples of the kinds of revisions writers typically make. We have annotated the examples to explain the changes the writer has made to make the paragraphs unified and clear to readers. The first example is from a later draft of the essay on the dorm room carpets from Chapter 11 (pp. 287–288).

Revision–Topic Sentence First

*Another reason for the university not to buy carpets is the cost.*

ʌAccording to Rachel Jones, Assistant Director of Housing Services,

*Topic sentence placed first*

the initial purchase and installation of carpeting would cost $300 per room.

Considering the number of rooms in the three residence halls, carpeting amounts

to a substantial investment. Additionally, once the carpets are installed, the

university would need to maintain them through the purchase of more vacuum

cleaners and shampoo machines. This money would be better spent on other

dorm improvements that would benefit more residents, such as expanded kitchen

facilities and improved recreational space. ~~Thus carpets would be too expensive.~~

In the original draft, the writer states the point at the end of the paragraph. In his revision he states the point in an opening topic sentence that links back to the thesis statement, which promises "several reasons" that the university should not buy carpets for the dorms. The words "Another reason" thus link the topic sentence to the argument's big picture.

## Revising Paragraphs for Unity

In addition to placing topic sentences at the heads of paragraphs, writers often need to revise topic sentences to better match what the paragraph actually says, or revise the paragraph to better match the topic sentence. Paragraphs have unity when all their sentences develop the point stated in the topic sentence. Paragraphs in rough drafts are often not unified because they reflect the writer's shifting, evolving, thinking-while-writing process. Consider the following paragraph from an early draft of an argument against euthanasia by student writer Dao Do. Her peer reviewer labeled it "confusing." What makes it confusing?

*We look at more examples from Dao's essay later in this chapter.*

Early Draft–Confusing

First, euthanasia is wrong because no one has the right to take the life of another person. Some people say that euthanasia or suicide will end suffering and pain. But what proofs do they have for such a claim? Death is still mysterious to us; therefore, we do not know whether death will end suffering and pain or not. What seems to be the real claim is that death to those with illnesses will end *our* pain. Such pain involves worrying over them, paying their medical bills, and giving up so much of our time. Their deaths end our pain rather than theirs. And for that reason, euthanasia is a selfish act, for the outcome of euthanasia benefits us, the nonsufferers, more. Once the sufferers pass away, we can go back to our normal lives.

The paragraph opens with an apparent topic sentence: "Euthanasia is wrong because no one has the right to take the life of another person." But the rest of the paragraph doesn't focus on that point. Instead, it focuses on how euthanasia benefits the survivors more than the sick person. Dao had two choices: to revise the paragraph to fit the topic sentence or to revise the topic sentence to fit the paragraph. Here is her revision, which includes a different topic sentence and an additional sentence midparagraph to keep particulars focused on the opening point. Dao unifies this paragraph by keeping all its parts focused on her main point: "Euthanasia...benefits the survivors more than the sick person."

Revision for Unity

*Revised topic sentence better forecasts focus of paragraph*

*Keeps focus on "sick person"*

*First, euthanasia is wrong because it benefits the survivors more than the sick person.*
~~First, euthanasia is wrong because no one has the right to take the~~

~~life of another person.~~ Some people say that euthanasia or suicide will
    *the sick person's*
end suffering and pain. But what proofs do they have for such a claim?

Death is still mysterious to us; therefore, we do not know whether death

*Moreover, modern pain killers can relieve most of the pain a sick person has to endure.* ←

will end suffering and pain or not. What seems to be the real claim is

that death to those with illnesses will end *our* pain. Such pain involves

worrying over them, paying their medical bills, and giving up so much

of our time. Their deaths end our pain rather than theirs. And for that

reason, euthanasia is a selfish act, for the outcome of euthanasia benefits

us, the nonsufferers, more. Once the sufferers pass away, we can go back

to our normal lives.

*Concludes subpoint about sick person*

*Supports subpoint about how euthanasia benefits survivors*

A paragraph may lack unity for a variety of reasons. It may shift to a new direction in the middle, or one or two sentences may simply be irrelevant to the point. The key is to make sure that all the sentences in the paragraph fulfill the reader's expectations based on the topic sentence.

## Adding Particulars to Support Points

Just as writers of rough drafts often omit point sentences from paragraphs, they also sometimes leave out the particulars needed to support a point. In such cases, the writer needs to add particulars such as facts, statistics, quotations, research summaries, examples, or further subpoints. Consider how adding additional particulars to the following draft paragraph strengthens a student writer's argument opposing the logging of old-growth forests.

### DRAFT PARAGRAPH: PARTICULARS MISSING

One reason that it is not necessary to log old-growth forests is that the timber industry can supply the world's lumber needs without doing so. For example, we have plenty of new-growth forest from which timber can be taken (Sagoff 89). We could also reduce the amount of trees used for paper products by using other materials besides wood for paper pulp. In light of the fact that we have plenty of trees and ways of reducing our wood demands, there is no need to harvest old-growth forests.

### REVISED PARAGRAPH: PARTICULARS ADDED

One reason that it is not necessary to log old-growth forests is that the timber industry can supply the world's lumber needs without doing so. For example, we have plenty of new-growth forest from which timber can be taken as a result of major reforestation efforts all over the United States (Sagoff 89). In the Northwest, for instance, Oregon law requires every acre of timber harvested to be replanted. According to Robert Sedjo, a forestry expert, the world's demand for industrial wood could be met by a widely implemented tree farming system (Sagoff 90). We could also reduce the amount of trees used for paper products by using a promising new innovation called Kenaf, a fast-growing annual herb which is fifteen feet tall and is native to Africa. It has been used for making rope for many years, but recently it was found to work just as well for paper pulp. In light of the fact that we have plenty of trees and ways of reducing our wood demands, there is no need to harvest old-growth forests.

*Added particulars support subpoint that we have plenty of new-growth forest*

*Added particulars support second subpoint that wood alternatives are available*

## Revising Paragraphs for Points-First Structure

**Individual task:** Bring to class a draft-in-progress for a closed-form essay. Pick out several paragraphs in the body of your essay and analyze them for "points-first" structure. For each paragraph, ask the following questions:

- Does my paragraph have a topic sentence near the beginning?
- If so, does my topic sentence accurately forecast what the paragraph says?
- Does my topic sentence link to my thesis statement or to a higher-order point that my paragraph develops?
- Does my paragraph have enough particulars to develop and support my topic sentence?

**Group task:** Then exchange your draft with a partner and do a similar analysis of your partner's selected paragraphs. Discuss your analyses of each other's paragraphs and then help each other plan appropriate revision strategies. If time permits, revise your paragraphs and show your results to your partner. [Note: Sometimes you can revise simply by adding a topic sentence to a paragraph, rewording a topic sentence, or making other kinds of local revisions. At other times, you may need to cross out whole paragraphs and start over, rewriting from scratch after you rethink your ideas.]

---

**12.5**
Guide readers
with transitions.

## SKILL 12.5  Guide your reader with transitions and other signposts.

As we have explained, when readers read closed-form prose, they expect each new sentence, paragraph, and section to link clearly to what they have already read. They need a well-marked trail with signposts signaling the twists and turns along the way. They also need resting spots at major junctions where they can review where they've been and survey what's coming. In this lesson, we show you how transition words as well as summary and forecasting passages can keep your readers securely on the trail.

### Using Common Transition Words to Signal Relationships

Transitions are like signposts that signal where the road is turning and limit the possible directions that an unfolding argument might take. Consider how the use of "therefore" and "nevertheless" limits the range of possibilities in the following examples:

> While on vacation, Suzie caught the chicken pox. Therefore, _____.
> While on vacation, Suzie caught the chicken pox. Nevertheless, _____.

"Therefore" signals to the reader that what follows is a consequence. Most readers will imagine a sentence similar to this one:

> Therefore, she spent her vacation lying in bed itchy, feverish, and miserable.

In contrast, "nevertheless" signals an unexpected or denied consequence, so the reader might anticipate a sentence such as this:

> Nevertheless, she enjoyed her two weeks off, thanks to a couple of bottles of calamine lotion, some good books, and a big easy chair overlooking the ocean.

Here is a list of the most common transition words and phrases and what they signal to the reader:*

| Words or Phrases | What They Signal |
|---|---|
| first, second, third, next, finally, earlier, later, meanwhile, afterward | *sequence*—First we went to dinner; then we went to the movies. |
| that is, in other words, to put it another way, — (dash), : (colon) | *restatement*—He's so hypocritical that you can't trust a word he says. To put it another way, he's a complete phony. |
| rather, instead | *replacement*—We shouldn't use the money to buy opera tickets; rather, we should use it for a nice gift. |
| for example, for instance, a case in point | *example*—Mr. Carlyle is very generous. For example, he gave the janitors a special holiday gift. |
| because, since, for | *reason*—Taxes on cigarettes are unfair because they place a higher tax burden on the working class. |
| therefore, hence, so, consequently, thus, then, as a result, accordingly, as a consequence | *consequence*—I failed to turn in the essay; therefore I flunked the course. |
| still, nevertheless | *denied consequence*—The teacher always seemed grumpy in class; nevertheless, I really enjoyed the course. |
| although, even though, granted that (*with* still) | *concession*—Even though the teacher was always grumpy, I still enjoyed the course. |
| in comparison, likewise, similarly | *similarity*—Teaching engineering takes a lot of patience. Likewise, so does teaching accounting. |
| however, in contrast, conversely, on the other hand, but | *contrast*—I disliked my old backpack immensely; however, I really like this new one. |
| in addition, also, too, moreover, furthermore | *addition*—Today's cars are much safer than those of ten years ago. In addition, they get better gas mileage. |
| in brief, in sum, in conclusion, finally, to sum up, to conclude | *conclusion or summary*—In sum, the plan presented by Mary is the best choice. |

## Using Transitions

**FOR WRITING AND DISCUSSION**

This exercise is designed to show you how transition words govern relationships between ideas. Working in groups or on your own, finish each of the following statements using ideas of your own invention. Make sure what you add fits the logic of the transition word.

1. Writing is difficult; therefore _____.
2. Writing is difficult; however, _____.

*Although all the words on the list serve as transitions or connectives, grammatically they are not all equivalent, nor are they all punctuated the same way.

3. Writing is difficult because _____.
4. Writing is difficult. For example, _____.
5. Writing is difficult. To put it another way, _____.
6. Writing is difficult. Likewise, _____.
7. Although writing is difficult, _____.

In the following paragraph, various kinds of linking devices have been omitted. Fill in the blanks with words or phrases that would make the paragraph coherent. Clues are provided in brackets.

Writing an essay is a difficult process for most people. _____ [contrast] the process can be made easier if you learn to practice three simple techniques. _____ [sequence] learn the technique of nonstop writing. When you are first trying to think of ideas for an essay, put your pen to your paper and write nonstop for ten or fifteen minutes without letting your pen leave the paper. Stay loose and free. Let your pen follow the waves of thought. Don't worry about grammar or spelling. _____ [concession] this technique won't work for everyone, it helps many people get a good cache of ideas to draw on. A _____ [sequence] technique is to write your rough draft rapidly without worrying about being perfect. Too many writers try to get their drafts right the first time. _____ [contrast] by learning to live with imperfection, you will save yourself headaches and a wastepaper basket full of crumpled paper. Think of your first rough draft as a path hacked out of the jungle—as part of an exploration, not as a completed highway. As a _____ [sequence] technique, try printing out a triple-spaced copy to allow space for revision. Many beginning writers don't leave enough space to revise. _____ [consequence] these writers never get in the habit of crossing out chunks of their rough draft and writing revisions in the blank spaces. After you have revised your rough draft until it is too messy to work from anymore, you can _____ [sequence] enter your changes into your word processor and print out a fresh draft, again setting your text on triple-space. The resulting blank space invites you to revise.

## Writing Major Transitions between Parts

In long closed-form pieces, writers often put *resting places* between major parts—transitional passages that allow readers to shift their attention momentarily away from the matter at hand to get a sense of where they've been and where they're going. Often such passages sum up the preceding major section, refer back to the essay's thesis statement or opening blueprint plan, and then preview the next major section. Here are three typical examples:

So far I have looked at a number of techniques that can help people identify debilitating assumptions that block their self-growth. In the next section, I examine ways to question and overcome these assumptions.

Now that the difficulty of the problem is fully apparent, our next step is to examine some of the solutions that have been proposed.

These, then, are the major theories explaining why Hamlet delays. But let's see what happens to Hamlet if we ask the question in a slightly different way. In this next section, we shift our critical focus, looking not at Hamlet's actions, but at his language.

## Signaling Major Transitions with Headings

In many genres, particularly scientific and technical reports, government documents, business proposals, textbooks, and long articles in magazines or scholarly journals, writers conventionally break up long stretches of text with headings and subheadings. Headings are often set in different type sizes and fonts and mark transition points between major parts and subparts of the argument.

## SKILL 12.6   **Bind sentences together by placing old information before new information.**

**12.6**
Link sentences by placing old information before new.

The previous skill focused on marking the reader's trail with transitions. This skill will enable you to build a smooth trail without potholes or washed-out bridges.

## The Old/New Contract in Sentences

A powerful way to prevent gaps is to follow the old/new contract—a writing strategy derived from the principle of old before new that we explained and illustrated in Skill 12.1. Simply put, the old/new contract asks writers to begin sentences with something old—something that links to what has gone before—and then to end sentences with new information.

To understand the old/new contract more fully, try the following thought exercise. We'll show you two passages, both of which explain the old/new contract. One of them, however, follows the principle it describes; the other violates it.

**THOUGHT EXERCISE**

Which of these passages follows the old/new contract?

**VERSION 1**

The old/new contract is another principle for writing clear closed-form prose. Beginning your sentences with something old—something that links to what has gone before—and then ending your sentences with new information that advances the argument is what the old/new contract asks writers to do. An effect called *coherence*, which is closely related to *unity*, is created by following this principle. Whereas the clear relationship between the topic sentence and the body of the paragraph and between the parts and the whole is what *unity* refers to, the clear relationship between one sentence and the next is what *coherence* relates to.

**VERSION 2**

Another principle for writing clear closed-form prose is the old/new contract. The old/new contract asks writers to begin sentences with something old—something that links to what has gone before—and then to end sentences with new information that advances the argument. Following this principle creates an effect called *coherence*, which is closely related to unity. Whereas *unity* refers to the clear relationship between the body of a paragraph and its topic sentence and between the parts and the whole, *coherence* refers to the clear relationship between one sentence and the next, between part and part.

If you are like most readers, you have to concentrate much harder to understand Version 1 than Version 2 because Version 1 violates the old-before-new way that our minds normally process information. When a writer doesn't begin a sentence with old material, readers have to hold the new material in suspension until they have figured out how it connects to what has gone before. They can stay on the trail, but they have to keep jumping over the potholes between sentences.

To follow the old/new contract, place old information near the beginning of sentences in what we call the **topic position** and place new information that advances the argument in the predicate or **stress position** at the end of the sentence. We associate topics with the beginnings of sentences simply because in the standard English sentence, the topic (or subject) comes before the predicate—hence the notion of a "contract" by which we agree not to fool or frustrate our readers by breaking with the "normal" order of things. The contract says that the old, backward-linking material comes at the beginning of the sentence and that the new, argument-advancing material comes at the end.

**FOR WRITING AND DISCUSSION**

## Practicing the Old/New Contract

Here are two more passages, one of which obeys the old/new contract while the other violates it. Working in small groups or as a whole class, reach consensus on which of these passages follows the old/new contract. Explain your reasoning by showing how the beginning of each sentence links to something old.

### PASSAGE A

Play is an often-overlooked dimension of fathering. From the time a child is born until its adolescence, fathers emphasize caretaking less than play. Egalitarian feminists may be troubled by this, and spending more time in caretaking may be wise for fathers. There seems to be unusual significance in the father's style of play. Physical excitement and stimulation are likely to be part of it. With older children more physical games and teamwork that require the competitive testing of physical and mental skills are also what it involves. Resemblance to an apprenticeship or teaching relationship is also a characteristic of fathers' play: Come on, let me show you how.

### PASSAGE B

An often-overlooked dimension of fathering is play. From their children's birth through adolescence, fathers tend to emphasize play more than caretaking. This emphasis may be troubling to egalitarian feminists, and it would indeed be wise for most fathers to spend more time in caretaking. Yet the fathers' style of play seems to have unusual significance. It is likely to be both physically stimulating and exciting. With older children it involves more physical games and teamwork that require the competitive testing of physical and mental skills. It frequently resembles an apprenticeship or teaching relationship: Come on, let me show you how.

## How to Make Links to the "Old"

To understand how to link to "old information," you need to understand more fully what we mean by "old" or "familiar." In the context of sentence-level coherence, we mean everything in the text that the reader has read so far. Any upcoming sentence is new information, but once the reader has read it, it becomes old information. For example, when a reader is halfway through a text, everything previously read—the title, the introduction, half the body—is old information to which you can link to meet your readers' expectations for unity and coherence.

In making these backward links, writers have three targets:

1. They can link to a key word or concept in the immediately preceding sentence (creating coherence).
2. They can link to a key word or concept in a preceding point sentence (creating unity).
3. They can link to a preceding forecasting statement about structure (helping readers map their location in the text).

Writers have a number of textual strategies for making these links. In Figure 12.3 our annotations show how a professional writer links to old

**FIGURE 12.3** How a Professional Writer Follows the Old/New Contract

Recent research has given us much deeper—and more surprising—insights into the father's role in childrearing. It shows that in almost all of their interactions with children, fathers do things a little differently from mothers. What fathers do—their special parenting style—is not only highly complementary to what mothers do but is by all indications important in its own right.

For example, an often-overlooked dimension of fathering is play. From their children's birth through adolescence, fathers tend to emphasize play more than caretaking. This may be troubling to egalitarian feminists, and it would indeed be wise for most fathers to spend more time in caretaking.

Yet the fathers' style of play seems to have unusual significance. It is likely to be both physically stimulating and exciting. With older children it involves more physical games and teamwork that require the competitive testing of physical and mental skills. It frequently resembles an apprenticeship or teaching relationship: Come on, let me show you how.

*Refers to "research" in previous sentence*

*Rephrases idea of "childrearing"*

*Repeats "fathers" from previous sentence*

*Rephrases concept in previous paragraph*

*Pronoun sums up previous concept*

*"It" refers to fathers' style of play*

*Refers to "fathers" in previous sentence*

*Transition tells us new paragraph will be an example of previous concept*

*Refers to "fathers"*

*New information that becomes topic of this paragraph*

*Repeats words "father" and "play" from the topic sentence of the preceding paragraph*

David Popenoe, "Where's Papa?" from *Life Without Father: Compelling New Evidence that Fatherhood and Marriage Are Indispensable for the Good of Children and Society.*

information within the first five or six words of each sentence. What follows is a compendium of these strategies:

## Strategies for Linking to the "Old"

| What to Do | Example Shown in Figure 12.3 |
| --- | --- |
| **Repeat a key word** from the preceding sentence or an earlier point sentence. | Note the number of sentences that open with "father," "father's," or "fathering." Note also the frequent repetitions of "play." |
| **Use a pronoun** to substitute for a key word. | In our example, the second sentence opens with the pronouns "It," referring to "research," and "their," referring to "fathers." The last three sentences open with the pronoun "It," referring to "father's style of play." |
| **Summarize, rephrase, or restate earlier concepts.** | In the second sentence, "interactions with children" restates the concept of childrearing. Similarly, the phrase "an often-overlooked dimension" sums up a concept implied in the preceding paragraph—that recent research reveals something significant and not widely known about a father's role in childrearing. Finally, note that the pronoun "This" in the second paragraph sums up the main concept of the previous two sentences. (But see our warning on p. 317 about the overuse of "this" as a pronoun.) |
| **Use a transition word** such as *first…*, *second…*, *third…*, or *therefore* or *however* to cue the reader about the logical relationship between an upcoming sentence and the preceding ones. | Note how the second paragraph opens with "For example," indicating that the upcoming paragraph will illustrate the concept identified in the preceding paragraph. |

These strategies give you a powerful way to check and revise your prose. Comb your drafts for gaps between sentences where you have violated the old/new contract. If the opening of a new sentence doesn't refer back to an earlier word, phrase, or concept, your readers could derail, so use what you have learned to repair the tracks.

---

**FOR WRITING AND DISCUSSION**

### Applying the Old/New Contract to Your Own Draft

**Individual task:** Bring to class a draft-in-progress for a closed-form essay. On a selected page, examine the opening of each sentence. Place a vertical slash in front of any sentence that doesn't contain near the beginning some backward-looking element that links to old, familiar material. Then revise these sentences to follow the old/new contract.

**Group task:** Working with a partner, share the changes you each made on your drafts. Then on each other's pages, work together to identify the kinds of links made at the beginning of each sentence. (For example, does the opening of a sentence repeat a key word, use a pronoun to substitute for a key word, rephrase or restate an earlier concept, or use a transition word?)

As we discussed in Skill 12.1, the principle of old before new has great explanatory power in helping writers understand their choices when they compose. In this last section, we give you some further insights into the old/new contract.

## Avoiding Ambiguous Use of "This" to Fulfill the Old/New Contract

Some writers try to fulfill the old/new contract by frequent use of the pronoun *this* to sum up a preceding concept. Occasionally such usage is effective, as in our example passage on fathers' style of play when the writer says: "*This* may be troubling to egalitarian feminists." But frequent use of *this* as a pronoun creates lazy and often ambiguous prose. Consider how our example passage might read if many of the explicit links were replaced by *this*:

LAZY USE OF *THIS* AS PRONOUN

Recent research has given us much deeper—and more surprising—insights into **this.** It shows that in doing **this,** fathers do things a little differently from mothers. **This** is not only highly complementary to what mothers do but is by all indications important in its own right.

For example, an often-overlooked dimension of **this** is play.

Perhaps this passage helps you see why we refer to *this* (used by itself as a pronoun) as "the lazy person's all-purpose noun-slot filler."*

## SKILL 12.7  Use effective tables, graphs, and charts to present numeric data.

**12.7**
Present numerical data effectively through tables, graphs, and charts.

In contemporary analyses and arguments, writers often draw on quantitative data to support their points. Writers can make numbers speak powerfully by means of reader-effective graphics including tables, graphs, and charts. Generally, quantitative data displayed in tables invite the reader to tease out many different stories that the numbers might tell. In contrast, line graphs, bar graphs, or pie charts focus vividly on one story.

*It's acceptable to use *this* as an adjective, as in "this usage"; we refer here only to *this* used by itself as a pronoun.

## How Tables Tell Many Stories

Data displayed in tables usually have their origins in raw numbers collected from surveys, questionnaires, observational studies, scientific experiments, and so forth. These numbers are then consolidated and arranged in tables where they can be analyzed for potentially meaningful patterns. Consider, for example, Table 12.1, produced by the National Center for Education Statistics. It shows the number of postsecondary degrees earned by men and women from 1960 to 2007.

**Reading a Table** Tables are read in two directions: from top to bottom and from left to right. To read a table efficiently, begin with the title, *which always includes elements from both the vertical and horizontal dimensions of the table*. Note how this rule applies to Table 12.1.

- The table's horizontal dimension is indicated in the first part of the title: "Earned Degrees Conferred by Level and Sex." Reading horizontally, we see the names of the degrees (associate's, bachelor's, and so forth) with subcategories indicating male and female.
- The table's vertical dimension is indicated in the second part of the title: "1960 to 2007." Reading vertically, we see selected years between 1960 and 2007.

Beneath the title are further instructions: Numbers represent thousands except for one column labeled "percent."

We are now prepared to read specific information from the table. In 1994, for example, colleges and universities in the United States conferred 2,206,000 degrees, of which 45.1 percent were earned by men. In that same year, 532,000 men and 637,000 women earned bachelors's degrees while 27,000 men and 17,000 women earned doctoral degrees.

**Discovering Stories in the Data** You need to peruse the table carefully before interesting patterns begin to emerge. Among the stories the table tells are these:

- The percent of women receiving postsecondary degrees rose substantially between 1960 and 2007 (with a corresponding fall for men).
- This increased percentage of degrees given to women is more dramatic for associate's and bachelor's degrees than it is for master's, first professional, or doctoral degrees.

As we show in the next section, these two stories, which must be teased out of this table, can be told more dramatically with graphs.

## Using a Graphic to Tell a Story

Whereas tables can embed many stories and invite detailed examination of the numbers, a graph or chart makes one selected story immediately visible.

**Line Graph** A line graph converts numerical data to a series of points on a grid and connects them to create flat, rising, or falling lines. The result gives us a picture of the relationship between the variables represented on the horizontal and vertical axes.

Suppose you wanted to tell the story of the increasing percentage of women receiving bachelor's and doctoral degrees from 1960 to 2007. Using Table 12.1

**TABLE 12.1 Earned Degrees Conferred by Level and Sex: 1960 to 2007**

[In thousands (477 represents 477,000), except percent. Based on survey; see Appendix III]

| Year ending | All degrees Total | All degrees Percent male | Associate's Male | Associate's Female | Bachelor's Male | Bachelor's Female | Master's Male | Master's Female | First professional Male | First professional Female | Doctoral Male | Doctoral Female |
|---|---|---|---|---|---|---|---|---|---|---|---|---|
| 1960 [1] ......... | 477 | 65.8 | (NA) | (NA) | 254 | 138 | 51 | 24 | (NA) | (NA) | 9 | 1 |
| 1970 ......... | 1,271 | 59.2 | 117 | 89 | 451 | 341 | 126 | 83 | 33 | 2 | 26 | 4 |
| 1975 ......... | 1,666 | 56.0 | 191 | 169 | 505 | 418 | 162 | 131 | 49 | 7 | 27 | 7 |
| 1980 ......... | 1,731 | 51.1 | 184 | 217 | 474 | 456 | 151 | 147 | 53 | 17 | 23 | 10 |
| 1985 ......... | 1,828 | 49.3 | 203 | 252 | 483 | 497 | 143 | 143 | 50 | 25 | 22 | 11 |
| 1990 ......... | 1,940 | 46.6 | 191 | 264 | 492 | 560 | 154 | 171 | 44 | 27 | 24 | 14 |
| 1991 ......... | 2,025 | 45.8 | 199 | 283 | 504 | 590 | 156 | 181 | 44 | 2S | 25 | 15 |
| 1992 ......... | 2,108 | 45.6 | 207 | 297 | 521 | 616 | 162 | 191 | 45 | 29 | 26 | 15 |
| 1993 ......... | 2,167 | 45.5 | 212 | 303 | 533 | 632 | 169 | 200 | 45 | 30 | 26 | 16 |
| 1994 ......... | 2,206 | 45.1 | 215 | 315 | 532 | 637 | 176 | 211 | 45 | 31 | 27 | 17 |
| 1995 ......... | 2,218 | 44.9 | 218 | 321 | 526 | 634 | 179 | 219 | 45 | 31 | 27 | 18 |
| 1996 [2] ......... | 2,248 | 44.2 | 220 | 336 | 522 | 642 | 179 | 227 | 45 | 32 | 27 | 18 |
| 1997 [2] ......... | 2,288 | 43.6 | 224 | 347 | 521 | 652 | 181 | 238 | 46 | 33 | 27 | 19 |
| 1998 [2] ......... | 2,298 | 43.2 | 218 | 341 | 520 | 664 | 184 | 246 | 45 | 34 | 27 | 19 |
| 1999 [2] ......... | 2,323 | 42.7 | 218 | 342 | 519 | 682 | 186 | 254 | 44 | 34 | 25 | 19 |
| 2000 [2] ......... | 2,385 | 42.6 | 225 | 340 | 530 | 708 | 192 | 265 | 44 | 36 | 25 | 20 |
| 2001 [2] ......... | 2,416 | 42.4 | 232 | 347 | 532 | 712 | 194 | 274 | 43 | 37 | 25 | 20 |
| 2002 [2] ......... | 2,494 | 42.2 | 238 | 357 | 550 | 742 | 199 | 283 | 43 | 38 | 24 | 20 |
| 2003 [2] ......... | 2,621 | 42.1 | 253 | 380 | 573 | 775 | 211 | 301 | 42 | 39 | 24 | 22 |
| 2004 [2] ......... | 2,755 | 41.8 | 260 | 405 | 595 | 804 | 230 | 329 | 42 | 41 | 25 | 23 |
| 2005 [2] ......... | 2,850 | 41.6 | 268 | 429 | 613 | 826 | 234 | 341 | 44 | 43 | 27 | 26 |
| 2006 [2] ......... | 2,936 | 41.3 | 270 | 443 | 631 | 855 | 238 | 356 | 44 | 44 | 29 | 27 |
| 2007 [2] ......... | 3,007 | 41.2 | 275 | 453 | 650 | 875 | 238 | 366 | 45 | 45 | 30 | 30 |

NA Not available.

[1] First-professional degrees are included with bachelor's degrees.

[2] Beginning 1996, data reflect the new classification of institutions.

*Source:* U.S. National Center for Education Statistics, *Digest of Education Statistics,* annual.

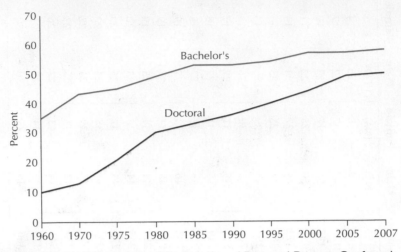

**FIGURE 12.4** Percentage of Bachelor's and Doctoral Degrees Conferred on Females: 1960–2007

you can calculate these percentages yourself and display them in a line graph as shown in Figure 12.4. To determine what a graph tells you, you need to clarify what's represented on the two axes. By convention, the horizontal axis of a graph contains the predictable, known variable that has no surprises, such as time or some other sequence—in this case, the years 1960 to 2007 in predictable chronological order. The vertical axis contains the unpredictable variable that tells the graph's story—in this case, the percent of degrees conferred on women in each year on the graph. The ascending lines tell the stories at a glance.

**Bar Graph** Bar graphs use bars of varying lengths, extending either horizontally or vertically, to contrast two or more quantities. To make the story of women's progress in earning doctoral degrees particularly vivid (the same story told in the "doctoral" line in Figure 12.4), you could use a bar graph as shown in Figure 12.5. To read a bar graph, note carefully the title and the axes to see what is compared to what. Bars are typically distinguished from each other by use of different colors, shades, or patterns of cross-hatching. The special power of bar graphs is that they can help you make quick comparisons. Figure 12.5 tells you at a glance that in 1960, women received far fewer doctoral degrees than men but that in 2007 they received an equal percentage.

**Pie Chart** A pie chart, also called a circle graph, depicts the different percentages of a total (the pie) represented by variously sized slices. Suppose you wanted to know the most popular undergraduate majors in American colleges and universities. These statistics, which are available in table format from the National Center for Education Statistics, can be quickly converted into a pie chart as shown in Figure 12.6. As you can see, a pie chart shows at a glance how the whole of something is divided into segments. In 2007, for example, 7 percent of graduating seniors majored in education while 22 percent majored in business. The effectiveness of pie charts diminishes as you add more slices. In most cases, you begin to confuse readers if you include more than five or six slices.

**FIGURE 12.5** Percentage of Doctoral Degrees Conferred on Males and Females: 1960 and 2007

## Incorporating a Graphic into Your Essay

Today, most word processing programs, often integrated with a spreadsheet, easily allow you to create a graphic and insert it into your document. In some cases, your instructor may give you permission to make a graphic with pen or pencil and paste it into your document.

**Designing Your Graphic**  In academic manuscripts, graphics are designed conservatively without bells and whistles such as three-dimensional effects or special fonts and patterns. Keep the graphic as simple and uncluttered as possible. Also in

**FIGURE 12.6**  Distribution of Bachelor's Degrees by Majors, 2007

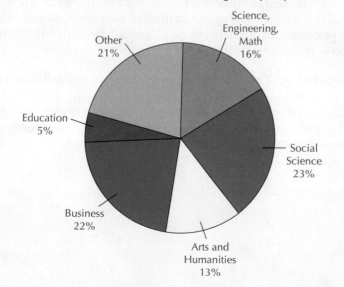

**FIGURE 12.7** Example of a Student Text with a Referenced Graph

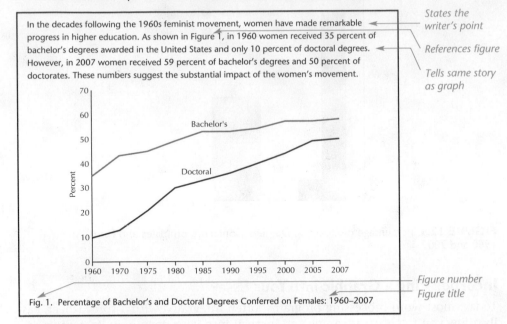

In the decades following the 1960s feminist movement, women have made remarkable ← *States the writer's point*
progress in higher education. As shown in Figure 1, in 1960 women received 35 percent of
bachelor's degrees awarded in the United States and only 10 percent of doctoral degrees. ← *References figure*
However, in 2007 women received 59 percent of bachelor's degrees and 50 percent of
doctorates. These numbers suggest the substantial impact of the women's movement. *Tells same story as graph*

*Figure number*
*Figure title*

Fig. 1.  Percentage of Bachelor's and Doctoral Degrees Conferred on Females: 1960–2007

academic manuscripts, do not wrap text around the graphic. In contrast, in popular published work, writers often use flashy fonts, three dimensions, text wrapping, and other effects that would undermine your *ethos* in an academic setting.

**Numbering, Labeling, and Titling the Graphic** In newspapers and popular magazines, writers often include graphics in boxes or sidebars without specifically referring to them in the text. However, in academic manuscripts or scholarly works, graphics are always labeled, numbered, titled, and referred to in the text. Tables are listed as "Tables," while line graphs, bar graphs, pie charts, or any other kinds of drawings or photographs are labeled as "Figures." By convention, the title for tables goes above the table, while the title for figures goes below.

**Referencing the Graphic in Your Text** Academic and professional writers follow a referencing convention called independent redundancy. The graphic should be understandable without the text; the text should be understandable without the graphic. In other words, the text should tell in words the same story that the graphic displays visually. An example is shown in Figure 12.7.

# STRATEGIES FOR COMPOSING MULTIMODAL TEXTS

**WHAT YOU WILL LEARN**

**13.1** To consider a range of multimodal options for accomplishing your rhetorical purpose.

**13.2** To design multimodal texts so that each mode contributes its own strengths to the message.

**13.3** To design texts in multimodal genres including posters, speeches with visual aids, podcasts, and videos.

This chapter gives practical advice for composing multimodal texts. As we explained in Chapter 4, a **multimodal text** uses two or more "modalities" of communication by variously combining words, images, and sounds. Multimodal productions can be low-tech (a speech with flip charts for visual aids), medium-tech (graphs or photographs embedded into a written text), or high-tech (Web sites, videos, podcasts, desktop published posters or brochures). It is beyond the scope of this text to explain the technological aspects of digital productions. However, many digitally native students already possess technological know-how, and many institutions provide instruction and backup support for multimodal projects. Our purpose in this chapter is to offer rhetorical advice on how to make your multimodal texts as effective as possible for your targeted audience.

## SKILL 13.1  Consider a range of multimodal options for accomplishing your rhetorical purpose.

One way to appreciate the power of multimedia texts is to imagine how a written text might be transformed or remixed to reach different audiences in different ways. Suppose, for example, that you have written an autobiographical narrative about your recovery from an accident when you were in the 8th grade. That essay might reach a wider audience if you transformed it into a podcast and posted a link to it on your Facebook page or blog. Perhaps you also have relevant and evocative photographs from this period. Instead of a podcast, you might then create a video screencast combining your photographs with a voice-over narrative. Both the podcast and the screencast could be enhanced with music. Or, to take another example, suppose you have written an op-ed piece for your school's newspaper

**13.1**
Consider
a range of
multimodal
options for
accomplishing
your rhetorical
purpose.

taking a stand on a controversial campus issue. You might widen the reach of your argument through a campaign that includes posters or brochures, a speech supported with PowerPoint or Prezi slides, and a batch of T-shirts embossed with your message in a verbal/visual design.

Of course, not all multimedia texts start off as written arguments. You might upload a funny video to YouTube purely for its entertainment value, or you might post on Flickr a slideshow, set to music, of beautiful photographs of flowers just for the aesthetic or inspirational appeal.

In all cases, when you design a multimodal text, you should think rhetorically about your audience and purpose. In Chapter 1 (Concept 1.2), we identified six common aims or purposes for written texts: to express, to explore, to inform, to analyze/synthesize, to persuade, and to reflect. Table 13.1 provides examples of multimodal texts designed for these aims. As the chart suggests, designing effective multimodal texts requires both purposeful thinking and creative imagination. There is lots of room for trial and error (and fun) when you experiment with multimodal texts.

**TABLE 13.1 Rhetorical Purposes and Multimodal Texts**

| Rhetorical Aim | Subject Matter/Focus of Writing | Possible Multimodal Forms |
| --- | --- | --- |
| Express | You share aspects of your life; you invite your audience to walk in your shoes, to experience your insights | Personal story narrated as a podcast or a video with images |
| Explore | You take your audience on your own intellectual journey by showing your inquiry process (raising questions, seeking evidence, considering alternative views) | A podcast or video that includes interviews with experts who progressively expand your thinking |
| Inform | You bring to your audience factual knowledge addressing a reader's need or curiosity | An informative poster; a report with graphics; a collaborative wiki article; a how-to video |
| Analyze/ Synthesize | You provide your audience with deeper insights by breaking an artifact or phenomenon into parts and putting them together in new ways for greater understanding | The text of a poem with marginal drawings that illustrate metaphors; an audioguide analyzing a museum exhibit |
| Persuade | You try to convince your audience, who may not share your values and beliefs, to accept your stance on an issue | Advocacy poster, podcast, or video; persuasive speech with PowerPoint or Prezi slides |
| Reflect | You look back retrospectively on an experience or journey and bring to your audience your evaluation of its significance or meaning | A collage of photographs, arranged in a way that represents retrospective thinking about value or meaning; same collage done as a pechakucha presentation |

### Thinking about Your Purpose and Audience

**Individually**: If you are planning to design a multimodal text, consider your answers to the following questions:

1. What will be the content or subject matter of your text?
2. What is your purpose? Where would you place your imagined text in Table 13.1 on rhetorical aims?
3. Who is your intended audience and what genre or medium will you use to reach them?

**In small groups or as a whole class:** Share your answers to these questions.

## SKILL 13.2   Design multimodal texts so that each mode contributes its own strengths to the message.

13.2
Design
multimodal
texts so that
each mode
contributes its
own strengths to
the message.

The main point of this lesson is intuitively simple: The various elements of a multimodal text should work together to send the same message. In a podcast, the music should match the content. In a poster, the images should work in harmony with the words. In a PowerPoint presentation, the slide on the screen should reinforce the speaker's point. However, the creative opportunities offered by multimodal composing can sometimes lead inadvertently to jumbled multimodal texts, causing audience members to scratch their heads and say "whuuuhh?" In the language of cognitive scientists, the audience members' confusion can be called "cognitive dissonance" or "cognitive overload."

### This Design Principle at Work in Successful Multimodal Texts

Let's consider some examples of successful multimodal texts, starting with children's picture books. For many children, their first introduction to multimodal texts comes from being read to while snuggled in a parent's lap. As the child listens to the story of Peter Rabbit, he or she enjoys the pictures, page by page, watching Peter wander into Mr. MacGregor's garden, hide in the watering can, and eventually end up drinking his chamomile tea. Picture books show how our brains can process both auditory information (the story) and visual information (the pictures) at the same time. Some children's books (such as *Pat the Bunny*) even introduce a third communication channel—touch. The child can both see the bunny and feel its cotton-soft ears.

But now imagine how we might create cognitive dissonance for the child. Suppose that we told the child the story of Peter Rabbit (which we had memorized), but actually held in our laps the picture book about Jemima Puddleduck. Suddenly the words she was hearing about Peter Rabbit would no longer match the pictures she was looking at about Jemima Puddleduck. Or suppose we just had the Peter Rabbit story out of sync: While the child looked at Peter drinking his chamomile tea, we told the story of Peter's being chased by Mr. MacGregor. The child would be frustrated by the disconnect between the auditory channel processing words and the visual channel processing images. Our point is that multimodal texts work successfully only when the various modes are in sync with each other.

**Function of Images in a Multimodal Text** Many multimodal texts rely extensively on images. We examined the power of images in Chapter 3 (Concept 3.4) and then more fully in Chapter 7 on visual rhetoric. As we explained in these chapters, insights that need to be built up slowly through words in the verbal-processing part of our brains might be apprehended almost instantaneously in the visual-processing part of our brains (hence the saying "A picture is worth a thousand words"). An effective image condenses an argument into a memorable scene or symbol that is apprehensible at a glance and taps deeply into our emotions and values. Images make implicit arguments (*logos*) while also appealing directly to our values and emotions (*pathos*). The creative challenge of multimodal composing is to find or design images that tell visually the same story that the words tell verbally. Typical images in a multimodal text (say a poster, brochure, advocacy ad, Web page, PowerPoint slide, cartoon, graphic novel, video) include still or moving photographs, drawings or animations, graphs, charts, maps, or words arranged in meaningful nonlinear designs to show relationships—for example, as components of flow charts, cause-effect diagrams with arrows, circle diagrams showing recursive processes, and so forth.

**Function of Words in a Multimodal Text** But images by themselves usually need accompanying words to focus the image's point. Because images have open-ended or multiple, ambiguous interpretive possibilities, designers of multimodal texts often use words to crystallize the intended meaning, thereby shaping the audience's response. A successful multimodal text thus usually includes some kind of "nutshell statement" that makes a claim and thereby identifies and sharpens the text's take-away message. This nutshell serves the same function for a multimodal text as a thesis statement serves for an essay or a topic sentence for a paragraph. Consider as an example the classic World War II poster alerting soldiers in jungle warfare to the dangers of unsafe drinking water.

The poster shows a soldier, a canteen cup in his hand and a look of horror on his face, peering into a pond in search of drinking water. The poster's message is conveyed visually by the reflection of the soldier's face transfigured into a skull—a powerful appeal to *pathos*. But the same message is also conveyed in the verbal channel through the words: "BEWARE … Drink Only Approved Water. Never give a germ a break." The words, which appeal primarily to *logos*, serve as a "nutshell" for the whole argument, making the poster's message unmistakably clear.

But note how the words themselves also register in the visual channel through the effect of layout and font size. In the top half of the poster, the large-font, all-caps "BEWARE" seems to shout a warning to the soldier. In the bottom half of the poster, the text next to the skull—"Drink Only Approved Water"—uses a smaller font and calm sentence case to convey the poster's take-away message. Finally the words along the bottom border of the poster ("Never Give a Germ a Break!") in still a different font offer a cause-and-effect explanation of why the water might kill you. Although the images alone convey the message at a glance, the poster's full punch comes from our registering the argument in both the visual and verbal parts of our brains.

### Dual Channel Effect of Words and Images

As cognitive scientists researching multimodal learning have shown, multimodal texts achieve their power by combining the strengths of two or more modes of communication. Because each mode or channel is processed in a different area of the brain, each mode contributes its own strengths to the message. This dual-channel effect can be seen in a wide range of multimodal texts. As we have suggested, an effective visual/verbal multimodal text typically has a nutshell claim that summarizes the text's takeaway message combined with images that support the claim through a visual channel. The location of the nutshell claim can vary depending on the design of the text, and it can be emphasized by font size, location on the page, or other means. Table 13.2 shows examples from multimodal posters in this text.

### Effect of Sounds in a Multimodal Text

Because a print textbook can't accommodate sounds or moving images, our examples have focused primarily on multimodal print genres combining words and images. But sounds can also be a powerful channel for multimedia compositions, particularly the qualities of voice in speeches, podcasts, or videos as well as the special powers of music. In our example of a child listening to Peter Rabbit, the parent's voice coming through the auditory channel is simultaneously an auditory experience and a word/verbal experience. The child sees both the pictures of Peter Rabbit and

| TABLE 13.2 | Use of Nutshell Claims and Images in Multimodal Texts | |
|---|---|---|
| **Multimodal text** | **Verbal nutshell, claim, or key assertion (stated in words)** | **Images used for visual support** |
| <br>Page 275 | This glacier was here in 1982. (Implied claim: Global warming is melting the glaciers.) | Photograph showing at a glance the extent to which the glacier has retreated since 1982 |
| <br>Page 250 | Black kids are much more likely to go to prison.<br>    The poster uses words interactively to elicit viewer response to the question "What's wrong with these pictures?" White kids are more likely to use and sell drugs, but black kids go to prison more often. Statistical data provides strong appeal to *logos* and *ethos*. | This poster uses simple black and white drawings to appeal to *pathos*: A black kid is shown behind bars while a white kid has no jail time. |

also the words on the page—an important first step in the process of learning to read. A PowerPoint presentation similarly provides words through both an auditory channel (the speech) but also a visual channel (words on a slide). So sounds in multimodal compositions can range from the language-centered employment of voice to nonlanguage sounds such as street noise, animal sounds, drums, music, and other sounds with powerful emotional and associational effects.

## Using This Design Principle to Revise a Jumbled Multimodal Text

Let's contrast effective multimodal texts with a jumbled one, in this case the "first draft" of a PowerPoint slide developed by student writer Joyce Keeley for an oral presentation of her research on the plight of African refugees (Figure 13.1). It is not quite clear what the function or focus of the slide is. The whole slide seems to be about "Life of a Refugee," but it doesn't make a nutshell claim or assertion of the kind we noted previously in the successful posters. The audience might ask, "What is this slide's point about the life of a refugee?" The top right photograph of a refugee camp seems to make the claim that the life of a refugee is harsh or dismal. But it is uncertain what the other photographs

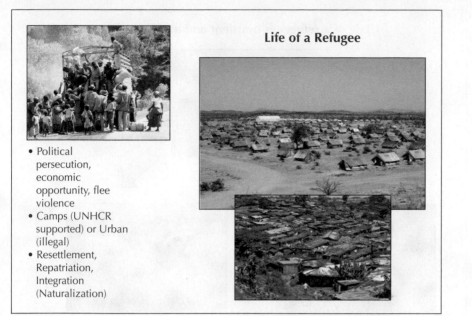

**FIGURE 13.1** A Jumbled Multimodal Slide

are doing. The top left photo shows refugees being loaded into the back of a truck while the bottom photo looks like an aerial view of a city, with no apparent connection to the life of a refugee. Additionally, none of the images seems connected to the bulleted list on the left side of the slide about political persecution, economic opportunity, violence, kinds of camps, resettlement, repatriation, integration, and naturalization. The slide is trying to do too many things at once. The words and the images aren't working together to send a single meaningful message.

When her peer reviewers said that they couldn't figure out what her PowerPoint slide was trying to say about the life of a refugee, Joyce decided to redesign it to follow more closely the multimodal principles explained in this lesson. As applied to PowerPoint slides using words and images, we can summarize these principles as follows:

- Make sure that each slide has a point that can be stated in a nutshell claim or assertion
- Make sure the audience knows that point (a presenter can state it in the speech or state it directly on the slide)
- Make sure that the words and images on the slide work together to develop or support that point

Figure 13.2 shows Joyce's revision of the slide to focus on just one of the points she originally intended.

For more on oral presentations using PowerPoint, see pp. 332–336.

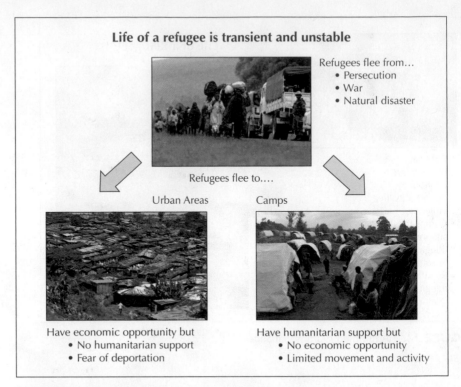

**FIGURE 13.2** Joyce's Redesign of Her "Jumbled" Slide

**FOR WRITING AND DISCUSSION**

## Purposeful Design of PowerPoint Slides

1. In small groups or as a whole class, identify the changes that Joyce made when she redesigned her original slide and then speculate on her thinking process. Do you agree that her redesigned slide is more effective than her original one? Why or how? How would you improve it?

2. Examine student writer Sam Rothchild's multimodal PowerPoint slides, which accompanied his speech outline (Chapter 10, p. 261). To what extent do Sam's slides follow the design principles outlined in this chapter? How do you imagine that he used each of these slides in his speech?

**13.3**
Design texts in multimodal genres including posters, speeches with visual aids, podcasts, and videos.

## SKILL 13.3 To design texts in multimodal genres including posters, speeches with visual aids, podcasts, and videos.

In this final lesson, we give some nuts-and-bolts advice connected to specific genres of multimodal texts.

## Informational or Advocacy Posters, Brochures, Flyers, and Ads

Posters and their cousin genres such as brochures, flyers, and newspaper ads—all of which can be published in print or posted to Web sites—typically have an informative purpose or a persuasive purpose. Effective posters try to maximize the power of both words and images.

To drive home the message presented in images, designers of posters pay attention to both the content and formatting of verbal text, including type sizes and fonts. Large-type text is frequently used to highlight slogans or condensed thesis statements (nutshells) written in an arresting style. They serve the function of complete sentence assertions, but for purposes of economy or impact may be grammatically incomplete. Here are two examples of large boldfaced copy from advocacy ads that the authors of this text have encountered recently:

- "Abstinence: It works every time.... " (from a newspaper advocacy ad sponsored by Focus on the Family, asking readers to donate money to promote abstinence education)
- "Expectant Mothers Deserve Compassionate Health Care—Not Prison!" (an advocacy advertisement from Common Sense for Drug Policy; this one appeared in the *National Review*)

To break up extended blocks of text, designers often put supporting reasons in bulleted lists and sometimes enclose carefully selected facts and quotations in boxed sidebars. To say a lot in a limited space, designers must be efficient in making words, images, and document design work effectively together. The following strategies will help you design a poster.

| Strategies for Designing Posters, Flyers, Brochures, and Ads | |
| --- | --- |
| **Features and Strategies to Consider** | **Questions to Ask** |
| ***Purpose, Genre, and Medium:*** Based on your purpose, choose the most appropriate genre and medium for your targeted audience. | Will your purpose be informative or persuasive? Should your genre be a poster, a flyer, a one-page advertisement, or a brochure? Should you publish it in print or post it on a Web site? |
| ***Giving Visual Presence to Your Message:*** Choose the most effective visual features to create appeals to *pathos*. | What would be the best visual means to establish the urgency and importance of your subject: graphic elements, cartoon images, photos, drawings? |
| ***Presenting the "Nutshell" of Your Message:*** Decide on how you will condense your argument into an assertion or focused point and convey it clearly. | What type size, font, and layout will be the most powerful in presenting your assertion and supporting it for your intended audience? How much verbal text do you want to use? How much will you rely on images alone? |

*(continued)*

| Features and Strategies to Consider | Questions to Ask |
| --- | --- |
| ***Accentuating Key Phrases:*** Decide what key phrases could highlight the parts or the main points of this argument. | What memorable phrases or slogans could you use to convey your argument? How condensed or detailed should your argument be? |
| ***Clarifying the Call for Action:*** Decide what you are asking your audience to know or do. | How can document design clarify the takeaway message of your poster? |
| ***Using Color for Impact:*** Decide whether you will use color. Note: For some media, color might be cost-prohibitive. | If color is an option, how could you use color to enhance the overall impact of your advocacy argument? How could you use black-and-white images effectively? |

## Speeches with Visual Aids (PowerPoint, Prezi, Pechakucha)

Another common multimodal form is a speech supported with visual aids, usually as digitally produced presentation slides. Such presentations are by definition multimodal because the audience receives information through an auditory channel, which processes the speaker's words, and a visual channel, which processes the slides. When the speaker's words and the slides are in sync, they can make the speech memorable and persuasive. But if they are out of sync, the audience is subjected to distracting multitasking.

Although PowerPoint remains the most common form of presentation software, Prezi—with its panning, zooming, and rotating features—is becoming increasingly popular. Also becoming popular is a **Pechakucha 20X20** presentation in which speakers must use exactly 20 slides displayed for 20 seconds each. Developed in Japan and named after the Japanese word for "chit chat," Pechakucha presentations are exactly six minutes and 40 seconds long. Whereas in PowerPoint or Prezi presentations the speaker controls the timing of the slides, in Pechakucha the slides are controlled by the computer timer, ensuring that a speaker can't drone on. Pechakucha evenings are now being sponsored in many cities where individuals can present their carefully timed speeches to welcoming audiences.

In all of these genres, the presenter is expected to speak extemporaneously. To speak **extemporaneously** means to spend ample time preparing the speech, but not to read it from a script or to recite it from memory. Instead, the speaker talks directly to the audience with the aid of an outline or note cards.

Long before the delivery of the speech, the speaker should have engaged in the same sort of composing process that precedes a finished essay. Effective speakers typically spend an hour of preparation time per minute of speaking time. Much of this work focuses on creating a well-developed sentence outline for the speech. Since you won't be writing out the complete argument in prose, this outline will be the written frame for your speech. The following chart suggests strategies for developing your speech outline.

## Strategies for Creating an Effective Speech Outline

| Strategies | Rationales and Explanations of How They Work |
|---|---|
| Plan the structure and content of your speech with the needs of your audience in mind. | How can you make the question or problem you are addressing come alive for your audience? What background information or defined terms does your audience need? What kinds of evidence will you need to support your argument? What objections will your listeners be apt to raise? How can you motivate action? |
| Create a complete-sentence outline of your argument; use parallel structures, coordination, and subordination to clarify relationships among ideas. | See Skill 12.2 for advice about different kinds of outlines, particularly the advantage of complete-sentence outlines, which state meanings rather than topics. Since you won't be writing out the complete argument in prose, this outline will be the written frame for your speech. |
| Build into your outline places for explicit signposting to help the audience follow your speech. | Indicate where you are in your speech: "My second reason is that...." "As I stated earlier...." |
| Early on, practice saying your speech in a normally paced speaking voice to determine its length. | Often speeches can cover much less ground than a written argument. By timing the speech when it is still in its rough-draft stage, you will know whether you must cut or add material. |

Once you have outlined your speech, you can design slides that follow the design principles that we explain in Skill 13.2 for maximizing the impact of both the auditory and visual channels of your presentation. Common mistakes are to make too many slides, to overdesign them, or to become enamored with special effects rather than with the ideas in the speech. Particularly avoid text-heavy slides that include passages cut and pasted from a print text. Unlike an image, which is apprehended almost instantaneously in the visual processing part of our brains, a text-heavy slide must be read to be understood. Text-heavy slides force the audience to multitask, moving back and forth between trying to listen to the speech and trying to read the slide. The only way to bring the speaker's words and the slide into sync is for the speaker to read the slide directly (boring!).

Another design flaw is to leave your audience confused about the slide's focus or purpose—its nutshell assertion or take-away point. This problem is particularly common with PowerPoint because its software encourages users to create short topic phrases for titles rather than points. This topic/subtopic approach violates the meaning-making principle that we emphasize in Chapter 12 (Skill 12.2), where we advocate complete sentence outlines rather than topic outlines. Meanings are expressed in predicates and thus require complete sentences. In Skill 12.2, we

The meaning-making function of complete sentence outlines can be found on pp. 294–298.

illustrated this distinction in the contrast between "Peanut butter" (a phrase) and "Peanut butter is nutritious" (an assertion requiring support). From this meaning-making perspective, PowerPoint's focus on topic phrases for titles often leads to slides that don't assert a nutshell point.

One solution to the problem of topic-only titles, advocated by some rhetoricians, is to make the slide's title a complete sentence rather than a phrase. Examples of assertion titles versus topic titles are shown in the following chart:

| Slide Title as Topic | Slide Title as a Claim or Assertion |
| --- | --- |
| Gender Stereotypes in Children's Birthday Cards | Children's birthday cards revealed extensive gender stereotyping. |
| Wage Comparison: CEO Versus Worker | Gap between CEO salaries and average worker salaries is increasing rapidly. |

Of course, the designer could choose to articulate the slide's point in the speech itself rather than stating it on the slide as a complete sentence title. Sometimes, too, a title can make an assertion or claim without having to be grammatically complete. The key is to make sure that the audience knows what the slide's take-away point is. (Using a grammatically complete sentence for the title is particularly helpful if you want the slide to stand on its own as an independent multimodal argument.)

Here are some additional strategies for creating your visual aids.

## Strategies for Creating Effective Visual Aids for a Presentation

| Strategies | Rationales and Explanations of How They Work |
| --- | --- |
| Limit the number of words per slide; avoid blocks of linear text. | Linear text must be read—a slow process different from the almost instantaneous apprehension of an image. Viewers can't listen to your speech and read the text on the screen simultaneously. |
| Use slides to enhance the points in your speech—either images or very limited number of words. | Effective slides reinforce the aural speech by being apprehended in a visual channel. The meaningful assertion made by the slide should be quickly apparent. |
| Use visual features that enhance meaning; don't use cutesy bells and whistles. | PowerPoint has special effects like exploding figures, words circling into position, and little buses wheeling across the screen. Using these special effects can distract the audience from the content of your speech, creating the *ethos* of a technical whiz rather than a serious presenter of a proposal. |

| Strategies | Rationales and Explanations of How They Work |
|---|---|
| Create your speech first and then design slides to drive home major points. Do not use slides simply to reproduce your speech outline. | If you convert your outline into slides, you simply replicate rather than enhance the speech. Use images (rather than words) wherever possible. Think visually. |
| Consider using complete sentences for the titles of your slides, particularly if you want them to stand alone as meaning-making arguments. | Complete sentence titles highlight each slide's meaningful point (see Skill 13.2). Note: To have enough room for a complete sentence, you'll need to change the default PowerPoint title font to make room for a complete sentence. It is OK to have a two-line title. |
| Limit the number of visual aids you use. | Communication experts advise no more than one visual aid per minute of presentation. In many parts of the speech, the screen can be blank. |

Once you have outlined your speech and developed your slides, you need to practice delivering your speech. You can stand before a mirror, make a video of a practice session, or practice in front of friends until you are confident about the length of your speech and your ability to deliver it with minimal prompting from your notes. In addition, you should think about these important strategies for successful speechmaking.

## Strategies for Successfully Delivering a Speech

| Strategies | What to Do |
|---|---|
| Control your volume and pace. | • Speak loudly enough to be heard and add emphasis by speaking louder or softer.<br>• Speed up to get through details quickly and slow down for points you want to stress. |
| Use posture and gestures to your advantage. | • Stand straight and tall to help your breathing and projection.<br>• Use natural gestures or a few carefully planned ones.<br>• Avoid distracting or nervous gestures. |
| Maintain eye contact with your audience and look at every member of your audience. | • Know your speech well enough that you can look at your audience, not read your note cards.<br>• Make steady and even eye contact with your audience. |

*(continued)*

| Strategies | What to Do |
|---|---|
| Show enthusiasm and passion for the issue of your speech. | • Make your audience care about your issue through your own enthusiasm.<br>• Show your audience that your issue is important by the energy you put into your delivery.<br>• Also, use your enthusiasm to help control nervousness. |
| Use your slides effectively; turn off the screen if you aren't currently referring to a slide. | • Click on slides at the appropriate time.<br>• Give slides air time. Talking through images and graphs is effective. Reading long text passages is not. |
| Overcome nervousness by controlling your hands, your breathing, and the volume of your voice. | • Take deep breaths and speak slightly louder than usual to help your body relax.<br>• Use a podium if one is available. |

## Scripted Speech (Podcasts, Video Voiceovers)

When you speak before a live audience, it is best to speak extemporaneously. However, if you are preparing a podcast or the voiceover on a video, you can read from a completed script. Give your script a tone and voice appropriate for your audience and purpose. For example, part of the drafting/revising process is to read your emerging text aloud to make sure the script sounds effective out loud, something you wouldn't necessarily do for a print-only paper. Features that might not be appropriate in an academic paper—slang, street language, or less-than-formal grammar—might be just what you need in your script. You'll also need to practice reading the script so that it sounds spontaneous and natural. If your script includes dialogue, you may need to practice adopting different voices. The most common problems to avoid include reading too rapidly, not enunciating clearly, or swallowing words at the ends of sentences. If you use music in the podcast or video, make sure that it is appropriate to the content of the words and sets an appropriate mood. Don't let the music muffle or overwhelm the words.

## Videos

Videos offer a range of production options. At the simplest level, you could make a video of a PowerPoint presentation (yours or a friend's) creating a multimodal text similar to a TED talk or a professor's recorded lecture. You could also make a video that was essentially a screencast of still photos enhanced with background music and voice-over narration. You could even splice in recorded interview segments, captions, or text. At a more complex level, you could make a short documentary or create your own original film with actors and a script. Such productions need to be carefully designed and executed, beginning with preproduction storyboarding, moving through production (where filmmakers often shoot a surprisingly high excess of footage), and concluding with purposeful postproduction editing.

As an example of a simple original production, one of our students, Alex Mullen, was selected to produce a short video to introduce the master of ceremonies at a student award ceremony. He wanted to parody the genre of the humorous "introduction" videos—often used at the Academy Awards or the Grammies—which take the audience backstage to see the Master or Mistress of Ceremonies getting ready. Alex wanted to show the MC getting his official invitation letter, putting on his tux, stopping to talk with friends in a dorm room on his way to the ceremony, forgetting the time, and then racing across campus in goofy circles, arriving breathless at the last moment. Selected scenes from Alex's storyboard are shown in Figure 13.3, and a corresponding screen shot from the video is shown

**FIGURE 13.3** Scenes from Alex's Storyboard

**FIGURE 13.4** Still Shot of MC Putting on Tux

For discussion
of camera shots
and angles see
Chapter 4
(pp. 68–70)
and Chapter 7
(pp. 148–152).

in Figure 13.4. The storyboard, which had more than twenty frames, suggests the kind of advance planning that Alex put into his three-minute video.

    If you are contemplating making a video, the following strategies will help guide your thinking.

## Strategies for Creating an Effective Video

| Strategy | What to Do |
|---|---|
| **Remember the Rhetorical Situation:** As always, consider your purpose and audience. What effect do you want your video to have on your targeted audience? | Articulating your rhetorical goal will help you plan appeals to *logos, ethos,* and *pathos* and decide your own role. Do you wish to appear in the video or stay behind the scenes? In some cases, your rhetorical purpose might call for multiple points of view; in other cases your goal is to move your audience toward one view. If your video has a persuasive aim, are you targeting opposing/neutral audiences or appealing to those who already hold your view? |
| **Use a Storyboard Approach:** Think about the text in terms of scenes. | Storyboards are like graphic organizers that help you see your video's big picture scene by scene. Organize the video according to individual shots the same way you might use paragraphs or sections in a written text. Also consider ways to transition, using strategies such as zooming, fading, or rapid cuts to a different camera angle. Many narratives seen in literary writing are analogous to film strategies including flashbacks and sequences of scenes. |

| Strategy | What to Do |
|---|---|
| ***Start with Visual Elements First:*** The text will be dominated by images. | Audiences of video texts expect to be engaged visually at all times. Avoid using monotonous or uninteresting visuals as filler for stretches of voice-over. Use camera angles to create a narrative "story." Consider particularly the use of establishing shots (medium or long shots), point-of-view shots through a character's eyes, and reaction shots (close-ups of faces). Consider also creative juxtapositions of image with graphics or words. |
| ***Incorporate Effective Verbal and Written Text:*** Use graphic and sound design to emphasize main points. | Video technology allows for more versatile text options than just about any other multimodal form. With the use of graphic design and sound options such as voice-overs and captions, the intended rhetorical impact of images can be underscored with written and spoken words to emphasize main points and highlight important information. Just as in other multimodal texts, be sure to present assertions rather than topics by using complete sentences whenever possible. |
| ***Use Musical Elements and Other Sound Options to Emphasize the Effect:*** As appropriate, underscore important rhetorical goals with auditory effects. | Sound can have a subtle but powerful impact on the viewers of a video text. Effective use of music, background sounds (street noise, café buzz, bird chirps, sudden silence), and qualities of voice (accent, pitch, emotional emphasis) can enhance the key ideas of your video. In shooting scenes, consider the placement of microphones as well as cameras. |

# A RHETORICAL GUIDE TO RESEARCH

These stills from the documentary *Gasland* by Josh Fox (2010) depict a homeowner demonstrating the flow of methane from his water faucet as a result of natural gas wells near his home. This anti-fracking film argues that the process of hydraulic fracturing (commonly called fracking) has not been sufficiently regulated to ensure safety to homeowners and their water supplies. The alarming images of dangerous gas issuing from water faucets elicit a powerful emotional response against fracking. The film builds its authority and credibility by including a number of images like these and interviews with residents around the country, showing fracking's contamination of groundwater with gas and chemicals. We return to the controversy surrounding fracking in the "For Writing and Discussion" exercise found on pages 336–337.

# 14 USING SOURCES

**WHAT YOU WILL LEARN**

**14.1** Evaluate sources for reliability, credibility, angle of vision, and degree of advocacy.

**14.2** Know when and how to use summary, paraphrase, and quotation.

**14.3** Use attributive tags to distinguish your ideas from a source's.

**14.4** Avoid plagiarism by following academic conventions for ethical use of sources.

Our goal in Part 4 is to explain the skills you'll need for successful college research papers. We'll show you how to apply your growing knowledge of rhetoric and composition to research tasks by explaining how to evaluate research sources and use them properly in your own writing.

## SKILL 14.1 Evaluate sources for reliability, credibility, angle of vision, and degree of advocacy.

When you read sources for your research project, you need to evaluate them as you go along. As you read each potential source, ask yourself questions about the author's reliability, credibility, angle of vision, and degree of advocacy.

### Reliability

"Reliability" refers to the accuracy of factual data in a source. If you check a writer's "facts" against other sources, do you find that the facts are correct? Does the writer distort facts, take them out of context, or otherwise use them unreasonably? In some controversies, key data are highly disputed—for example, the frequency of date rape or the risk factors for many diseases. A reliable writer acknowledges these controversies and doesn't treat disputed data as fact. Furthermore, if you check out the sources used by a reliable writer, they'll reveal accurate and careful research—respected primary sources rather than hearsay or secondhand reports. Journalists of reputable newspapers (not tabloids) pride themselves on meticulously checking out their facts, as do editors of serious popular magazines. Editing is often minimal for Web sources, however, and they can be notoriously unreliable. As you gain knowledge of your research question, you'll develop a good ear for writers who play fast and loose with data.

## Credibility

"Credibility" is similar to "reliability" but is based on internal rather than external factors. It refers to the reader's trust in the writer's honesty, goodwill, and trustworthiness and is apparent in the writer's tone, reasonableness, fairness in summarizing opposing views, and respect for different perspectives. Audiences differ in how much credibility they will grant to certain authors. Nevertheless, a writer can achieve a reputation for credibility, even among bitter political opponents, by applying to issues a sense of moral courage, integrity, and consistency of principle.

"Credibility" is synonymous with the classical term *ethos*. See pp. 57–58.

## Angle of Vision and Political Stance

By "angle of vision," we mean the way that a piece of writing is shaped by the underlying values, assumptions, and beliefs of its author, resulting in a text that reflects a certain perspective, worldview, or belief system. Of paramount importance are the underlying values or beliefs that the writer assumes his or her readers will share. You can get useful clues about a writer's angle of vision and intended audience by doing some quick research into the politics and reputation of the author on the Internet or by analyzing the genre, market niche, and political reputation of the publication in which the material appears.

Angle of vision is discussed in detail in Chapter 3, Concept 8. See also Chapter 5, pp. 97–98, which shows how analyzing angle of vision helps you read a text with and against the grain.

**Determining Political Stance**   Your awareness of angle of vision and political stance is especially important if you are doing research on contemporary cultural or political issues. In Table 14.1, we have categorized some well-known political commentators, publications, policy research institutes (commonly known as *think tanks*), and blogs across the political spectrum from left/liberal to right/conservative.

Although the terms *liberal* and *conservative* or *left* and *right* often have fuzzy meanings, they provide convenient shorthand for signaling a person's overall views about the proper role of government in relation to the economy and

**TABLE 14.1   Angles of Vision in U.S. Media and Think Tanks: A Sampling Across the Political Spectrum[1]**

### Commentators

| Left | Left Center | Center | Right Center | Right |
|---|---|---|---|---|
| Barbara Ehrenreich | E. J. Dionne | David Ignatius | David Brooks | Charles |
| Bob Herbert | Leonard Pitts | Thomas Friedman | Peggy Noonan | Krauthammer |
| Michael Moore | Eugene Robinson | Kathleen Hall | Jonah Goldberg | Cal Thomas |
| (film-maker) | Nicholas Kristof | Jamieson | Andrew Sullivan | Glenn Beck |
| Bill Moyers | Maureen Dowd | Kevin Phillips | George Will | (radio/TV) |
| (television) | Mark Shields | David Broder | Ruben Navarrette, Jr. | Rush Limbaugh |
| Paul Krugman | Frank Rich | William Saletan | | (radio/TV) |
| Thom Hartman | | Mary Sanchez | | Bill O'Reilly |
| (radio) | | | | (radio/TV) |
| Rachel Maddow | | | | Kathleen Parker |
| (radio) | | | | Thomas Sowell |

*(continued)*

**TABLE 14.1** *continued*

## Newspapers and Magazines[2]

| Left/Liberal | Center | Right/Conservative |
|---|---|---|
| *The American Prospect* | *Atlantic Monthly* | *American Spectator* |
| *Harper's* | *Business Week* | *Fortune* |
| *Los Angeles Times* | *Commentary* | *National Review* |
| *Mother Jones* | *Commonweal* | *Reader's Digest* |
| *The Nation* | *Foreign Affairs* | *Reason* |
| *New York Times* | *New Republic* | *Wall Street Journal* |
| *New Yorker* | *Slate* | *Washington Times* |
| *Salon* | *Washington Post* | *Weekly Standard* |
| *Sojourners* | | |

## Blogs

| Liberal/Left | Center | Right/Conservative |
|---|---|---|
| americablog.com | donklephant.com | watchingwashington.blogspot.com |
| atrios.blogspot.com | newmoderate.blogspot.com | conservativeblogger.com |
| crooksandliars.com | politics-central.blogspot.com | drudgereport.com |
| dailykos.com | rantingbaldhippie.com | instapundit.com |
| digbysblog.blogspot.com | stevesilver.net | littlegreenfootballs.com |
| firedoglake.com | themoderatevoice.com | michellemalkin.com |
| huffingtonpost.com | washingtonindependent.com | polipundit.com |
| mediamatters.com | | powerlineblog.com |
| talkingpointsmemo.com | | sistertoldjah.com |
| wonkette.com | | redstate.com |
| | | townhall.com |

## Think Tanks

| Left/Liberal | Center | Right/Conservative |
|---|---|---|
| Center for American Progress | The Brookings Institution | American Enterprise Institute |
| Center for Media and | Carnegie Endowment for | Cato Institute (Libertarian) |
| Democracy (sponsors | International Peace | Center for Strategic and |
| Disinfopedia.org) | Council on Foreign Relations | International Studies |
| Institute for Policy Studies | Jamestown Foundation | Heritage Foundation |
| Open Society Institute (Soros | National Bureau of Economic | (sponsors Townhall.com) |
| Foundation) | Research | Project for the New American |
| Progressive Policy Institute | | Century |
| Urban Institute | | |

[1]*For further information about the political leanings of publications or think tanks, ask your librarian about* Gale Directory of Publications and Broadcast Media *or* NIRA World Directory of Think Tanks.

[2]*Newspapers are categorized according to positions they take on their editorial page; any reputable newspaper strives for objectivity in news reporting and includes a variety of views on its op-ed pages. Magazines do not claim and are not expected to present similar breadth and objectivity.*

social values. Liberals, tending to sympathize with those potentially harmed by unfettered free markets (workers, consumers, plaintiffs, endangered species), are typically comfortable with government regulation of economic matters while conservatives, who tend to sympathize with business interests, typically assert faith in free markets and favor a limited regulatory role for government. On social issues, conservatives tend to espouse traditional family values and advocate laws that would maintain these values (for example, promoting a Constitutional amendment limiting marriage to a bond between a man and a woman). Liberals, on the other hand, tend to espouse individual choice regarding marital partnerships and a wide range of other issues. Some persons identify themselves as economic conservatives but social liberals; others side with workers' interests on economic issues but are conservative on social issues.

Finally, many persons regard themselves as "centrists." In Table 14.1 the column labeled "Center" includes commentators who seek out common ground between the left and the right and who often believe that the best civic decisions are compromises between opposing views. Likewise, centrist publications and institutes often approach issues from multiple points of view, looking for the most workable solutions.

## Degree of Advocacy

By "degree of advocacy" we mean the extent to which an author unabashedly takes a persuasive stance on a contested position as opposed to adopting a more neutral, objective, or exploratory stance. For example, publications affiliated with advocacy organizations (the Sierra Club, the National Rifle Association) will have a clear editorial bias. When a writer has an ax to grind, you need to weigh carefully the writer's selection of evidence, interpretation of data, and fairness to opposing views. Although no one can be completely neutral, it is always useful to seek out authors who offer a balanced assessment of the evidence. Evidence from a more detached and neutral writer may be more trusted by your readers than the arguments of a committed advocate. For example, if you want to persuade corporate executives on the dangers of global warming, evidence from scholarly journals may be more persuasive than evidence from an environmentalist Web site or from a freelance writer for a leftist popular magazine such as *Mother Jones*.

## Criteria for Evaluating a Web Source

When you evaluate a Web source, we suggest that you ask five different kinds of questions about the site in which the source appeared, as shown in Table 14.2. These questions, developed by scholars and librarians as points to consider when you are evaluating Web sites, will help you determine the usefulness of a site or source for your own purposes.

As a researcher, the first question you should ask about a potentially useful Web source should be, Who placed this piece on the Web and why? You can begin answering this question by analyzing the site's home page, where you will often find navigational buttons linking to "Mission," "About Us," or other identifying information about the site's sponsors. You can also get hints about the site's purpose by asking, What kind of Web site is it? Different kinds of Web sites have different purposes. You should be conscious of the purpose of the site, often revealed by the domain identifier, such as .com or .org

| TABLE 14.2 | **Criteria for Evaluating Web Sites** |
|---|---|
| **Criteria** | **Questions to Ask** |
| 1. Authority | • Is the document author or site sponsor clearly identified?<br>• Does the site identify the occupation, position, education, experience, or other credentials of the author?<br>• Does the home page or a clear link from the home page reveal the author's or sponsor's motivation for establishing the site?<br>• Does the site provide contact information for the author or sponsor such as an e-mail or organization address? |
| 2. Objectivity or Clear Disclosure of Advocacy | • Is the site's purpose clear (for example, to inform, entertain, or persuade)?<br>• Is the site explicit about declaring its point of view?<br>• Does the site indicate whether the author is affiliated with a specific organization, institution, or association?<br>• Does the site indicate whether it is directed toward a specific audience? |
| 3. Coverage | • Are the topics covered by the site clear?<br>• Does the site exhibit a suitable depth and comprehensiveness for its purpose?<br>• Is sufficient evidence provided to support the ideas and opinions presented? |
| 4. Accuracy | • Are the sources of information stated?<br>• Do the facts appear to be accurate?<br>• Can you verify this information by comparing this source with other sources in the field? |
| 5. Currency | • Are dates included in the Web site?<br>• Do the dates apply to the material itself, to its placement on the Web, or to the time the site was last revised and updated?<br>• Is the information current, or at least still relevant, for the site's purpose? For your purpose? |

**FOR WRITING AND DISCUSSION**

## Analyzing the Rhetorical Elements of Fracking Web Pages

Working in small groups or as a whole class, try to reach consensus answers to the following questions about how Web sites seek to draw in readers. Use Figures 14.1 and 14.2 as well as other pro-fracking and anti-fracking sites that you discover through Web searches.

1. What is your initial impression of the images, information, and layout of the Web pages for the organizations you have found? How do these Web pages frame the fracking issue? In the specific case of Energy from Shale (Figure 14.1) and Americans Against Fracking (Figure 14.2), how are the images of citizen involvement in the fracking debate depicted differently? (For a site with a different approach, investigate New Yorkers Against Fracking.)

2. How do various fracking Web sites use multimodal arguments (combinations of images and text) to make their case? What do you see as the rhetorical advantages of using photographs, including photos of real people, versus using schematic drawings or graphics? What rhetorical effect do you think the Web page designers were hoping to achieve for each of the sites you have observed?

3. How do these Web pages use *logos, ethos,* and *pathos* to sway readers toward their point of view?

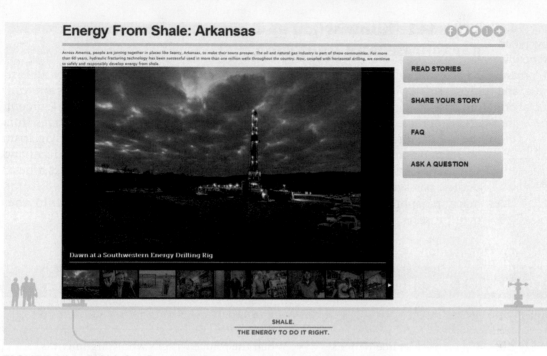

**FIGURE 14.1**  A Web Site Portraying Fracking Positively (Energy from Shale)

**FIGURE 14.2**  A Web Site Portraying Fracking Negatively (from Americans Against Fracking)

**14.2**
Know when
and how to
use summary,
paraphrase, and
quotation.

## SKILL 14.2 **Know when and how to use summary, paraphrase, and quotation.**

As a research writer, you need to incorporate sources gracefully into your own prose so that you stay focused on your own argument. Depending on your purpose, you might (1) summarize all or part of a source author's argument, (2) paraphrase a relevant portion of a source, or (3) quote small passages from the source directly. Whenever you use a source, you need to avoid plagiarism by referencing the source with an in-text citation, by putting paraphrases and summaries entirely in your own words, and by placing quotation marks around quoted passages. The following strategies chart gives you an overview of summary, paraphrase, and quotation as ways of incorporating sources into your own prose.

For an explanation of avoiding plagiarism in academic writing, see Skill 14.4. For in-text citations, see Chapter 15.

### Strategies for Incorporating Sources into Your Own Prose

| Strategies | What to Do | When to Use These Strategies |
|---|---|---|
| Summarize the source. | Condense a source writer's argument by keeping main ideas and omitting details (see Chapter 5, pp. 88–89 and 102–105). | • When the source writer's whole argument is relevant to your purpose<br>• When the source writer presents an alternative or opposing view that you want to push against<br>• When the source writer's argument can be used in support of your own |
| Paraphrase the source. | Reproduce an idea from a source writer but translate the idea entirely into your own words; a paraphrase should be approximately the same length as the original. | • When you want to incorporate factual information from a source or to use one specific idea from a source<br>• When the source passage is overly complex or technical for your targeted audience<br>• When you want to incorporate a source's point in your own voice without interrupting the flow of your argument |
| Quote short passages from the source using quotation marks. | Work brief quotations from the source smoothly into the grammar of your own sentences. | • When you need testimony from an authority (state the authority's credentials in an attributive tag—see Skill 14.3)<br>• In summaries, when you want to reproduce a source's voice, particularly if the language is striking or memorable<br>• In lieu of paraphrase when the source language is memorable |

| Strategies | What to Do | When to Use These Strategies |
|---|---|---|
| Quote long passages from the source using the block method. | Results in a page with noticeably lengthy block quotations | • When you intend to analyze or critique the quotation—the quotation is followed by your detailed analysis of its ideas or rhetorical features<br>• When the flavor and language of testimonial evidence is important |

With practice, you'll be able to use all these strategies smoothly and effectively.

## Summarizing

Detailed instructions on how to write a summary of an article and incorporate it into your own prose are provided in Chapter 5, "Reading Rhetorically" (pp. 88–90 and 102–105). Summaries can be as short as a single sentence or as long as a paragraph. Make the summary as concise as possible so that you don't distract the reader from your own argument.

## Paraphrasing

Unlike a summary, which is a condensation of a source's whole argument, a **paraphrase** translates a short passage from a source's words into the writer's own words. Writers often choose to paraphrase when the details of a source passage are particularly important or when the source is overly technical and needs to be simplified for the intended audience. When you paraphrase, be careful to avoid reproducing the original writer's grammatical structure and syntax. If you mirror the original sentence structure while replacing occasional words with synonyms or small structural changes, you will be doing what composition specialists call "**patchwriting**"—that is, patching some of your language into someone else's writing.* Patchwriting is a form of academic dishonesty because you aren't fully composing your own sentences and thus misrepresent both your own work and that of the source writer. An acceptable paraphrase needs to be entirely in your own words. To understand patchwriting more fully, track the differences between unacceptable patchwriting and acceptable paraphrase in the following examples.

ORIGINAL

• The evidence is "strong " that vegetarians have (a) a lower risk of becoming alcoholic, constipated, or obese and (b) a lower risk of developing lung cancer.
• The evidence is "good " that vegetarians have a lower risk of developing adult-onset diabetes mellitus, coronary artery disease, hypertension, and gallstones.

*We are indebted to the work of Rebecca Moore Howard and others who have led composition researchers to reexamine the use of sources and plagiarism from a cultural and rhetorical perspective. See especially Rebecca Moore Howard, *Standing in the Shadow of Giants: Plagiarists, Authors, Collaborators*. Stamford, CT: Ablex Pub., 1999.

UNACCEPTABLE PATCHWRITING

*Identification of source*

*Note phrases taken word for word from original.*

According to the American Council on Science and Health, there is strong evidence that vegetarians have a lower risk of becoming alcoholic, constipated, or obese. The evidence is also strong that they have a lower risk of lung cancer. The evidence is good that vegetarians are less apt to develop adult-onset diabetes, coronary artery disease, hypertension, or gallstones.

ACCEPTABLE PARAPHRASE

*Identification of source*

*Doesn't follow original sentence structure*

*Quotes "strong" and "good" to indicate distinction made in original*

The Council summarizes "strong" evidence from the scientific literature showing that vegetarians have reduced risk of lung cancer, obesity, constipation, and alcoholism. The council also cites "good" evidence that they have a reduced risk of adult-onset diabetes, high blood pressure, gallstones, or hardening of the arteries.

Both the patchwriting example and the acceptable paraphrase reproduce the same ideas as the original in approximately the same number of words. But the writer of the acceptable paraphrase has been more careful to change the sentence structure substantially and not copy exact phrases. In contrast, the patchwritten version contains longer strings of borrowed language without quotation marks.

Among novice writers, the ease of copying Web sources can particularly lead to patchwriting. You may be tempted to copy and paste a Web-based passage into your own draft and then revise it slightly by changing some of the words. Such patchwriting won't occur if you write in your own voice—that is, if you convert information from a source into your own words in order to make your own argument.

When you first practice paraphrasing, try paraphrasing a passage twice to avoid patchwriting:

- The first time, read the passage carefully and put it into your own words, looking at the source as little as possible.
- The second time, paraphrase your own paraphrase. Then recheck your final version against the original to make sure you have eliminated similar sentence structures or word-for-word strings.

We'll return to the problem of patchwriting in our discussion of plagiarism (Skill 14.4).

**Quoting**  Besides summary and paraphrase, writers often choose to quote directly in order to give the reader the flavor and style of the source author's prose or to make a memorable point in the source author's own voice. Be careful not to quote a passage that you don't fully understand. (Sometimes novice writers quote a passage because it sounds impressive.) When you quote, you must reproduce the source author's original words exactly without change, unless you indicate changes with ellipses or brackets. Also be careful to represent the author's intention and meaning fairly; don't change the author's meaning by taking quotations out of context.

# SKILL 14.3   Use attributive tags to distinguish your ideas from a source's.

Whenever you use sources in your writing, you need to signal to your reader which words and ideas come from your source and which are your own. There are generally two ways of doing so:

- ***State source author's name in an attributive tag.*** You can identify the source by using a short phrase (called an **attributive tag** or sometimes a **signal phrase** or **signal tag**) such as "according to the American Council on Science and Health, " "Kent Ansen says, " "in Ansen's view, " and so on. In the humanities, the source author's full name is commonly used the first time the author is mentioned. If the tag refers to a specific passage or quotation in the source, then a page number is placed in parentheses at the end of the quotation as shown in the second sentence below.

> According to Kent Ansen, a year of public service should be required of all American young adults.

*Attributive tag*

> Ansen explains that "mandated national service could be built upon the model of AmeriCorps" (406).

*Attributive tag*

Page number of quotation

- ***State source author's name in a parenthetical citation.*** You can identify a source by placing the author's name in parentheses at the end of the material taken from the source (called a **parenthetical citation**).

> A year of public service should be required of all American young adults (Ansen).

*Source identified in parentheses*

> "Mandated national service could be built upon the model of AmeriCorps" (Ansen 406).

Page number of quotation

Of these two methods, attributive tags are generally preferred, especially when you are writing for general rather than specialist audiences. The attributive tag method has three advantages:

- It signals where borrowed material starts and ends.
- It avoids ambiguities about what is "fact" versus what is filtered through a source's angle of vision.
- It allows the writer to frame the borrowed material rhetorically.

Let's look at each of these in turn.

## Attributive Tags Mark Where Source Material Starts and Ends

The parenthetical method requires readers to wait until the end of the writer's use of source material before the source is identified. Attributive tags, in contrast, identify the source from the moment it is first used. Here is an example of a writer's summary of an article from the American Council on Science and Health, in which we have highlighted the attributive tags. Note the frequency with which the writer informs the reader that this material comes from the Council.

### USE OF ATTRIBUTIVE TAGS IN WRITER 2'S SUMMARY

Not only will a vegetarian diet help stop cruelty to animals, but it is also good for your health. According to the American Council on Science and Health, vegetarians have longer life expectancy than nonvegetarians and suffer from fewer chronic diseases. The Council cites "strong" evidence from the scientific literature showing that vegetarians have reduced risk of lung cancer, obesity, constipation, and alcoholism. They also cite "good" evidence that they have a reduced risk of adult-onset diabetes, high blood pressure, gallstones, or hardening of the arteries....

Here the attributive tags signal the use of the Council's ideas throughout the summary. The reader is never confused about which words and ideas come from the original article.

## Attributive Tags Avoid Ambiguities That Can Arise with Parenthetical Citations

Not only does the parenthetical method fail to mark where the source material begins, it also tends to imply that the source material is a "fact " rather than the view of the source author. In contrast, attributive tags always call attention to the source's angle of vision. Note this ambiguity in the following passage, where parenthetical citations are used without attributive tags:

### AMBIGUOUS ATTRIBUTIONS

There are many arguments in favor of preserving old-growth forests. First, it is simply unnecessary to log these forests to supply the world's lumber. We have plenty of new-growth forest from which lumber can be taken (Sagoff 89–90). Recently there have been major reforestation efforts all over the United States, and it is common practice now for loggers to replant every tree that is harvested. These new-growth forests, combined with extensive planting of tree farms, provide more than enough wood for the world's needs. Tree farms alone can supply the world's demand for industrial lumber (Sedjo 90).

When confronted with this passage, skeptical readers might ask, "Who are Sagoff and Sedjo? I've never heard of them." It is also difficult to tell how much of the passage is the writer's own argument and how much is borrowed from Sagoff and Sedjo. Is this whole passage a paraphrase? Finally, the writer tends to treat Sagoff's and Sedjo's assertions as uncontested facts rather than as professional opinions. Compare the preceding version with this one, in which attributive tags are added:

**CLEAR ATTRIBUTION**

There are many arguments in favor of preserving old-growth forests. First, it is simply unnecessary to log these forests to supply the world's lumber. According to environmentalist Carl Sagoff, we have plenty of new-growth forest from which lumber can be taken (89–90). Recently there have been major reforestation efforts all over the United States, and it is common practice now for loggers to replant every tree that is harvested. These new-growth forests, combined with extensive planting of tree farms, provide more than enough wood for the world's needs. According to forestry expert Robert Sedjo, tree farms alone can supply the world's demand for industrial lumber (90).

We can now see that most of the paragraph is the writer's own argument, into which she has inserted the expert testimony of Sagoff and Sedjo, whose views are treated not as indisputable facts but as the opinions of authorities in this field.

## Attributive Tags Frame the Source Material Rhetorically

When you introduce a source for the first time, you can use the attributive tag not only to introduce the source but also to shape your readers's attitudes toward the source. In the previous example, the writer wants readers to respect Sagoff and Sedjo, so she identifies Sagoff as an "environmentalist" and Sedjo as a "forestry expert." If the writer favored logging old-growth forests and supported the logging industry's desire to create more jobs, she might have used different tags: "Carl Sagoff, an outspoken advocate for spotted owls over people," or "Robert Sedjo, a forester with limited knowledge of world lumber markets."

When you compose an initial tag, you can add to it any combination of the following kinds of information, depending on your purpose, your audience's values, and your sense of what the audience already knows or doesn't know about the source:

| Strategies for Modifying Attributive Tags to Shape Reader Response | |
| --- | --- |
| **Add to Attributive Tags** | **Examples** |
| Author's credentials or relevant specialty (enhances credibility) | Civil engineer David Rockwood, a noted authority on stream flow in rivers |
| Author's lack of credentials (decreases credibility) | City Council member Dilbert Weasel, a local politician with no expertise in international affairs |

*(continued)*

| Add to Attributive Tags | Examples |
|---|---|
| Author's political or social views | Left-wing columnist Alexander Cockburn [has negative feeling]; Alexander Cockburn, a longtime champion of labor [has positive feeling] |
| Title of source if it provides context | In her book *Fasting Girls: The History of Anorexia Nervosa*, Joan Jacobs Brumberg shows that [establishes credentials for comments on eating disorders] |
| Publisher of source if it adds prestige or otherwise shapes audience response | Dr. Carl Patrona, in an article published in the prestigious *New England Journal of Medicine* |
| Historical or cultural information about a source that provides context or background | In his 1960s book popularizing the hippie movement, Charles Reich claims that |
| Indication of source's purpose or angle of vision | Feminist author Naomi Wolfe, writing a blistering attack on the beauty industry, argues that |

Our point here is that you can use attributive tags rhetorically to help your readers understand the significance and context of a source when you first introduce it and to guide your readers' attitudes toward the source.

---

**FOR WRITING AND DISCUSSION**

## Evaluating Different Ways to Use and Cite a Source

What follow are four different ways that a writer can use the same passage from a source to support a point about the greenhouse effect. Working in groups or as a whole class, rank the four methods from "most effective " to "least effective. " Assume that you are writing a researched argument addressed to your college classmates.

1. ***Quotation with parenthetical citation*** The greenhouse effect will have a devastating effect on the earth's environment: "Potential impacts include increased mortality and illness due to heat stress and worsened air pollution, as in the 1995 Chicago heat wave that killed hundreds of people. … Infants, children and other vulnerable populations—especially in already-stressed regions of the world—would likely suffer disproportionately from these impacts " (Hall 19).

2. ***Quotation with attributive tag*** The greenhouse effect will have a devastating effect on the earth's environment. David C. Hall, president of Physicians for Social Responsibility, claims the following: "Potential impacts include increased mortality and illness due to heat stress and worsened air pollution, as in the 1995 Chicago heat wave that killed hundreds

of people. ... Infants, children and other vulnerable populations—especially in already-stressed regions of the world—would likely suffer disproportionately from these impacts " (19).

3. ***Paraphrase with parenthetical citation*** The greenhouse effect will have a devastating effect on the earth's environment. One of the most frightening effects is the threat of diseases stemming from increased air pollution and heat stress. Infants and children would be most at risk (Hall 19).

4. ***Paraphrase with attributive tag*** The greenhouse effect will have a devastating effect on the earth's environment. One of the most frightening effects, according to David C. Hall, president of Physicians for Social Responsibility, is the threat of diseases stemming from increased air pollution and heat stress. Infants and Children would be most at risk (19).

# SKILL 14.4   Avoid plagiarism by following academic conventions for ethical use of sources.

In the next chapter, we proceed to the nuts and bolts of citing and documenting sources—a skill that will enhance your *ethos* as a skilled researcher and as a person of integrity. Unethical use of sources—called **plagiarism**—is a major concern not only for writing teachers but for teachers in all disciplines. To combat plagiarism, many instructors across the curriculum use plagiarism-detection software like turnitin.com. Their purpose, of course, is to discourage students from cheating. But sometimes students who have no intention of cheating can fall into producing papers that look like cheating. That is, they produce papers that might be accused of plagiarism even though the students had no intention of deceiving their readers.* Our goal in this section is to explain the concept of plagiarism more fully and to sum up the strategies needed to avoid it.

## Why Some Kinds of Plagiarism May Occur Unwittingly

To understand how unwitting plagiarism might occur, consider Table 14.2, where the middle column—"Misuse of Sources"—shows common mistakes of novice writers. Everyone agrees that the behaviors in the "Fraud" column constitute deliberate cheating and deserve appropriate punishment. Everyone also agrees that good scholarly work meets the criteria in the "Ethical Use of Sources" column. Novice researchers, however, may find themselves unwittingly in the middle column until they learn the academic community's conventions for using research sources.

You might appreciate these conventions more fully if you recognize how they have evolved from Western notions of intellectual property and patent law associated with the rise of modern science in the seventeenth and eighteenth centuries. A person not only could own a house or a horse, but also could own an idea and the words used to express that idea. You can see these cultural conventions

*See Rebecca Moore Howard, *Standing in the Shadow of Giants: Plagiarists, Authors, Collaborators.* Stamford, CT: Ablex Pub., 1999.

**TABLE 14.2    Plagiarism and the Ethical Use of Sources**

| Plagiarism | | Ethical Use of Sources |
|---|---|---|
| **Fraud** | **Misuse of Sources** *(Common Mistakes Made by New Researchers)* | |
| The writer | The writer | The writer |
| • buys paper from a paper mill<br>• submits someone else's work as his own<br>• copies chunks of text from sources with obvious intention of not being detected<br>• fabricates data or makes up evidence<br>• intends to deceive | • copies passages directly from a source, references the source with an in-text citation, but fails to use quotation marks or block indentation<br>• in attempting to paraphrase a source, makes some changes, but follows too closely the wording of the original ("patchwriting")<br>• fails to indicate the sources of some ideas or data (often is unsure what needs to be cited or has lost track of sources through poor note taking)<br>• in general, misunderstands the conventions for using sources in academic writing | • writes paper entirely in her own words or uses exact quotations from sources<br>• indicates all quotations with quotation marks or block indentation<br>• indicates her use of all sources through attribution, in-text citation, and an end-of-paper list of works cited |

at work—in the form of laws or professional codes of ethics—whenever a book author is disgraced for lifting words or ideas from another author or whenever an artist or entrepreneur is sued for stealing song lyrics, publishing another person's photographs without permission, or infringing on some inventor's patent.

This understanding of plagiarism may seem odd in some non-Western cultures where collectivism is valued more than individualism. In these cultures, words written or spoken by ancestors, elders, or other authority figures may be regarded with reverence and shared with others without attribution. Also in these cultures, it might be disrespectful to paraphrase certain passages or to document them in a way that would suggest the audience didn't recognize the ancient wisdom.

However, such collectivist conventions won't work in research communities committed to building new knowledge. In the academic world, the conventions separating ethical from unethical use of sources are essential if research findings are to win the community's confidence. Effective research can occur only within ethical and responsible research communities where people do not fabricate data and where current researchers respect and acknowledge the work of those who have gone before them.

## Strategies for Avoiding Plagiarism

The following chart will help you review strategies for using source material ethically and avoiding plagiarism.

## Strategies for Avoiding Plagiarism or the Appearance of Plagiarism

| What to Do | Why to Do It | Where to Find More Information |
|---|---|---|
| **At the beginning** | | |
| Read your college's policy on plagiarism as well as statements from your teachers in class or on course syllabi. | Understanding policies on plagiarism and academic integrity will help you research and write ethically. | Chapter 2 |
| Pose a research question rather than a topic area. | Arguing your own thesis gives you a voice, establishes your *ethos,* and urges you to write ethically. | Chapter 1, Concept 2 |
| **At the note-taking stage** | | |
| Create a bibliographic entry for each source. | This action makes it easy to create an end-of-paper bibliography and encourages rhetorical reading. | Chapter 6, page 131 |
| When you copy a passage into your notes, copy word for word and enclose it within quotation marks. | It is important to distinguish a source's words from your own words. | Chapter 6, page 126 |
| When you enter summaries or paraphrases into your notes, avoid patchwriting. | If your notes contain any strings of a source's original wording, you might later assume that these words are your own. | Skill 14.2 |
| Distinguish your informational notes from your personal exploratory notes. | Keeping these kinds of notes separate will help you identify borrowed ideas when it's time to incorporate the source material into your paper. | Chapter 6, page 127 |
| **When writing your draft** | | |
| Except for exact quotations, write the paper entirely in your own words. | This strategy keeps you from patchwriting when you summarize or paraphrase. | Skill 14.2 |
| Indicate all quotations with quotation marks or block indentation. Use ellipses or brackets to make changes to fit your own grammar. | Be careful to represent the author fairly; don't change meaning by taking quotations out of context. | Skill 14.2; for use of ellipses and brackets consult a good handbook |

*(continued)*

| What to Do | Why to Do It | Where to Find More Information |
|---|---|---|
| When you summarize or paraphrase, avoid patchwriting. | Word-for-word strings from a source must either be avoided or placed in quotation marks. Also avoid mirroring the source's grammatical structure. | Skill 14.2 |
| Never cut and paste a Web passage directly into your draft. Paste it into a separate note file and put quotation marks around it. | Pasted passages are direct invitations to patchwrite. | Skill 14.2 |
| Inside your text, use attributive tags or parenthetical citations to identify all sources. List all sources alphabetically in a concluding works cited or references list. | This strategy makes it easy for readers to know when you are using a source and where to find it. | Skills 14.3, 15.1, and 15.2 |
| Cite with attributive tags or parenthetical citations all quotations, paraphrases, summaries, and any other references to specific sources. | These are the most common in-text citations in a research paper. | Skills 15.1 and 15.2 |
| Use in-text citations to indicate sources for all visuals and media such as graphs, maps, photographs, films, videos, broadcasts, and recordings. | The rules for citing words and ideas apply equally to visuals and media cited in your paper. | Skill 15.1 |
| Use in-text citations for all ideas and facts that are not common knowledge. | Although you don't need to cite widely accepted and noncontroversial facts and information, it is better to cite them if you are unsure. | Skill 15.1 |

# CITING AND DOCUMENTING SOURCES

# 15

I n the previous chapter we explained how to evaluate sources and incorporate them into your writing; in this chapter we focus on the nuts and bolts of documenting those sources in a way appropriate to your purpose, audience, and genre, using the systems of the Modern Language Association (MLA) and the American Psychological Association (APA).* Accurate documentation not only helps other researchers locate your sources but also contributes substantially to your own *ethos* as a writer.

## SKILL 15.1  Cite and document sources using MLA style.

**15.1**
Cite and document sources using MLA style.

An in-text citation and its corresponding Works Cited entry are linked in a chicken-and-egg system: You can't cite a source in the text without first knowing how the source's entry will be alphabetized in the Works Cited list. However, since most Works Cited entries are alphabetized by the first author's last name, for convenience we start with in-text citations.

### In-Text Citations in MLA Style

A typical in-text citation contains two elements: (1) the last name of the author and (2) the page number of the quoted or paraphrased passage. However, in some cases a work is identified by something other than an author's last name, and sometimes no page number is required. Let's begin with the most common cases.

Typically, an in-text citation uses one of these two methods:

- **Parenthetical method.**  Place the author's last name and the page number in parentheses immediately after the material being cited.

---

*Our discussion of MLA style is based on the *MLA Handbook for Writers of Research Papers*, 7th ed. (2009). Our discussion of APA style is based on the *Publication Manual of the American Psychological Association*, 6th ed. (2010).

The Spanish tried to reduce the status of Filipina women who had been able to do business, get divorced, and sometimes become village chiefs (Karnow 41).

- ***Attributive tag method.*** Place the author's name in an attributive tag at the beginning of the source material and the page number in parentheses at the end.

According to Karnow, the Spanish tried to reduce the status of Filipina women, who had been able to do business, get divorced, and sometimes become village chiefs (41).

Once you have cited an author and it is clear that the same author's material is being used, you need cite only the page numbers in parentheses in subsequent citations. A reader who wishes to look up the source will find the bibliographic information in the Works Cited section by looking for the entry under "Karnow."

Let's now turn to the variations. Table 15.1 identifies the typical variations and shows again the one-to-one connection between the in-text citation and the Works Cited list.

**When to Use Page Numbers in In-Text Citations** When the materials you are citing are available in print or in .pdf format, you can provide accurate page numbers for parenthetical citations. If you are working with Web sources or HTML files, however, do not use the page numbers obtained from a

**TABLE 15.1  In-Text Citations in MLA Style**

| Type of Source | Works Cited Entry at End of Paper (*Construct the entry while taking notes on each source.*) | In-Text Citation in Body of Paper (*Use the first word of the Works Cited entry in parentheses or an attributive tag; add page number at end of quoted or paraphrased passage.*) |
|---|---|---|
| **One author** | Pollan, Michael. *The Omnivore's Dilemma: A Natural History of Four Meals.* New York: Penguin, 2006. Print. | …(Pollan 256). OR According to Pollan, …(256). |
| **More than one author** | Pollay, Richard W., Jung S. Lee, and David Carter-Whitney. "Separate, but Not Equal: Racial Segmentation in Cigarette Advertising." *Journal of Advertising* 21.1 (1992): 45–57. Print. | …race" (Pollay, Lee, and Carter-Whitney 52). OR Pollay, Lee, and Carter-Whitney have argued that "advertisers…race" (52). *For the in-text citation, cite the specific page number rather than the whole range of pages given in the Works Cited entry.* |

**TABLE 15.1**  *continued*

| Type of Source | Works Cited Entry at End of Paper (*Construct the entry while taking notes on each source.*) | In-Text Citation in Body of Paper (*Use the first word of the Works Cited entry in parentheses or an attributive tag; add page number at end of quoted or paraphrased passage.*) |
|---|---|---|
| **Author has more than one work in Works Cited list** | Dombrowski, Daniel A. *Babies and Beasts: The Argument from Marginal Cases*. Urbana: U of Illinois P, 1997. Print. <br><br> ---. *The Philosophy of Vegetarianism*. Amherst: U of Massachusetts P, 1984. Print. | …(Dombrowski, *Babies* 207). <br> …(Dombrowski, *Philosophy* 328). OR <br> According to Dombrowski,…(*Babies* 207). <br> Dombrowski claims that… <br> (*Philosophy* 328). <br><br> *Because author has more than one work in Works Cited, include a short version of title to distinguish between entries.* |
| **Corporate author** | American Red Cross. *Standard First Aid*. St. Louis: Mosby Lifeline, 1993. Print. | …(American Red Cross 102). OR Snake bite instructions from the American Red Cross show that…(102). |
| **No named author** (Work is therefore alphabetized by title.) | "Ouch! Body Piercing." *Menstuff*. National Men's Resource Center, n.d. Web. 17 July 2013. | …("Ouch!"). <br> According to the National Men's Resource Center,…("Ouch!"). <br> • *Add "Ouch!" in parentheses to show that work is alphabetized under "Ouch!" not "National."* <br> • *No page numbers are shown because Web site pages aren't stable. "n.d." state for "no date."* |
| **Indirect citation of a source that you found in another source** <br> *Suppose you want to use a quotation from Peter Singer that you found in a book by Daniel Dombrowski. Include Dombrowski but not Singer in Works Cited.* | Dombrowski, Daniel A. *Babies and Beasts: The Argument from Marginal Cases*. Urbana: U of Illinois P, 1997. Print. | Animal rights activist Peter Singer argues that…(qtd. in Dombrowski 429). <br> • *Singer is used for the attributive tag, but the in-text citation is to Dombrowski.* <br> • *"qtd. in" stands for "quoted in."* |

printout because they will not be consistent from printer to printer. If the item has numbered paragraphs, cite them with the abbreviation *par.* or *pars.*—for example, "(Jones, pars. 22–24)." In the absence of reliable page numbers for the original material, MLA says to omit page references from the parenthetical citation.

## Works Cited List in MLA Style

In the MLA system, you place a complete Works Cited list at the end of the paper. The list includes all the sources that you mention in your paper. However, it does *not* include works you read but did not use. Entries in the Works Cited list follow these general guidelines:

- Entries are arranged alphabetically by author, or by title if there is no author.
- Each entry includes the medium of publication of the source you consulted— for example, *Print, Web, DVD, Performance, Oil on canvas,* and so on.
- If there is more than one entry per author, the works are arranged alphabetically by title. For the second and all additional entries, type three hyphens and a period in place of the author's name.

> Dombrowski, Daniel A. *Babies and Beasts: The Argument from Marginal Cases.* Urbana: U of Illinois P, 1997. Print.
>
> ---. *The Philosophy of Vegetarianism.* Amherst: U of Massachusetts P, 1984. Print.

## MLA Citation Models

### Print Articles in Scholarly Journals

#### General Format for Print Article in Scholarly Journal

To see what citations look like when typed in a research paper, see Kent Ansen's Works Cited list on p. 272

Author. "Article Title." *Journal Title* volume number.issue number (year): page numbers. Print.

Note that all scholarly journal entries include both volume number and issue number, regardless of how the journal is paginated. For articles published in a scholarly e-journal, see page 365. For scholarly journal articles retrieved from an online database, see pages 363–364.

*One author*

Herrera-Sobek, Maria. "Border Aesthetics: The Politics of Mexican Immigration in Film and Art." *Western Humanities Review* 60.2 (2006): 60–71. Print.

*Two or three authors*

Pollay, Richard W., Jung S. Lee, and David Carter-Whitney. "Separate, but Not Equal: Racial Segmentation in Cigarette Advertising." *Journal of Advertising* 21.1 (1992): 45–57. Print.

*Four or more authors*

Either list all the authors in the order in which they appear, or use "et al." (meaning "and others") to replace all but the first author.

Buck, Gayle A., et al. "Examining the Cognitive Processes Used by Adolescent Girls and Women Scientists in Identifying Science Role Models: A Feminist Approach." *Science Education* 92.4 (2008): 688–707. Print.

## Print Articles in Magazines and Newspapers

### General Format for Magazines and Newspapers

Author. "Article Title." *Magazine Title* day Month year: page numbers. Print.

*Magazine article with named author*

Snyder, Rachel L. "A Daughter of Cambodia Remembers: Loung Ung's Journey." *Ms.*
      Aug.–Sept. 2001: 62–67. Print.

*Magazine article without named author*

"Sacred Geese." *Economist* 1 June 2013: 24–25. Print.

*Newspaper article*

Henriques, Diana B. "Hero's Fall Teaches Wall Street a Lesson." *Seattle Times* 27 Sept.
      1998: A1+. Print.

Page numbers in newspapers are typically indicated by a section letter or number as well as a page number. The "+" indicates that the article continues on one or more pages later in the newspaper.

*Newspaper editorial*

"Dr. Frankenstein on the Hill." Editorial. *New York Times* 18 May 2002, natl. ed.: A22. Print.

## Print Books

### General Format for Print Books

Author. *Title*. City of publication: Publisher, year of publication. Print.

Pollan, Michael. *The Omnivore's Dilemma: A Natural History of Four Meals*. New York:
      Penguin, 2006. Print.

*Second, later, or revised edition*

Montagu, Ashley. *Touching: The Human Significance of the Skin*. 3rd ed. New York:
      Perennial, 1986. Print.

*Anthology article*

Royer, Ann. "The Role of the Transcendental Meditation Technique in Promoting
      Smoking Cessation: A Longitudinal Study." *Self Recovery: Treating Addictions Using*
      *Transcendental Meditation and Maharishi Ayur-Veda*. Ed. David F. O'Connell and
      Charles N. Alexander. New York: Haworth, 1994. 221–39. Print.

## Articles or Books from an Online Database

### General Format for Material from Online Databases

Author. "Title." *Periodical Name* Print publication data including date and volume/ issue
      numbers: pagination. *Database*. Web. Date of access.

*Journal article from online database*

Rosenman, Mark. "A Call for National Service." *Chronicle of Philanthropy* 20.1 (18 Oct.

2007). *Academic Search Complete*. Web. 12 Feb. 2013.

*E-book from online database*

Hanley, Wayne. *The Genesis of Napoleonic Propaganda, 1796–1799*. New York: Columbia

UP, 2002. *Gutenberg-e*. Web. 31 July 2010.

Machiavelli, Niccolo. *Prince*. 1513. *Bibliomania*. Web. 31 July 2013.

## Other Internet Sources

**General Format for Web Sources** Since Web sources are often unstable, MLA recommends that you download or print out your Web sources. The goal in citing these sources is to enable readers to locate the material. To that end, use the basic citation model and adapt it as necessary.

Author, editor, director, narrator, performer, compiler, or producer of the work, if

available. *Title of a long work, italicized.* OR "Title of page or document that is

part of a larger work, in quotation marks." *Title of the overall site, usually taken*

*from the home page, if this is different from the title of the work.* Publisher or sponsor

of the site (if none, use N.p.), day Month year of publication online or last

update of the site (if not available, use n.d.). Web. day Month year you accessed

the site.

Saucedo, Robert. "A Bad Idea for a Movie." *theeagle.com*. Bryan College Station Eagle,

1 July 2010. Web. 7 July 2010.

MLA assumes that readers will use a search engine to locate a Web source, so do not include a URL *unless* the item would be hard to locate without it. If you do include a URL, it goes at the end of the citation, after the access date. Enclose it in angle brackets <> followed by a period. If you need to break the URL from one line to the next, divide it only after a slash. Do not hyphenate a URL. See the blog entry on page 365 for an example of a citation with a URL.

*Entire Web site*

*BlogPulse*. Intelliseek, n.d. Web. 24 July 2012.

Padgett, John B., ed. *William Faulkner on the Web*. U of Mississippi, 26 Mar. 2007. Web.

25 June 2013.

*Document within a Web site*

Marks, John. "Overview: Letter from the President." *Search for Common Ground*. Search

for Common Ground, n.d. Web. 25 June 2007.

***Article from a newspaper or newswire site***

Bounds, Amy. "Thinking Like Scientists." *Daily Camera* [Boulder]. Scripps Interactive

Newspaper Group, 26 June 2007. Web. 26 June 2007.

"Great Lakes: Rwanda Backed Dissident Troops in DRC-UN Panel." *IRIN*. UN Office for

the Coordination of Humanitarian Affairs, 21 July 2004. Web. 31 July 2004.

***Article from a scholarly e-journal***

Welch, John R., and Ramon Riley. "Reclaiming Land and Spirit in the Western Apache

Homeland." *American Indian Quarterly* 25.4 (2001): 5–14. Web. 19 Dec. 2012.

***Blog posting***

Dyer, Bob, and Ella Barnes. "The 'Greening' of the Arctic." *Greenversations*. U.S.

Environmental Protection Agency, 7 Oct. 2008. Web. 11 Oct. 2010. http://blog.

epa.gov/blog/2008/10/07/the-greening-of-the-artic/.

***Social media posting***

"Rattlesnake Figure (Aluminum) by Thomas Houseago." *Storm King Art Center*.

Facebook, 30 May 2013. Web. 3 June 2013.

***Web video***

Beck, Roy. "Immigration Gumballs." *YouTube*. YouTube, 2 Nov. 2006. Web. 23 July 2009.

***Home Page***

*African Studies Program*. Home page. School of Advanced International Study, Johns

Hopkins U, n.d. Web. 31 July 2007.

***E-mail***

Rubino, Susanna. "Reasons for Unemployment." Message to the author. 12 Dec. 2013.

E-mail.

## Miscellaneous Sources

***Television or radio program***

"Lie Like a Rug." *NYPD Blue*. Dir. Steven Bochco and David Milch. ABC. KOMO, Seattle.

6 Nov. 2001. Television.

Ashbrook, Tom. "Turf Wars and the American Lawn." *On Point*. Natl. Public Radio,

22 July 2008. Web. 23 July 2009.

***Film or video recording***

*Shakespeare in Love*. Dir. John Madden. Perf. Joseph Fiennes and Gwyneth Paltrow.

Screenplay by Marc Norman and Tom Stoppard. Universal Miramax, 1998. Film.

Use "DVD" or "Videocassette" rather than "Film" as the medium of publication if that is the medium you consulted. If you accessed a film or video on the Web, omit the original medium of publication, include the Web site or database name (italicized), the sponsor and posting date, "Web" as medium of publication, and the date of access.

*Shakespeare in Love*. Dir. John Madden. Perf. Joseph Fiennes and Gwyneth Paltrow.

> Screenplay by Marc Norman and Tom Stoppard. Universal Miramax, 1998.
>
> *Netflix*. Netflix, n.d. Web. 9 Mar. 2010.

*Interview*

Castellucci, Marion. Personal interview. 7 Oct. 2013.

*Lecture, speech, or conference presentation*

Sharples, Mike. "Authors of the Future." Conference of European Teachers of Academic

> Writing. U of Groningen. Groningen, Neth. 20 June 2001. Lecture.

## MLA Format Research Paper

For an illustration of a student research paper written and formatted in MLA style, see "Engaging Young Adults to Meet America's Challenges: A Proposal for Mandatory National Service" by Kent Ansen (Chapter 10, pp. 263–272). Kent's process in producing this paper has been discussed in various places throughout the text.

# SKILL 15.2   **Cite and document sources using APA style.**

**15.2**
Cite and
document
sources using
APA style.

In many respects, the APA style and the MLA style are similar and the basic logic is the same. In the APA system, the list where readers can find full bibliographic information is titled "References"; as in MLA format, it includes only the sources cited in the body of the paper. The distinguishing features of APA citation style are highlighted in the following sections.

## In-Text Citations in APA Style

A typical APA-style in-text citation contains three elements: (1) the last name of the author, (2) the date of the publication, and (3) the page number of the quoted or paraphrased passage. Table 15.2 identifies some typical variations and shows again the one-to-one connection between the in-text citation and the References list.

For an example of a student paper in APA style, see the classical argument by Claire Giordano in Chapter 9, pp. 234–243.

**TABLE 15.2   In-Text Citations in APA Style**

| Type of Source | References Entry at End of Paper | In-Text Citation in Body of Paper |
|---|---|---|
| **One author** | Pollan, M. (2006). *The omnivore's dilemma: A natural history of four meals*. New York, NY: Penguin. | …(Pollan, 2006, p. 256). OR According to Pollan (2006),… (p. 256). |
| **Two authors** | Kwon, O., & Wen, Y. (2010). An empirical study of the factors affecting social network service use. *Computers in Human Behavior, 26*, 254–263. doi:10.1016/j.chb.2009.04.011 | …(Kwon & Wen, 2010, p. 262). OR Kwon and Wen (2010) claim that…(p. 262). |
| **Three to five authors** | Pollay, R. W., Lee, J. S., & Carter-Whitney, D. (1992). Separate, but not equal: Racial segmentation in cigarette advertising. *Journal of Advertising, 21*(1), 45–57. | …race" (Pollay, Lee, & Carter-Whitney, 1992, p. 52). OR Pollay, Lee, and Carter-Whitney have argued that "advertisers… race" (1992, p. 52). *For subsequent citations, use* Pollay et al. *For a quotation, use the specific page number, not the whole range of pages.* |

*(continued)*

**TABLE 15.2** *continued*

| Type of Source | References Entry at End of Paper | In-Text Citation in Body of Paper |
|---|---|---|
| **Author has more than one work in References list** | Dombrowski, D. A. (1984). *The philosophy of vegetarianism.* Amherst, MA: University of Massachusetts Press.<br><br>Dombrowski, D. A. (1997). *Babies and beasts: The argument from marginal cases.* Urbana: University of Illinois Press. | …(Dombrowski, 1984, p. 207).<br>…(Dombrowski, 1997, p. 328).<br>OR<br>Dombrowski (1984) claims that…(p. 207).<br>According to Dombrowski (1997),…(p. 328). |
| **Indirect citation of a source that you found in another source**<br>*You use a quotation from Peter Singer from a book by Dombrowski. Include Dombrowski, not Singer, in References.* | Dombrowski, D. A. (1997). *Babies and beasts: The argument from marginal cases.* Urbana: University of Illinois Press. | Animal rights activist Peter Singer argues that…(as cited in Dombrowski, 1997, p. 429).<br>*Singer is used for the attributive tag, but the in-text citation is to Dombrowski.* |

## References List in APA Style

The APA References list at the end of a paper presents entries alphabetically. If you cite more than one item for an author, repeat the author's name each time and arrange the items in chronological order, beginning with the earliest. In cases where two works by an author appeared in the same year, arrange them in the list alphabetically by title, and then add a lowercase "a" or "b" (etc.) after the date so that you can distinguish between them in the in-text citations:

A formatted References list appears on pp. 242–243

Smith, R. (1999a). *Body image in non-Western cultures, 1750–present.* London, England: Bonanza Press.

Smith, R. (1999b). Eating disorders reconsidered. *Journal of Appetite Studies, 45,* 295–300.

## APA Citation Models

### Print Articles in Scholarly Journals

### General Format for Print Article in Scholarly Journal

Author. (Year of Publication). Article title. *Journal Title, volume number,* page numbers.
    doi: xx.xxxx/x.xxxx.xx [or] http://dx.doi.org/10.xxxx/xxxxxx

If there is one, include the **DOI** (digital object identifier), a number that is uniquely assigned to many journal articles, in numeric or URL form. Note the style for capitalizing article titles and for italicizing the volume number.

*One author*

Herrera-Sobek, M. (2006). Border aesthetics: The politics of Mexican immigration in

film and art. *Western Humanities Review, 60,* 60–71. doi:10.1016/j.chb.2009.04.011

*Two to seven authors*

McElroy, B. W., & Lubich, B. H. (2013). Predictors of course outcomes: Early indicators

of delay in online classrooms. *Distance Education,* 34(1). http://dx.doi.org/10.1080/

01587919.2013.770433

When a source has more than seven authors, list the first six and the last one by name. Use ellipses ( … ) to indicate the authors whose names have been omitted.

*Scholarly journal that restarts page numbering with each issue*

Pollay, R. W., Lee, J. S., & Carter-Whitney, D. (1992). Separate, but not equal: Racial seg-

mentation in cigarette advertising. *Journal of Advertising, 21*(1), 45–57.

Note that the issue number and the parentheses are *not* italicized.

## Print Articles in Magazines and Newspapers

### General Format for Print Article in Magazine or Newspaper

Author. (Year, Month Day). Article title. *Periodical Title, volume number,* page numbers.

If page numbers are discontinuous, identify every page, separating numbers with a comma.

*Magazine article*

Hall, S. S. (2001, March 11). Prescription for profit. *The New York Times Magazine,* 40–45,

59, 91–92, 100.

*Newspaper article*

Dougherty, C. (2013, June 4). The latest urban trend: Less elbow room. *Wall Street*

*Journal,* pp. A1, A12.

## Print Books

### General Format for Print Books

Author. (Year of publication). *Book title: Subtitle.* City, State [abbreviated]: Name of

Publisher.

Brumberg, J. J. (1997). *The body project: An intimate history of American girls.* New York,

NY: Vintage.

If the publisher's name indicates the state in which it is located, list the city but omit the state.

Reid, H., & Taylor, B. (2010). *Recovering the commons: Democracy, place, and global justice.*

Champaign: University of Illinois Press.

*Second, later, or revised edition*

Montagu, A. (1986). *Touching: The human significance of the skin* (3rd ed.). New York, NY: Perennial Press.

*Anthology article*

Royer, A. (1994). The role of the transcendental meditation technique in promoting smoking cessation: A longitudinal study. In D. F. O'Connell & C. N. Alexander (Eds.), *Self recovery: Treating addictions using transcendental meditation and Maharishi Ayur-Veda* (pp. 221–239). New York, NY: Haworth Press.

## Articles or Books from an Online Database

*Article from database with digital object identifier (DOI)*

Scharrer, E., Daniel, K. D., Lin, K.-M., & Liu, Z. (2006). Working hard or hardly working? Gender, humor, and the performance of domestic chores in television commercials. *Mass Communication and Society, 9*(2), 215–238. doi:10.1207/s15327825mcs0902_5

Omit the database name. If an article or other document has been assigned a digital object identifier (DOI), include the DOI at the end.

*Article from database without DOI*

Highland, R. A., & Dabney, D. A. (2009). Using Adlerian theory to shed light on drug dealer motivations. *Applied Psychology in Criminal Justice, 5*(2), 109–138. Retrieved from http://www.apcj.org

Omit the database name. Instead, use a search engine to locate the publication's home page, and cite that URL. If you need to break a URL at the end of a line, do not use a hyphen. Instead, break it *before* a punctuation mark or *after* http://.

## Other Internet Sources

### General Format for Web Documents

Author, editor, director, narrator, performer, compiler, or producer of the work, if available. (Year, Month Day of posting). *Title of web document, italicized.* Retrieved from Name of website if different from author or title: URL of home page

Barrett, J. (2007, January 17). *MySpace is a natural monopoly.* Retrieved from ECommerce Times website: http://www.ecommercetimes.com

Marks, J. (n.d.). "Overview: Letter from the president." Retrieved June 3, 2010, from the Search for Common Ground website: http://www.sfcg.org

*Entire Web site*

BlogPulse. (n.d.). Retrieved September 3, 2010, from the Intelliseek website: http://www.intelliseek.com

*Article from a newspaper site*

Bounds, A. (2007, June 26). Thinking like scientists. *Daily Camera* [Boulder]. Retrieved
from http://www.dailycamera.com

*Article from a scholarly e-journal*

Welch, J. R., & Riley, R. (2001). Reclaiming land and spirit in the western Apache homeland. *American Indian Quarterly, 25*, 5–14. Retrieved from http://muse.jhu.edu/
journals/american_indian_quarterly

*E-book*

Hoffman, F. W. (1981). *The literature of rock: 1954–1978*. Retrieved from http://www.
netlibrary.com

*E-mail, interviews, and personal correspondence*

Cite personal correspondence in the body of your text, but not in the References
list: "Rubino (personal communication, December 12, 2013) claims that .... "

*Blog Posting*

Dyer, B., & Barnes, E. (2008, October 7). The "greening" of the Arctic [Web log post].
Retrieved from http://blog.epa.gov/blog/2008/10/07/the-greening-of-the-arctic

*Social media posting*

Storm King Art Centers. (2013, May 30). Rattlesnake figure (aluminums) by Thomas
Houseago. [Facebook update]. Retrieved from http://www.facebook.com/
StormKingArtCenter

*Web video*

Beck, R. (2006, November 2). Immigration gumballs [Video file]. Retrieved from http://
www.youtube.com/watch?v=n7WJeqxuOfQ

## Miscellaneous Sources

*Television program*

Bochco, S., & Milch, D. (Directors). (2001, November 6). Lie like a rug [Television series
episode]. In *NYPD blue*. New York, NY: American Broadcasting Company.

*Film*

Madden, J. (Director). (1998). *Shakespeare in love* [Motion picture]. United States:
Universal Miramax.

## Student Example of an APA-Style Research Paper

An example of a paper in APA style is shown on pages 234–243.

# CREDITS

## Text

**Page 2.** Reprinted by permission of Rodney Kilcup.

**Page 15.** David Rockwood. "Letter to the Editor", *The Oregonian*, January 1, 1993. Reprinted by permission of Rosalie Rockwood Bean.

**Page 15.** Thomas Merton. From "Rain and the Rhinoceros" from *Raids on the Unspeakable*, copyright © 1966 by The Abbey of Gethsemani, Inc. Reprinted by permission of New Directions Publishing Corp.

**Page 22.** Walvoord, Barbara E. and McCarthy, Lucile P., "Thinking and Writing in College: A Naturalistic Study of Students in Four Disciplines." Urbana, IL: National Council of Teachers of English (NCTE), 1990, p. 51.

**Page 31.** "next to of course god america i". Copyright 1926, 1954, © 1991 by the Trustees for the E. E. Cummings Trust. Copyright © 1985 by George James Firmage, from *Complete Poems: 1904-1962* by E. E. Cummings, edited by George J. Firmage. Used by permission of Liveright Publishing Corporation.

**Page 42.** Kenneth Burke. From *Permanence and Change: An Anatomy of Purpose* by Kenneth Burke, © 1984 by Kenneth Burke. Reprinted by permission of the publisher, University of California Press and The Kenneth Burke Literary Trust.

**Page 46.** From "Which One is the REAL ANWR?" Arctic Power–Arctic National Wildlife Refuge, p. 1, www.anwr.org. Reprinted by permission of Arctic Power.

**Page 66.** Kirby Ferguson. From *Everything's a Remix: The TED Talk*, TED.com, June 2012. Reprinted by permission of Kirby Ferguson.

**Page 98.** Kyle Madsen.

**Page 114.** "Why Bother" by Michael Pollan from *The New York Times*, April 20, 2008. Copyright (c) 2008 by Michael Pollan for The New York Times. Reprinted by permission of International Creative Management, Inc.

**Page 136.** Kent Ansen (pseudonym) "Should the United States Establish Mandatory Public Service for Young Adults?" Reprinted by permission.

**Page 172.** Student Writing by Lydia Wheeler.

**Page 178.** Review of "The Accordion Family: Boomerang Kids, Anxious Parents, and the Private Toll of Global Competition" from *Publishers Weekly*, August 29, 2011.

**Page 230.** Student Essay by Ross Taylor.

**Page 234.** Claire Giordano. "Virtual Promise: Why Online Courses Will Not Adequately Prepare Us for the Future." Reprinted by permission of the author.

**Page 252.** Lucy Morsen (pseudonym) "A proposal to improve the campus learning environment." Reprinted by permission.

**Page 256.** Sam Rothchild (pseudonym) "Reward Work, Not Wealth" Reprinted by permission.

**Page 259.** Kent Ansen (pseudonym) "Should the United States Establish Mandatory Public Service for Young Adults?" Reprinted by permission.

**Page 315.** David Popenoe, "Where's Papa?" condensed from *Life Without Father: Compelling New Evidence that Fatherhood and Marriage Are Indispensable for the Good of Children and Society.* Reprinted by permission of the author

**Page 347.** "Arkansas" page from Energy for Shale website. © 2013 EnergyFromShale.org. All rights reserved. Reprinted by permission of American Petroleum Institute. (top). Reprinted by permission of Food & Water Watch/Americans Against Fracking (bottom).

## Images

**Page 1.** CNAC/MNAM/Dist. RMN-Grand Palais/Art Resource, NY. ©2013 Artists Rights Society (ARS), New York/ADAGP, Paris.

**Page 7.** Billie G. Lynn

**Page 44.** Jonathan Carr

**Page 58.** Peter Sobolev/Shutterstock

**Page 60.** Montana Fish Wildlife and Parks/AP Images (top left). 4FR/Getty Images (top right). Thomas Kitchin & Victoria Hurst/Design Pics Inc./Alamy (bottom left). Image Source/Getty Images (bottom right).

**Page 62.** Peter Jordan/Alamy (top left). Digital Vision/Thinkstock (top right). Creatas/Thinkstock (bottom left). Wavebreakmedia/Shutterstock (bottom right).

**Page 69.** John Bean (3 images)

**Page 77.** Roz Chast/The Cartoon Bank

**Page 81.** U.S. Air Force

**Page 145.** Leslie Stone/The Image Works (top left). Guillermo Arias/AP Images (top right). J. Emilio Flores/Corbis (bottom left). Carlos Barria/Reuters/Corbis (bottom right).

**Page 147.** Steven James Silva/Reuters/Landov (top left). Det. Greg Semendinger/NYPD/AP Images (top right). David Turnley/Corbis (bottom).

**Page 153.** Peter Turnley/Corbis

**Page 156.** Scala/Art Resource, NY

**Page 158.** Albright-Knox Art Gallery/Art Resource, NY

**Page 159.** June Johnson (two images)

# INDEX

# How *The Allyn & Bacon Guide to Writing* Will Help You Achieve the Learning Outcomes Endorsed by the Council of Writing Program Administrators

| WPA Outcomes for First-Year Composition | Where *The Allyn & Bacon Guide* Addresses These Outcomes |
|---|---|
| **RHETORICAL KNOWLEDGE**<br>By the end of first-year composition, students should:<br>• Focus on a purpose<br>• Respond to the needs of different audiences<br>• Respond appropriately to different kinds of rhetorical situations<br>• Use conventions of format and structure appropriate to the rhetorical situation<br>• Adopt appropriate voice, tone, and level of formality<br>• Understand how genres shape reading and writing<br>• Write in several genres | Part 1 "A Rhetoric for Writers"<br>Chapter 5 "Reading Rhetorically"<br>Chapter 12 "Composing Closed-Form Prose"<br>Chapter 13 "Composing Multimodal Texts"<br>Part 4 "A Rhetorical Guide to Research"<br>Additionally, all Writing Project chapters in Part 2 have a strong rhetorical and genre dimension. |
| **CRITICAL THINKING, READING, AND WRITING**<br>By the end of first-year composition, students should:<br>• Use writing and reading for inquiry, learning, thinking, and communicating<br>• Understand a writing assignment as a series of tasks, including finding, evaluating, analyzing, and synthesizing appropriate primary and secondary sources<br>• Integrate their own ideas with those of others<br>• Understand the relationships among language, knowledge, and power | Part 1 "A Rhetoric for Writers"<br>Chapter 5 "Reading Rhetorically"<br>Part 4 "A Rhetorical Guide to Research"<br>Additionally, all Writing Project chapters in Part 2 emphasize problem posing, critical thinking, critical reading, and marshaling of evidence. |
| **PROCESSES**<br>By the end of first-year composition, students should:<br>• Be aware that it usually takes multiple drafts to create and complete a successful text<br>• Develop flexible strategies for generating, revising, editing, and proofreading<br>• Understand writing as an open process that permits writers to use later invention and rethinking to revise their work<br>• Understand the collaborative and social aspects of writing processes<br>• Learn to critique their own and others' works<br>• Learn to balance the advantages of relying on others with the responsibility of doing their part<br>• Use a variety of technologies to address a range of audiences | Part 3 "A Guide to Composing and Revising"<br>All Writing Project chapters in Part 2 have substantial process components, including questions for peer review.<br>A variety of technologies is used to produce genres such as advocacy ads, blog posts, online reviews, podcasts, videos, presentation visuals, and desktop-published material, as well as conventional print essays, in Part 2. |